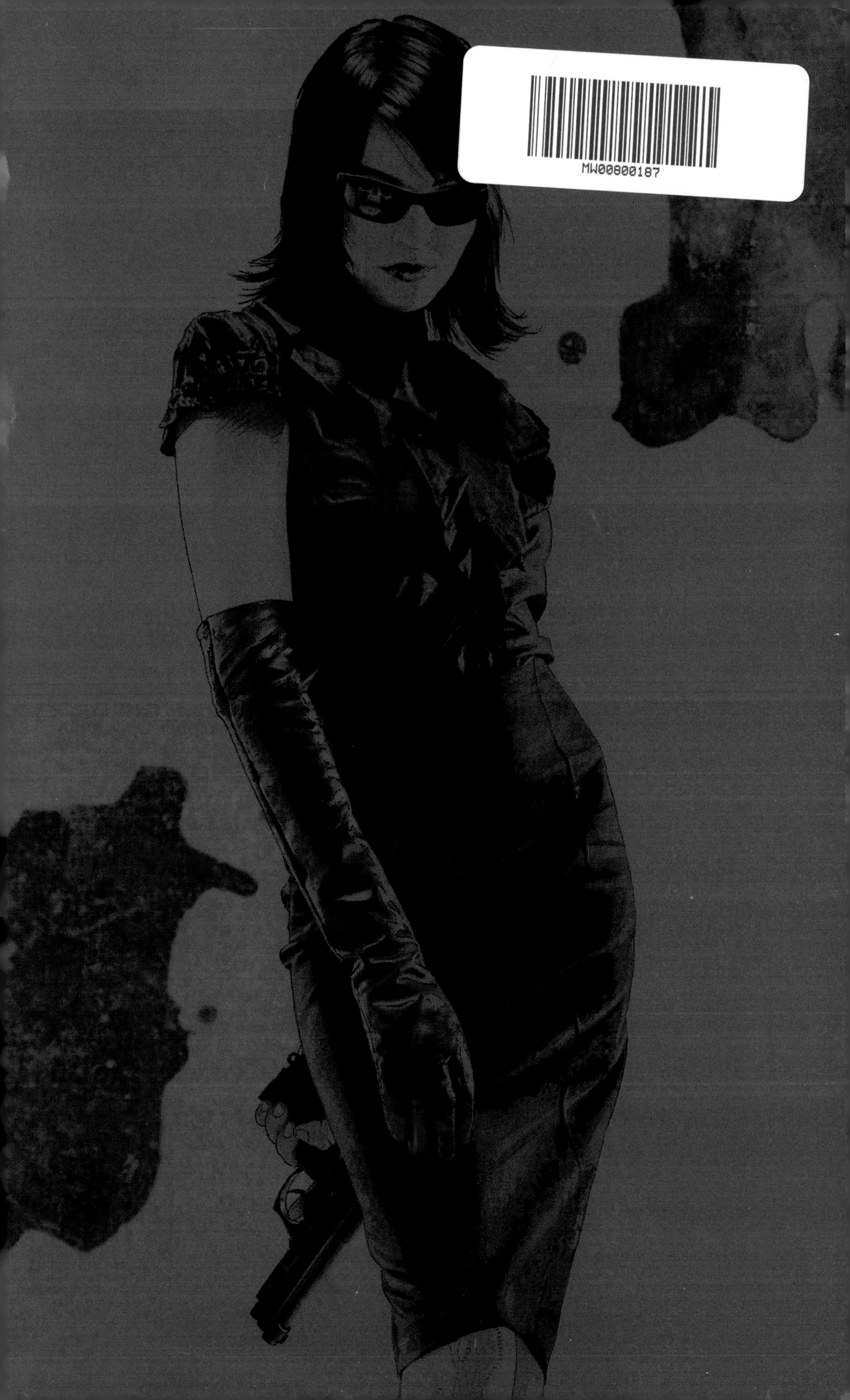

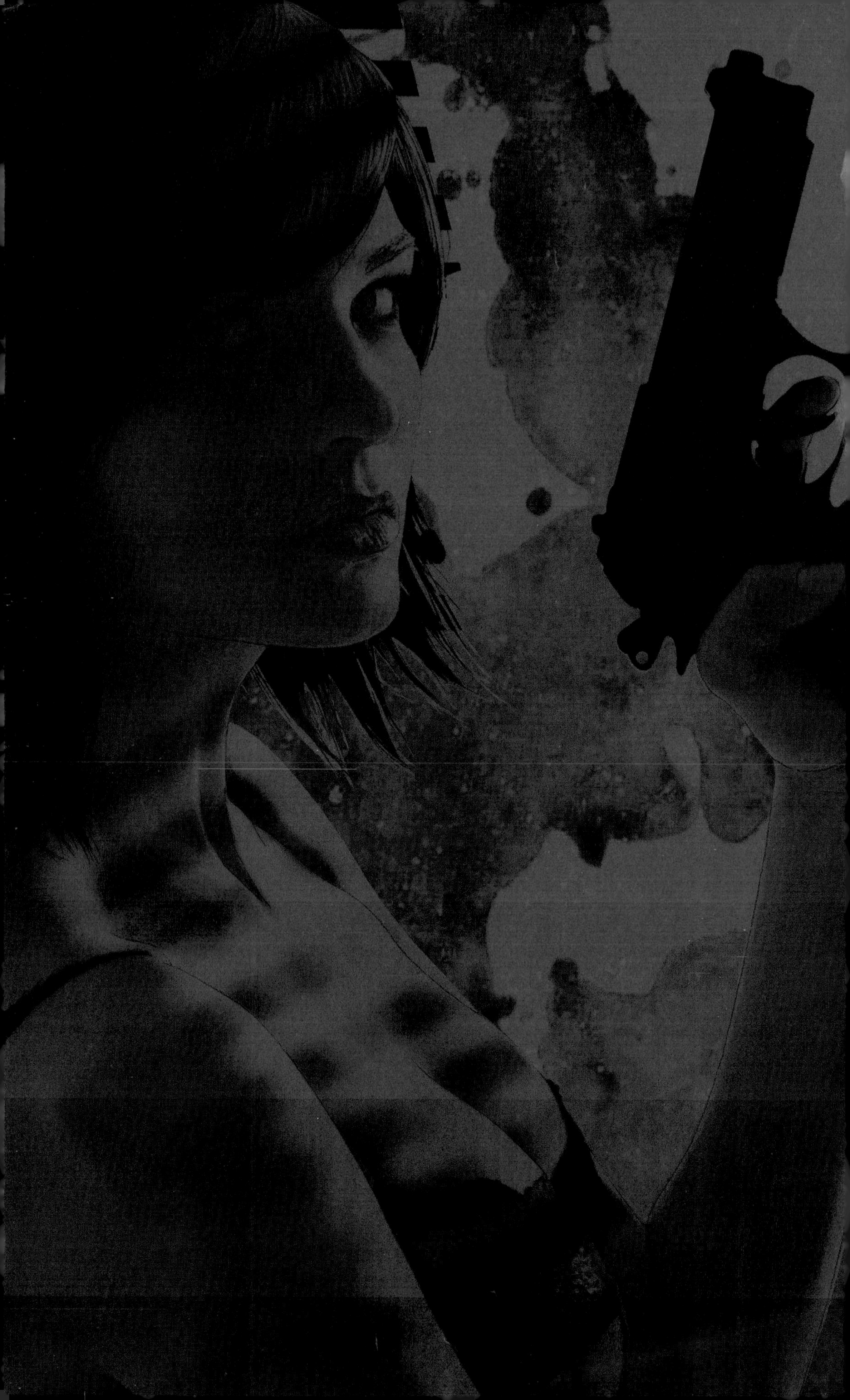

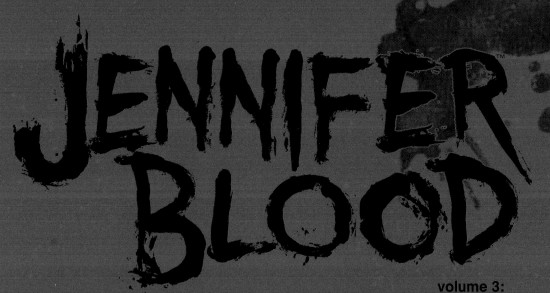

JENNIFER BLOOD

volume 3:
NEITHER TARNISHED NOR AFRAID

written by
AL EWING

illustrated by
KEWBER BAAL (issues 13-15, 17)
EMAN CASALLOS (issues 16, 18)

colored by
INLIGHT STUDIOS

lettered by
ROB STEEN

collection cover by
TIM BRADSTREET

collection design by
JASON ULLMEYER

This volume collects issues thirteen through eighteen of
the Dynamite Entertainment series, Jennifer Blood.

Visit us online at **www.DYNAMITE.com**
Follow us on Twitter @dynamitecomics
Like us on Facebook /Dynamitecomics
Watch us on YouTube /Dynamitecomics

Nick Barrucci, CEO / Publisher
Juan Collado, President / COO
Joe Rybandt, Senior Editor
Josh Johnson, Art Director
Rich Young, Director Business Development
Jason Ullmeyer, Senior Graphic Designer
Keith Davidsen, Marketing Manager
Josh Green, Traffic Coordinator
Chris Caniano, Production Assistant

ISBN-10: 1-60690-386-1   ISBN-13: 978-1-60690-386-5   First Printing   10 9 8 7 6 5 4 3 2 1

PREVIOUSLY IN
JENNIFER BLOOD:

In 1987, Sam Blute, head of the Blute crime family, was murdered by his five brothers. His wife Jennifer committed suicide, leaving behind their only daughter, Jessie.

It's 2011. Jessie – now calling herself Jen Fellows – just finished killing off her uncles one by one, along with their lawyer, Marcus Goldhagen, a trio of college girls turned amateur assassins called The Ninjettes, waffle magnate Katashi Oshiro, private military contractor Mason Buwick and two dozen of his best mercenaries, and Hollywood power couple Nate LaZarr and Cilla Vale. For the coup de grace, she blew up homicide detectives Mike Fulsom and Elaine Pruitt along with her next-door neighbor Jack Thomas.

She's managed to achieve all this while keeping the whole enterprise from her husband Andrew and her daughter Alice. Her son, Mark, caught a glimpse of her staggering armament, but he's keeping his mouth shut so far.

All in all, things could be much worse. For instance, Elaine Pruitt could have survived the explosion, and she might know that Jen Fellows and The Jennifer Blood Killer are one and the same.
What? She did? And she does?

Oh.

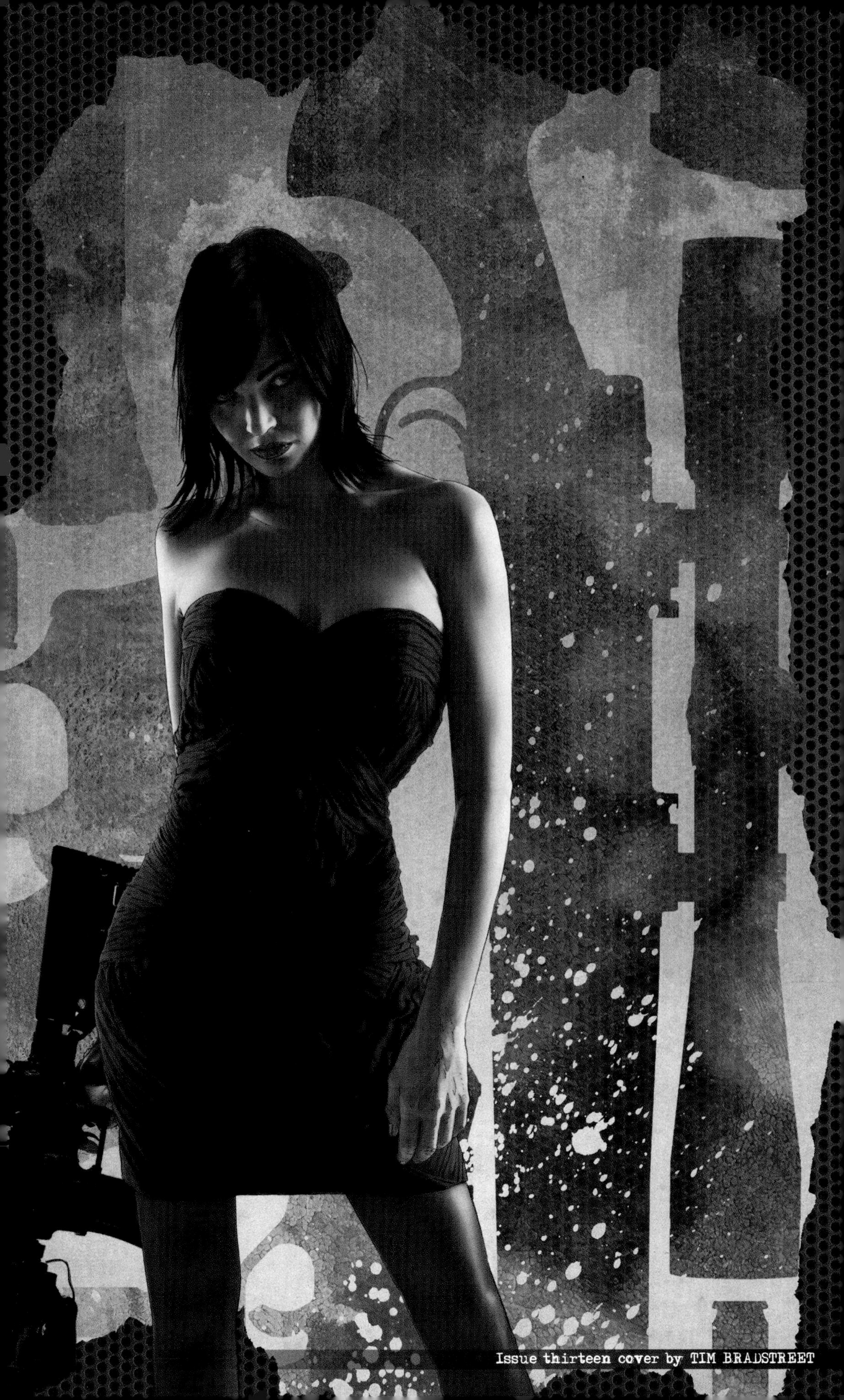

Issue thirteen cover by TIM BRADSTREET

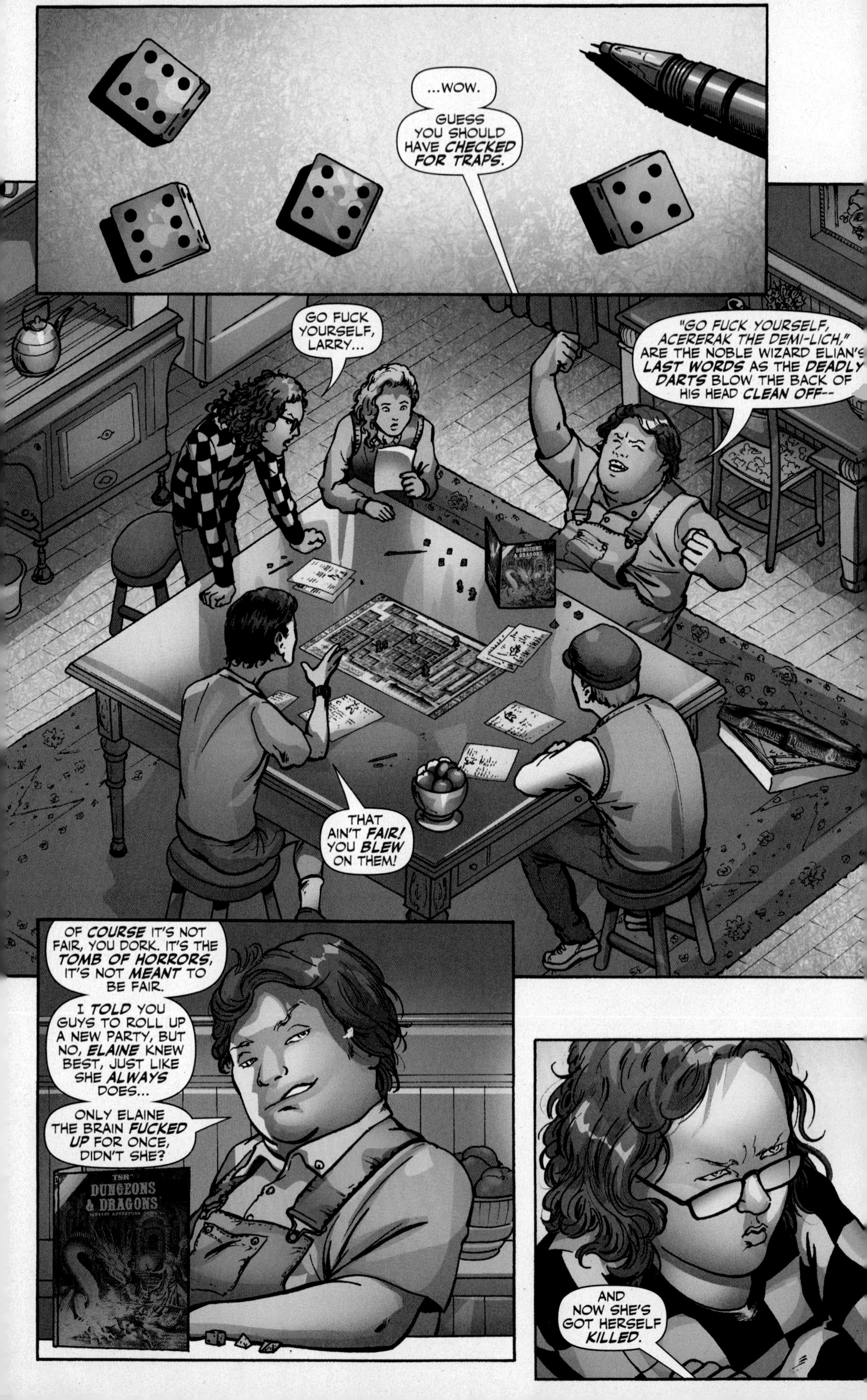
...WOW.
GUESS YOU SHOULD HAVE CHECKED FOR TRAPS.
GO FUCK YOURSELF, LARRY...
"GO FUCK YOURSELF, ACERERAK THE DEMI-LICH," ARE THE NOBLE WIZARD ELIAN'S LAST WORDS AS THE DEADLY DARTS BLOW THE BACK OF HIS HEAD CLEAN OFF--
DUNGEONS & DRAGONS
THAT AIN'T FAIR! YOU BLEW ON THEM!
OF COURSE IT'S NOT FAIR, YOU DORK. IT'S THE TOMB OF HORRORS, IT'S NOT MEANT TO BE FAIR.
I TOLD YOU GUYS TO ROLL UP A NEW PARTY, BUT NO, ELAINE KNEW BEST, JUST LIKE SHE ALWAYS DOES...
ONLY ELAINE THE BRAIN FUCKED UP FOR ONCE, DIDN'T SHE?
TSR
DUNGEONS & DRAGONS
AND NOW SHE'S GOT HERSELF KILLED.

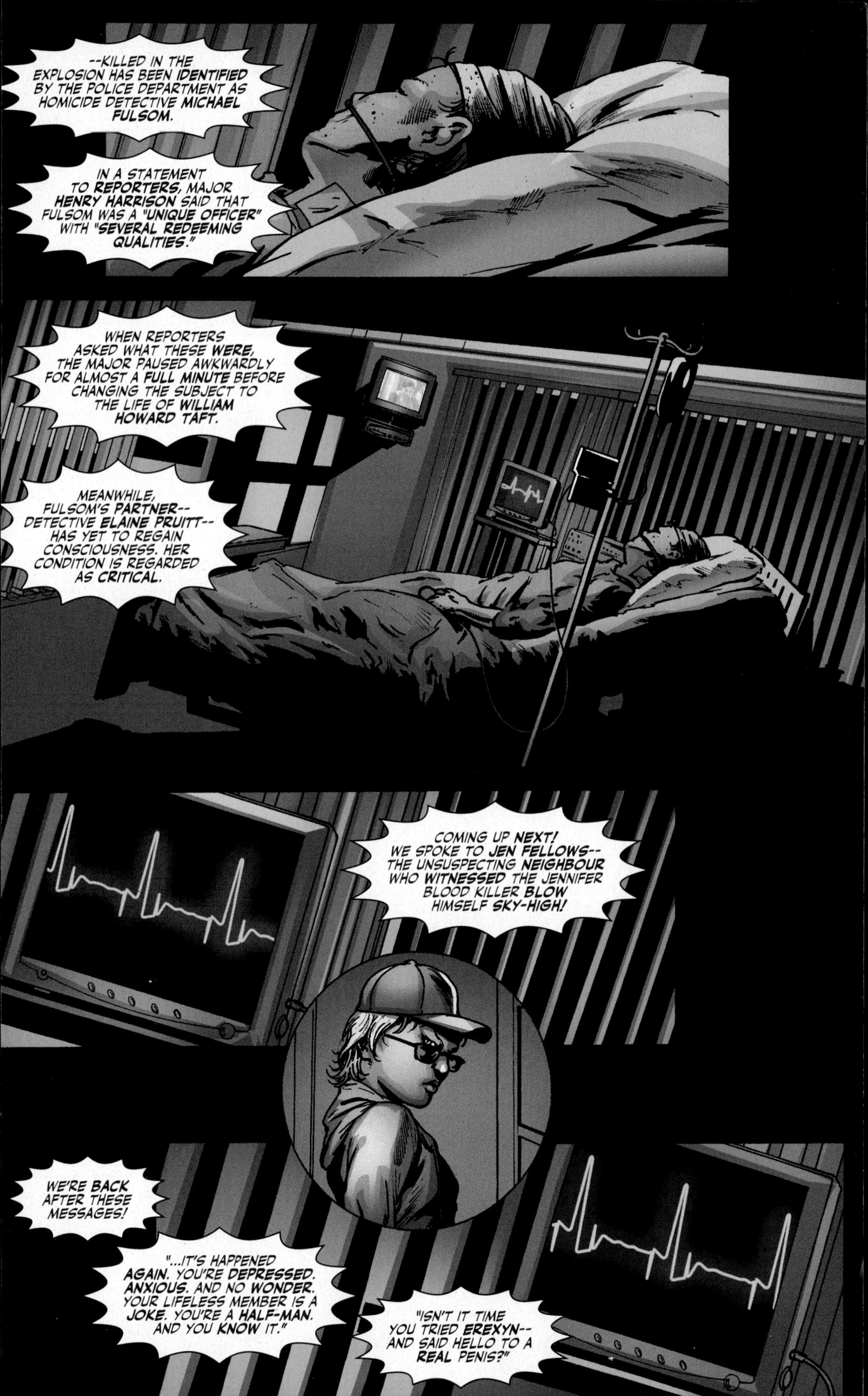
--KILLED IN THE EXPLOSION HAS BEEN IDENTIFIED BY THE POLICE DEPARTMENT AS HOMICIDE DETECTIVE MICHAEL FULSOM.
IN A STATEMENT TO REPORTERS, MAJOR HENRY HARRISON SAID THAT FULSOM WAS A "UNIQUE OFFICER" WITH "SEVERAL REDEEMING QUALITIES."
WHEN REPORTERS ASKED WHAT THESE WERE, THE MAJOR PAUSED AWKWARDLY FOR ALMOST A FULL MINUTE BEFORE CHANGING THE SUBJECT TO THE LIFE OF WILLIAM HOWARD TAFT.
MEANWHILE, FULSOM'S PARTNER--DETECTIVE ELAINE PRUITT--HAS YET TO REGAIN CONSCIOUSNESS. HER CONDITION IS REGARDED AS CRITICAL.
COMING UP NEXT! WE SPOKE TO JEN FELLOWS--THE UNSUSPECTING NEIGHBOUR WHO WITNESSED THE JENNIFER BLOOD KILLER BLOW HIMSELF SKY-HIGH!
WE'RE BACK AFTER THESE MESSAGES!
"...IT'S HAPPENED AGAIN. YOU'RE DEPRESSED. ANXIOUS. AND NO WONDER. YOUR LIFELESS MEMBER IS A JOKE. YOU'RE A HALF-MAN. AND YOU KNOW IT."
"ISN'T IT TIME YOU TRIED EREXYN--AND SAID HELLO TO A REAL PENIS?"

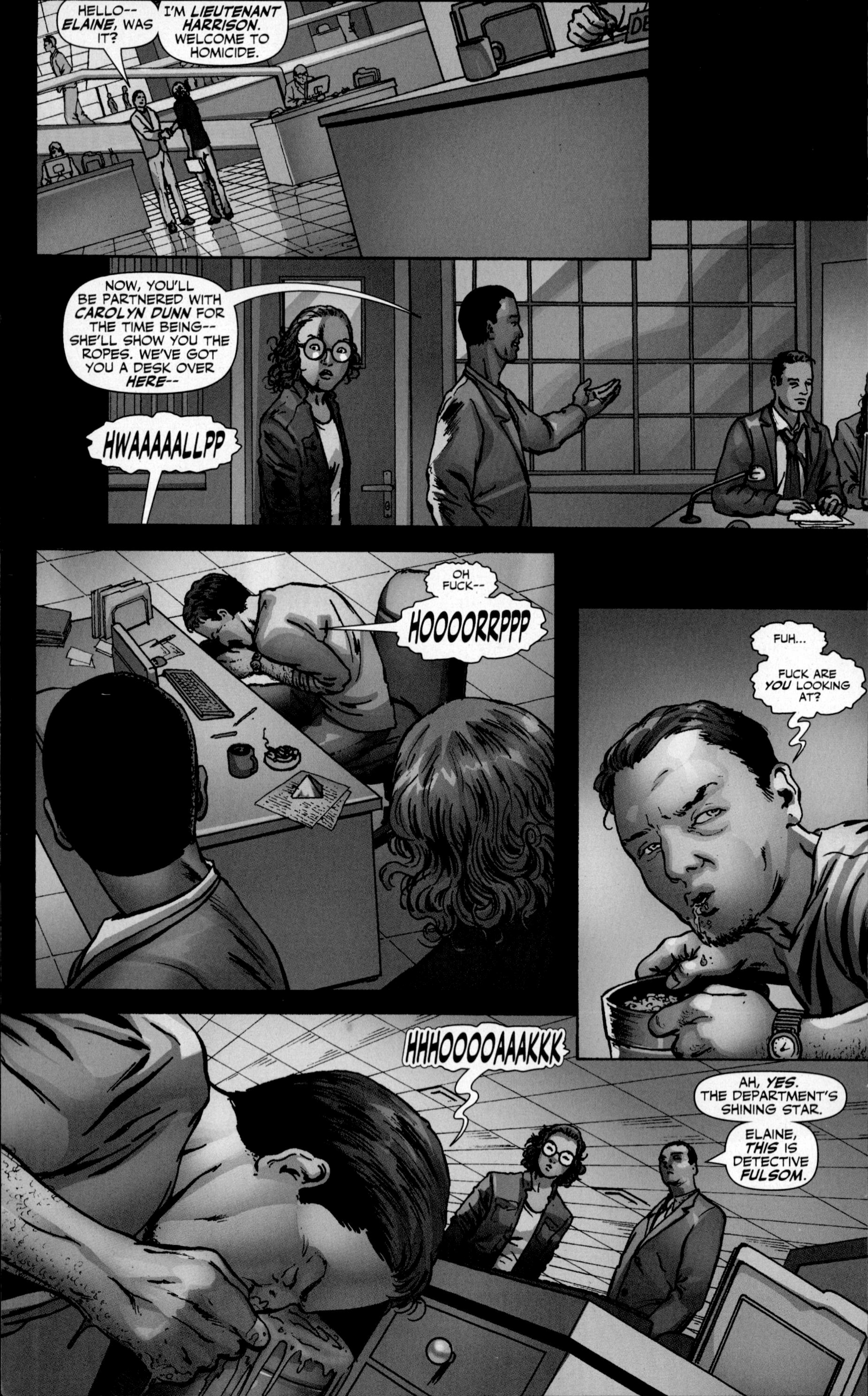
HELLO-- ELAINE, WAS IT?
I'M LIEUTENANT HARRISON. WELCOME TO HOMICIDE.
NOW, YOU'LL BE PARTNERED WITH CAROLYN DUNN FOR THE TIME BEING-- SHE'LL SHOW YOU THE ROPES. WE'VE GOT YOU A DESK OVER HERE--
HWAAAAALLPP
OH FUCK--
HOOOORRPPP
FUH...
FUCK ARE YOU LOOKING AT?
HHHOOOOAAAKKK
AH, YES. THE DEPARTMENT'S SHINING STAR.
ELAINE, THIS IS DETECTIVE FULSOM.

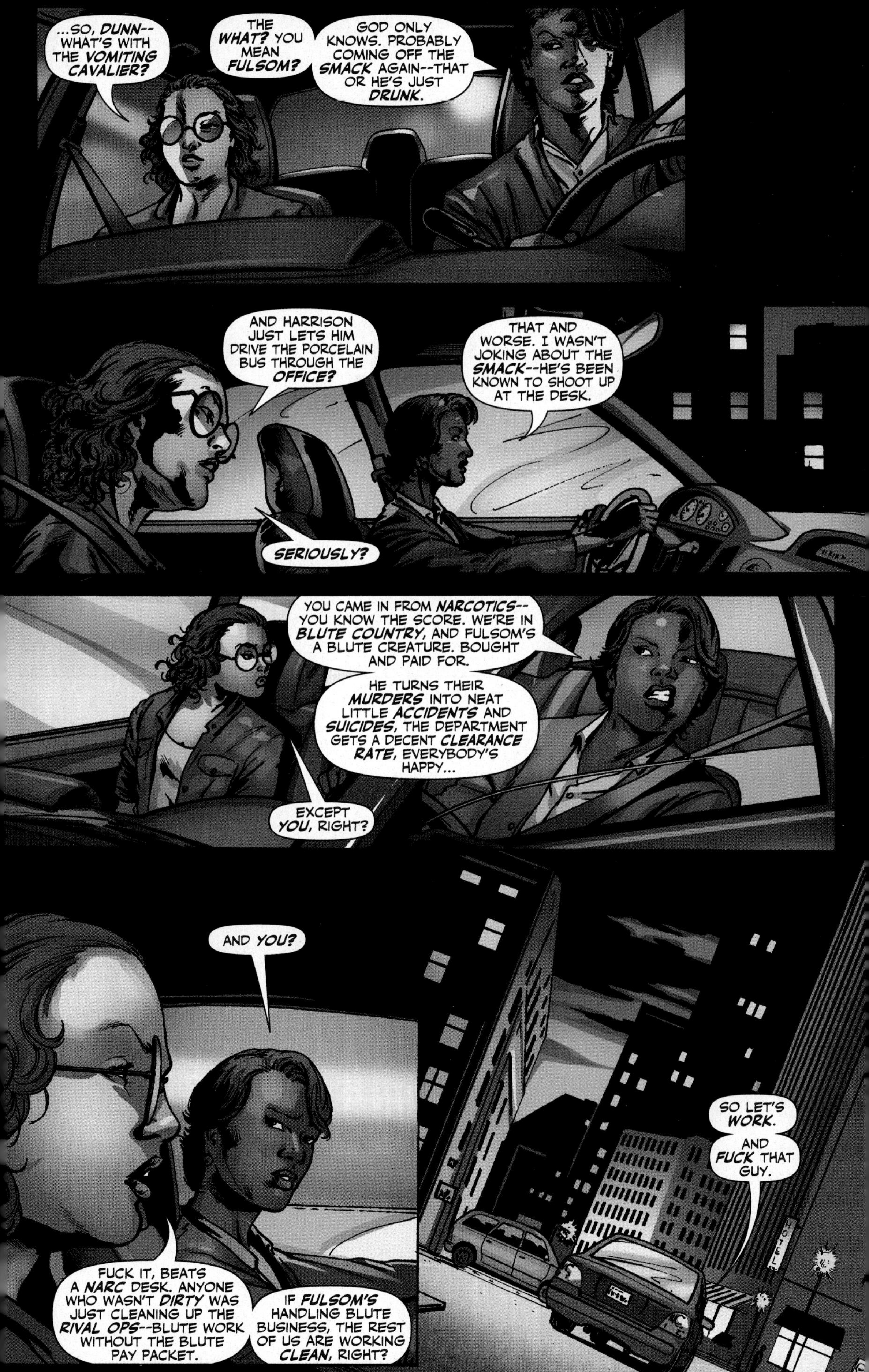
...SO, DUNN--WHAT'S WITH THE VOMITING CAVALIER?
THE WHAT? YOU MEAN FULSOM?
GOD ONLY KNOWS. PROBABLY COMING OFF THE SMACK AGAIN--THAT OR HE'S JUST DRUNK.
AND HARRISON JUST LETS HIM DRIVE THE PORCELAIN BUS THROUGH THE OFFICE?
THAT AND WORSE. I WASN'T JOKING ABOUT THE SMACK--HE'S BEEN KNOWN TO SHOOT UP AT THE DESK.
SERIOUSLY?
YOU CAME IN FROM NARCOTICS--YOU KNOW THE SCORE. WE'RE IN BLUTE COUNTRY, AND FULSOM'S A BLUTE CREATURE. BOUGHT AND PAID FOR.
HE TURNS THEIR MURDERS INTO NEAT LITTLE ACCIDENTS AND SUICIDES, THE DEPARTMENT GETS A DECENT CLEARANCE RATE, EVERYBODY'S HAPPY...
EXCEPT YOU, RIGHT?
AND YOU?
FUCK IT, BEATS A NARC DESK. ANYONE WHO WASN'T DIRTY WAS JUST CLEANING UP THE RIVAL OPS--BLUTE WORK WITHOUT THE BLUTE PAY PACKET.
IF FULSOM'S HANDLING BLUTE BUSINESS, THE REST OF US ARE WORKING CLEAN, RIGHT?
SO LET'S WORK.
AND FUCK THAT GUY.
HOTEL

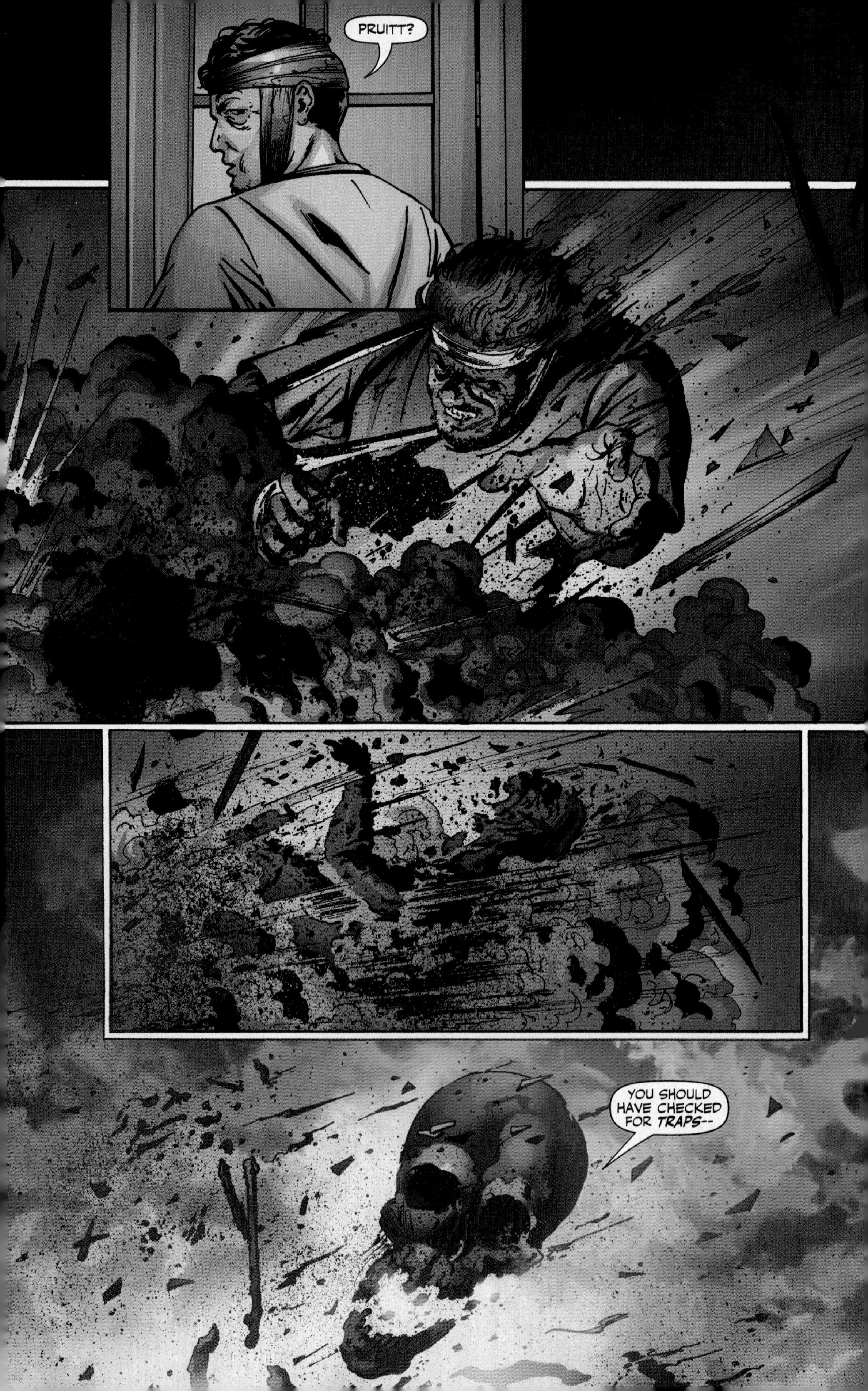
PRUITT?
YOU SHOULD HAVE CHECKED FOR *TRAPS*--

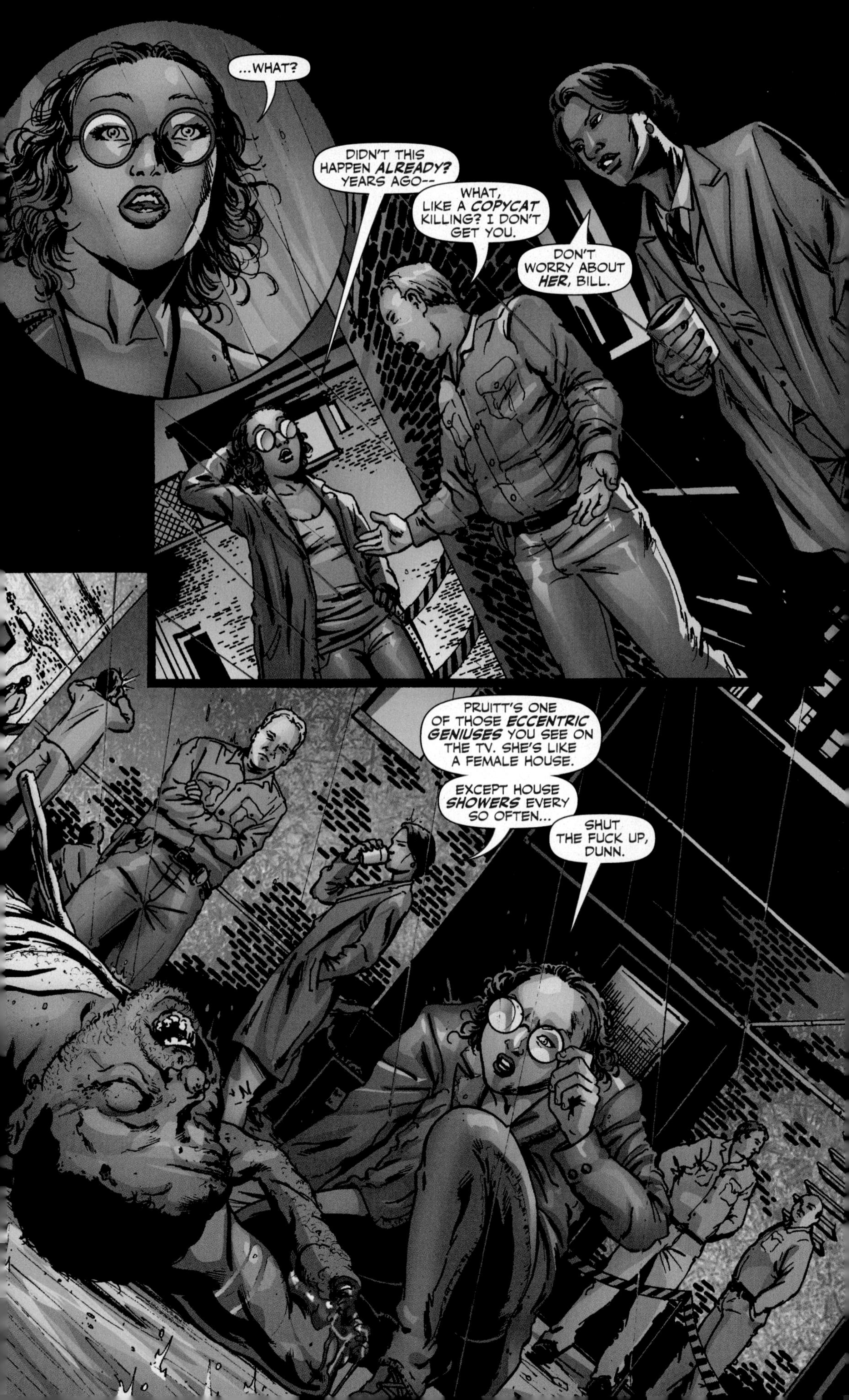
...WHAT?
DIDN'T THIS HAPPEN ***ALREADY?*** YEARS AGO--
WHAT, LIKE A ***COPYCAT*** KILLING? I DON'T GET YOU.
DON'T WORRY ABOUT ***HER***, BILL.
PRUITT'S ONE OF THOSE ***ECCENTRIC GENIUSES*** YOU SEE ON THE TV. SHE'S LIKE A FEMALE HOUSE.
EXCEPT HOUSE ***SHOWERS*** EVERY SO OFTEN...
SHUT THE FUCK UP, DUNN.

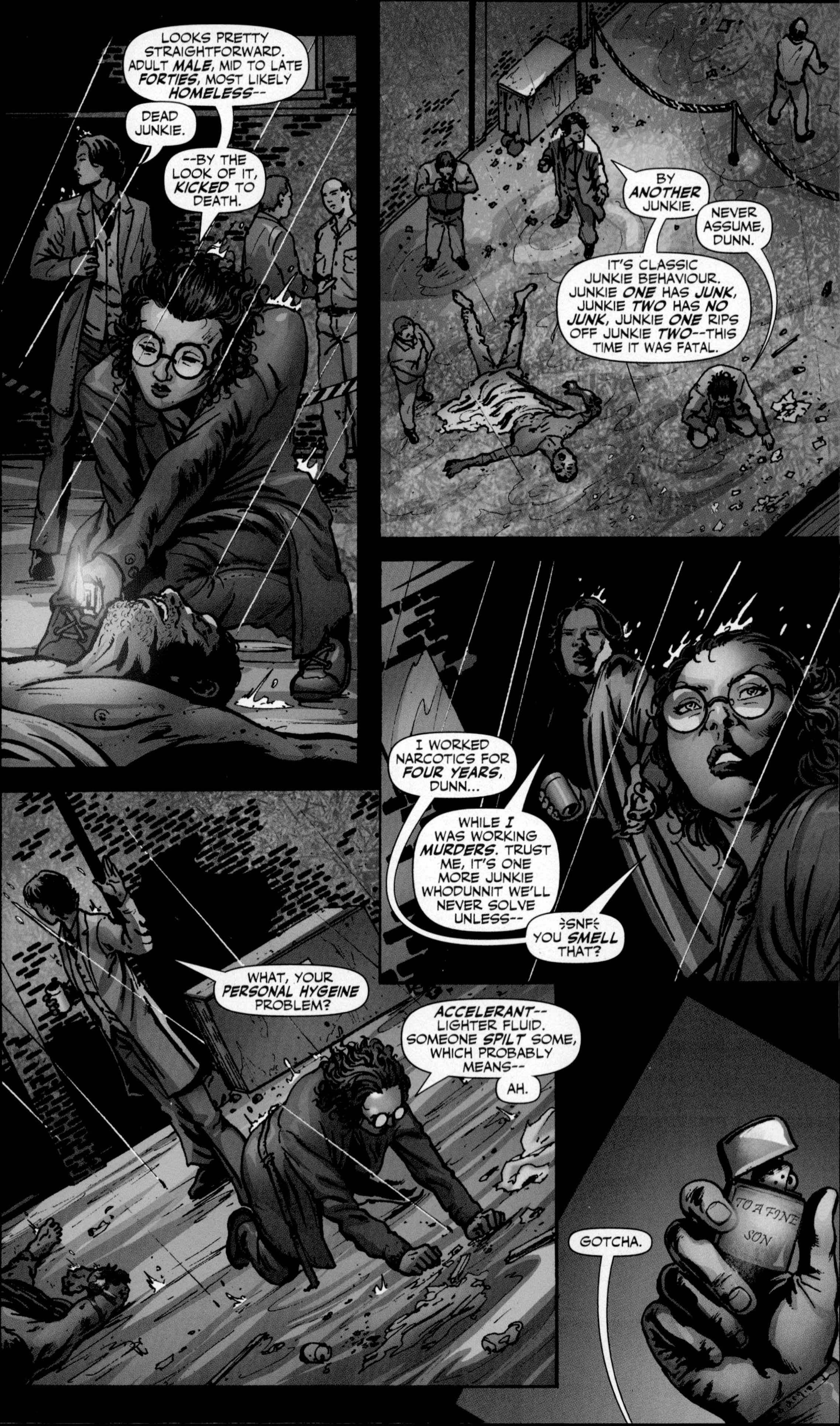
LOOKS PRETTY STRAIGHTFORWARD. ADULT MALE, MID TO LATE FORTIES, MOST LIKELY HOMELESS--
DEAD JUNKIE.
--BY THE LOOK OF IT, KICKED TO DEATH.
BY ANOTHER JUNKIE.
NEVER ASSUME, DUNN.
IT'S CLASSIC JUNKIE BEHAVIOUR. JUNKIE ONE HAS JUNK, JUNKIE TWO HAS NO JUNK, JUNKIE ONE RIPS OFF JUNKIE TWO--THIS TIME IT WAS FATAL.
I WORKED NARCOTICS FOR FOUR YEARS, DUNN...
WHILE I WAS WORKING MURDERS. TRUST ME, IT'S ONE MORE JUNKIE WHODUNNIT WE'LL NEVER SOLVE UNLESS--
SNF
YOU SMELL THAT?
WHAT, YOUR PERSONAL HYGEINE PROBLEM?
ACCELERANT-- LIGHTER FLUID. SOMEONE SPILT SOME, WHICH PROBABLY MEANS--
AH.
TO A FINE SON
GOTCHA.

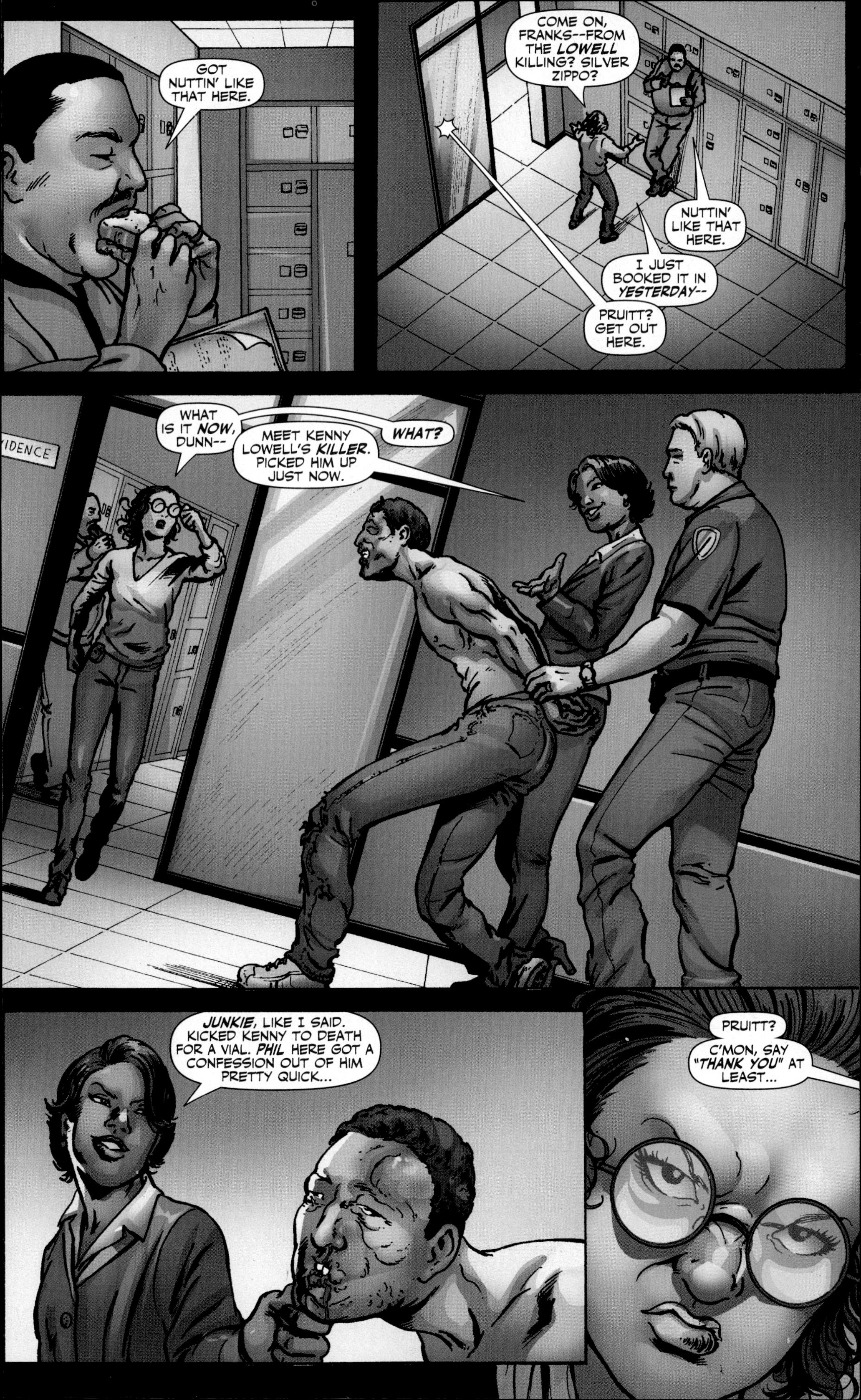
GOT NUTTIN' LIKE THAT HERE.
COME ON, FRANKS--FROM THE LOWELL KILLING? SILVER ZIPPO?
NUTTIN' LIKE THAT HERE.
I JUST BOOKED IT IN YESTERDAY--
PRUITT? GET OUT HERE.
WHAT IS IT NOW, DUNN--
MEET KENNY LOWELL'S KILLER. PICKED HIM UP JUST NOW.
WHAT?
IDENCE
JUNKIE, LIKE I SAID. KICKED KENNY TO DEATH FOR A VIAL. PHIL HERE GOT A CONFESSION OUT OF HIM PRETTY QUICK...
PRUITT?
C'MON, SAY "THANK YOU" AT LEAST...

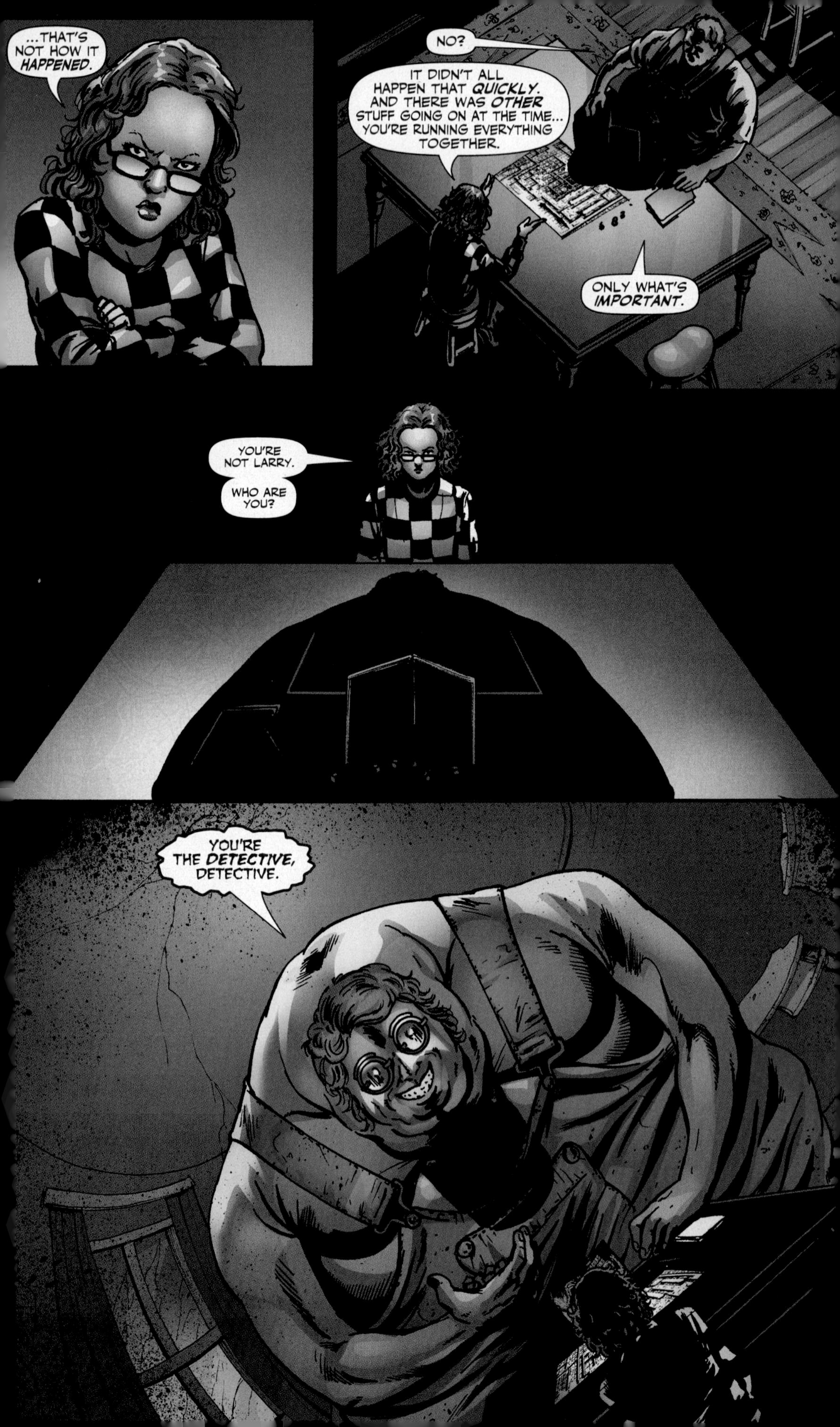
...THAT'S NOT HOW IT HAPPENED.
NO?
IT DIDN'T ALL HAPPEN THAT QUICKLY. AND THERE WAS OTHER STUFF GOING ON AT THE TIME... YOU'RE RUNNING EVERYTHING TOGETHER.
ONLY WHAT'S IMPORTANT.
YOU'RE NOT LARRY.
WHO ARE YOU?
YOU'RE THE DETECTIVE, DETECTIVE.

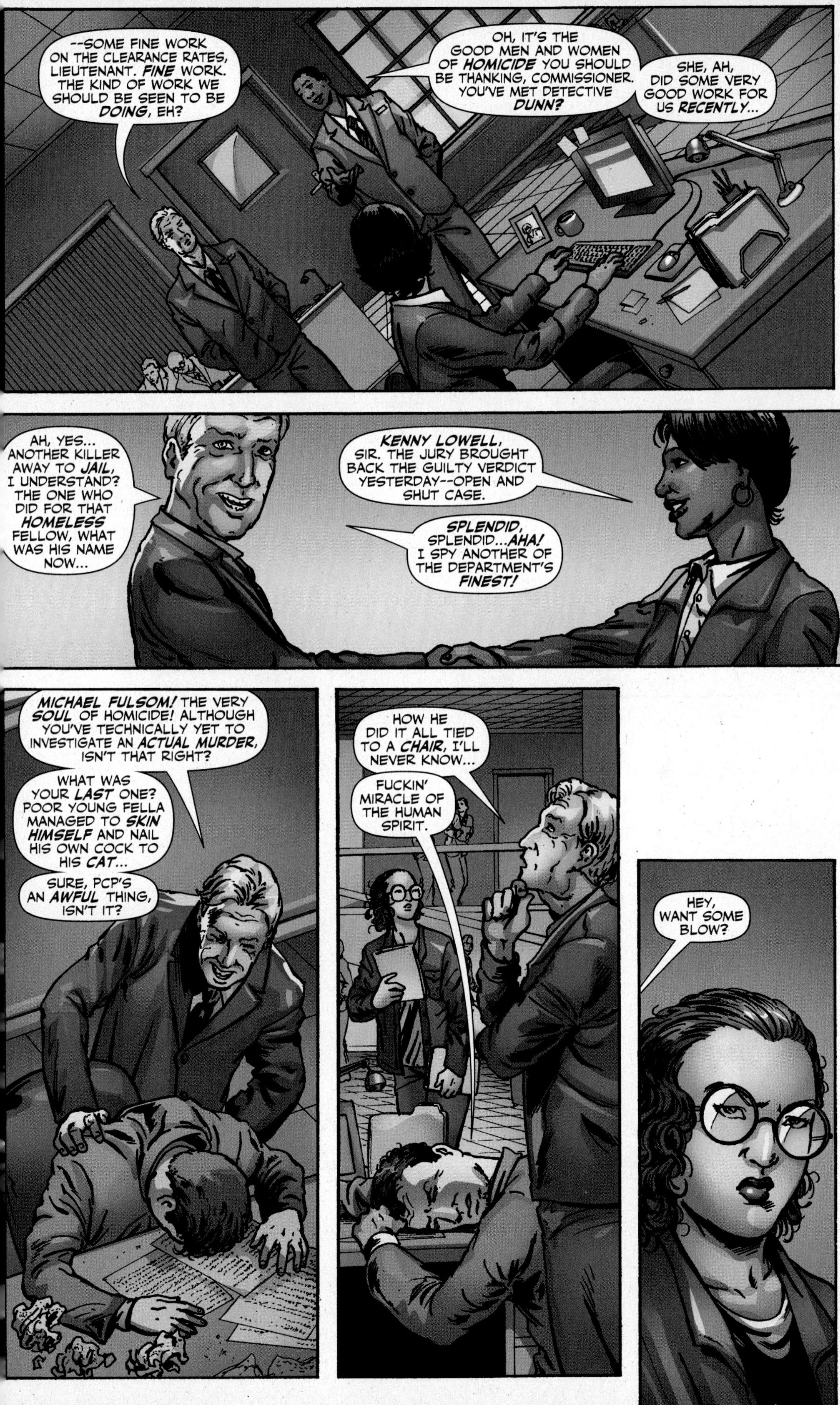
--SOME FINE WORK ON THE CLEARANCE RATES, LIEUTENANT. FINE WORK. THE KIND OF WORK WE SHOULD BE SEEN TO BE DOING, EH?
OH, IT'S THE GOOD MEN AND WOMEN OF HOMICIDE YOU SHOULD BE THANKING, COMMISSIONER. YOU'VE MET DETECTIVE DUNN?
SHE, AH, DID SOME VERY GOOD WORK FOR US RECENTLY...
AH, YES... ANOTHER KILLER AWAY TO JAIL, I UNDERSTAND? THE ONE WHO DID FOR THAT HOMELESS FELLOW, WHAT WAS HIS NAME NOW...
KENNY LOWELL, SIR. THE JURY BROUGHT BACK THE GUILTY VERDICT YESTERDAY--OPEN AND SHUT CASE.
SPLENDID, SPLENDID...AHA! I SPY ANOTHER OF THE DEPARTMENT'S FINEST!
MICHAEL FULSOM! THE VERY SOUL OF HOMICIDE! ALTHOUGH YOU'VE TECHNICALLY YET TO INVESTIGATE AN ACTUAL MURDER, ISN'T THAT RIGHT?
WHAT WAS YOUR LAST ONE? POOR YOUNG FELLA MANAGED TO SKIN HIMSELF AND NAIL HIS OWN COCK TO HIS CAT...
SURE, PCP'S AN AWFUL THING, ISN'T IT?
HOW HE DID IT ALL TIED TO A CHAIR, I'LL NEVER KNOW...
FUCKIN' MIRACLE OF THE HUMAN SPIRIT.
HEY, WANT SOME BLOW?

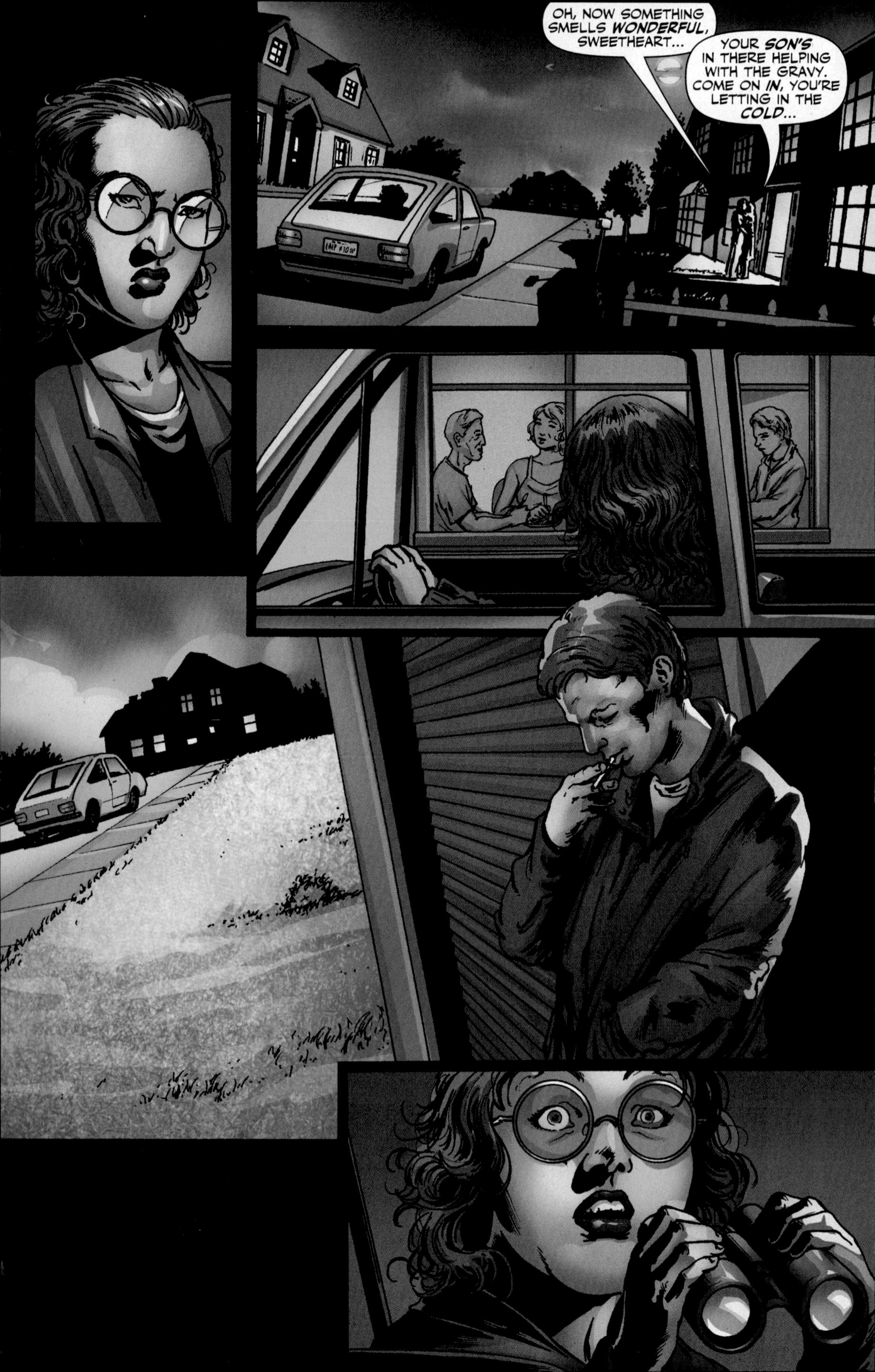
OH, NOW SOMETHING SMELLS WONDERFUL, SWEETHEART...
YOUR SON'S IN THERE HELPING WITH THE GRAVY. COME ON IN, YOU'RE LETTING IN THE COLD...

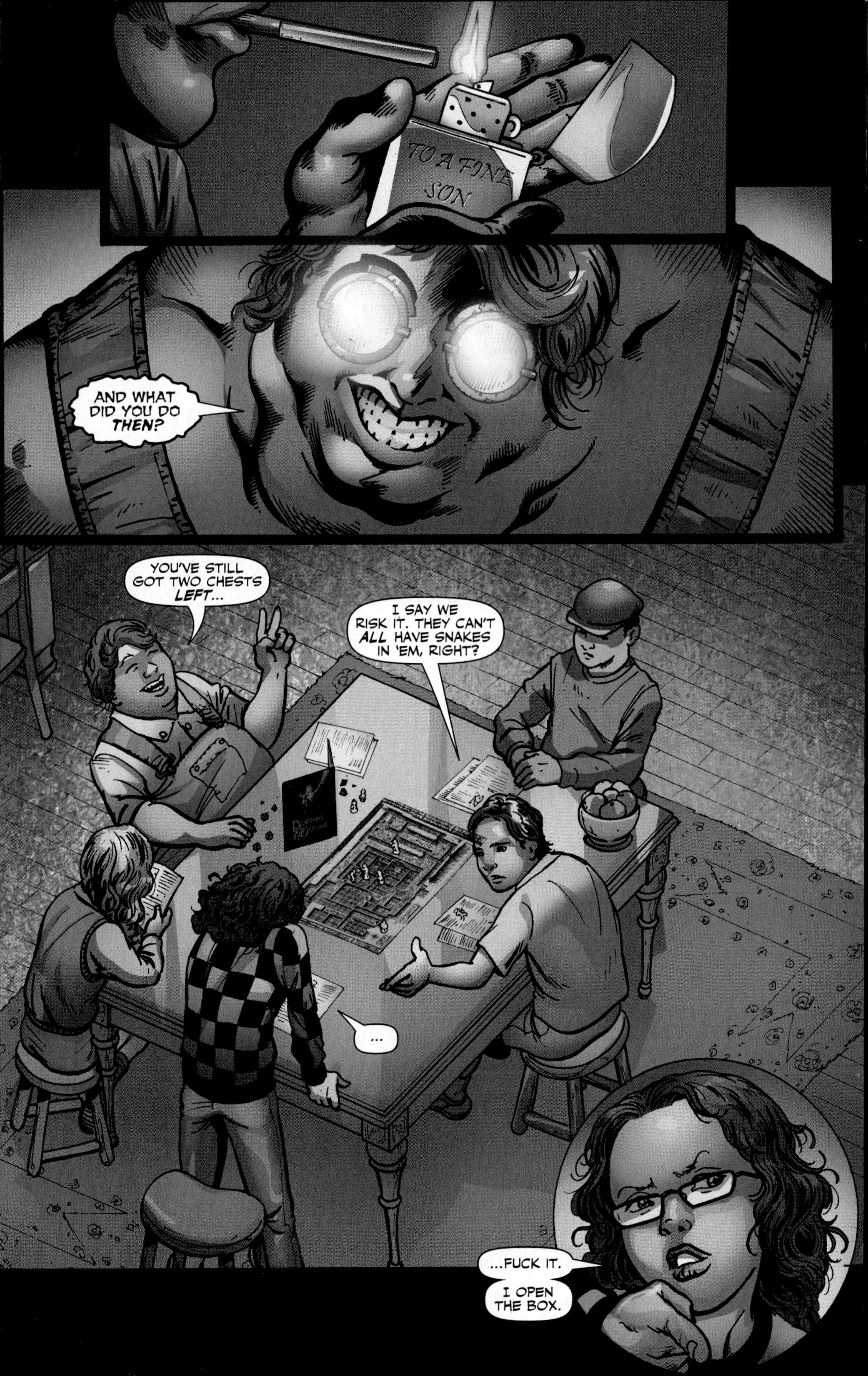

TO A FINE SON
AND WHAT DID YOU DO *THEN?*
YOU'VE STILL GOT TWO CHESTS *LEFT*...
I SAY WE RISK IT. THEY CAN'T *ALL* HAVE SNAKES IN 'EM, RIGHT?
...
...FUCK IT.
I OPEN THE BOX.

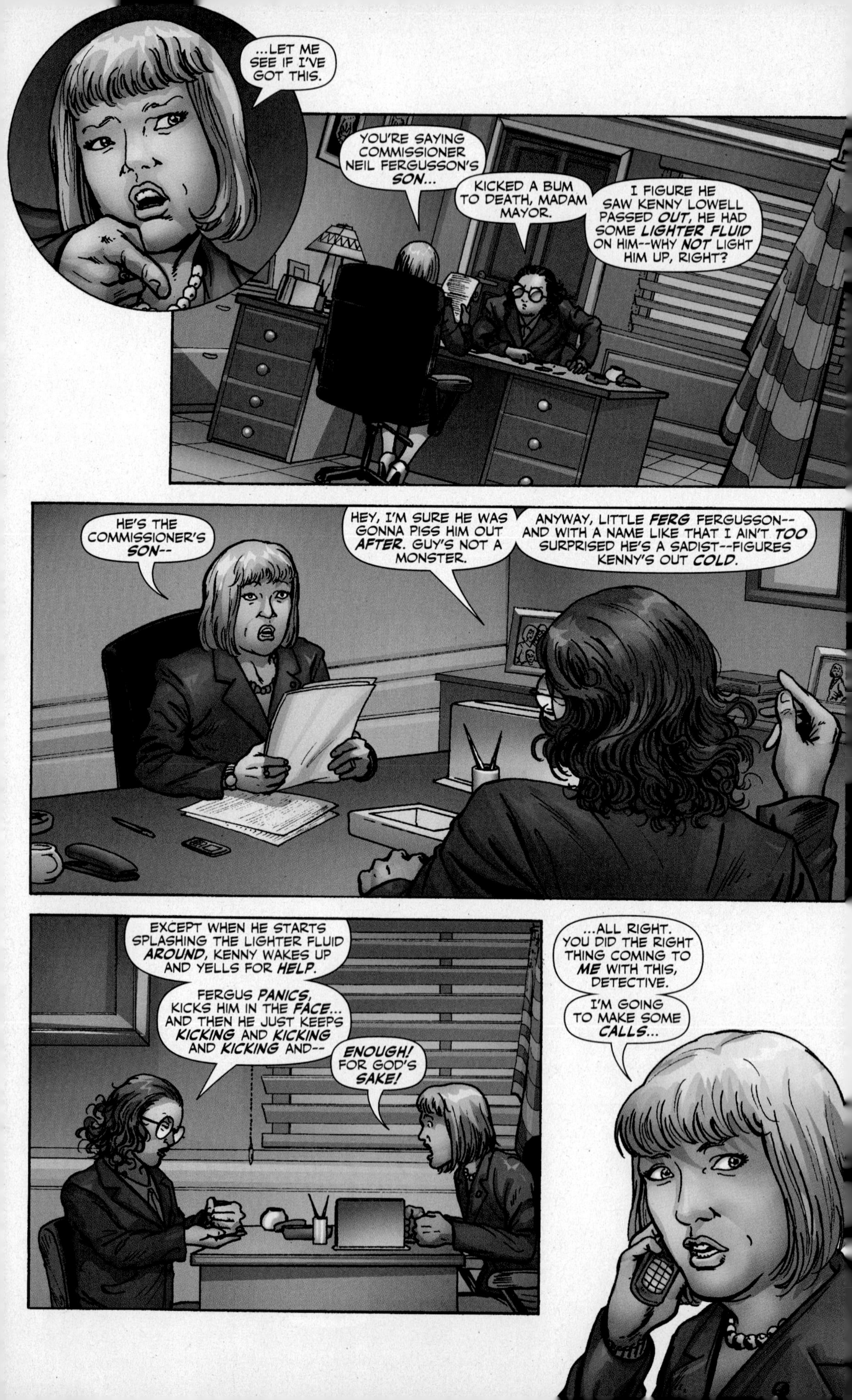
...LET ME SEE IF I'VE GOT THIS.
YOU'RE SAYING COMMISSIONER NEIL FERGUSSON'S SON...
KICKED A BUM TO DEATH, MADAM MAYOR.
I FIGURE HE SAW KENNY LOWELL PASSED OUT, HE HAD SOME LIGHTER FLUID ON HIM--WHY NOT LIGHT HIM UP, RIGHT?
HE'S THE COMMISSIONER'S SON--
HEY, I'M SURE HE WAS GONNA PISS HIM OUT AFTER. GUY'S NOT A MONSTER.
ANYWAY, LITTLE FERG FERGUSSON--AND WITH A NAME LIKE THAT I AIN'T TOO SURPRISED HE'S A SADIST--FIGURES KENNY'S OUT COLD.
EXCEPT WHEN HE STARTS SPLASHING THE LIGHTER FLUID AROUND, KENNY WAKES UP AND YELLS FOR HELP.
FERGUS PANICS, KICKS HIM IN THE FACE... AND THEN HE JUST KEEPS KICKING AND KICKING AND KICKING AND--
ENOUGH! FOR GOD'S SAKE!
...ALL RIGHT. YOU DID THE RIGHT THING COMING TO ME WITH THIS, DETECTIVE.
I'M GOING TO MAKE SOME CALLS...

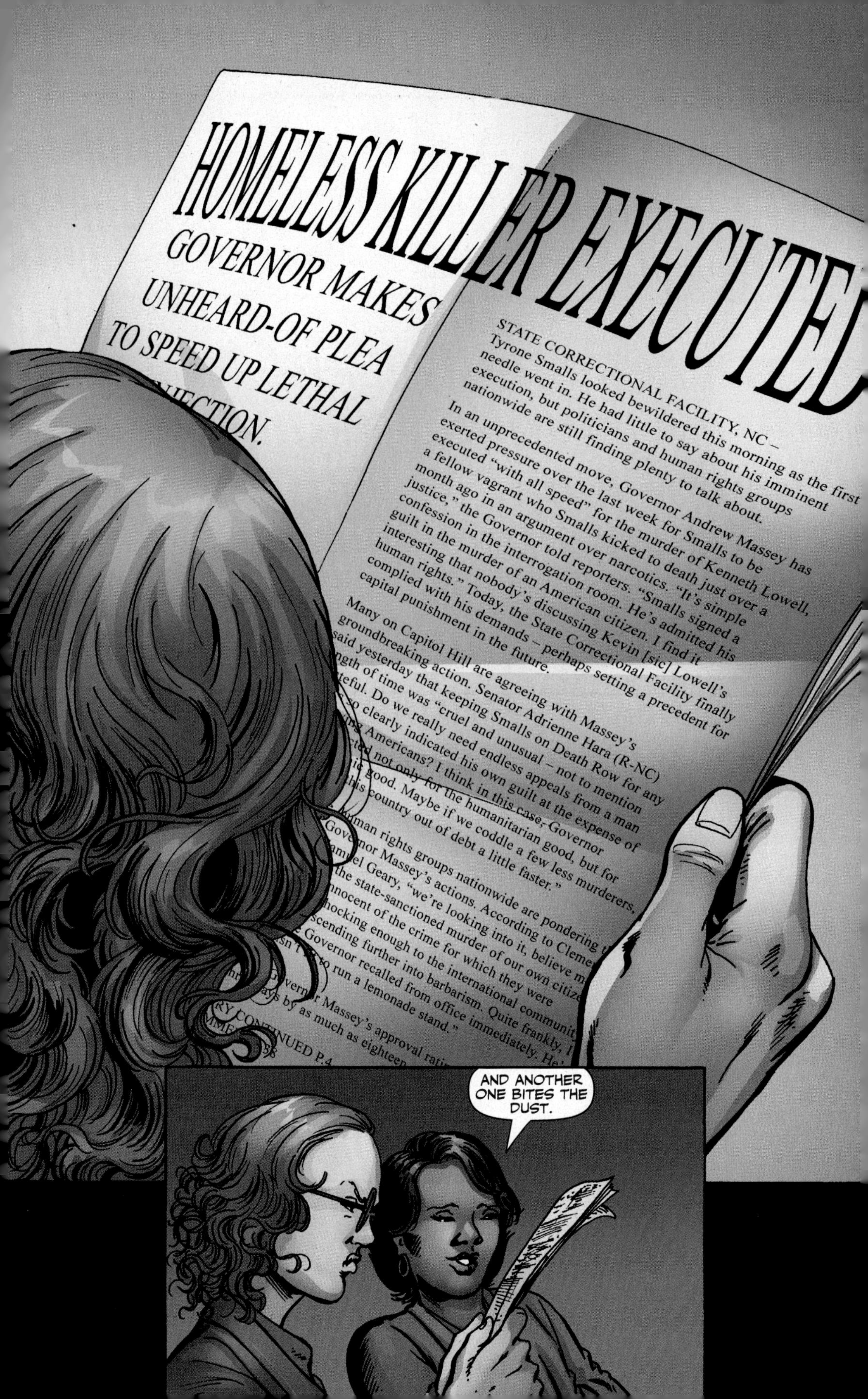
HOMELESS KILLER EXECUTED
GOVERNOR MAKES UNHEARD-OF PLEA TO SPEED UP LETHAL INJECTION.
STATE CORRECTIONAL FACILITY, NC – Tyrone Smalls looked bewildered this morning as the first needle went in. He had little to say about his imminent execution, but politicians and human rights groups nationwide are still finding plenty to talk about.
In an unprecedented move, Governor Andrew Massey has exerted pressure over the last week for Smalls to be executed "with all speed" for the murder of Kenneth Lowell, a fellow vagrant who Smalls kicked to death just over a month ago in an argument over narcotics. "It's simple justice," the Governor told reporters. "Smalls signed a confession in the interrogation room. He's admitted his guilt in the murder of an American citizen. I find it interesting that nobody's discussing Kevin [sic] Lowell's human rights." Today, the State Correctional Facility finally complied with his demands – perhaps setting a precedent for capital punishment in the future.
Many on Capitol Hill are agreeing with Massey's groundbreaking action. Senator Adrienne Hara (R-NC) said yesterday that keeping Smalls on Death Row for any ngth of time was "cruel and unusual – not to mention teful. Do we really need endless appeals from a man so clearly indicated his own guilt at the expense of Americans? I think in this case, Governor ted not only for the humanitarian good, but for ic good. Maybe if we coddle a few less murderers, this country out of debt a little faster."
human rights groups nationwide are pondering Governor Massey's actions. According to Clem amuel Geary, "we're looking into it, believe m the state-sanctioned murder of our own citiz nnocent of the crime for which they were hocking enough to the international communit scending further into barbarism. Quite frankly, Governor recalled from office immediately. He sn't to run a lemonade stand."
Governor Massey's approval rati ays by as much as eighteen
RY CONTINUED P.4
AND ANOTHER ONE BITES THE DUST.

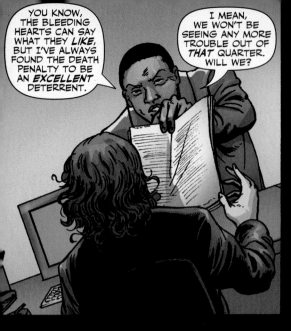

YOU KNOW, THE BLEEDING HEARTS CAN SAY WHAT THEY *LIKE*, BUT I'VE ALWAYS FOUND THE DEATH PENALTY TO BE AN *EXCELLENT* DETERRENT.

I MEAN, WE WON'T BE SEEING ANY MORE TROUBLE OUT OF *THAT* QUARTER. WILL WE?

CASE *CLOSED.*

WHICH BRINGS ME TO MY *NEXT* BIT OF NEWS. I KNOW YOU AND CAROLYN HAVE BEEN GETTING ON LIKE A *HOUSE ON FIRE*--

--A HOUSE THAT'S *BURNT TO THE GROUND* WITH A SCREAMING CHORUS OF ASSORTED *ORPHANS* AND *NUNS* TRAPPED IN IT, EVEN--

--BUT I HAVE A FEELING YOU'LL LIKE YOUR *NEW* PARTNER EVEN *MORE.*

NEW PARTNER?

OH YES.

HHHOOORRRPP

HEY, PRUITT. GOOD TO BE WORKING WITH YOU.

GIMME A SEC.

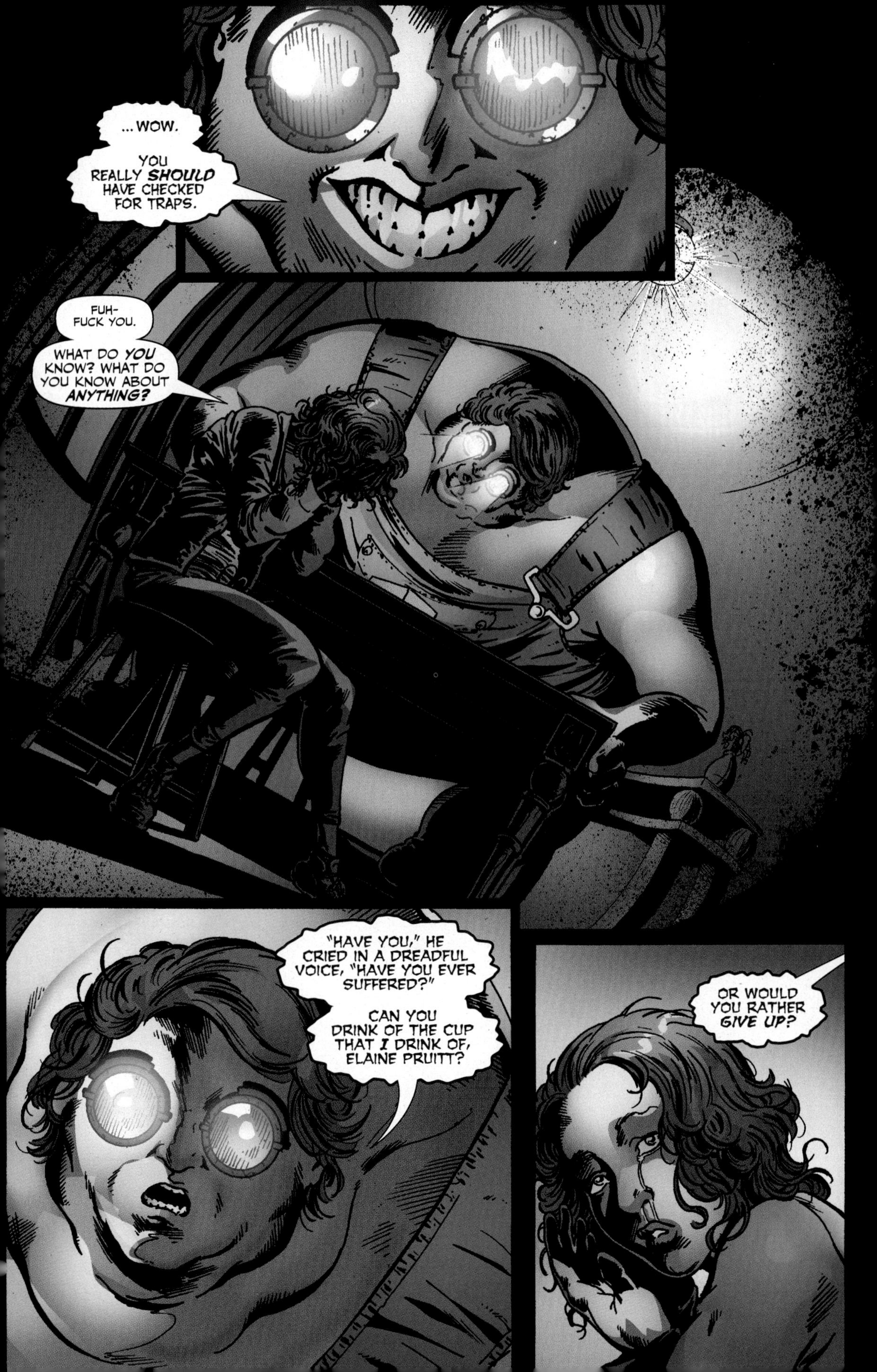
...WOW.
YOU REALLY *SHOULD* HAVE CHECKED FOR TRAPS.
FUH-FUCK YOU.
WHAT DO *YOU* KNOW? WHAT DO YOU KNOW ABOUT *ANYTHING?*
"HAVE YOU," HE CRIED IN A DREADFUL VOICE, "HAVE YOU EVER SUFFERED?"
CAN YOU DRINK OF THE CUP THAT *I* DRINK OF, ELAINE PRUITT?
OR WOULD YOU RATHER *GIVE UP?*

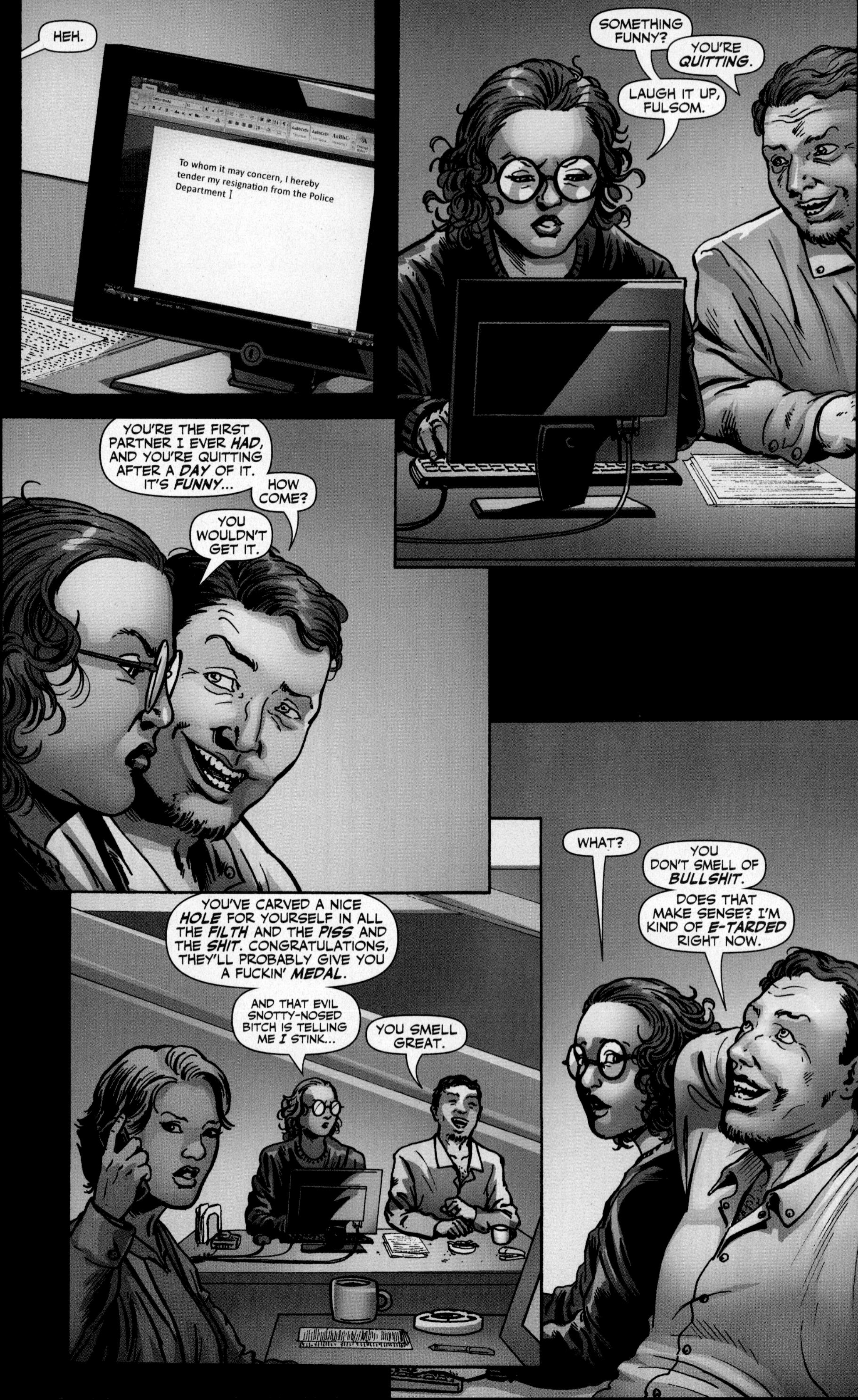
HEH.
To whom it may concern, I hereby tender my resignation from the Police Department I
SOMETHING FUNNY?
YOU'RE QUITTING.
LAUGH IT UP, FULSOM.
YOU'RE THE FIRST PARTNER I EVER HAD, AND YOU'RE QUITTING AFTER A DAY OF IT. IT'S FUNNY...
HOW COME?
YOU WOULDN'T GET IT.
WHAT?
YOU DON'T SMELL OF BULLSHIT.
DOES THAT MAKE SENSE? I'M KIND OF E-TARDED RIGHT NOW.
YOU'VE CARVED A NICE HOLE FOR YOURSELF IN ALL THE FILTH AND THE PISS AND THE SHIT. CONGRATULATIONS, THEY'LL PROBABLY GIVE YOU A FUCKIN' MEDAL.
AND THAT EVIL SNOTTY-NOSED BITCH IS TELLING ME I STINK...
YOU SMELL GREAT.

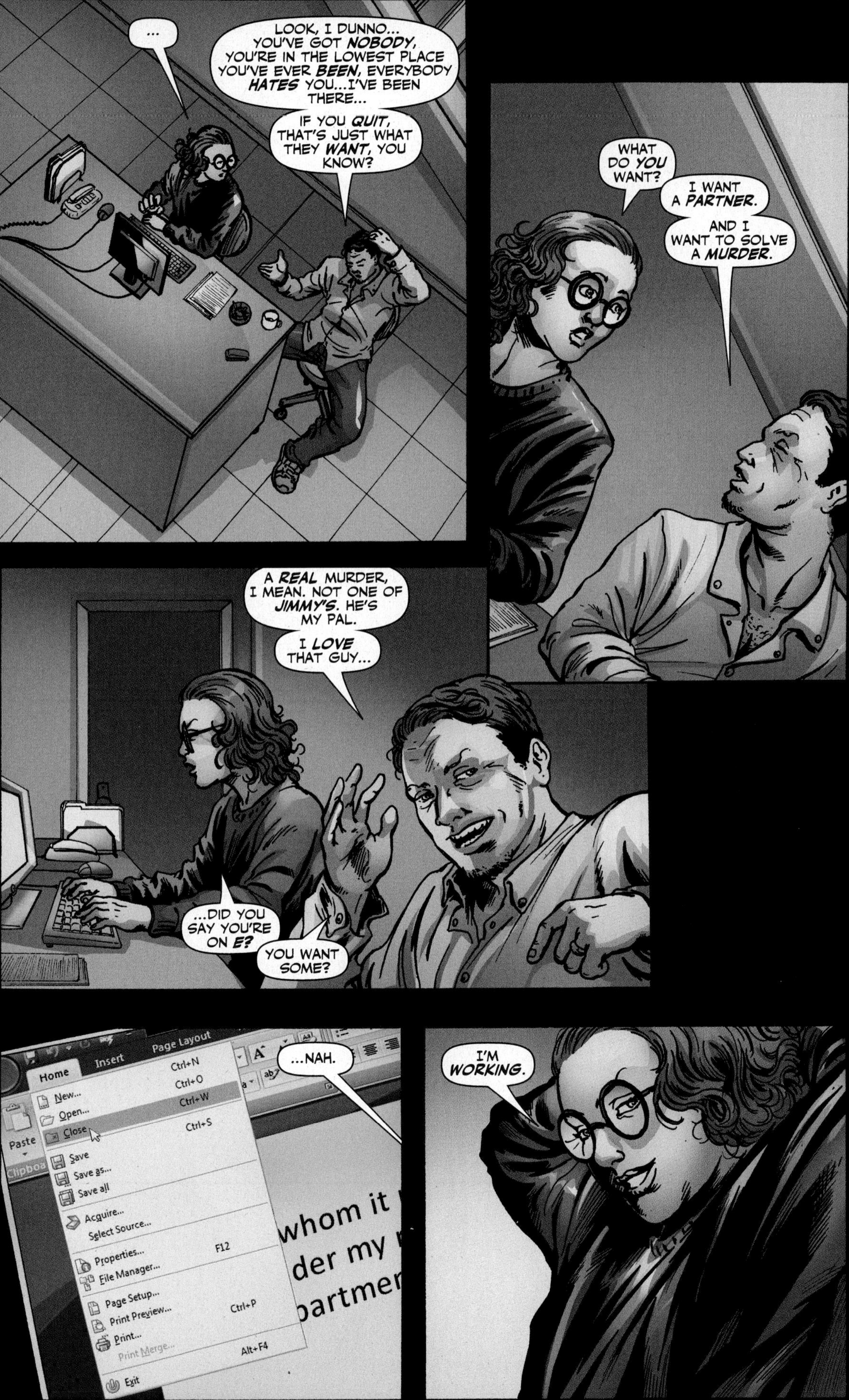
...
LOOK, I DUNNO... YOU'VE GOT NOBODY, YOU'RE IN THE LOWEST PLACE YOU'VE EVER BEEN, EVERYBODY HATES YOU...I'VE BEEN THERE...
IF YOU QUIT, THAT'S JUST WHAT THEY WANT, YOU KNOW?
WHAT DO YOU WANT?
I WANT A PARTNER.
AND I WANT TO SOLVE A MURDER.
A REAL MURDER, I MEAN. NOT ONE OF JIMMY'S. HE'S MY PAL.
I LOVE THAT GUY...
...DID YOU SAY YOU'RE ON E?
YOU WANT SOME?
Home
Insert
Page Layout
New... Ctrl+N
Open... Ctrl+O
Close Ctrl+W
Save Ctrl+S
Save as...
Save all
Acquire...
Select Source...
Properties... F12
File Manager...
Page Setup...
Print Preview... Ctrl+P
Print...
Print Merge...
Exit Alt+F4
Paste
whom it
der my
partmer
...NAH.
I'M WORKING.

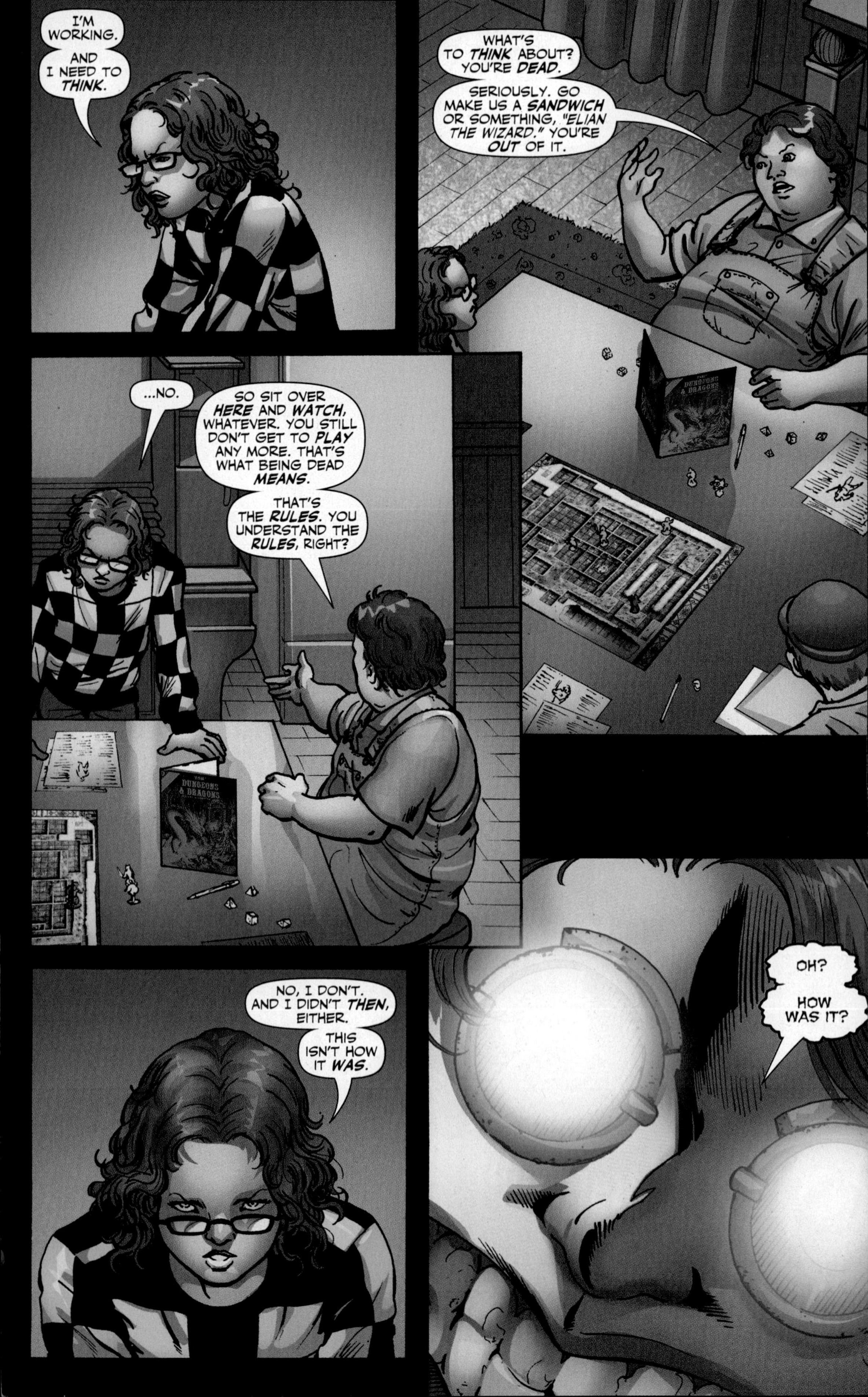
I'M WORKING.
AND I NEED TO THINK.
WHAT'S TO THINK ABOUT? YOU'RE DEAD.
SERIOUSLY. GO MAKE US A SANDWICH OR SOMETHING, "ELIAN THE WIZARD." YOU'RE OUT OF IT.
...NO.
SO SIT OVER HERE AND WATCH, WHATEVER. YOU STILL DON'T GET TO PLAY ANY MORE. THAT'S WHAT BEING DEAD MEANS.
THAT'S THE RULES. YOU UNDERSTAND THE RULES, RIGHT?
NO, I DON'T. AND I DIDN'T THEN, EITHER.
THIS ISN'T HOW IT WAS.
OH?
HOW WAS IT?

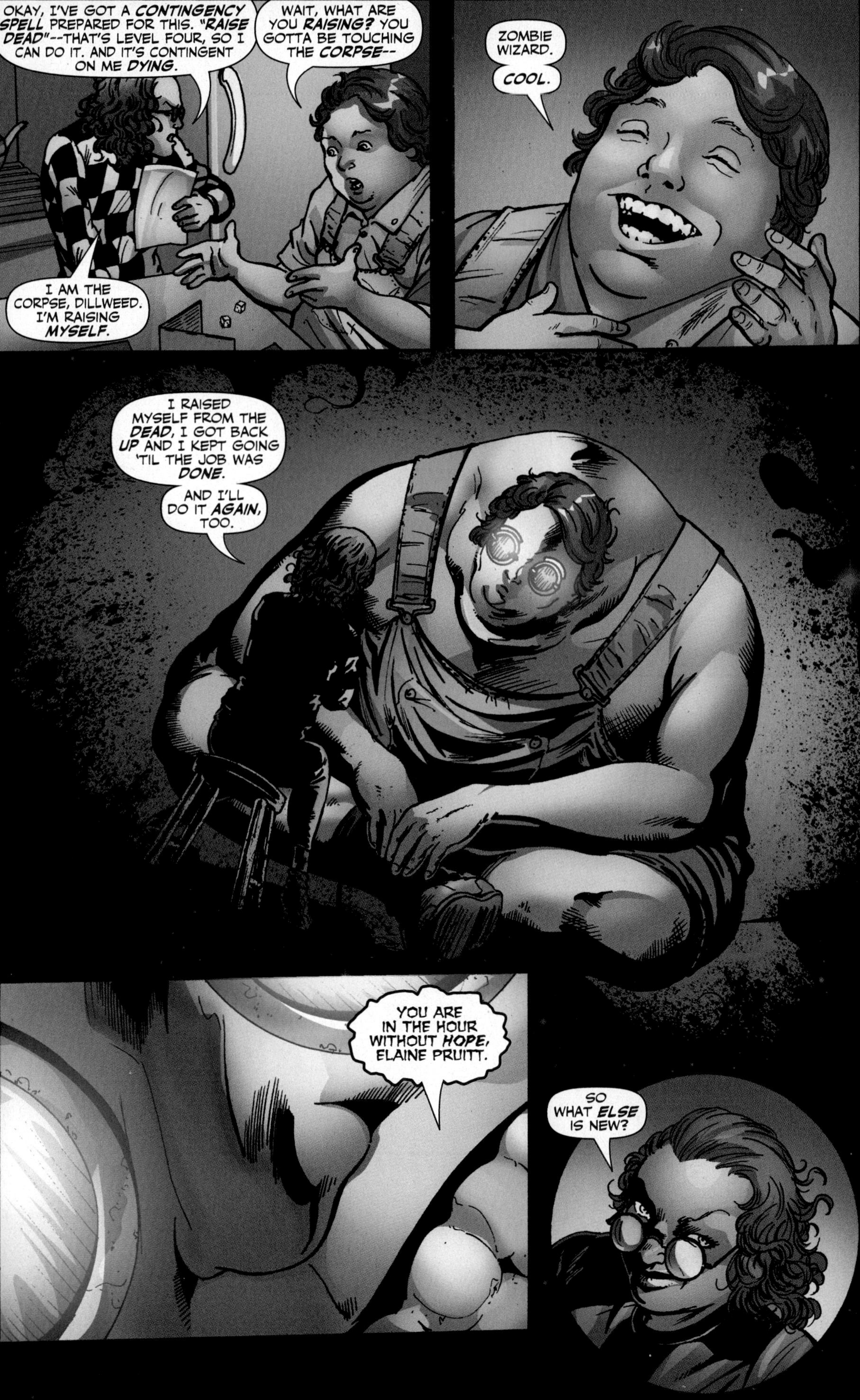
OKAY, I'VE GOT A CONTINGENCY SPELL PREPARED FOR THIS. "RAISE DEAD"--THAT'S LEVEL FOUR, SO I CAN DO IT. AND IT'S CONTINGENT ON ME DYING.
WAIT, WHAT ARE YOU RAISING? YOU GOTTA BE TOUCHING THE CORPSE--
I AM THE CORPSE, DILLWEED. I'M RAISING MYSELF.
ZOMBIE WIZARD.
COOL.
I RAISED MYSELF FROM THE DEAD, I GOT BACK UP AND I KEPT GOING 'TIL THE JOB WAS DONE.
AND I'LL DO IT AGAIN, TOO.
YOU ARE IN THE HOUR WITHOUT HOPE, ELAINE PRUITT.
SO WHAT ELSE IS NEW?

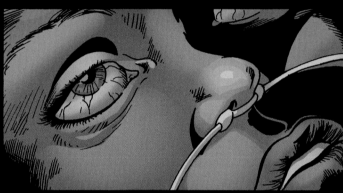

...FUCK.

YOU SAID IT.

SO WHAT NOW?

WELL, I DON'T KNOW ABOUT *YOU*, BUT I FEEL LIKE SHIT. I'M TAKING A FEW DAYS.

AFTER *THAT*, I FIGURE WE GET UP, GO BACK TO WORK AND WE TAKE DOWN *JENNIFER BLOOD*.

YOU *IN*?

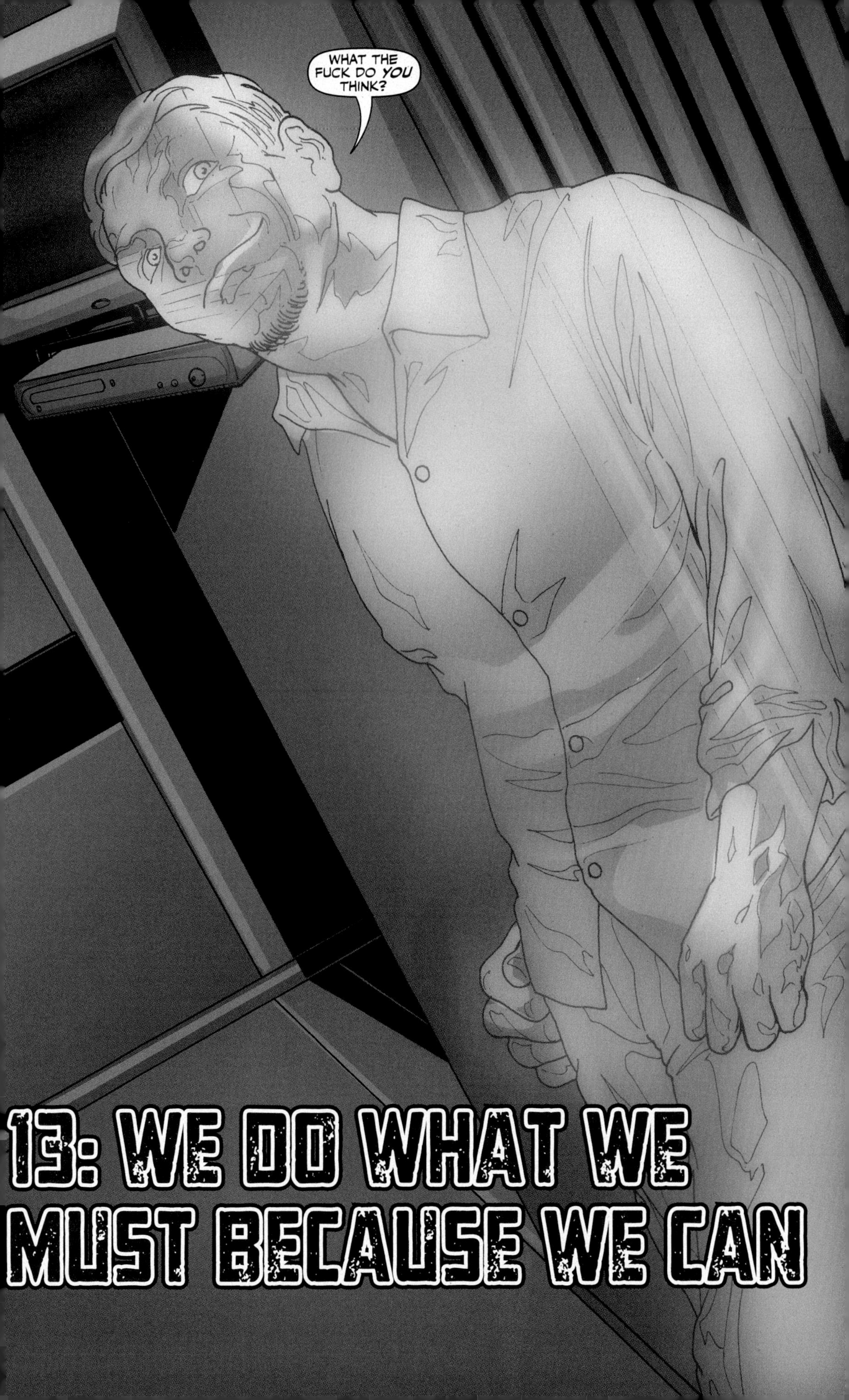
WHAT THE FUCK DO YOU THINK?
13: WE DO WHAT WE MUST BECAUSE WE CAN

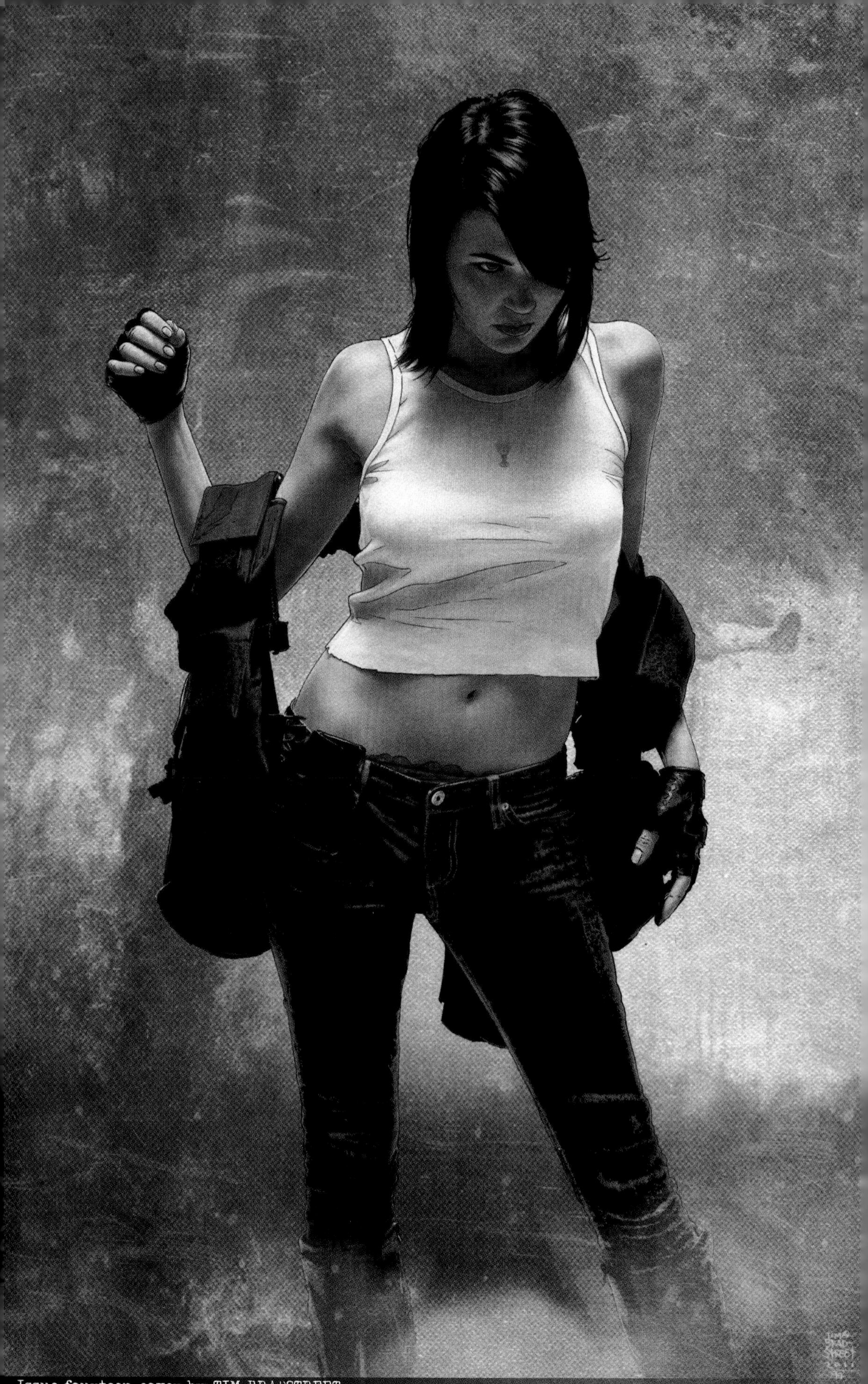

Issue fourteen cover by TIM BRADSTREET

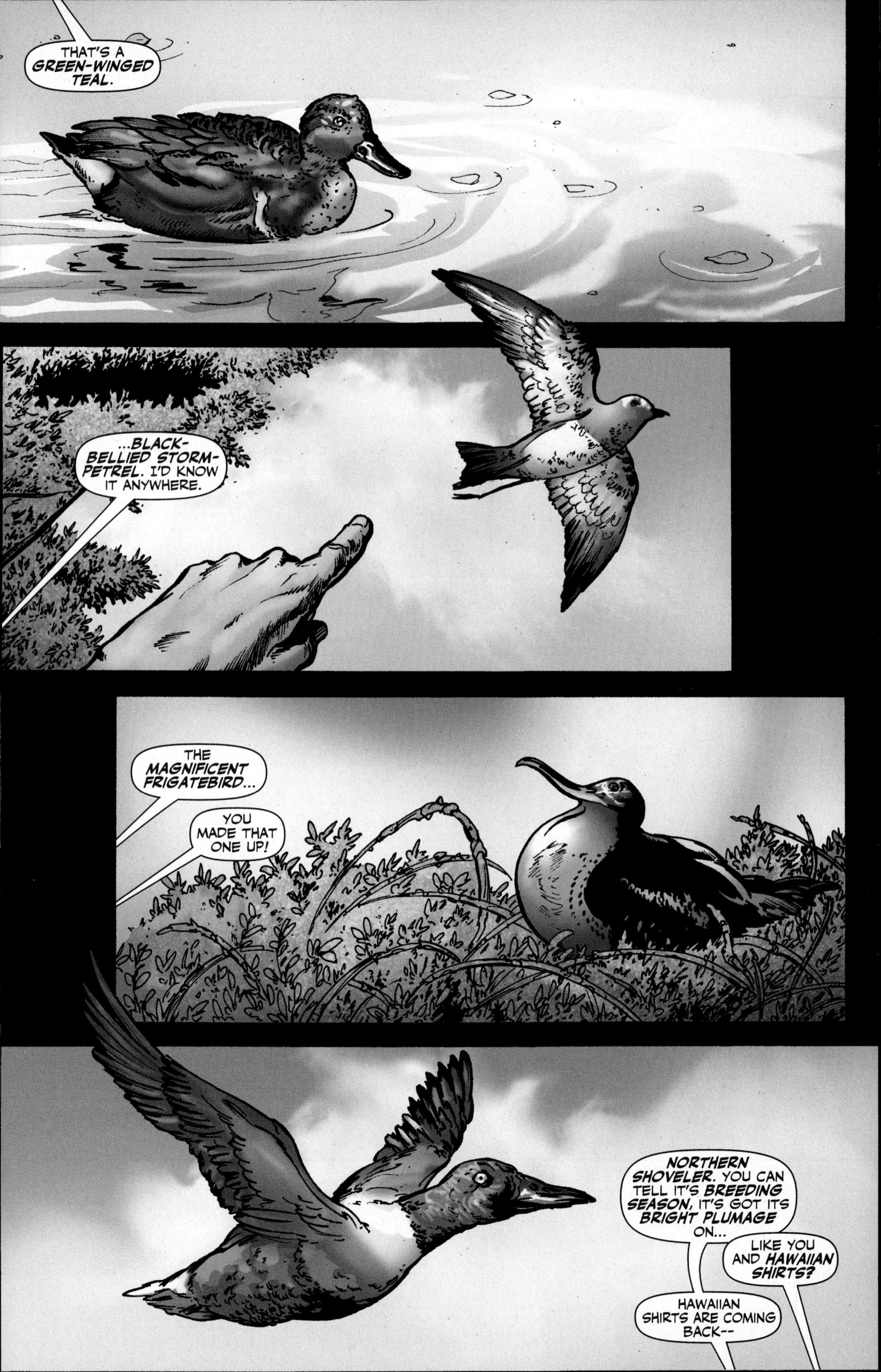

THAT'S A GREEN-WINGED TEAL.
...BLACK-BELLIED STORM-PETREL. I'D KNOW IT ANYWHERE.
THE MAGNIFICENT FRIGATEBIRD...
YOU MADE THAT ONE UP!
NORTHERN SHOVELER. YOU CAN TELL IT'S BREEDING SEASON, IT'S GOT ITS BRIGHT PLUMAGE ON...
LIKE YOU AND HAWAIIAN SHIRTS?
HAWAIIAN SHIRTS ARE COMING BACK--

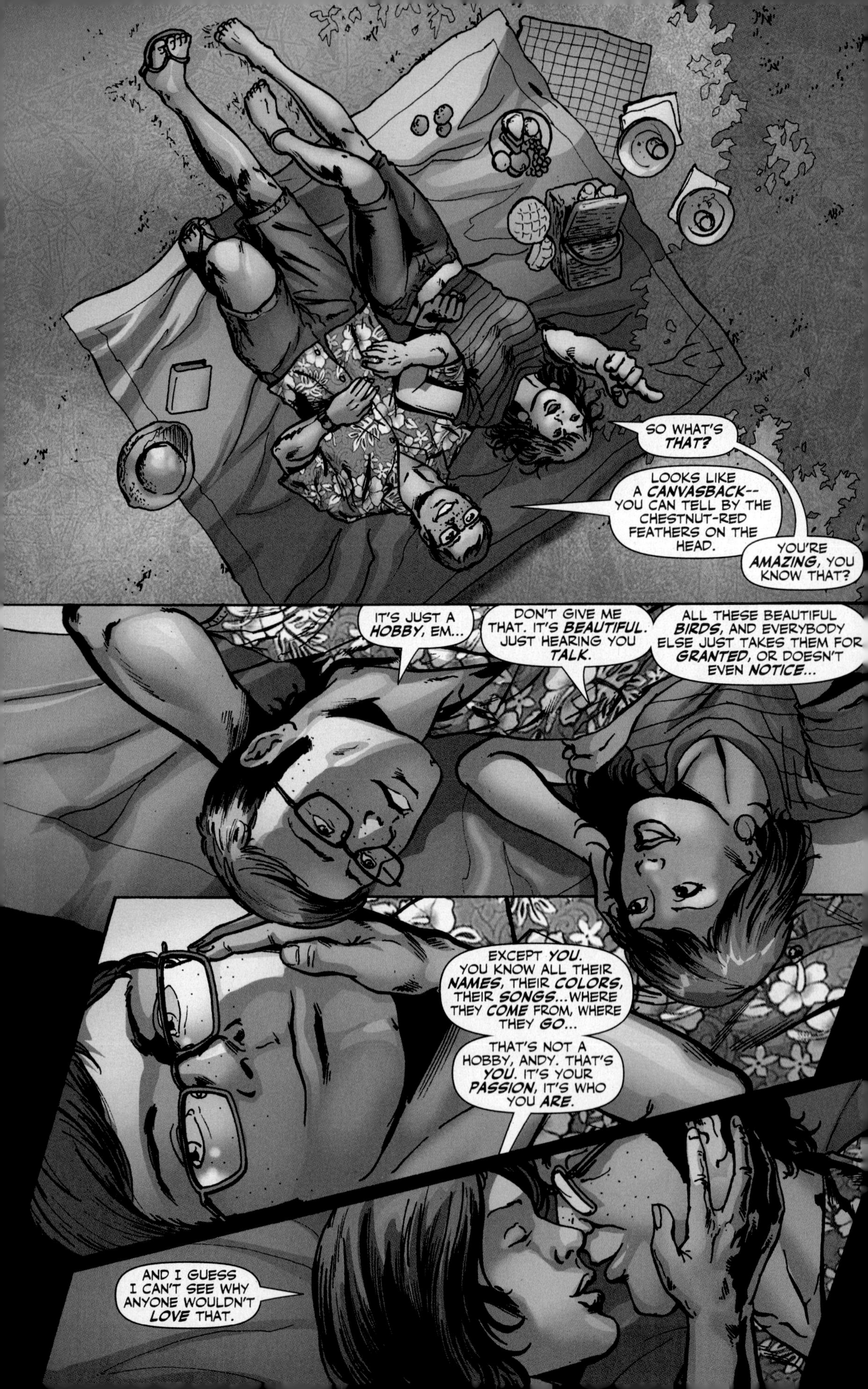
SO WHAT'S THAT?
LOOKS LIKE A CANVASBACK-- YOU CAN TELL BY THE CHESTNUT-RED FEATHERS ON THE HEAD.
YOU'RE AMAZING, YOU KNOW THAT?
IT'S JUST A HOBBY, EM...
DON'T GIVE ME THAT. IT'S BEAUTIFUL. JUST HEARING YOU TALK.
ALL THESE BEAUTIFUL BIRDS, AND EVERYBODY ELSE JUST TAKES THEM FOR GRANTED, OR DOESN'T EVEN NOTICE...
EXCEPT YOU. YOU KNOW ALL THEIR NAMES, THEIR COLORS, THEIR SONGS...WHERE THEY COME FROM, WHERE THEY GO...
THAT'S NOT A HOBBY, ANDY. THAT'S YOU. IT'S YOUR PASSION, IT'S WHO YOU ARE.
AND I GUESS I CAN'T SEE WHY ANYONE WOULDN'T LOVE THAT.

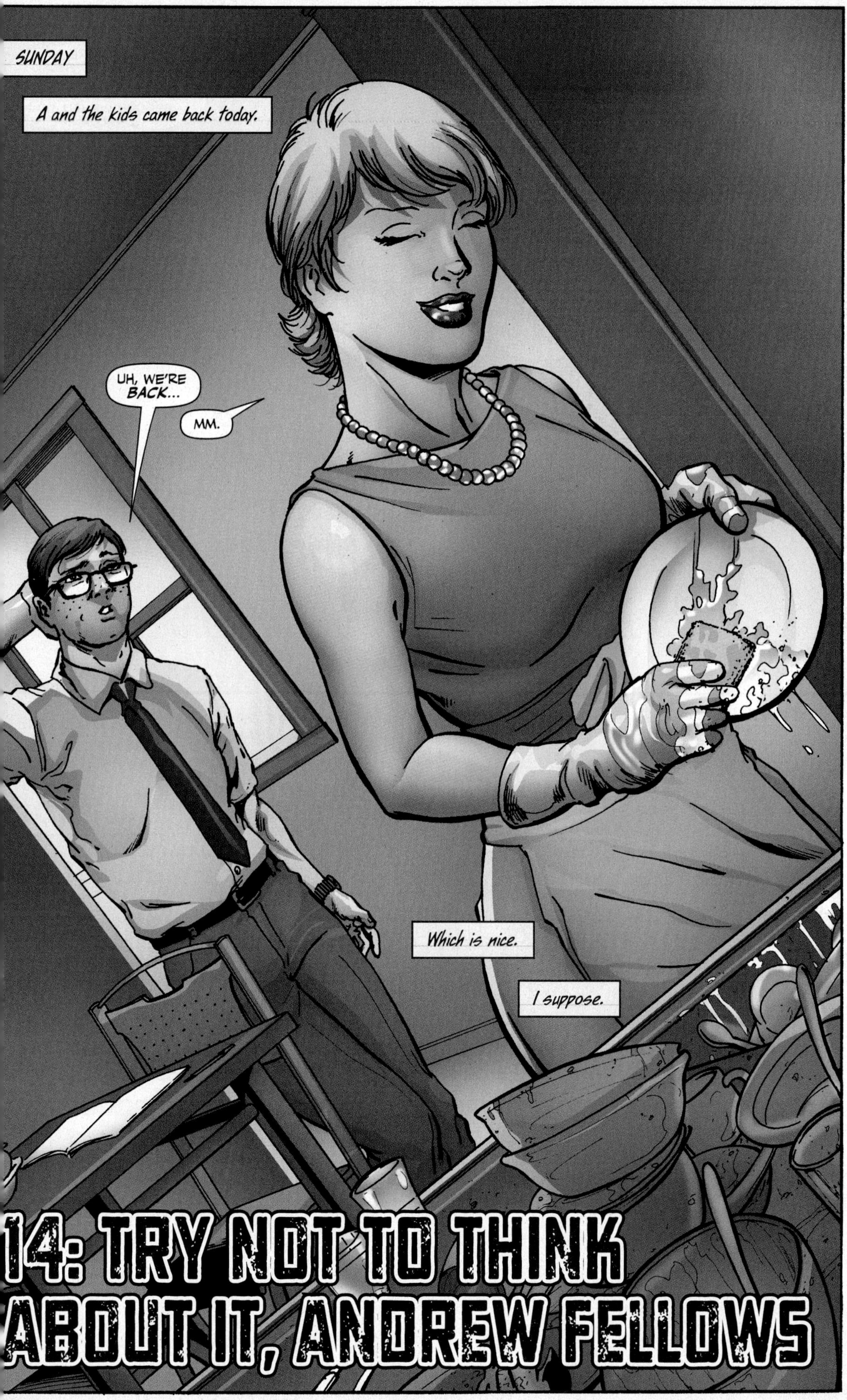
SUNDAY
A and the kids came back today.
UH, WE'RE BACK...
MM.
Which is nice.
I suppose.
14: TRY NOT TO THINK ABOUT IT, ANDREW FELLOWS

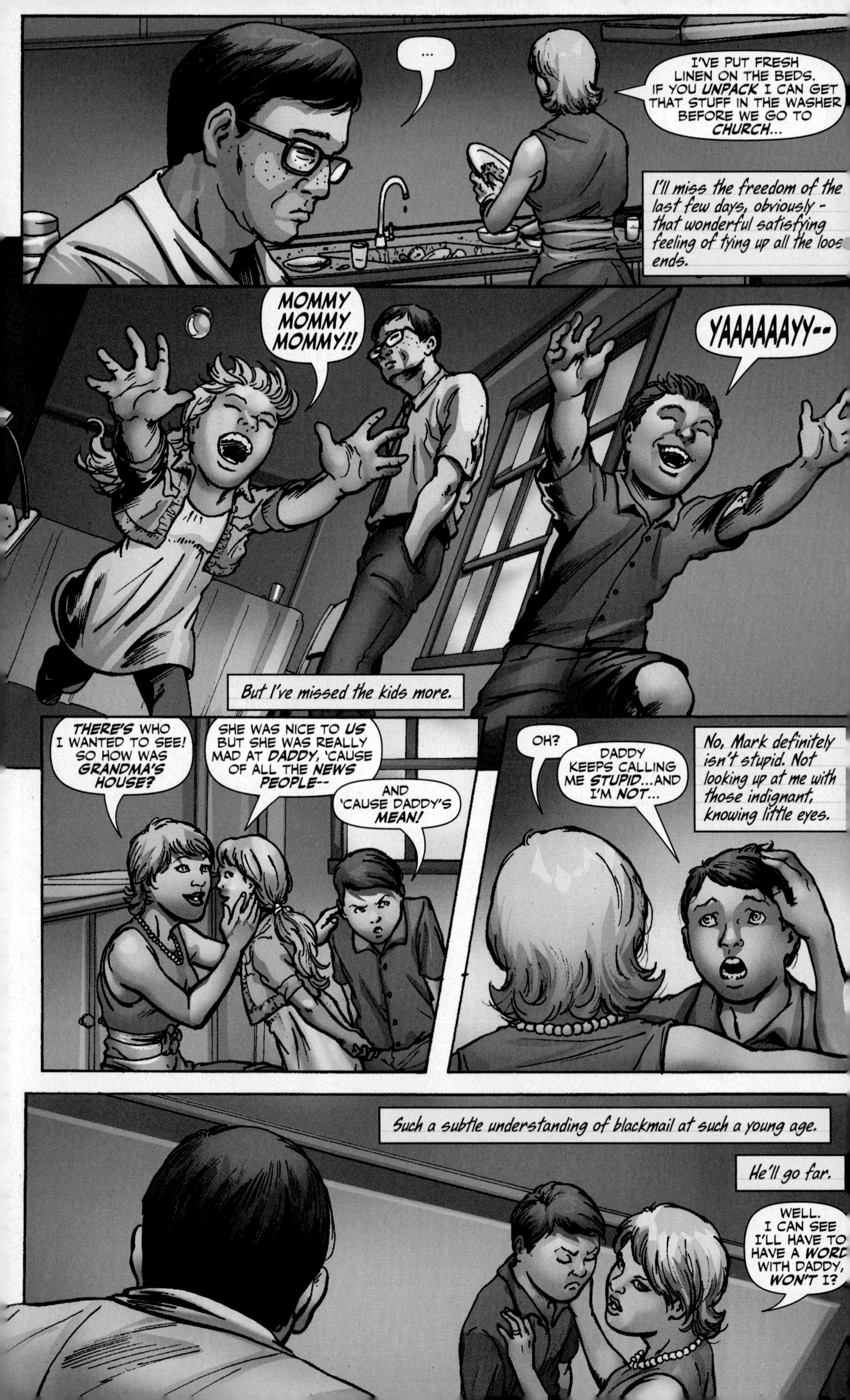
...
I'VE PUT FRESH LINEN ON THE BEDS. IF YOU UNPACK I CAN GET THAT STUFF IN THE WASHER BEFORE WE GO TO CHURCH...
I'll miss the freedom of the last few days, obviously - that wonderful satisfying feeling of tying up all the loos ends.
MOMMY MOMMY MOMMY!!
YAAAAAAYY--
But I've missed the kids more.
THERE'S WHO I WANTED TO SEE! SO HOW WAS GRANDMA'S HOUSE?
SHE WAS NICE TO US BUT SHE WAS REALLY MAD AT DADDY, 'CAUSE OF ALL THE NEWS PEOPLE--
AND 'CAUSE DADDY'S MEAN!
OH?
DADDY KEEPS CALLING ME STUPID...AND I'M NOT...
No, Mark definitely isn't stupid. Not looking up at me with those indignant, knowing little eyes.
Such a subtle understanding of blackmail at such a young age.
He'll go far.
WELL. I CAN SEE I'LL HAVE TO HAVE A WORD WITH DADDY, WON'T I?

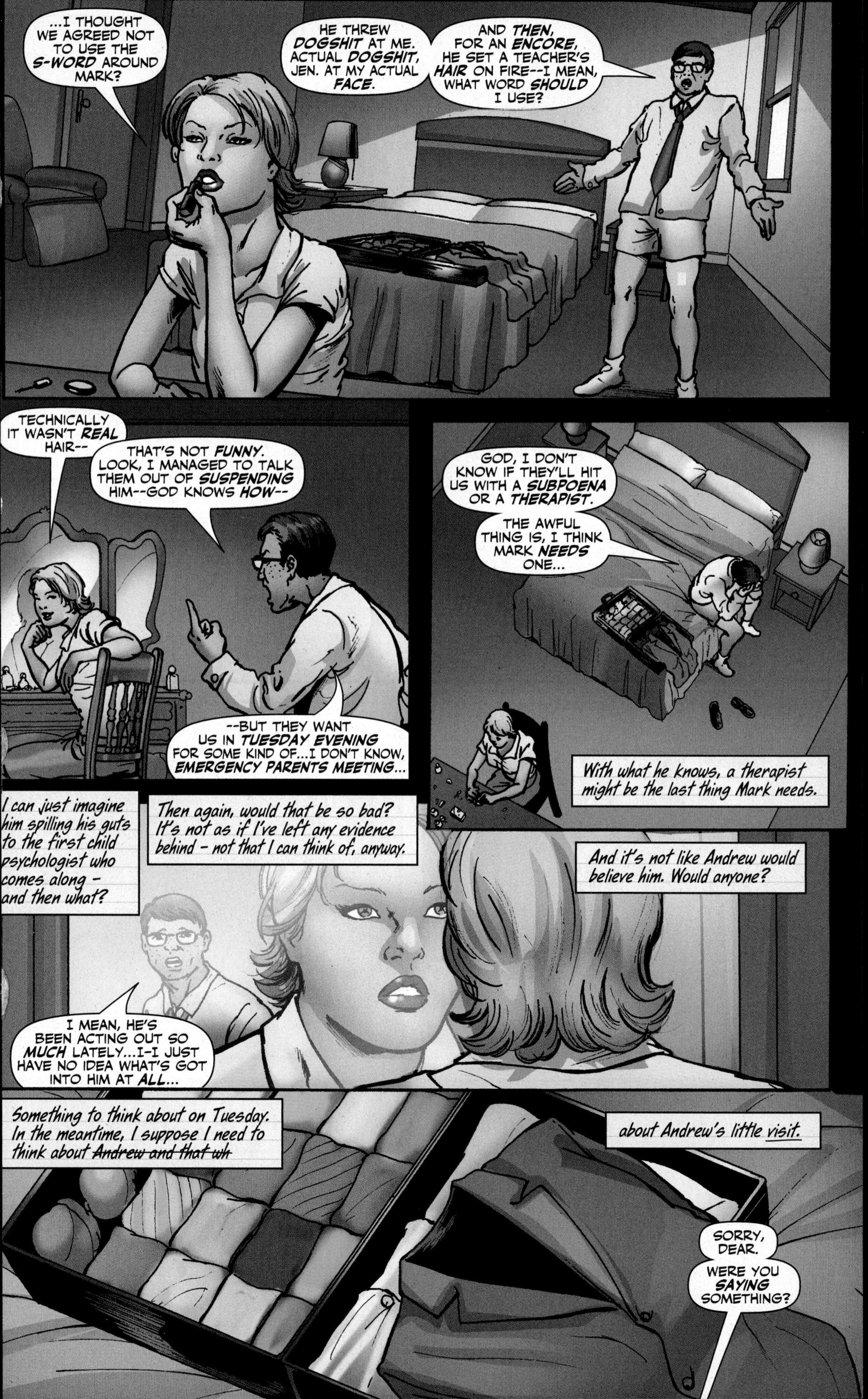

...I THOUGHT WE AGREED NOT TO USE THE S-WORD AROUND MARK?
HE THREW DOGSHIT AT ME. ACTUAL DOGSHIT, JEN. AT MY ACTUAL FACE.
AND THEN, FOR AN ENCORE, HE SET A TEACHER'S HAIR ON FIRE--I MEAN, WHAT WORD SHOULD I USE?
TECHNICALLY IT WASN'T REAL HAIR--
THAT'S NOT FUNNY. LOOK, I MANAGED TO TALK THEM OUT OF SUSPENDING HIM--GOD KNOWS HOW--
--BUT THEY WANT US IN TUESDAY EVENING FOR SOME KIND OF...I DON'T KNOW, EMERGENCY PARENTS MEETING...
GOD, I DON'T KNOW IF THEY'LL HIT US WITH A SUBPOENA OR A THERAPIST.
THE AWFUL THING IS, I THINK MARK NEEDS ONE...
With what he knows, a therapist might be the last thing Mark needs.
I can just imagine him spilling his guts to the first child psychologist who comes along - and then what?
Then again, would that be so bad? It's not as if I've left any evidence behind - not that I can think of, anyway.
And it's not like Andrew would believe him. Would anyone?
I MEAN, HE'S BEEN ACTING OUT SO MUCH LATELY...I-I JUST HAVE NO IDEA WHAT'S GOT INTO HIM AT ALL...
Something to think about on Tuesday. In the meantime, I suppose I need to think about ~~Andrew and that wh~~
about Andrew's little visit.
SORRY, DEAR.
WERE YOU SAYING SOMETHING?

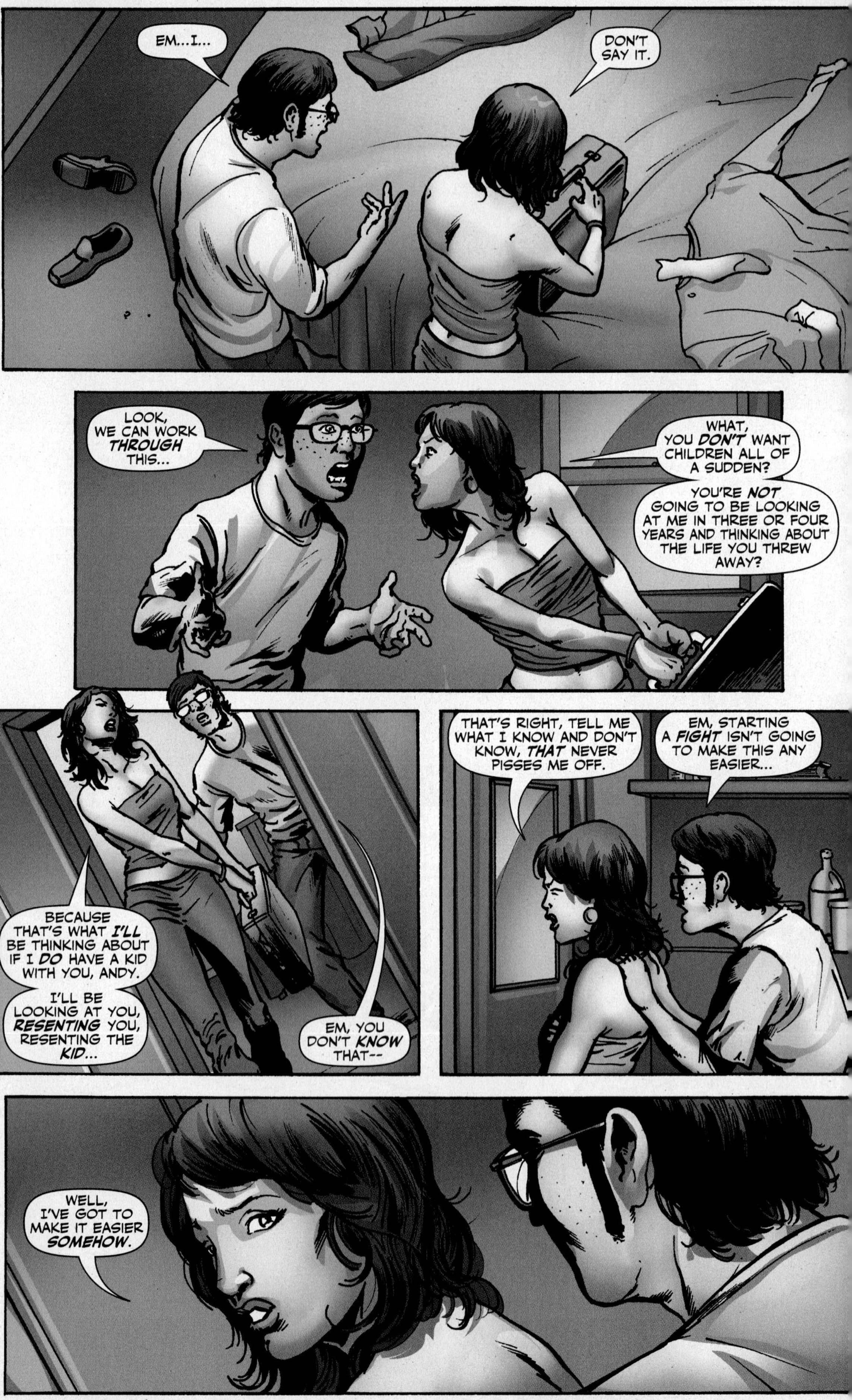
EM...I...
DON'T SAY IT.
LOOK, WE CAN WORK *THROUGH* THIS...
WHAT, YOU *DON'T* WANT CHILDREN ALL OF A SUDDEN?
YOU'RE *NOT* GOING TO BE LOOKING AT ME IN THREE OR FOUR YEARS AND THINKING ABOUT THE LIFE YOU THREW AWAY?
BECAUSE THAT'S WHAT *I'LL* BE THINKING ABOUT IF I *DO* HAVE A KID WITH YOU, ANDY.
I'LL BE LOOKING AT YOU, *RESENTING* YOU, RESENTING THE *KID*...
EM, YOU DON'T *KNOW* THAT--
THAT'S RIGHT, TELL ME WHAT I KNOW AND DON'T KNOW, *THAT* NEVER PISSES ME OFF.
EM, STARTING A *FIGHT* ISN'T GOING TO MAKE THIS ANY EASIER...
WELL, I'VE GOT TO MAKE IT EASIER *SOMEHOW*.

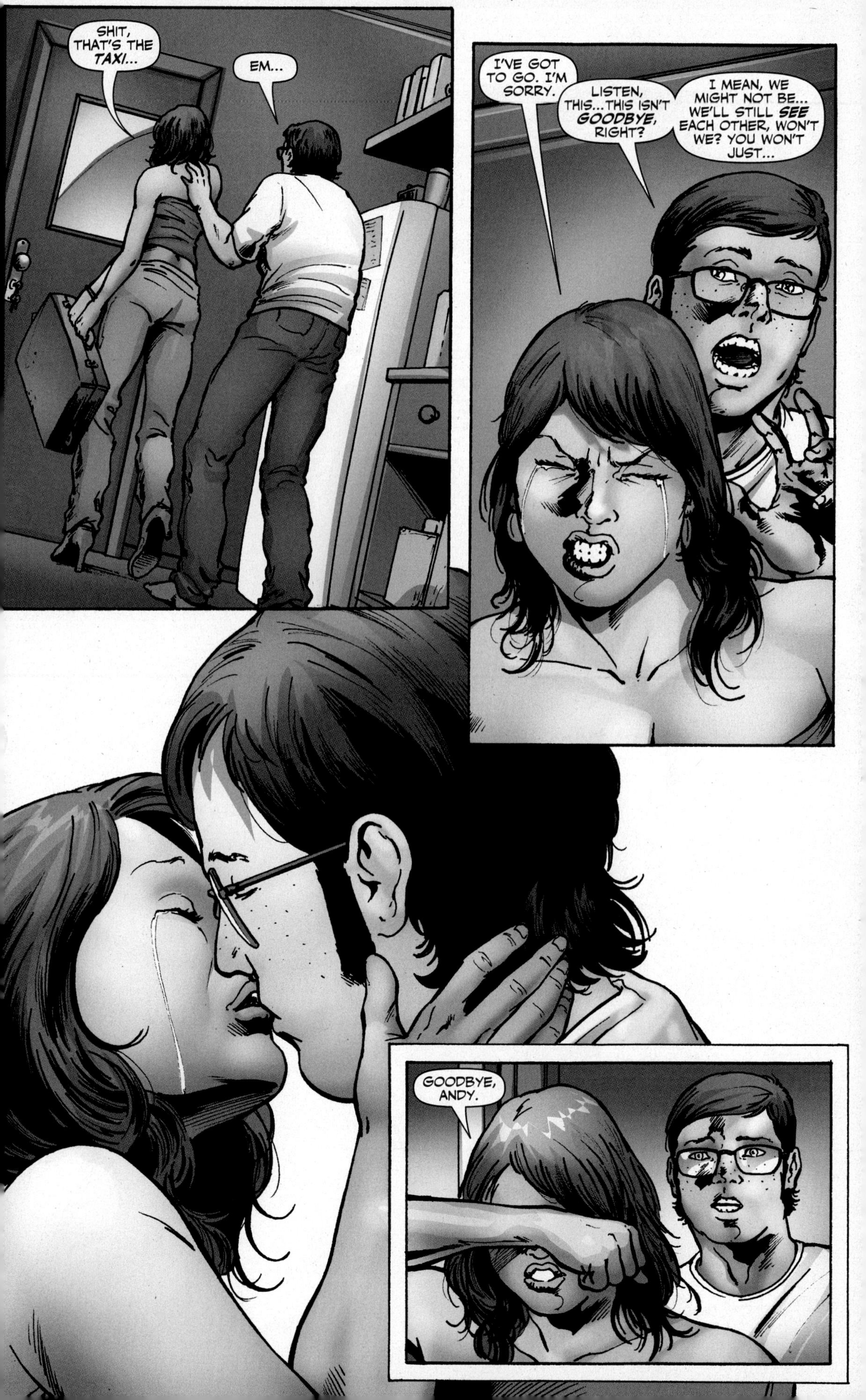
SHIT, THAT'S THE TAXI...
EM...
I'VE GOT TO GO. I'M SORRY.
LISTEN, THIS...THIS ISN'T GOODBYE, RIGHT?
I MEAN, WE MIGHT NOT BE... WE'LL STILL SEE EACH OTHER, WON'T WE? YOU WON'T JUST...
GOODBYE, ANDY.

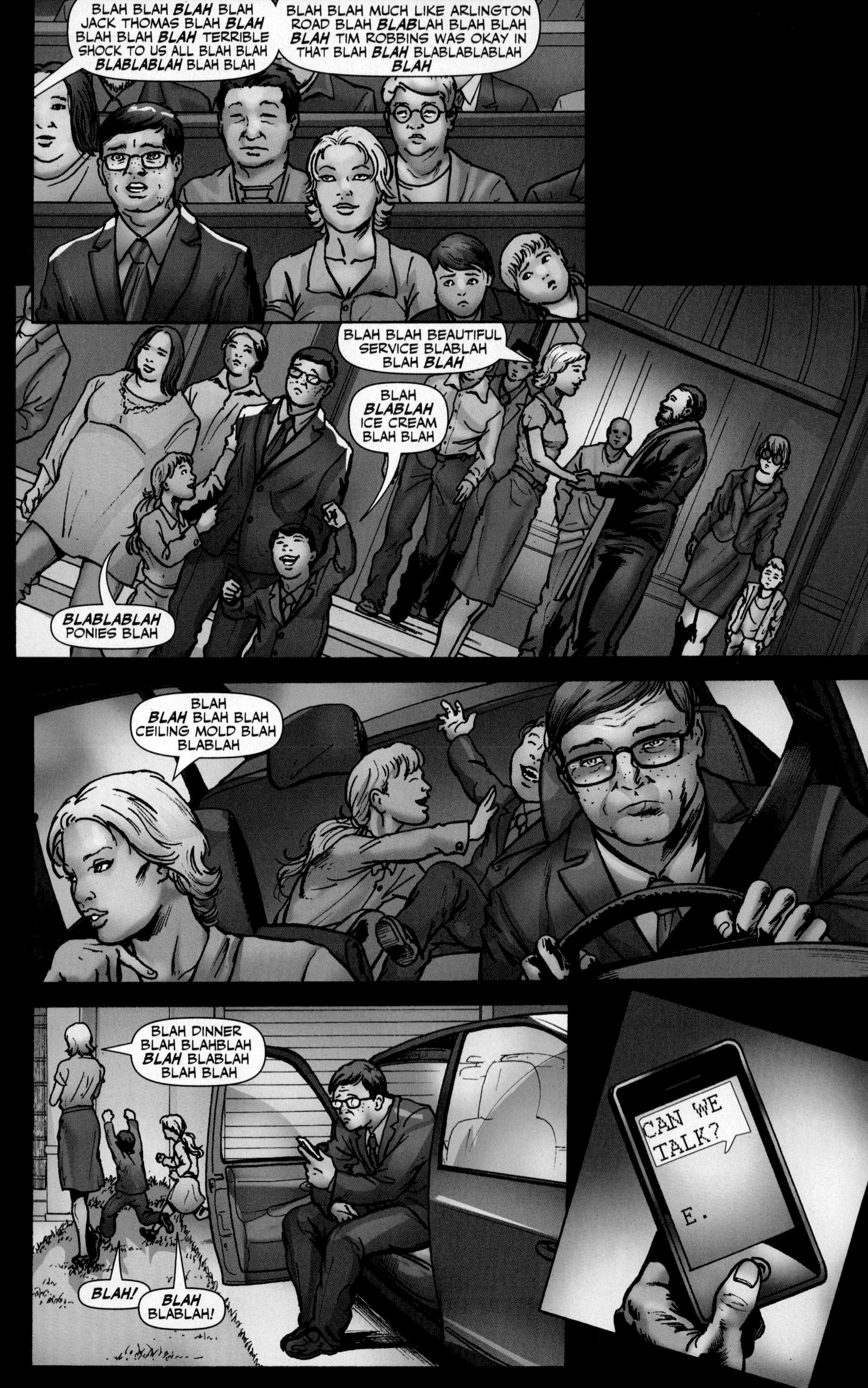
BLAH BLAH BLAH BLAH JACK THOMAS BLAH BLAH BLAH BLAH BLAH TERRIBLE SHOCK TO US ALL BLAH BLAH BLABLABLAH BLAH BLAH
BLAH BLAH MUCH LIKE ARLINGTON ROAD BLAH BLABLAH BLAH BLAH BLAH TIM ROBBINS WAS OKAY IN THAT BLAH BLAH BLABLABLABLAH BLAH
BLAH BLAH BEAUTIFUL SERVICE BLABLAH BLAH BLAH
BLAH BLABLAH ICE CREAM BLAH BLAH
BLABLABLAH PONIES BLAH
BLAH BLAH BLAH BLAH CEILING MOLD BLAH BLABLAH
BLAH DINNER BLAH BLAHBLAH BLAH BLABLAH BLAH BLAH
BLAH!
BLAH BLABLAH!
CAN WE TALK?
E.

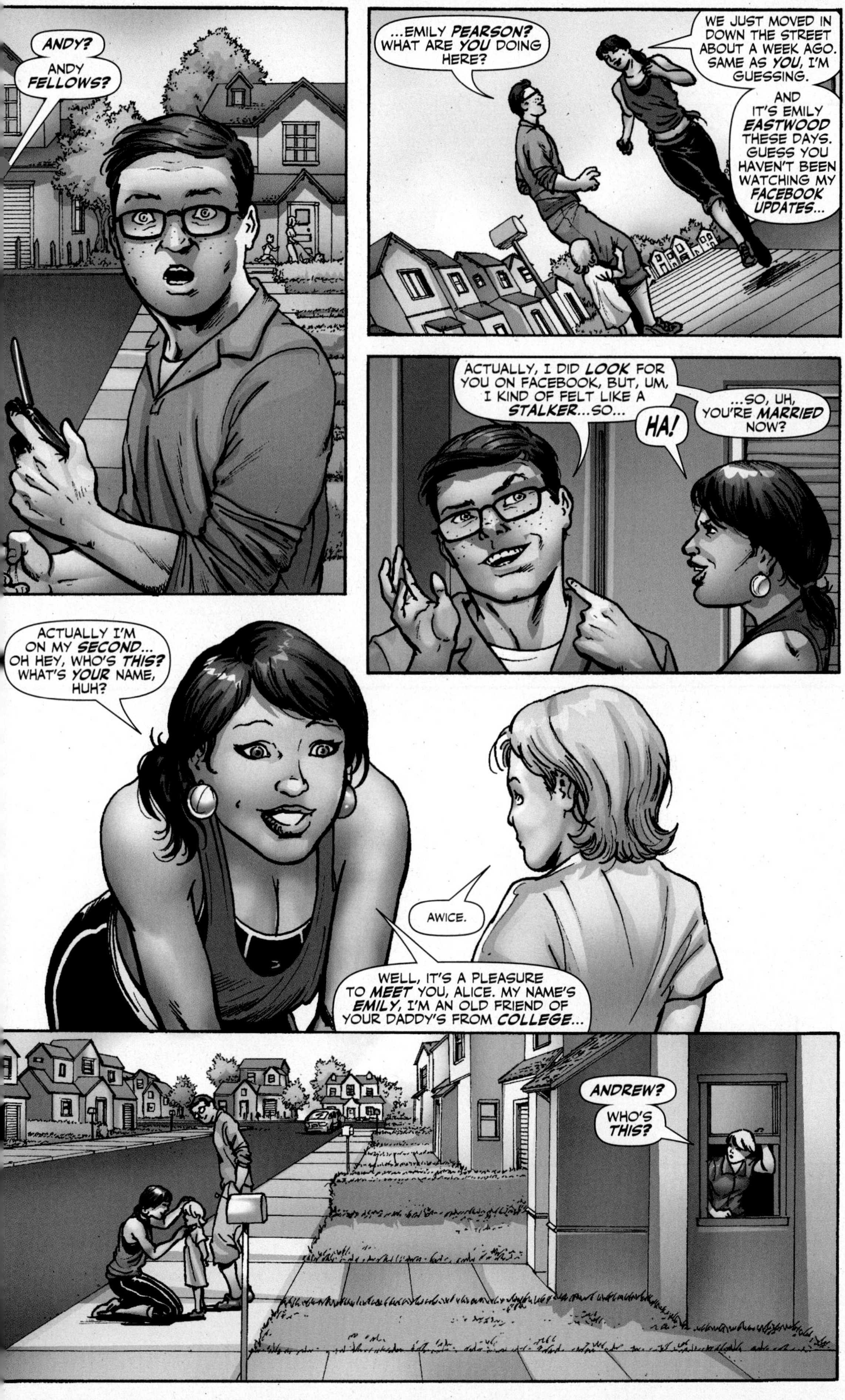
ANDY? ANDY FELLOWS?
...EMILY PEARSON? WHAT ARE YOU DOING HERE?
WE JUST MOVED IN DOWN THE STREET ABOUT A WEEK AGO. SAME AS YOU, I'M GUESSING.
AND IT'S EMILY EASTWOOD THESE DAYS. GUESS YOU HAVEN'T BEEN WATCHING MY FACEBOOK UPDATES...
ACTUALLY, I DID LOOK FOR YOU ON FACEBOOK, BUT, UM, I KIND OF FELT LIKE A STALKER...SO...
HA!
...SO, UH, YOU'RE MARRIED NOW?
ACTUALLY I'M ON MY SECOND... OH HEY, WHO'S THIS? WHAT'S YOUR NAME, HUH?
AWICE.
WELL, IT'S A PLEASURE TO MEET YOU, ALICE. MY NAME'S EMILY, I'M AN OLD FRIEND OF YOUR DADDY'S FROM COLLEGE...
ANDREW? WHO'S THIS?

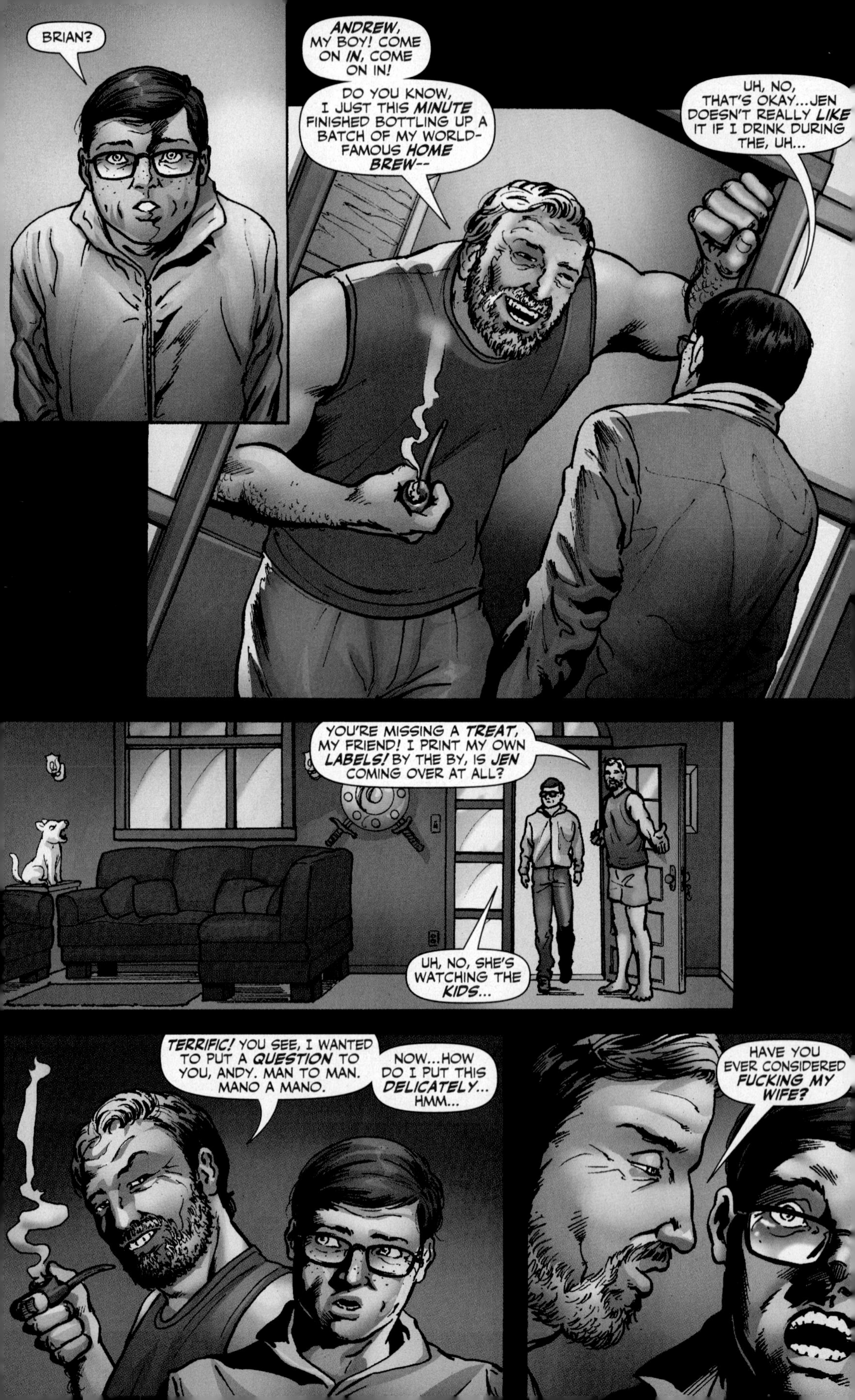
BRIAN?
ANDREW, MY BOY! COME ON IN, COME ON IN!
DO YOU KNOW, I JUST THIS MINUTE FINISHED BOTTLING UP A BATCH OF MY WORLD-FAMOUS HOME BREW--
UH, NO, THAT'S OKAY...JEN DOESN'T REALLY LIKE IT IF I DRINK DURING THE, UH...
YOU'RE MISSING A TREAT, MY FRIEND! I PRINT MY OWN LABELS! BY THE BY, IS JEN COMING OVER AT ALL?
UH, NO, SHE'S WATCHING THE KIDS...
TERRIFIC! YOU SEE, I WANTED TO PUT A QUESTION TO YOU, ANDY. MAN TO MAN. MANO A MANO.
NOW...HOW DO I PUT THIS DELICATELY... HMM...
HAVE YOU EVER CONSIDERED FUCKING MY WIFE?

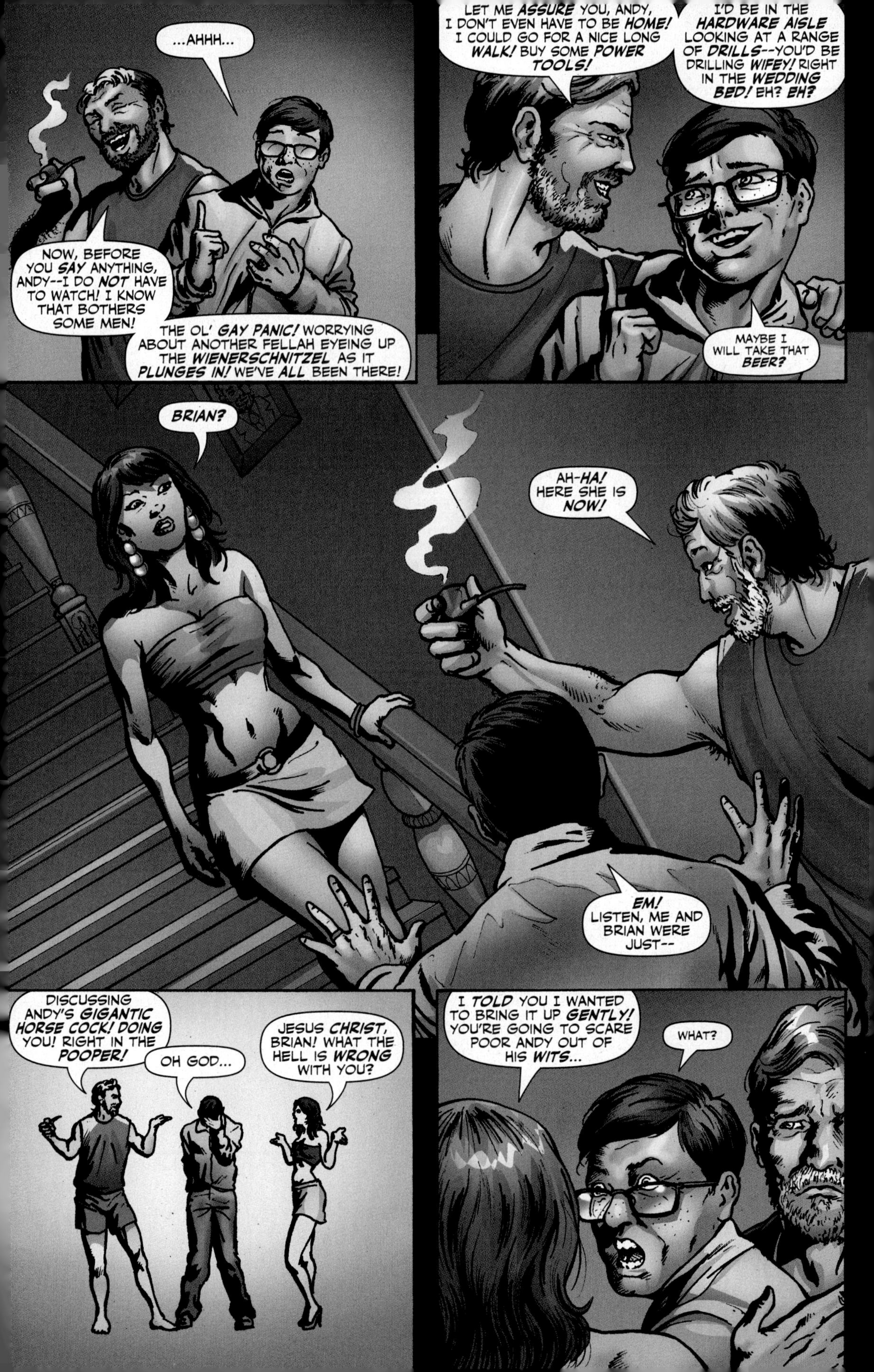
...AHHH...
NOW, BEFORE YOU SAY ANYTHING, ANDY--I DO NOT HAVE TO WATCH! I KNOW THAT BOTHERS SOME MEN!
THE OL' GAY PANIC! WORRYING ABOUT ANOTHER FELLAH EYEING UP THE WIENERSCHNITZEL AS IT PLUNGES IN! WE'VE ALL BEEN THERE!
LET ME ASSURE YOU, ANDY, I DON'T EVEN HAVE TO BE HOME! I COULD GO FOR A NICE LONG WALK! BUY SOME POWER TOOLS!
I'D BE IN THE HARDWARE AISLE LOOKING AT A RANGE OF DRILLS--YOU'D BE DRILLING WIFEY! RIGHT IN THE WEDDING BED! EH? EH?
MAYBE I WILL TAKE THAT BEER?
BRIAN?
AH-HA! HERE SHE IS NOW!
EM! LISTEN, ME AND BRIAN WERE JUST--
DISCUSSING ANDY'S GIGANTIC HORSE COCK! DOING YOU! RIGHT IN THE POOPER!
OH GOD...
JESUS CHRIST, BRIAN! WHAT THE HELL IS WRONG WITH YOU?
I TOLD YOU I WANTED TO BRING IT UP GENTLY! YOU'RE GOING TO SCARE POOR ANDY OUT OF HIS WITS...
WHAT?

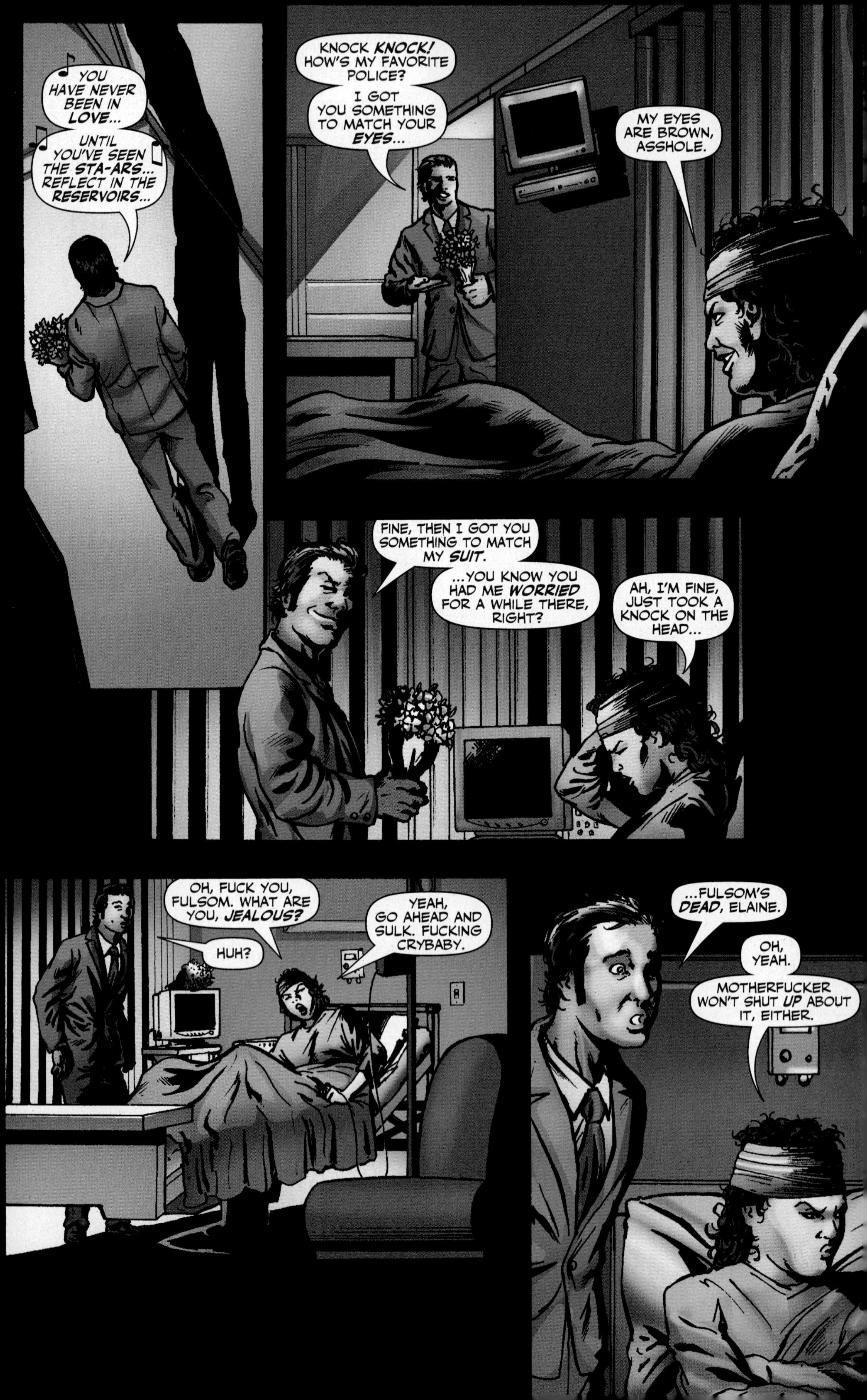
YOU HAVE NEVER BEEN IN LOVE...
UNTIL YOU'VE SEEN THE STA-ARS... REFLECT IN THE RESERVOIRS...
KNOCK KNOCK! HOW'S MY FAVORITE POLICE?
I GOT YOU SOMETHING TO MATCH YOUR EYES...
MY EYES ARE BROWN, ASSHOLE.
FINE, THEN I GOT YOU SOMETHING TO MATCH MY SUIT.
...YOU KNOW YOU HAD ME WORRIED FOR A WHILE THERE, RIGHT?
AH, I'M FINE, JUST TOOK A KNOCK ON THE HEAD...
OH, FUCK YOU, FULSOM. WHAT ARE YOU, JEALOUS?
HUH?
YEAH, GO AHEAD AND SULK. FUCKING CRYBABY.
...FULSOM'S DEAD, ELAINE.
OH, YEAH.
MOTHERFUCKER WON'T SHUT UP ABOUT IT, EITHER.

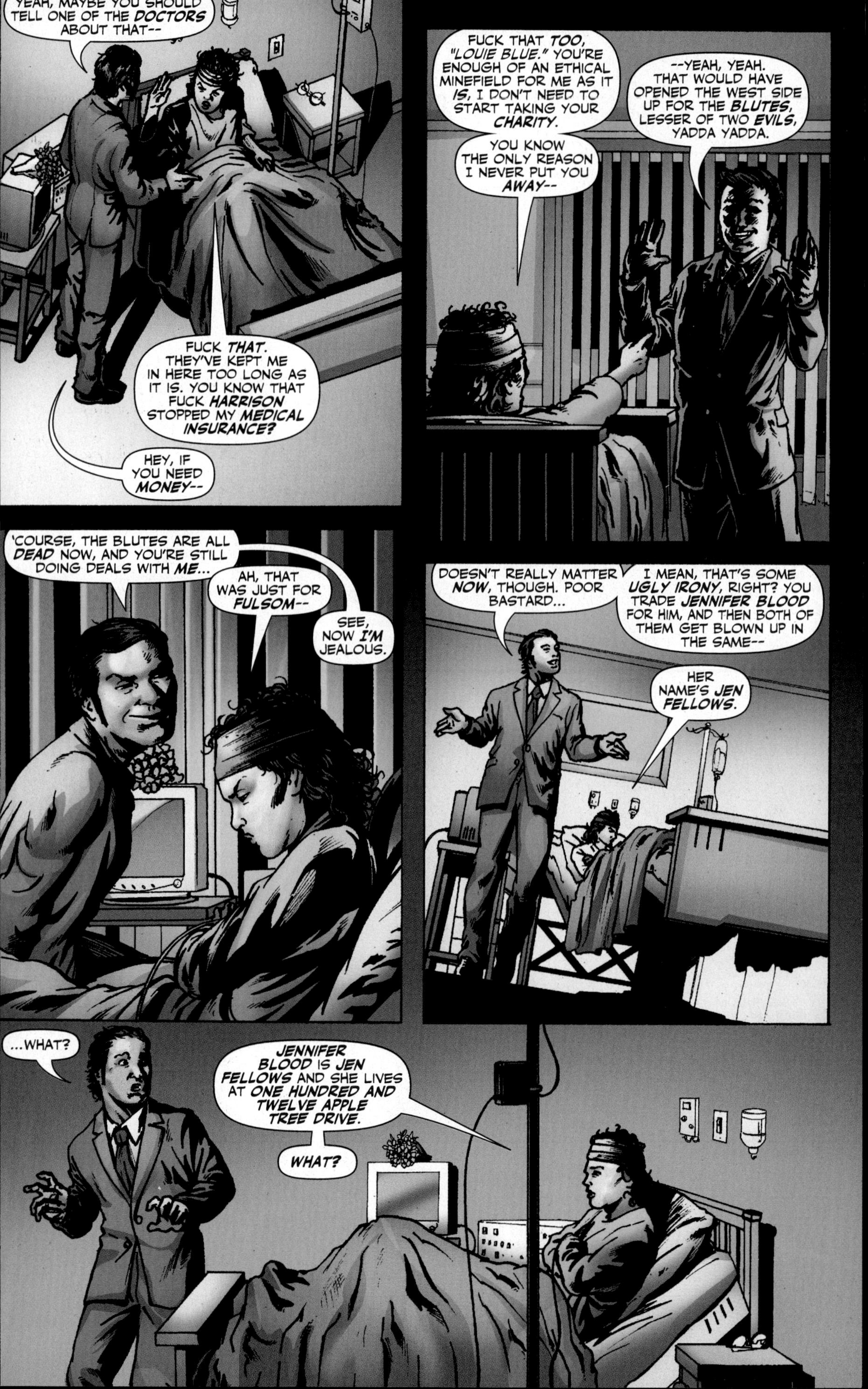
YEAH, MAYBE YOU SHOULD TELL ONE OF THE DOCTORS ABOUT THAT--
FUCK THAT. THEY'VE KEPT ME IN HERE TOO LONG AS IT IS. YOU KNOW THAT FUCK HARRISON STOPPED MY MEDICAL INSURANCE?
HEY, IF YOU NEED MONEY--
FUCK THAT TOO, "LOUIE BLUE." YOU'RE ENOUGH OF AN ETHICAL MINEFIELD FOR ME AS IT IS, I DON'T NEED TO START TAKING YOUR CHARITY.
YOU KNOW THE ONLY REASON I NEVER PUT YOU AWAY--
--YEAH, YEAH. THAT WOULD HAVE OPENED THE WEST SIDE UP FOR THE BLUTES, LESSER OF TWO EVILS, YADDA YADDA.
'COURSE, THE BLUTES ARE ALL DEAD NOW, AND YOU'RE STILL DOING DEALS WITH ME...
AH, THAT WAS JUST FOR FULSOM--
SEE, NOW I'M JEALOUS.
DOESN'T REALLY MATTER NOW, THOUGH. POOR BASTARD...
I MEAN, THAT'S SOME UGLY IRONY, RIGHT? YOU TRADE JENNIFER BLOOD FOR HIM, AND THEN BOTH OF THEM GET BLOWN UP IN THE SAME--
HER NAME'S JEN FELLOWS.
...WHAT?
JENNIFER BLOOD IS JEN FELLOWS AND SHE LIVES AT ONE HUNDRED AND TWELVE APPLE TREE DRIVE.
WHAT?

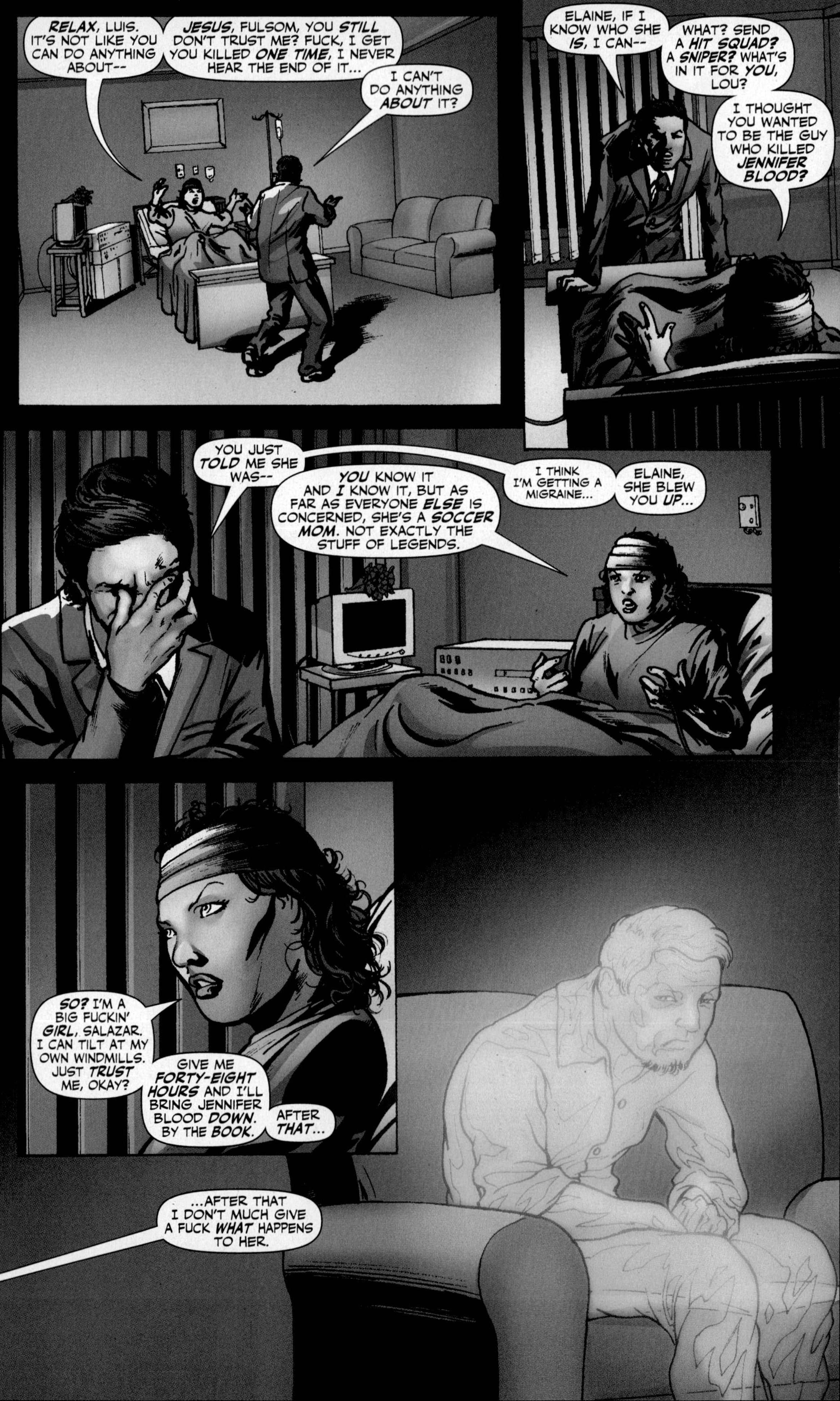
RELAX, LUIS. IT'S NOT LIKE YOU CAN DO ANYTHING ABOUT--
JESUS, FULSOM, YOU STILL DON'T TRUST ME? FUCK, I GET YOU KILLED ONE TIME, I NEVER HEAR THE END OF IT...
I CAN'T DO ANYTHING ABOUT IT?
ELAINE, IF I KNOW WHO SHE IS, I CAN--
WHAT? SEND A HIT SQUAD? A SNIPER? WHAT'S IN IT FOR YOU, LOU?
I THOUGHT YOU WANTED TO BE THE GUY WHO KILLED JENNIFER BLOOD?
YOU JUST TOLD ME SHE WAS--
YOU KNOW IT AND I KNOW IT, BUT AS FAR AS EVERYONE ELSE IS CONCERNED, SHE'S A SOCCER MOM. NOT EXACTLY THE STUFF OF LEGENDS.
I THINK I'M GETTING A MIGRAINE...
ELAINE, SHE BLEW YOU UP...
SO? I'M A BIG FUCKIN' GIRL, SALAZAR. I CAN TILT AT MY OWN WINDMILLS. JUST TRUST ME, OKAY?
GIVE ME FORTY-EIGHT HOURS AND I'LL BRING JENNIFER BLOOD DOWN. BY THE BOOK.
AFTER THAT...
...AFTER THAT I DON'T MUCH GIVE A FUCK WHAT HAPPENS TO HER.

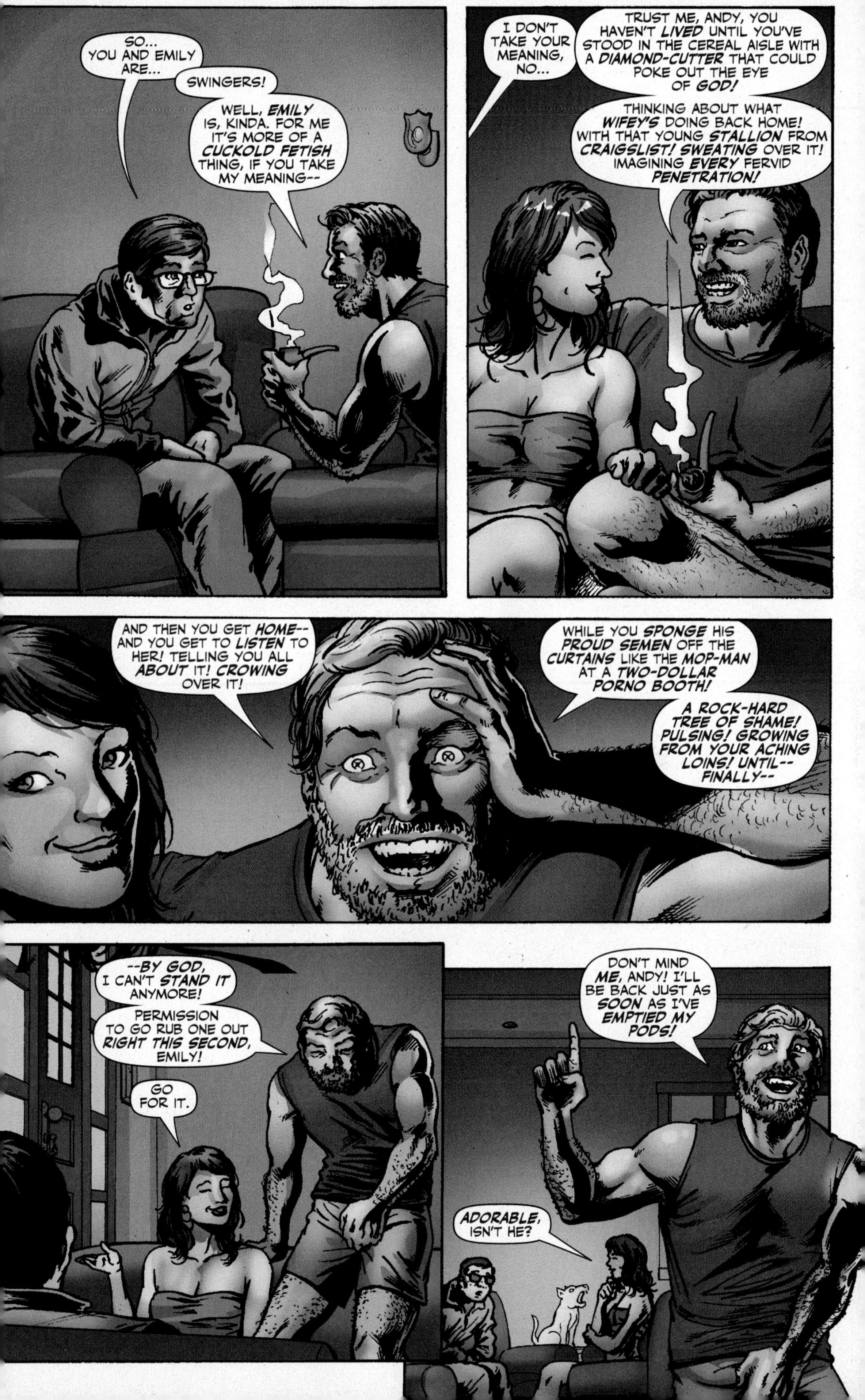
SO... YOU AND EMILY ARE...
SWINGERS!
WELL, EMILY IS, KINDA. FOR ME IT'S MORE OF A CUCKOLD FETISH THING, IF YOU TAKE MY MEANING--
I DON'T TAKE YOUR MEANING, NO...
TRUST ME, ANDY, YOU HAVEN'T LIVED UNTIL YOU'VE STOOD IN THE CEREAL AISLE WITH A DIAMOND-CUTTER THAT COULD POKE OUT THE EYE OF GOD!
THINKING ABOUT WHAT WIFEY'S DOING BACK HOME! WITH THAT YOUNG STALLION FROM CRAIGSLIST! SWEATING OVER IT! IMAGINING EVERY FERVID PENETRATION!
AND THEN YOU GET HOME-- AND YOU GET TO LISTEN TO HER! TELLING YOU ALL ABOUT IT! CROWING OVER IT!
WHILE YOU SPONGE HIS PROUD SEMEN OFF THE CURTAINS LIKE THE MOP-MAN AT A TWO-DOLLAR PORNO BOOTH!
A ROCK-HARD TREE OF SHAME! PULSING! GROWING FROM YOUR ACHING LOINS! UNTIL-- FINALLY--
--BY GOD, I CAN'T STAND IT ANYMORE!
PERMISSION TO GO RUB ONE OUT RIGHT THIS SECOND, EMILY!
GO FOR IT.
DON'T MIND ME, ANDY! I'LL BE BACK JUST AS SOON AS I'VE EMPTIED MY PODS!
ADORABLE, ISN'T HE?

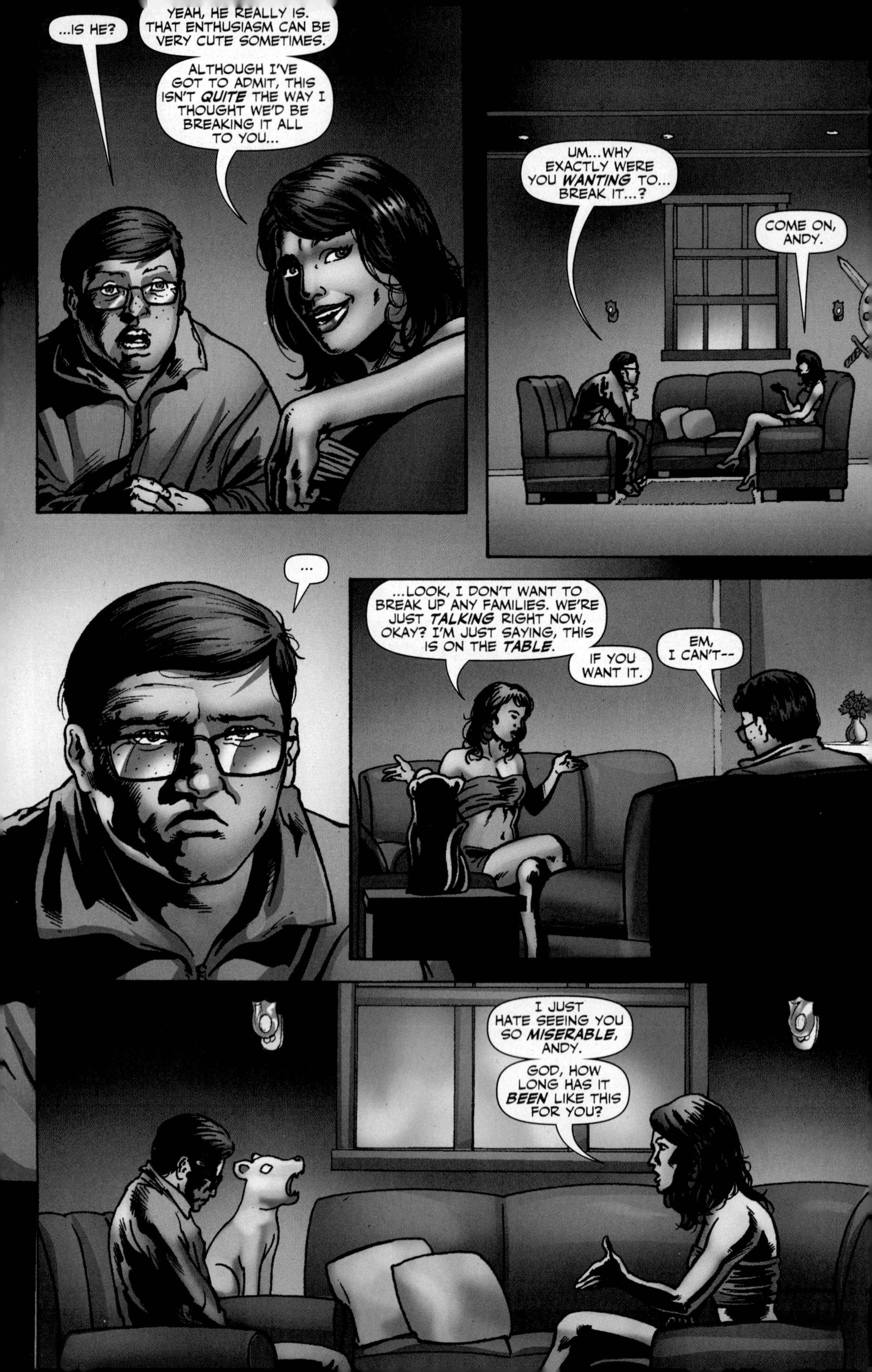

...IS HE?
YEAH, HE REALLY IS. THAT ENTHUSIASM CAN BE VERY CUTE SOMETIMES.
ALTHOUGH I'VE GOT TO ADMIT, THIS ISN'T QUITE THE WAY I THOUGHT WE'D BE BREAKING IT ALL TO YOU...
UM...WHY EXACTLY WERE YOU WANTING TO... BREAK IT...?
COME ON, ANDY.
...
...LOOK, I DON'T WANT TO BREAK UP ANY FAMILIES. WE'RE JUST TALKING RIGHT NOW, OKAY? I'M JUST SAYING, THIS IS ON THE TABLE.
IF YOU WANT IT.
EM, I CAN'T--
I JUST HATE SEEING YOU SO MISERABLE, ANDY.
GOD, HOW LONG HAS IT BEEN LIKE THIS FOR YOU?

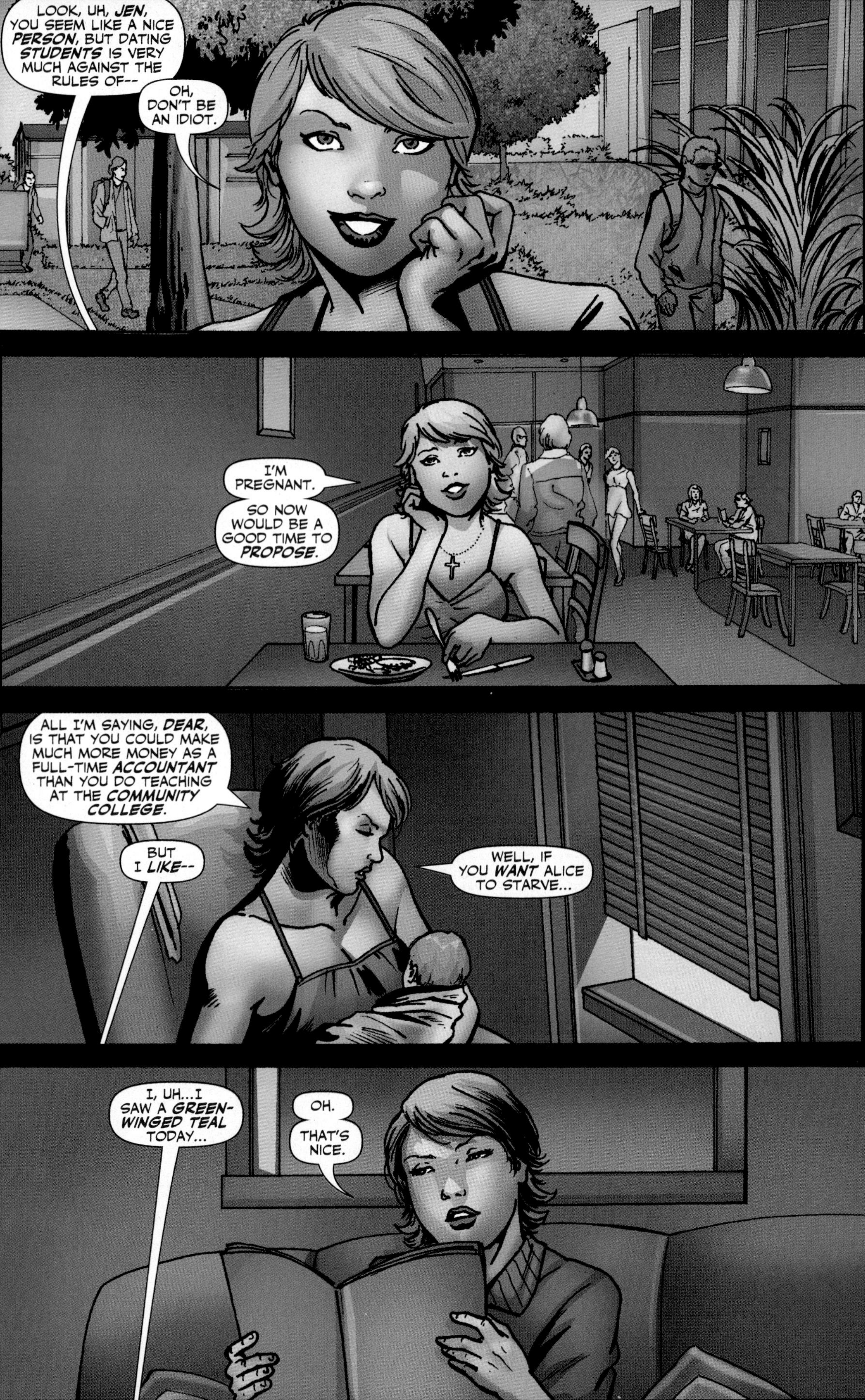

LOOK, UH, JEN, YOU SEEM LIKE A NICE PERSON, BUT DATING STUDENTS IS VERY MUCH AGAINST THE RULES OF--
OH, DON'T BE AN IDIOT.
I'M PREGNANT.
SO NOW WOULD BE A GOOD TIME TO PROPOSE.
ALL I'M SAYING, DEAR, IS THAT YOU COULD MAKE MUCH MORE MONEY AS A FULL-TIME ACCOUNTANT THAN YOU DO TEACHING AT THE COMMUNITY COLLEGE.
BUT I LIKE--
WELL, IF YOU WANT ALICE TO STARVE...
I, UH...I SAW A GREEN-WINGED TEAL TODAY...
OH.
THAT'S NICE.

UH, I'M *HOME*...

MM.

WHAT ARE YOU *LISTENING* TO?

ONE OF MY AUDIOBOOKS. THE KIDS ARE PLAYING *UPSTAIRS* IF YOU WANT TO SAY HELLO.

UM, OKAY.

I managed to keep the anger out of my voice, but I'm sure A. could tell something was up. Not that he'd ever say anything.

I suppose I should be grateful, really.

He didn't find the bug.

He didn't put his hand in his jacket pocket, which I was worried about.

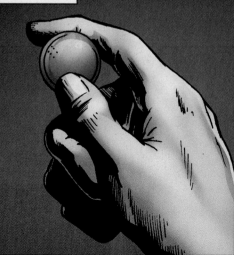

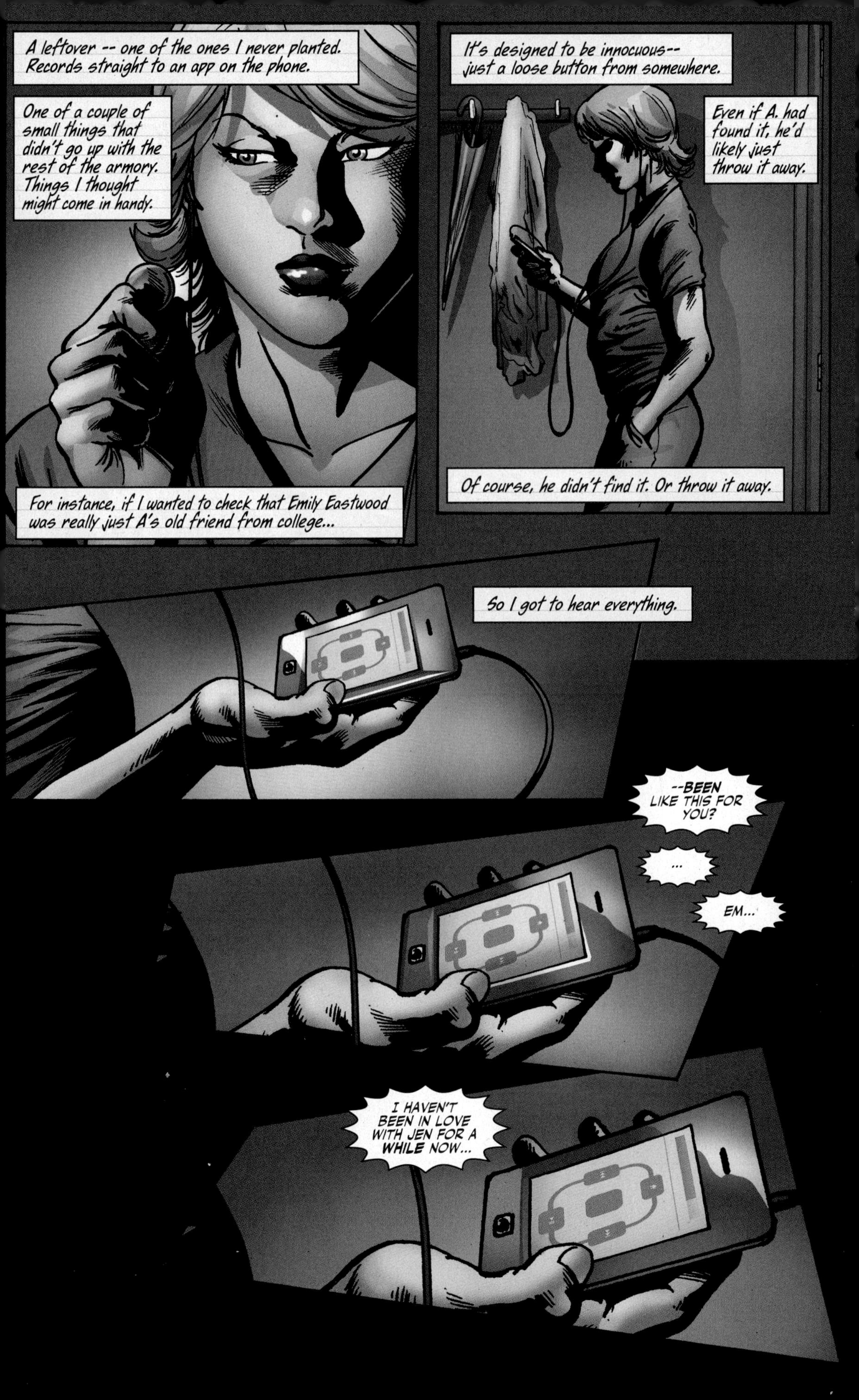

A leftover -- one of the ones I never planted. Records straight to an app on the phone.
One of a couple of small things that didn't go up with the rest of the armory. Things I thought might come in handy.
For instance, if I wanted to check that Emily Eastwood was really just A's old friend from college...
It's designed to be innocuous--just a loose button from somewhere.
Even if A. had found it, he'd likely just throw it away.
Of course, he didn't find it. Or throw it away.
So I got to hear everything.
--BEEN LIKE THIS FOR YOU?
...
EM...
I HAVEN'T BEEN IN LOVE WITH JEN FOR A WHILE NOW...

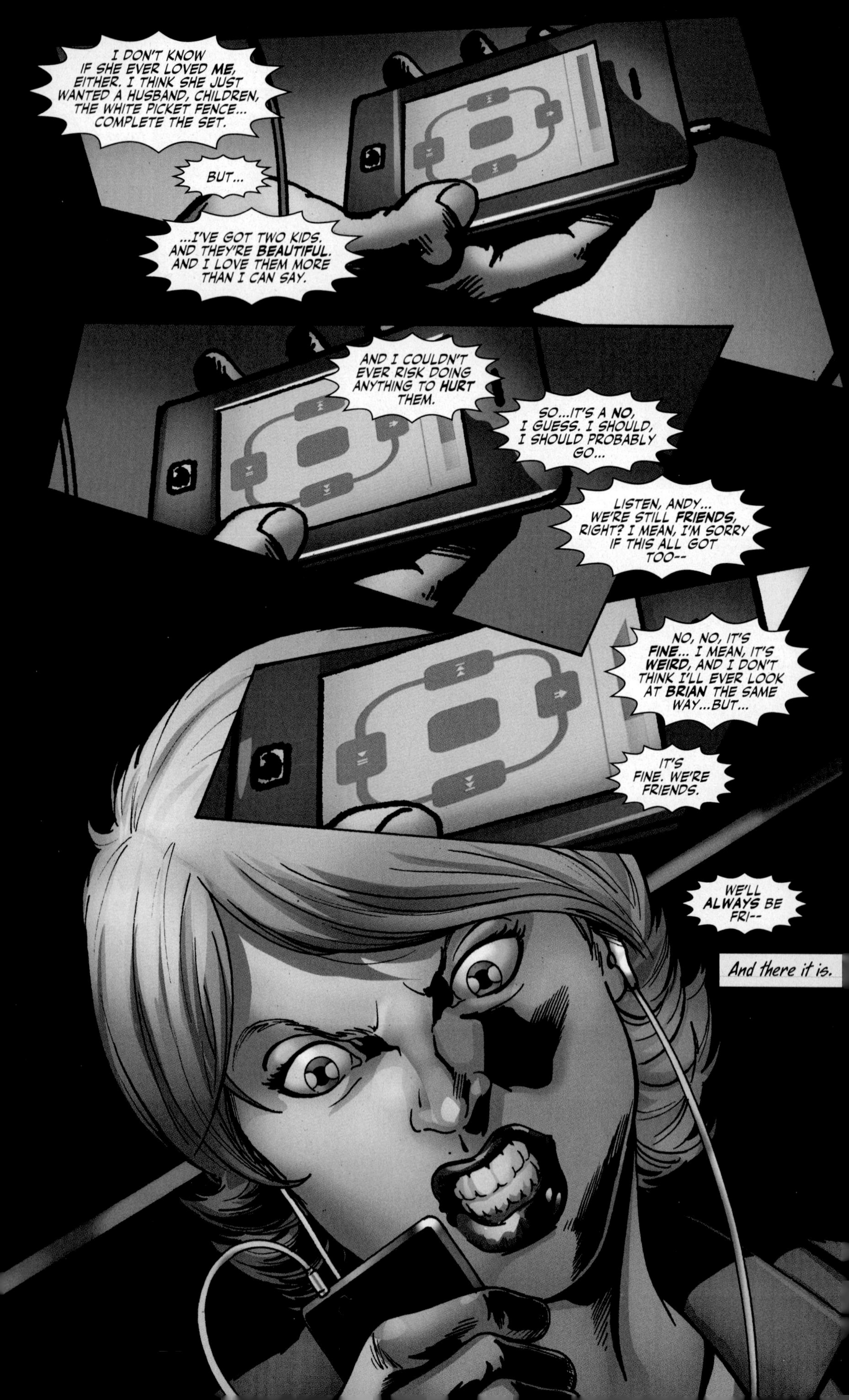
I DON'T KNOW IF SHE EVER LOVED ME, EITHER. I THINK SHE JUST WANTED A HUSBAND, CHILDREN, THE WHITE PICKET FENCE... COMPLETE THE SET.
BUT...
...I'VE GOT TWO KIDS. AND THEY'RE BEAUTIFUL. AND I LOVE THEM MORE THAN I CAN SAY.
AND I COULDN'T EVER RISK DOING ANYTHING TO HURT THEM.
SO...IT'S A NO, I GUESS. I SHOULD, I SHOULD PROBABLY GO...
LISTEN, ANDY... WE'RE STILL FRIENDS, RIGHT? I MEAN, I'M SORRY IF THIS ALL GOT TOO--
NO, NO, IT'S FINE... I MEAN, IT'S WEIRD, AND I DON'T THINK I'LL EVER LOOK AT BRIAN THE SAME WAY...BUT...
IT'S FINE. WE'RE FRIENDS.
WE'LL ALWAYS BE FRI--
And there it is.

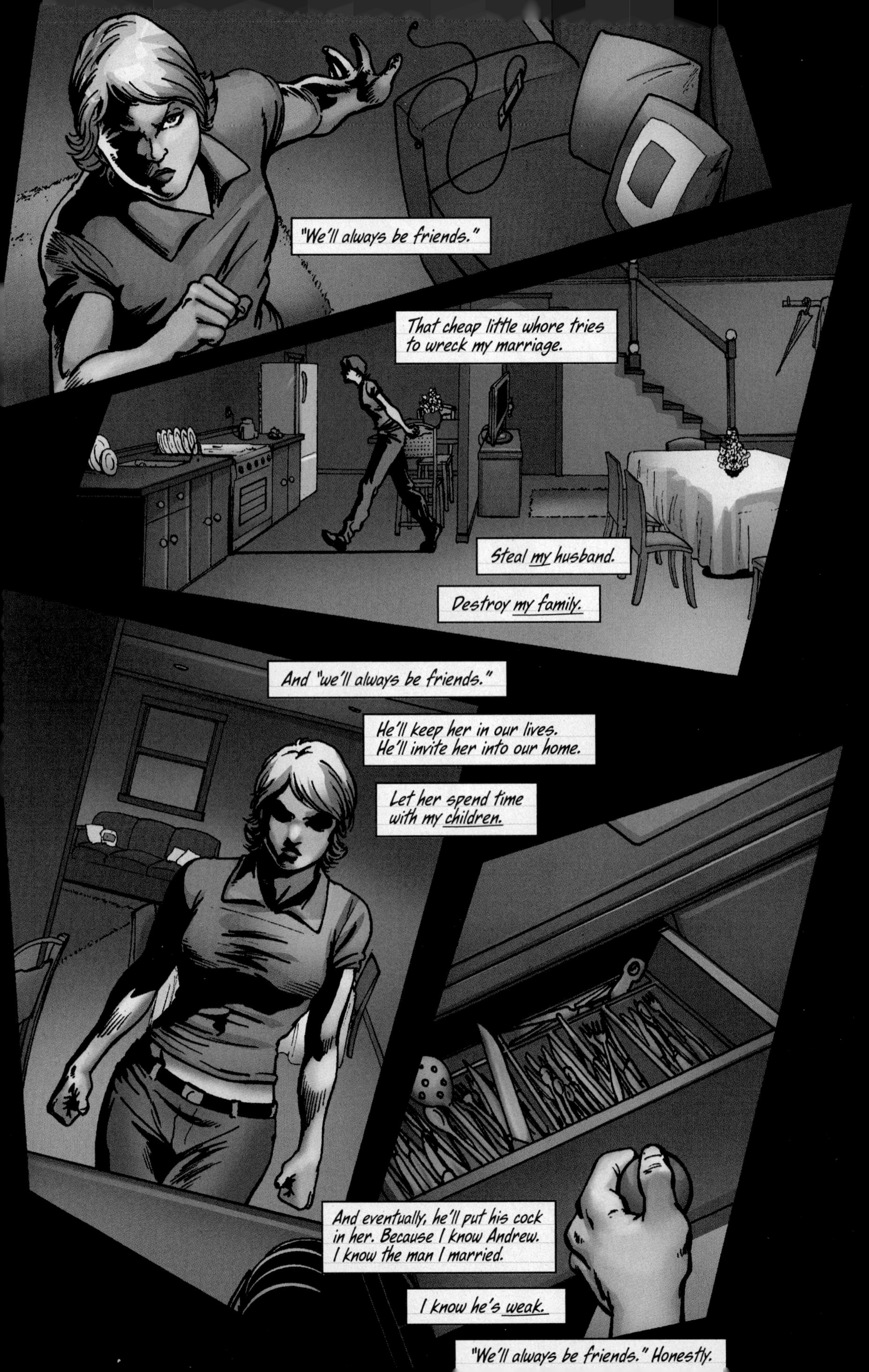
"We'll always be friends."
That cheap little whore tries to wreck my marriage.
Steal my husband.
Destroy my family.
And "we'll always be friends."
He'll keep her in our lives. He'll invite her into our home.
Let her spend time with my children.
And eventually, he'll put his cock in her. Because I know Andrew. I know the man I married.
I know he's weak.
"We'll always be friends." Honestly.

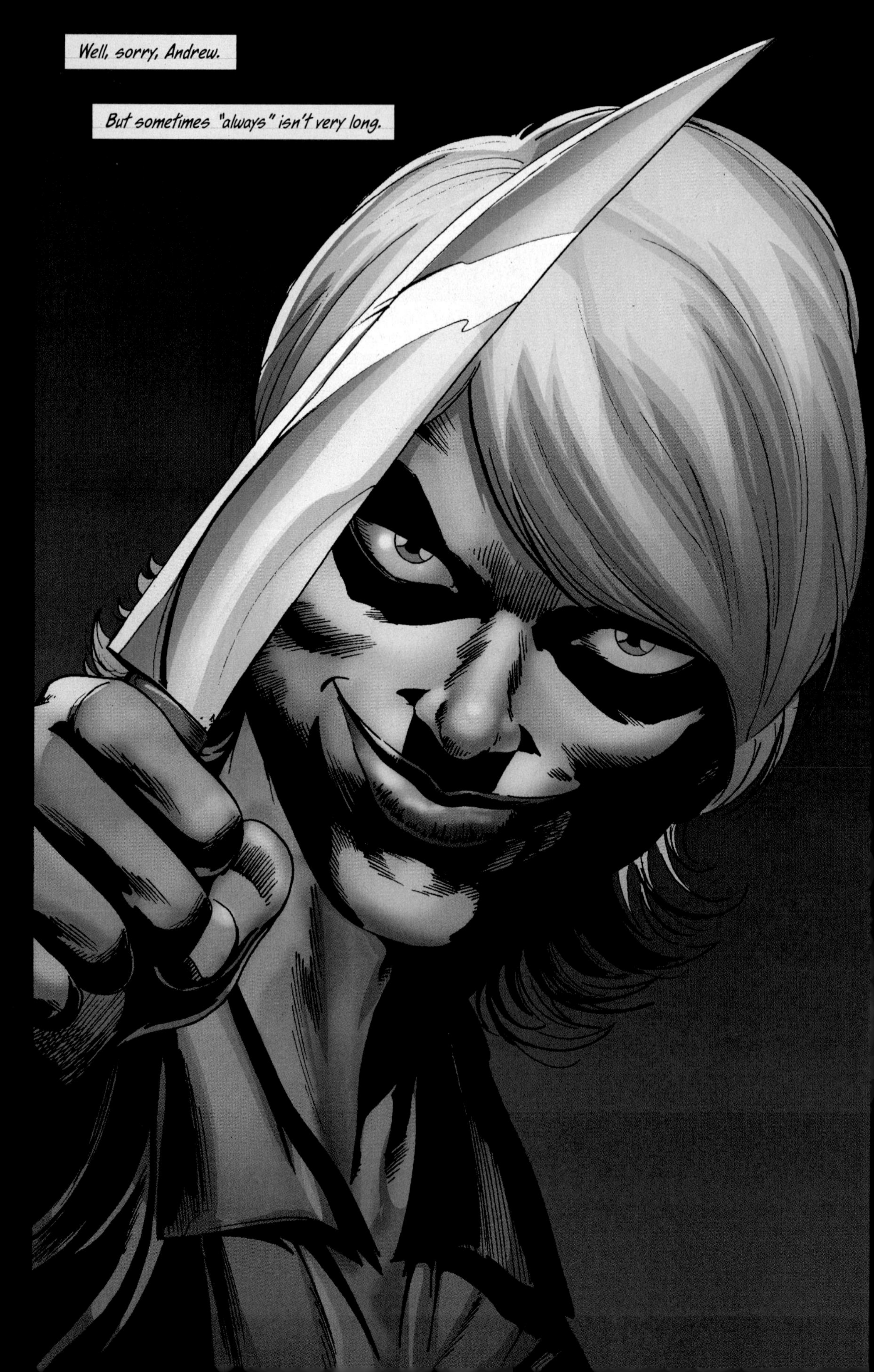
Well, sorry, Andrew.
But sometimes "always" isn't very long.

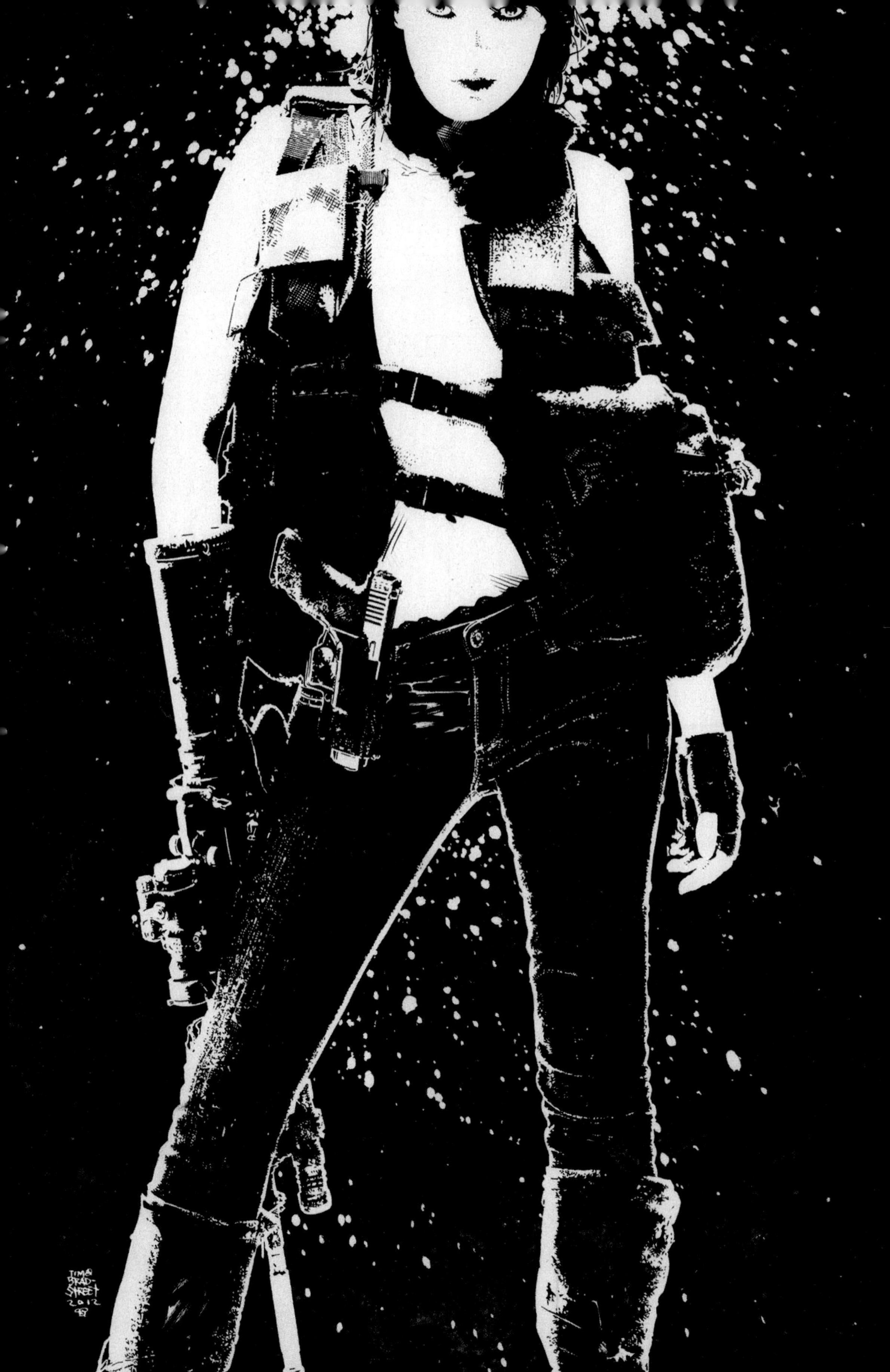
TIM BRAD-STREET 2012

Issue fifteen cover by TIM BRADSTREET

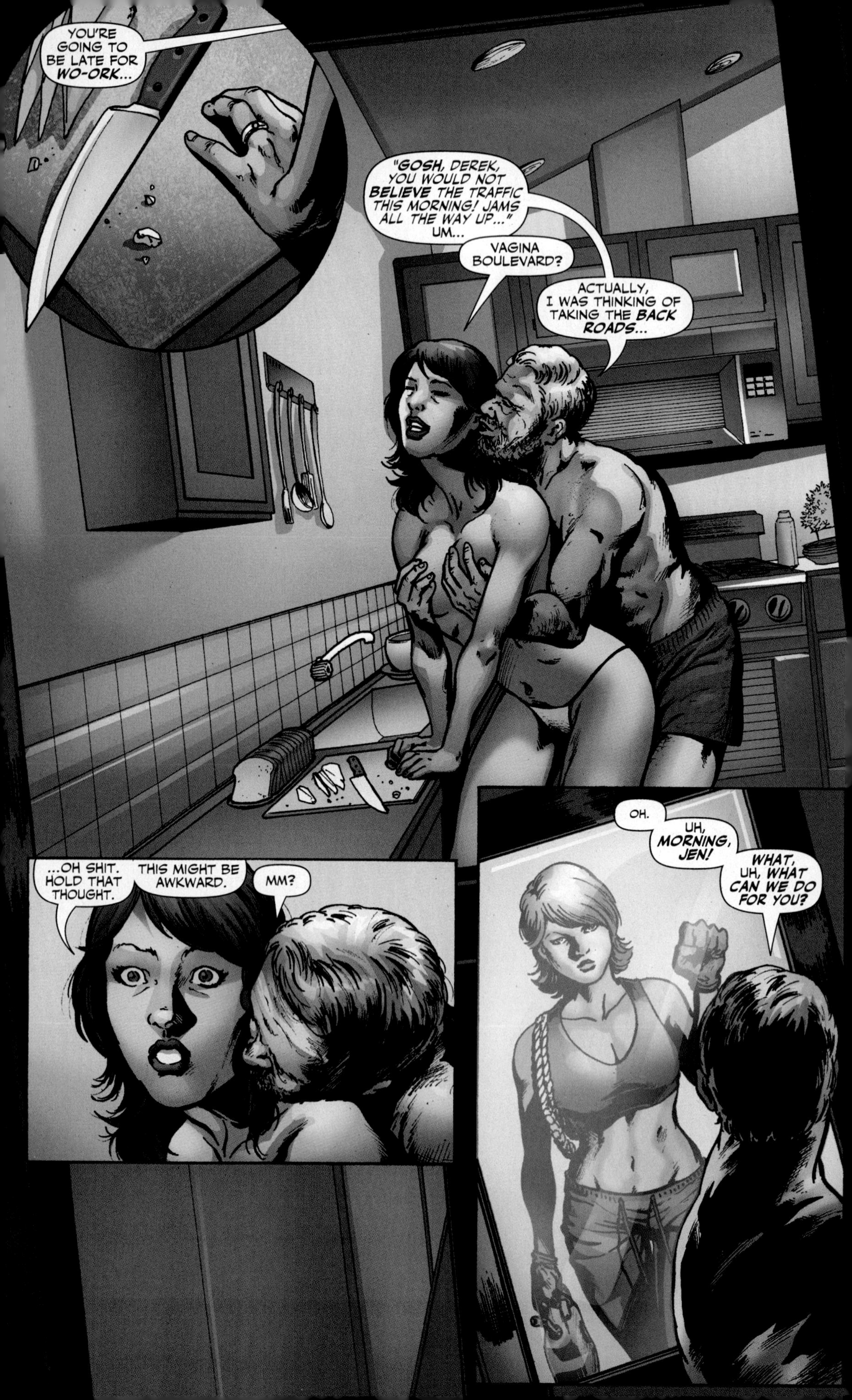

YOU'RE GOING TO BE LATE FOR *WO-ORK*...
"*GOSH*, DEREK, YOU WOULD NOT *BELIEVE* THE TRAFFIC THIS MORNING! JAMS ALL THE WAY UP..." UM...
VAGINA BOULEVARD?
ACTUALLY, I WAS THINKING OF TAKING THE *BACK ROADS*...
...OH SHIT. HOLD THAT THOUGHT.
THIS MIGHT BE AWKWARD.
MM?
OH.
UH, *MORNING, JEN!*
WHAT, UH, *WHAT CAN WE DO FOR YOU?*

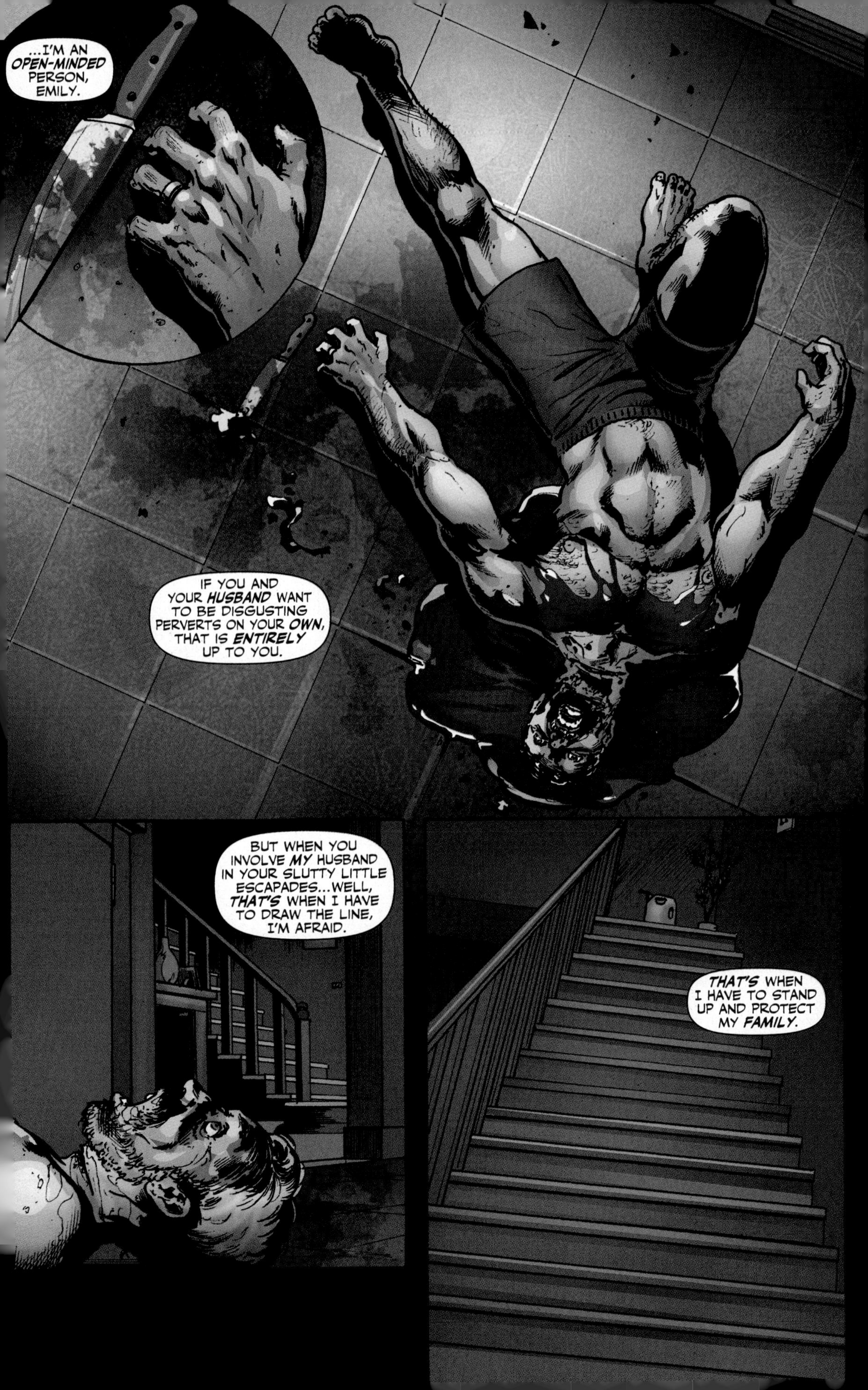
...I'M AN OPEN-MINDED PERSON, EMILY.
IF YOU AND YOUR HUSBAND WANT TO BE DISGUSTING PERVERTS ON YOUR OWN, THAT IS ENTIRELY UP TO YOU.
BUT WHEN YOU INVOLVE MY HUSBAND IN YOUR SLUTTY LITTLE ESCAPADES...WELL, THAT'S WHEN I HAVE TO DRAW THE LINE, I'M AFRAID.
THAT'S WHEN I HAVE TO STAND UP AND PROTECT MY FAMILY.

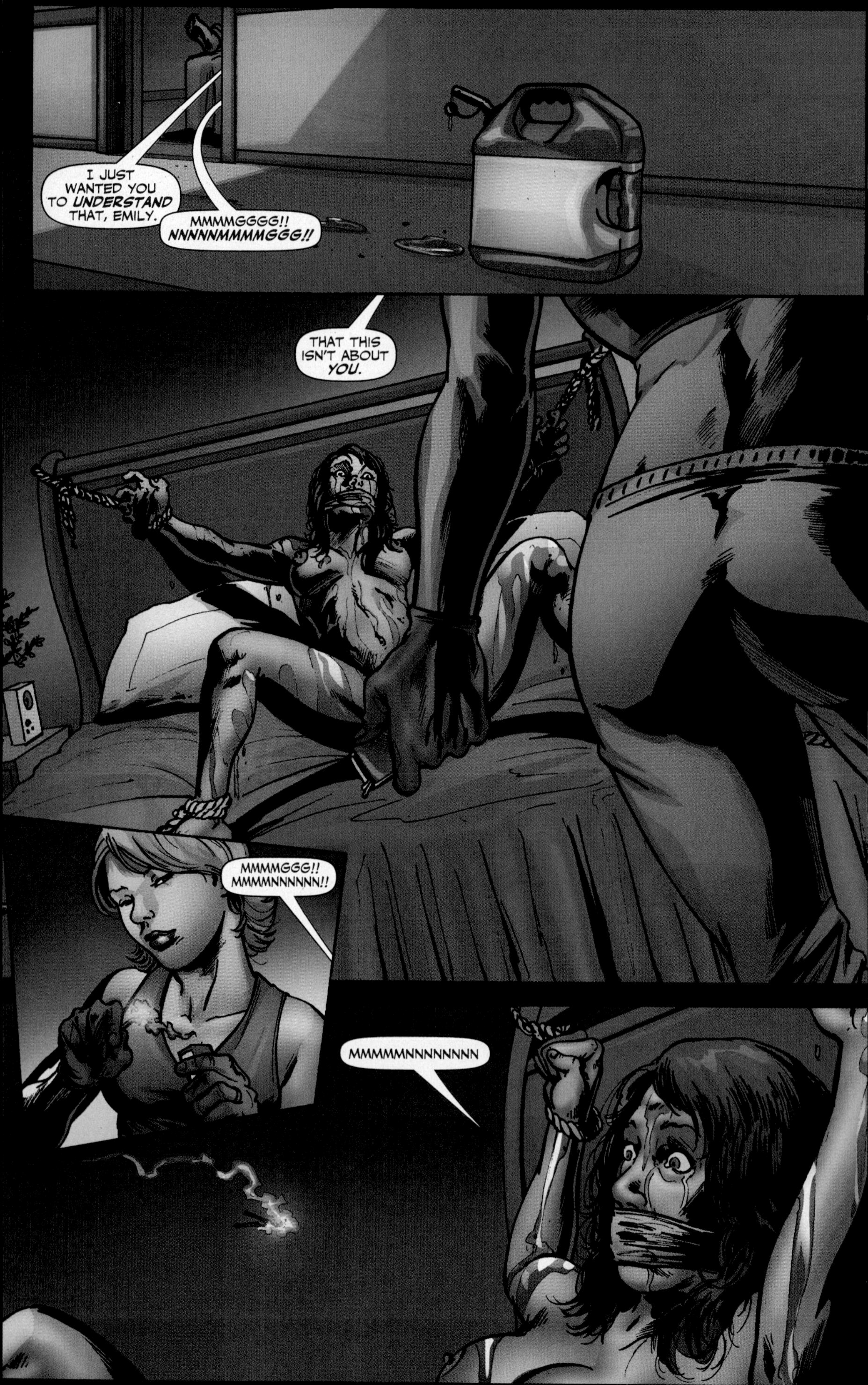

I JUST WANTED YOU TO UNDERSTAND THAT, EMILY.
MMMMGGGG!! NNNNNMMMMGGG!!
THAT THIS ISN'T ABOUT YOU.
MMMMGGG!! MMMMNNNNNN!!
MMMMMNNNNNNNN

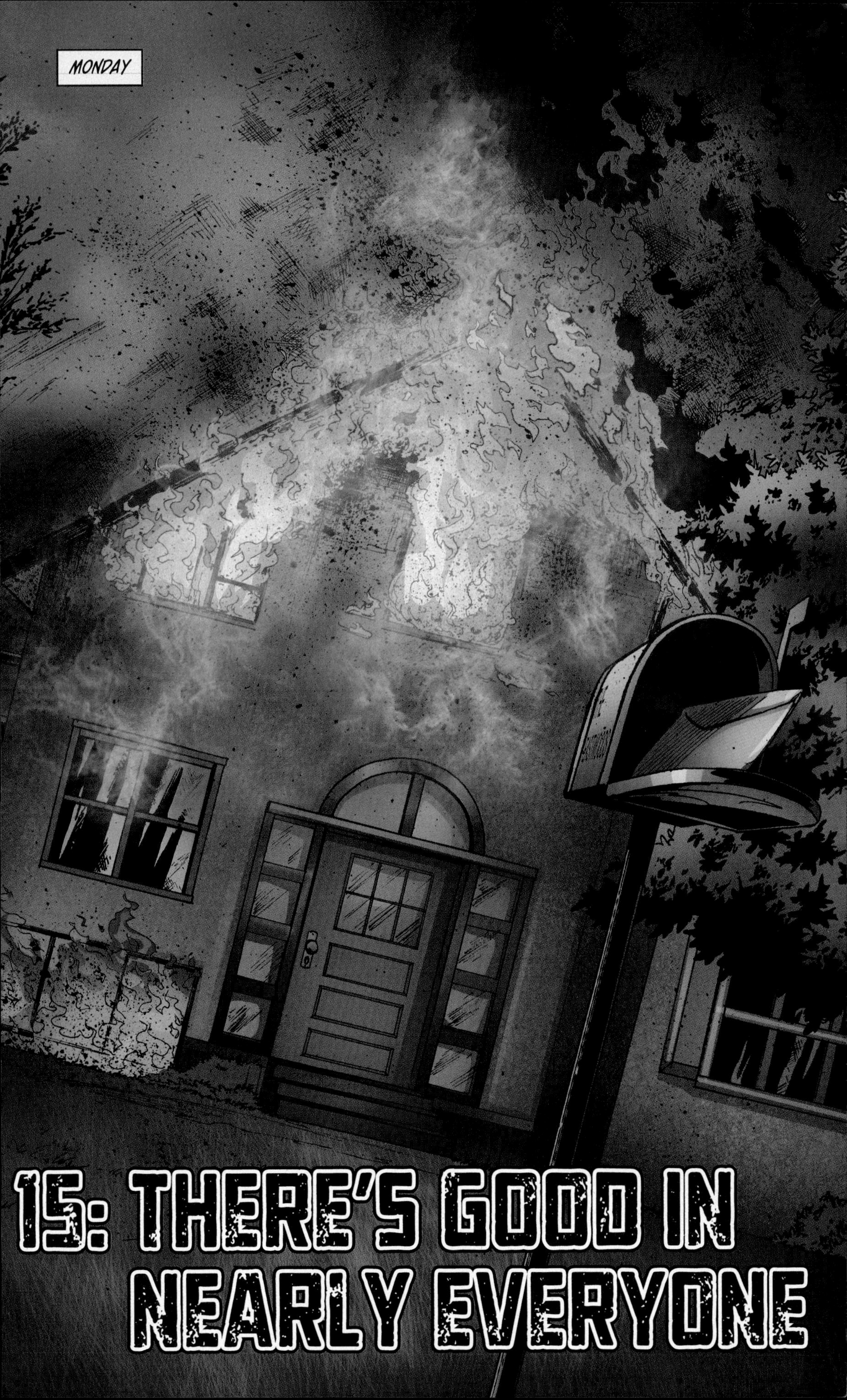
MONDAY
15: THERE'S GOOD IN NEARLY EVERYONE

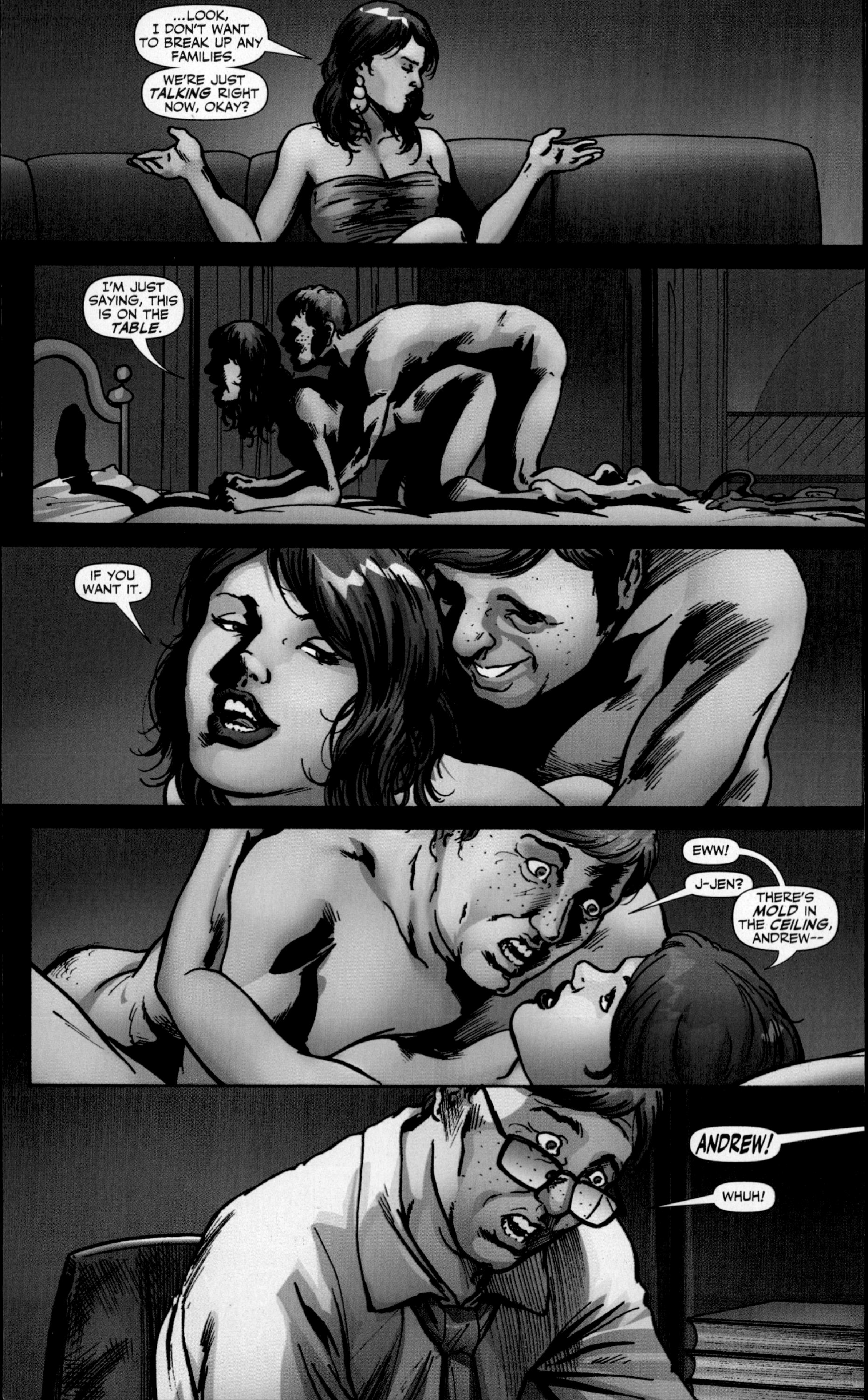
...LOOK, I DON'T WANT TO BREAK UP ANY FAMILIES.
WE'RE JUST *TALKING* RIGHT NOW, OKAY?
I'M JUST SAYING, THIS IS ON THE *TABLE*.
IF YOU WANT IT.
EWW!
J-JEN?
THERE'S *MOLD* IN THE *CEILING*, ANDREW--
ANDREW!
WHUH!

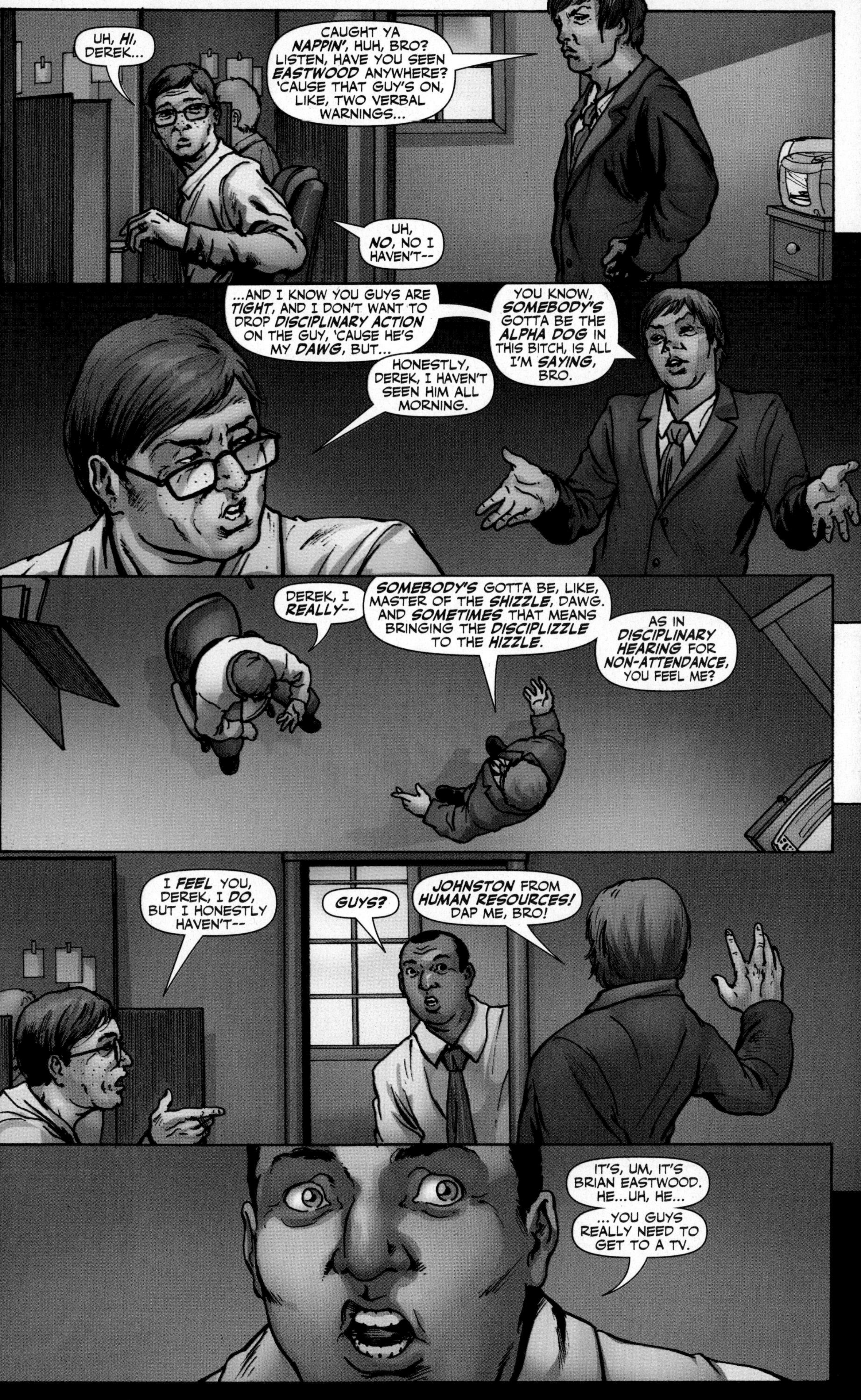
UH, HI, DEREK...
CAUGHT YA NAPPIN', HUH, BRO? LISTEN, HAVE YOU SEEN EASTWOOD ANYWHERE? 'CAUSE THAT GUY'S ON, LIKE, TWO VERBAL WARNINGS...
UH, NO, NO I HAVEN'T--
...AND I KNOW YOU GUYS ARE TIGHT, AND I DON'T WANT TO DROP DISCIPLINARY ACTION ON THE GUY, 'CAUSE HE'S MY DAWG, BUT...
HONESTLY, DEREK, I HAVEN'T SEEN HIM ALL MORNING.
YOU KNOW, SOMEBODY'S GOTTA BE THE ALPHA DOG IN THIS BITCH, IS ALL I'M SAYING, BRO.
DEREK, I REALLY--
SOMEBODY'S GOTTA BE, LIKE, MASTER OF THE SHIZZLE, DAWG. AND SOMETIMES THAT MEANS BRINGING THE DISCIPLIZZLE TO THE HIZZLE.
AS IN DISCIPLINARY HEARING FOR NON-ATTENDANCE, YOU FEEL ME?
I FEEL YOU, DEREK, I DO, BUT I HONESTLY HAVEN'T--
GUYS?
JOHNSTON FROM HUMAN RESOURCES! DAP ME, BRO!
IT'S, UM, IT'S BRIAN EASTWOOD. HE...UH, HE...
...YOU GUYS REALLY NEED TO GET TO A TV.

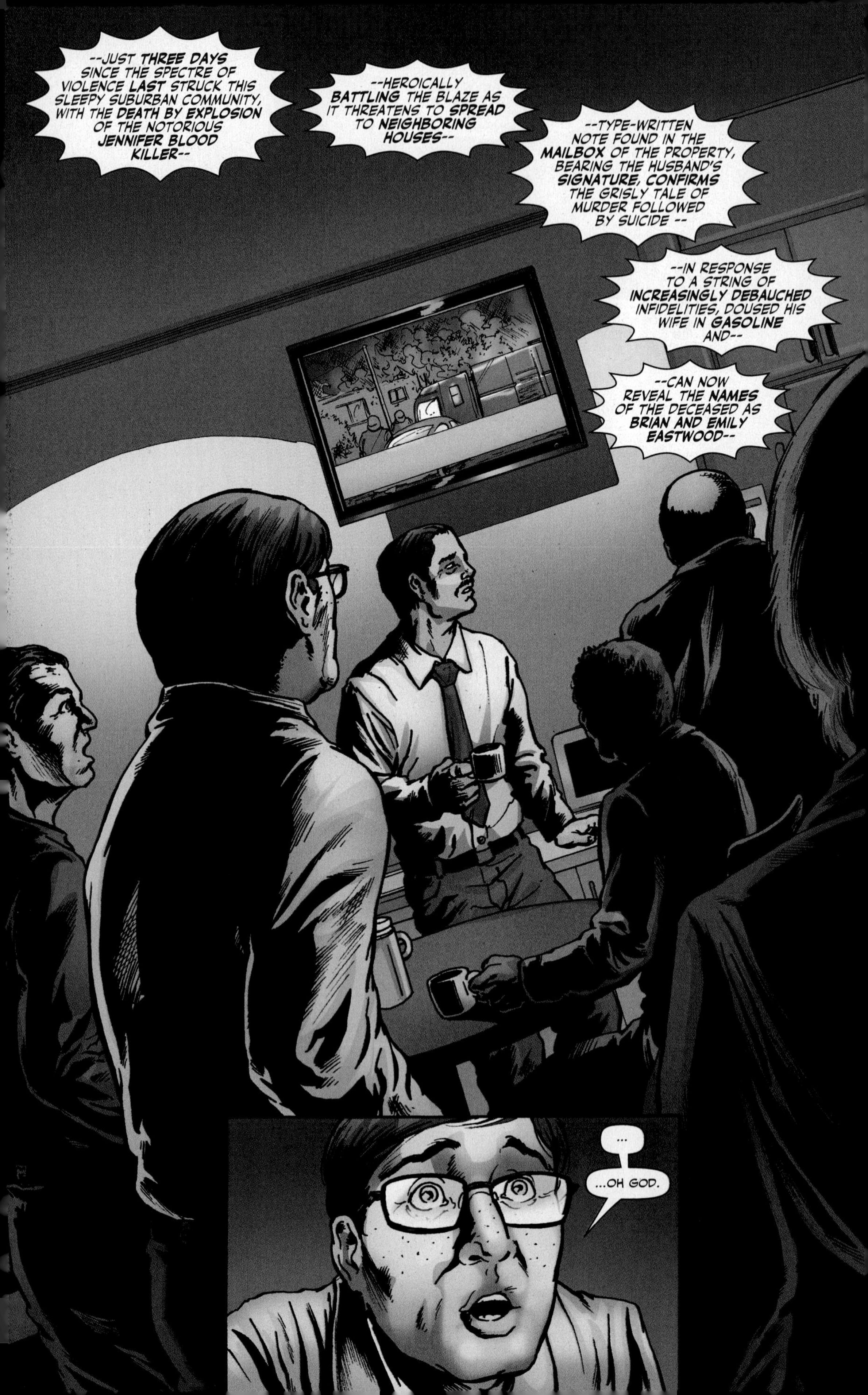
--JUST THREE DAYS SINCE THE SPECTRE OF VIOLENCE LAST STRUCK THIS SLEEPY SUBURBAN COMMUNITY, WITH THE DEATH BY EXPLOSION OF THE NOTORIOUS JENNIFER BLOOD KILLER--
--HEROICALLY BATTLING THE BLAZE AS IT THREATENS TO SPREAD TO NEIGHBORING HOUSES--
--TYPE-WRITTEN NOTE FOUND IN THE MAILBOX OF THE PROPERTY, BEARING THE HUSBAND'S SIGNATURE, CONFIRMS THE GRISLY TALE OF MURDER FOLLOWED BY SUICIDE --
--IN RESPONSE TO A STRING OF INCREASINGLY DEBAUCHED INFIDELITIES, DOUSED HIS WIFE IN GASOLINE AND--
--CAN NOW REVEAL THE NAMES OF THE DECEASED AS BRIAN AND EMILY EASTWOOD--
...
...OH GOD.

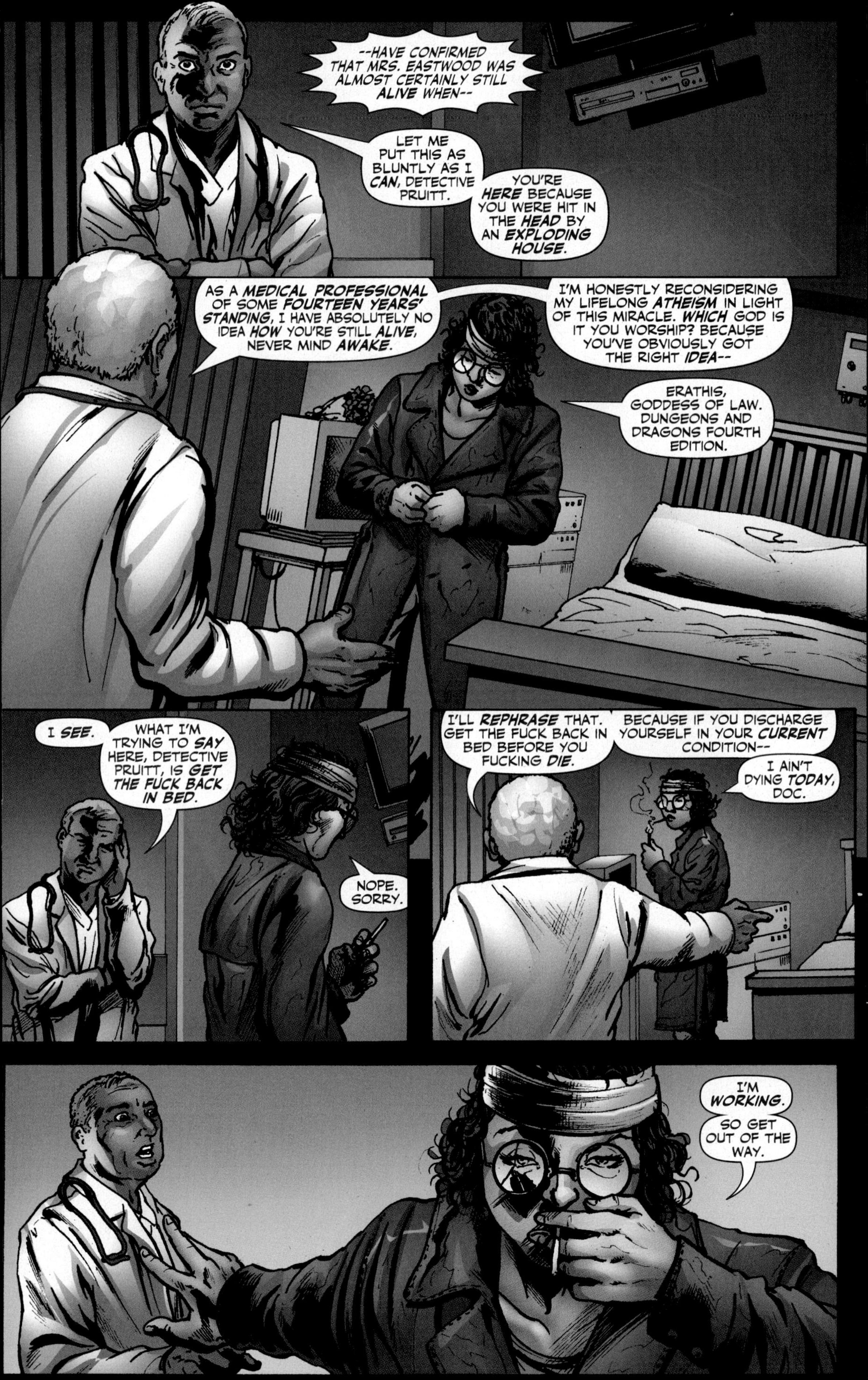
--HAVE CONFIRMED THAT MRS. EASTWOOD WAS ALMOST CERTAINLY STILL ALIVE WHEN--
LET ME PUT THIS AS BLUNTLY AS I CAN, DETECTIVE PRUITT.
YOU'RE HERE BECAUSE YOU WERE HIT IN THE HEAD BY AN EXPLODING HOUSE.
AS A MEDICAL PROFESSIONAL OF SOME FOURTEEN YEARS' STANDING, I HAVE ABSOLUTELY NO IDEA HOW YOU'RE STILL ALIVE, NEVER MIND AWAKE.
I'M HONESTLY RECONSIDERING MY LIFELONG ATHEISM IN LIGHT OF THIS MIRACLE. WHICH GOD IS IT YOU WORSHIP? BECAUSE YOU'VE OBVIOUSLY GOT THE RIGHT IDEA--
ERATHIS, GODDESS OF LAW. DUNGEONS AND DRAGONS FOURTH EDITION.
I SEE.
WHAT I'M TRYING TO SAY HERE, DETECTIVE PRUITT, IS GET THE FUCK BACK IN BED.
NOPE. SORRY.
I'LL REPHRASE THAT. GET THE FUCK BACK IN BED BEFORE YOU FUCKING DIE.
BECAUSE IF YOU DISCHARGE YOURSELF IN YOUR CURRENT CONDITION--
I AIN'T DYING TODAY, DOC.
I'M WORKING.
SO GET OUT OF THE WAY.

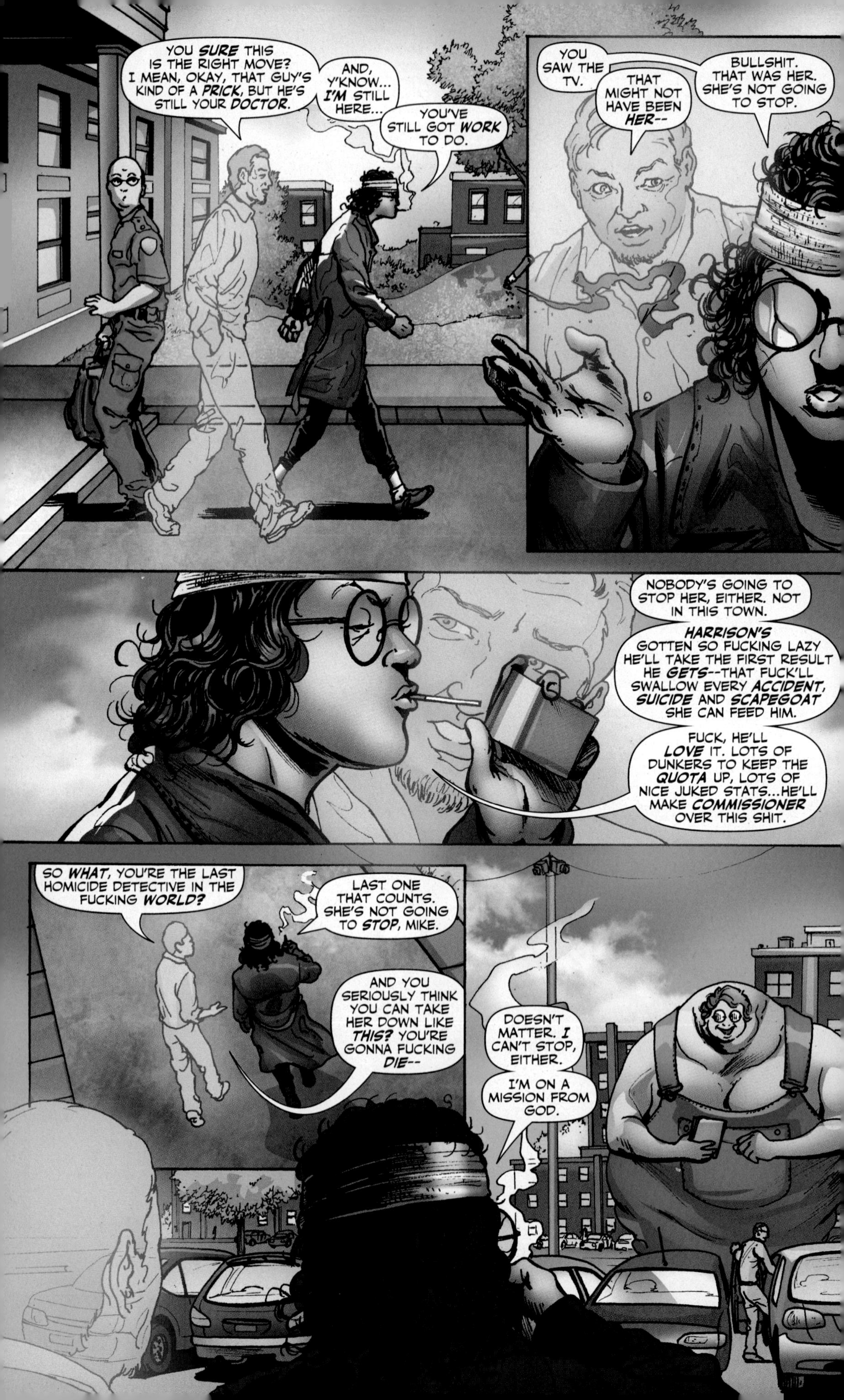
YOU SURE THIS IS THE RIGHT MOVE? I MEAN, OKAY, THAT GUY'S KIND OF A PRICK, BUT HE'S STILL YOUR DOCTOR.
AND, Y'KNOW... I'M STILL HERE...
YOU'VE STILL GOT WORK TO DO.
YOU SAW THE TV.
THAT MIGHT NOT HAVE BEEN HER--
BULLSHIT. THAT WAS HER. SHE'S NOT GOING TO STOP.
NOBODY'S GOING TO STOP HER, EITHER. NOT IN THIS TOWN.
HARRISON'S GOTTEN SO FUCKING LAZY HE'LL TAKE THE FIRST RESULT HE GETS--THAT FUCK'LL SWALLOW EVERY ACCIDENT, SUICIDE AND SCAPEGOAT SHE CAN FEED HIM.
FUCK, HE'LL LOVE IT. LOTS OF DUNKERS TO KEEP THE QUOTA UP, LOTS OF NICE JUKED STATS...HE'LL MAKE COMMISSIONER OVER THIS SHIT.
SO WHAT, YOU'RE THE LAST HOMICIDE DETECTIVE IN THE FUCKING WORLD?
LAST ONE THAT COUNTS. SHE'S NOT GOING TO STOP, MIKE.
AND YOU SERIOUSLY THINK YOU CAN TAKE HER DOWN LIKE THIS? YOU'RE GONNA FUCKING DIE--
DOESN'T MATTER. I CAN'T STOP, EITHER.
I'M ON A MISSION FROM GOD.

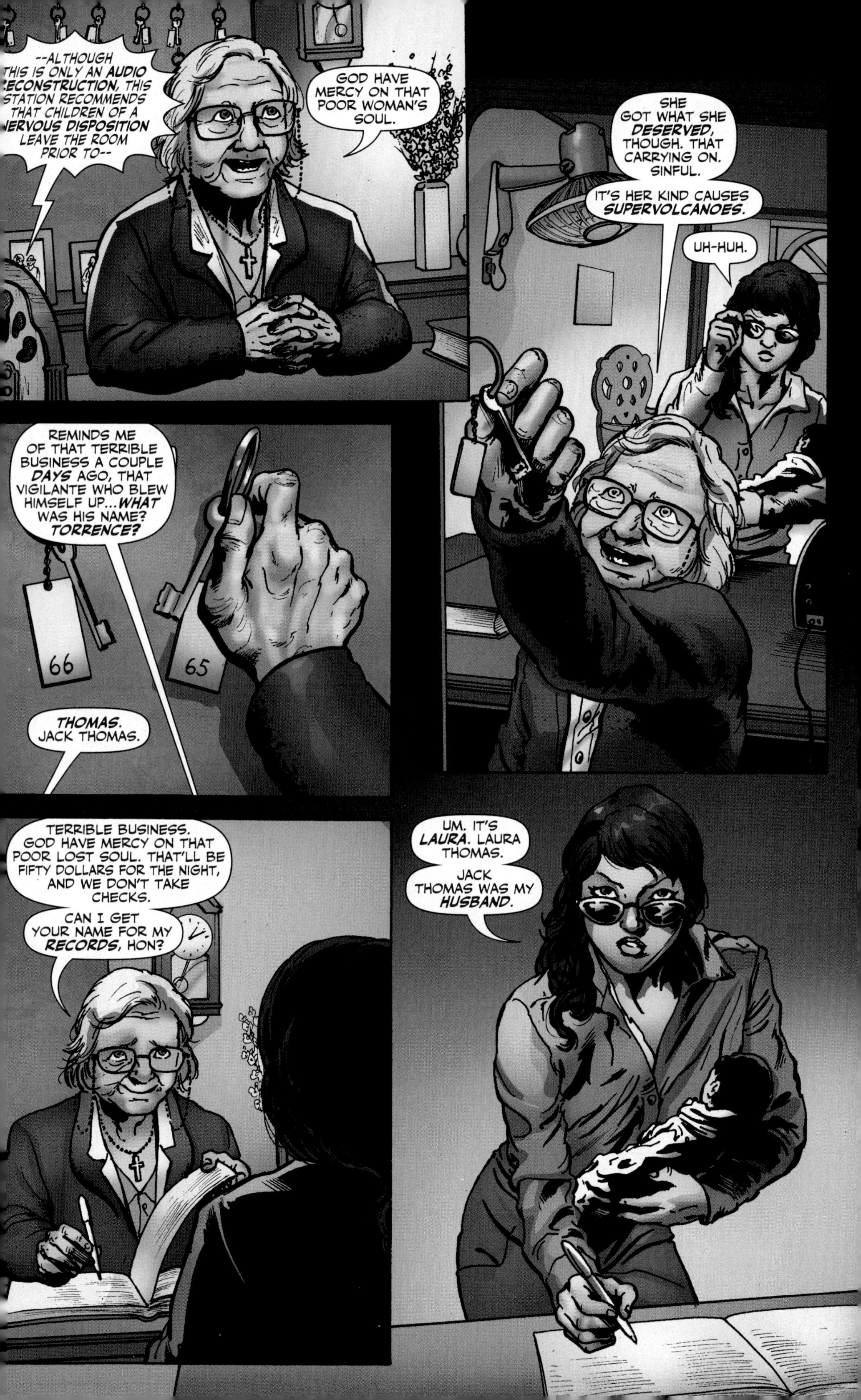
--ALTHOUGH THIS IS ONLY AN AUDIO RECONSTRUCTION, THIS STATION RECOMMENDS THAT CHILDREN OF A NERVOUS DISPOSITION LEAVE THE ROOM PRIOR TO--
GOD HAVE MERCY ON THAT POOR WOMAN'S SOUL.
SHE GOT WHAT SHE DESERVED, THOUGH. THAT CARRYING ON. SINFUL.
IT'S HER KIND CAUSES SUPERVOLCANOES.
UH-HUH.
REMINDS ME OF THAT TERRIBLE BUSINESS A COUPLE DAYS AGO, THAT VIGILANTE WHO BLEW HIMSELF UP... WHAT WAS HIS NAME? TORRENCE?
66
65
THOMAS. JACK THOMAS.
TERRIBLE BUSINESS. GOD HAVE MERCY ON THAT POOR LOST SOUL. THAT'LL BE FIFTY DOLLARS FOR THE NIGHT, AND WE DON'T TAKE CHECKS.
CAN I GET YOUR NAME FOR MY RECORDS, HON?
UM. IT'S LAURA. LAURA THOMAS.
JACK THOMAS WAS MY HUSBAND.

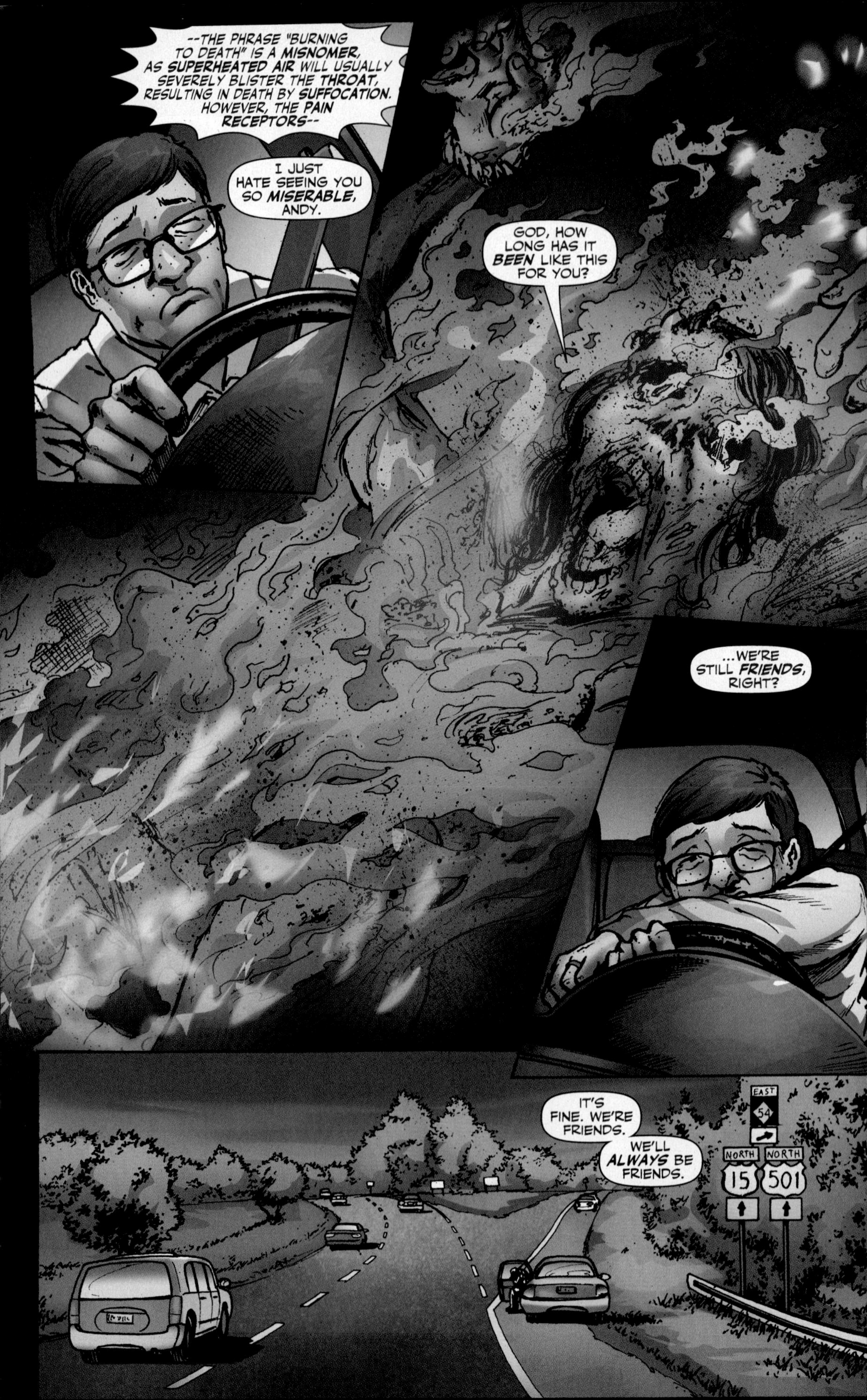
--THE PHRASE "BURNING TO DEATH" IS A MISNOMER, AS SUPERHEATED AIR WILL USUALLY SEVERELY BLISTER THE THROAT, RESULTING IN DEATH BY SUFFOCATION. HOWEVER, THE PAIN RECEPTORS--
I JUST HATE SEEING YOU SO MISERABLE, ANDY.
GOD, HOW LONG HAS IT BEEN LIKE THIS FOR YOU?
...WE'RE STILL FRIENDS, RIGHT?
IT'S FINE. WE'RE FRIENDS.
WE'LL ALWAYS BE FRIENDS.
EAST
54
NORTH
15
NORTH
501

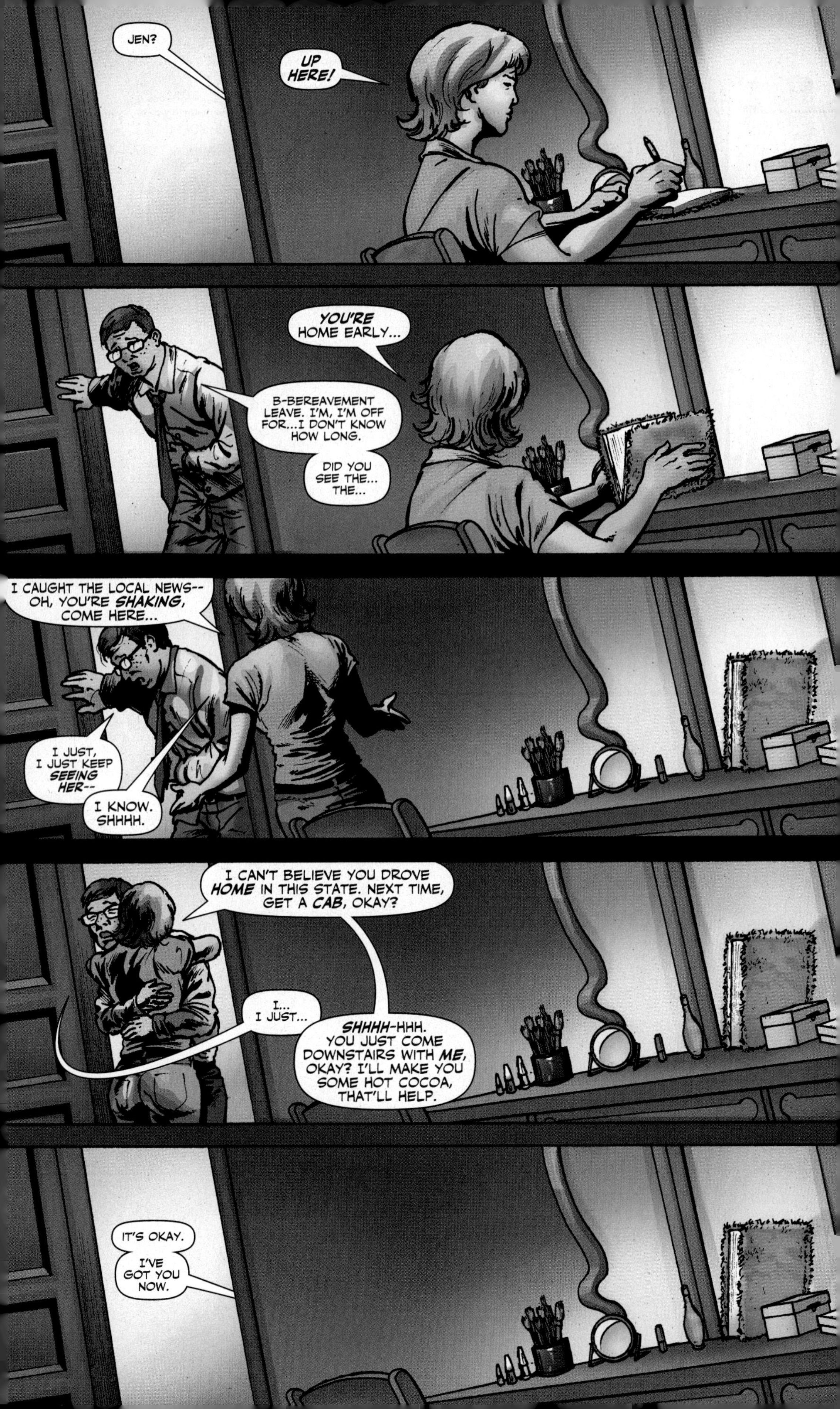
JEN?
UP HERE!
YOU'RE HOME EARLY...
B-BEREAVEMENT LEAVE. I'M, I'M OFF FOR...I DON'T KNOW HOW LONG.
DID YOU SEE THE... THE...
I CAUGHT THE LOCAL NEWS--OH, YOU'RE SHAKING, COME HERE...
I JUST, I JUST KEEP SEEING HER--
I KNOW. SHHHH.
I CAN'T BELIEVE YOU DROVE HOME IN THIS STATE. NEXT TIME, GET A CAB, OKAY?
I... I JUST...
SHHHH-HHH. YOU JUST COME DOWNSTAIRS WITH ME, OKAY? I'LL MAKE YOU SOME HOT COCOA, THAT'LL HELP.
IT'S OKAY.
I'VE GOT YOU NOW.

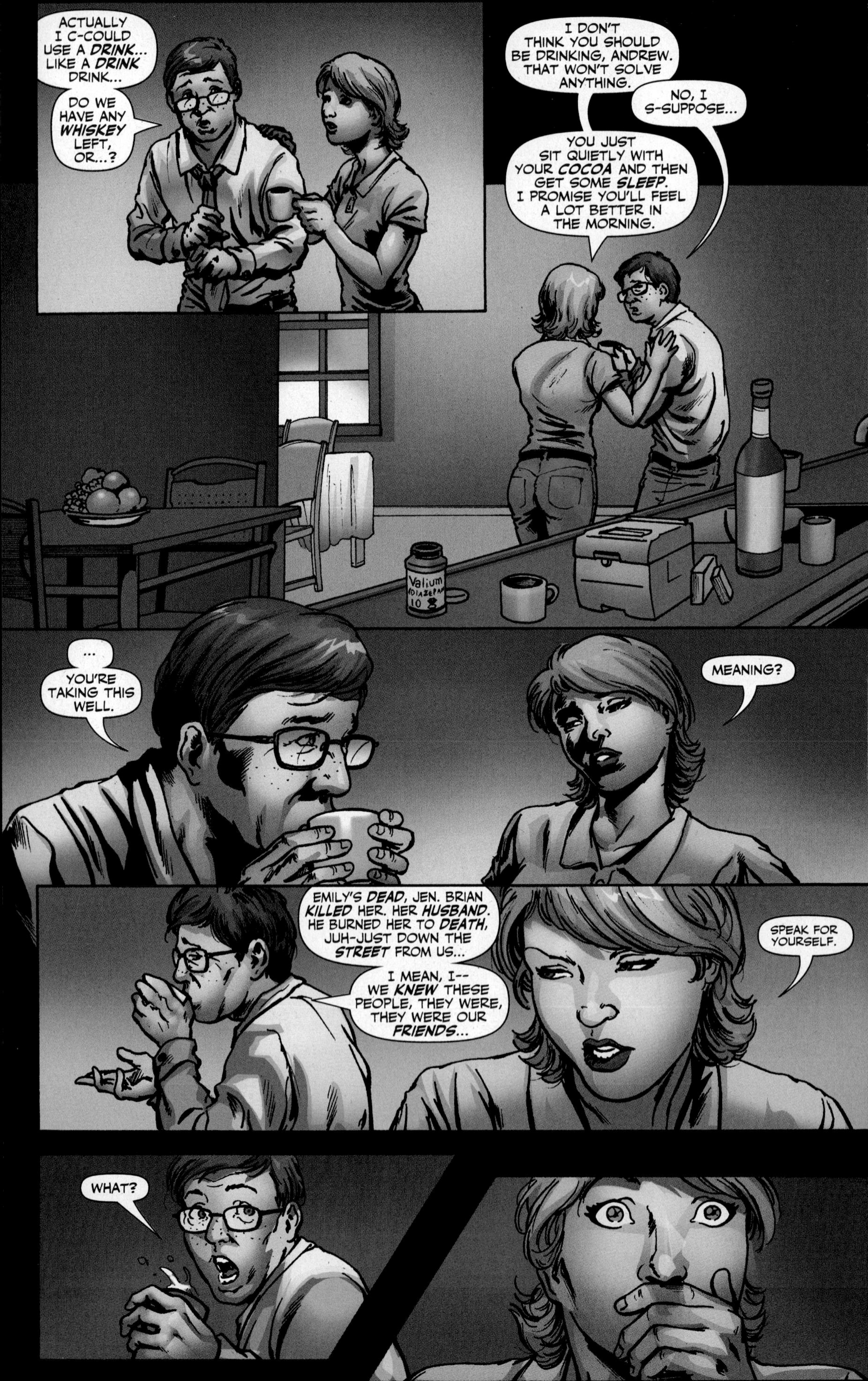
ACTUALLY I C-COULD USE A DRINK... LIKE A DRINK DRINK...
DO WE HAVE ANY WHISKEY LEFT, OR...?
I DON'T THINK YOU SHOULD BE DRINKING, ANDREW. THAT WON'T SOLVE ANYTHING.
NO, I S-SUPPOSE...
YOU JUST SIT QUIETLY WITH YOUR COCOA AND THEN GET SOME SLEEP. I PROMISE YOU'LL FEEL A LOT BETTER IN THE MORNING.
Valium DIAZEPAM 10
... YOU'RE TAKING THIS WELL.
MEANING?
EMILY'S DEAD, JEN. BRIAN KILLED HER. HER HUSBAND. HE BURNED HER TO DEATH, JUH-JUST DOWN THE STREET FROM US...
I MEAN, I-- WE KNEW THESE PEOPLE, THEY WERE, THEY WERE OUR FRIENDS...
SPEAK FOR YOURSELF.
WHAT?

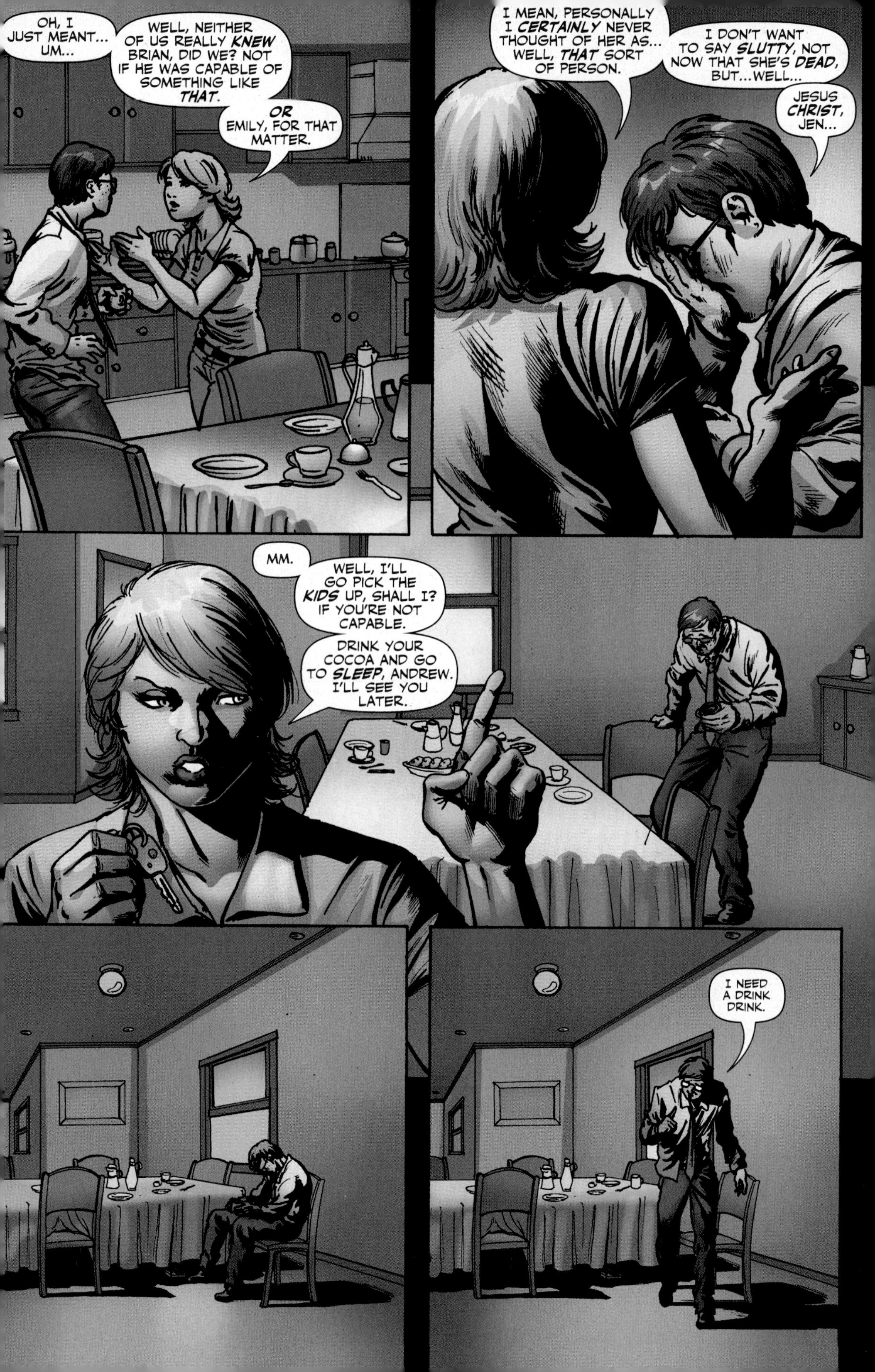
OH, I JUST MEANT... UM...
WELL, NEITHER OF US REALLY KNEW BRIAN, DID WE? NOT IF HE WAS CAPABLE OF SOMETHING LIKE THAT.
OR EMILY, FOR THAT MATTER.
I MEAN, PERSONALLY I CERTAINLY NEVER THOUGHT OF HER AS... WELL, THAT SORT OF PERSON.
I DON'T WANT TO SAY SLUTTY, NOT NOW THAT SHE'S DEAD, BUT...WELL...
JESUS CHRIST, JEN...
MM.
WELL, I'LL GO PICK THE KIDS UP, SHALL I? IF YOU'RE NOT CAPABLE.
DRINK YOUR COCOA AND GO TO SLEEP, ANDREW. I'LL SEE YOU LATER.
I NEED A DRINK DRINK.

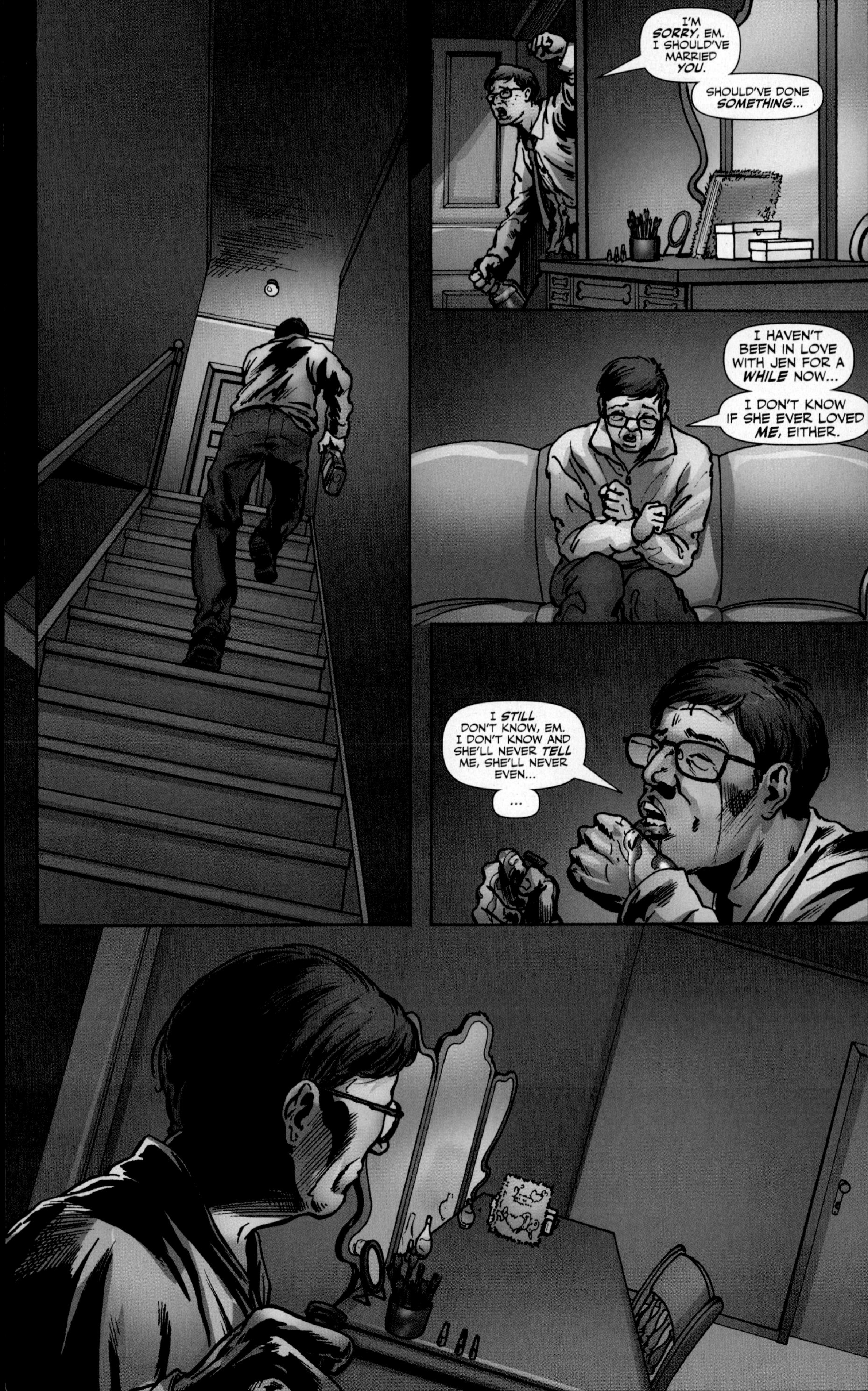
I'M SORRY, EM. I SHOULD'VE MARRIED YOU.
SHOULD'VE DONE SOMETHING...
I HAVEN'T BEEN IN LOVE WITH JEN FOR A WHILE NOW...
I DON'T KNOW IF SHE EVER LOVED ME, EITHER.
I STILL DON'T KNOW, EM. I DON'T KNOW AND SHE'LL NEVER TELL ME, SHE'LL NEVER EVEN...
...

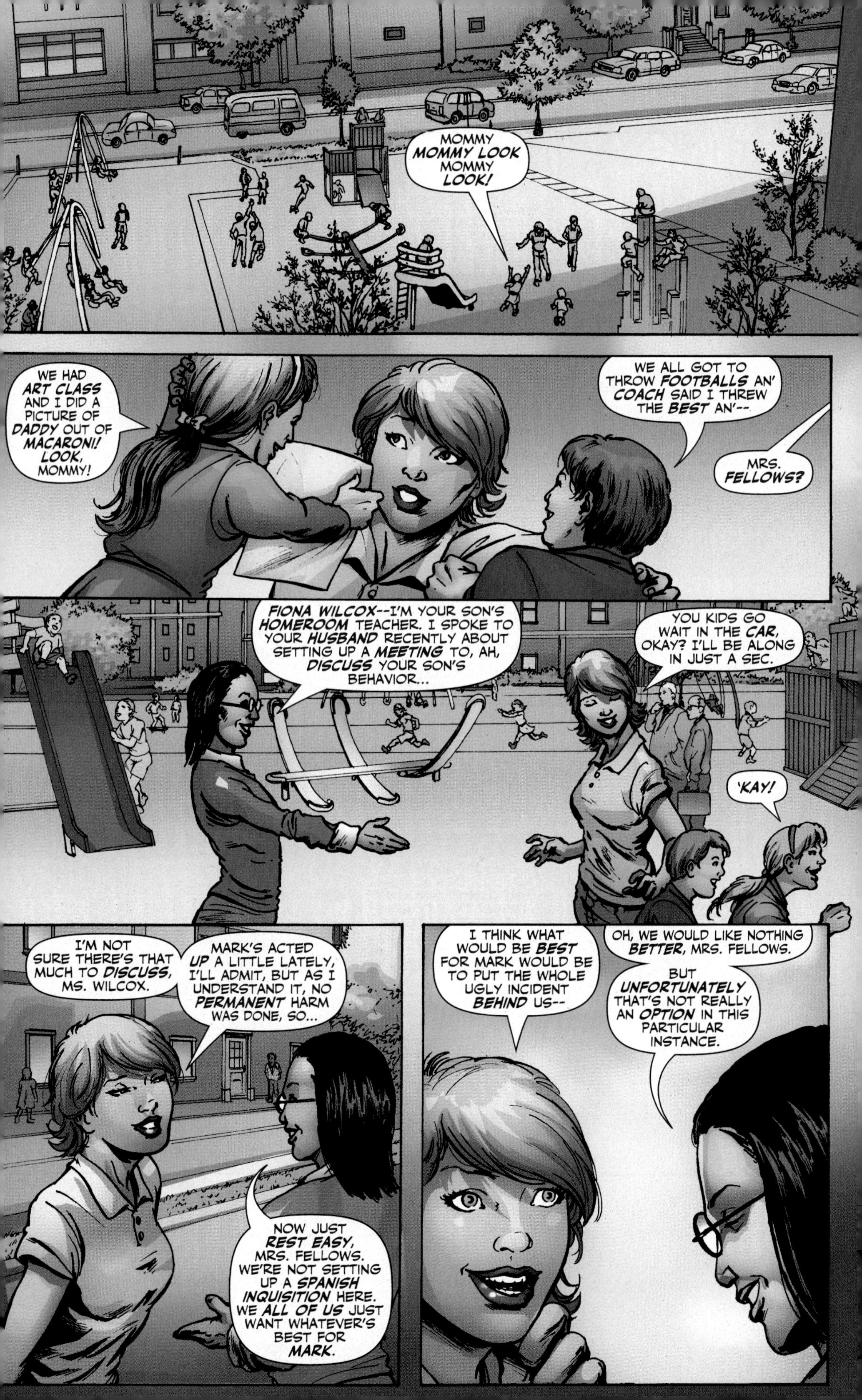
MOMMY MOMMY LOOK MOMMY LOOK!
WE HAD ART CLASS AND I DID A PICTURE OF DADDY OUT OF MACARONI! LOOK, MOMMY!
WE ALL GOT TO THROW FOOTBALLS AN' COACH SAID I THREW THE BEST AN'--
MRS. FELLOWS?
FIONA WILCOX--I'M YOUR SON'S HOMEROOM TEACHER. I SPOKE TO YOUR HUSBAND RECENTLY ABOUT SETTING UP A MEETING TO, AH, DISCUSS YOUR SON'S BEHAVIOR...
YOU KIDS GO WAIT IN THE CAR, OKAY? I'LL BE ALONG IN JUST A SEC.
'KAY!
I'M NOT SURE THERE'S THAT MUCH TO DISCUSS, MS. WILCOX.
MARK'S ACTED UP A LITTLE LATELY, I'LL ADMIT, BUT AS I UNDERSTAND IT, NO PERMANENT HARM WAS DONE, SO...
NOW JUST REST EASY, MRS. FELLOWS. WE'RE NOT SETTING UP A SPANISH INQUISITION HERE. WE ALL OF US JUST WANT WHATEVER'S BEST FOR MARK.
I THINK WHAT WOULD BE BEST FOR MARK WOULD BE TO PUT THE WHOLE UGLY INCIDENT BEHIND US--
OH, WE WOULD LIKE NOTHING BETTER, MRS. FELLOWS.
BUT UNFORTUNATELY THAT'S NOT REALLY AN OPTION IN THIS PARTICULAR INSTANCE.

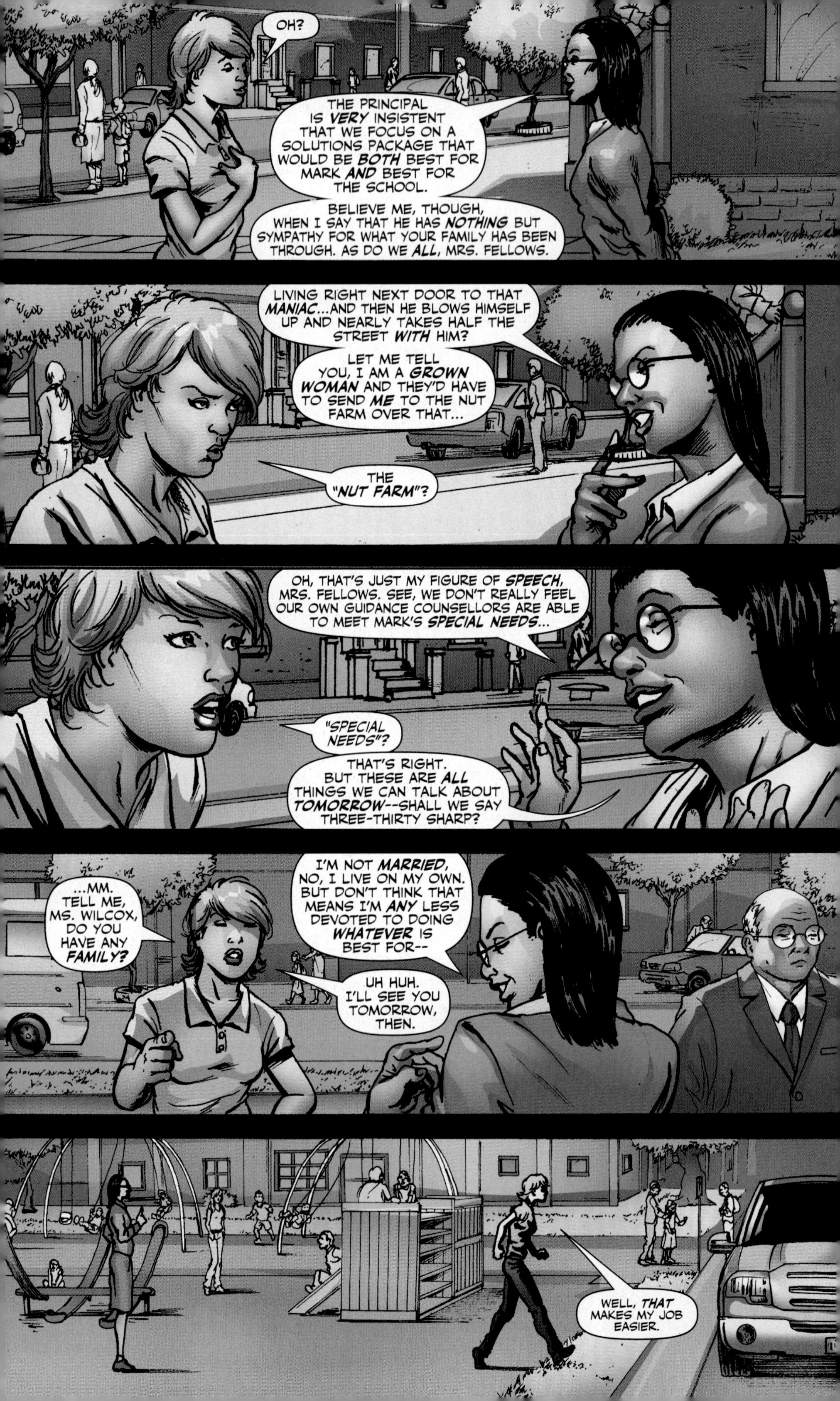
OH?
THE PRINCIPAL IS VERY INSISTENT THAT WE FOCUS ON A SOLUTIONS PACKAGE THAT WOULD BE BOTH BEST FOR MARK AND BEST FOR THE SCHOOL.
BELIEVE ME, THOUGH, WHEN I SAY THAT HE HAS NOTHING BUT SYMPATHY FOR WHAT YOUR FAMILY HAS BEEN THROUGH. AS DO WE ALL, MRS. FELLOWS.
LIVING RIGHT NEXT DOOR TO THAT MANIAC...AND THEN HE BLOWS HIMSELF UP AND NEARLY TAKES HALF THE STREET WITH HIM?
LET ME TELL YOU, I AM A GROWN WOMAN AND THEY'D HAVE TO SEND ME TO THE NUT FARM OVER THAT...
THE "NUT FARM"?
OH, THAT'S JUST MY FIGURE OF SPEECH, MRS. FELLOWS. SEE, WE DON'T REALLY FEEL OUR OWN GUIDANCE COUNSELLORS ARE ABLE TO MEET MARK'S SPECIAL NEEDS...
"SPECIAL NEEDS"?
THAT'S RIGHT. BUT THESE ARE ALL THINGS WE CAN TALK ABOUT TOMORROW--SHALL WE SAY THREE-THIRTY SHARP?
...MM. TELL ME, MS. WILCOX, DO YOU HAVE ANY FAMILY?
I'M NOT MARRIED, NO, I LIVE ON MY OWN. BUT DON'T THINK THAT MEANS I'M ANY LESS DEVOTED TO DOING WHATEVER IS BEST FOR--
UH HUH. I'LL SEE YOU TOMORROW, THEN.
WELL, THAT MAKES MY JOB EASIER.

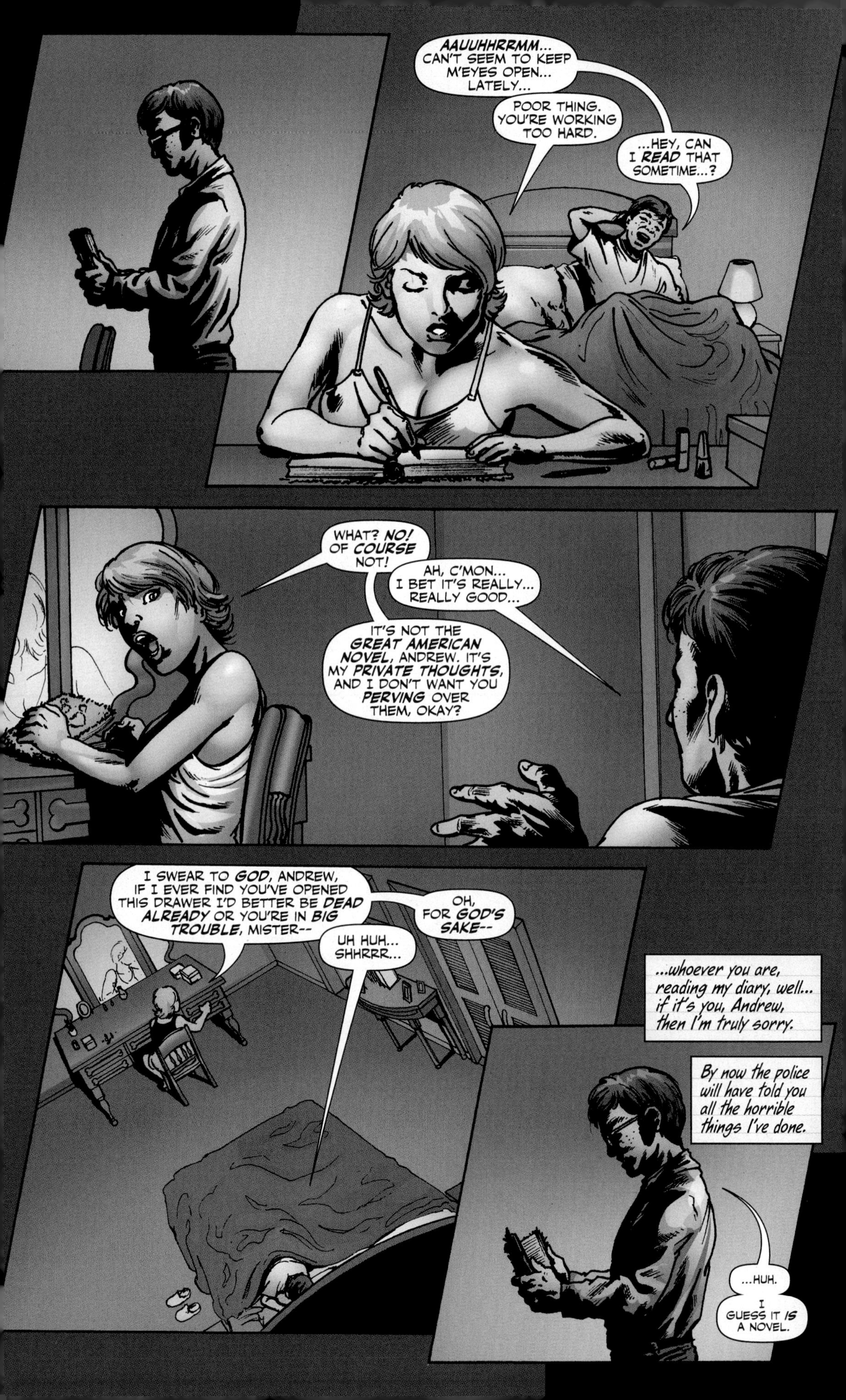
AAUUHHRRMM... CAN'T SEEM TO KEEP M'EYES OPEN... LATELY...
POOR THING. YOU'RE WORKING TOO HARD.
...HEY, CAN I READ THAT SOMETIME...?
WHAT? NO! OF COURSE NOT!
AH, C'MON... I BET IT'S REALLY... REALLY GOOD...
IT'S NOT THE GREAT AMERICAN NOVEL, ANDREW. IT'S MY PRIVATE THOUGHTS, AND I DON'T WANT YOU PERVING OVER THEM, OKAY?
I SWEAR TO GOD, ANDREW, IF I EVER FIND YOU'VE OPENED THIS DRAWER I'D BETTER BE DEAD ALREADY OR YOU'RE IN BIG TROUBLE, MISTER--
OH, FOR GOD'S SAKE--
UH HUH... SHHRRR...
...whoever you are, reading my diary, well... if it's you, Andrew, then I'm truly sorry.
By now the police will have told you all the horrible things I've done.
...HUH.
I GUESS IT IS A NOVEL.

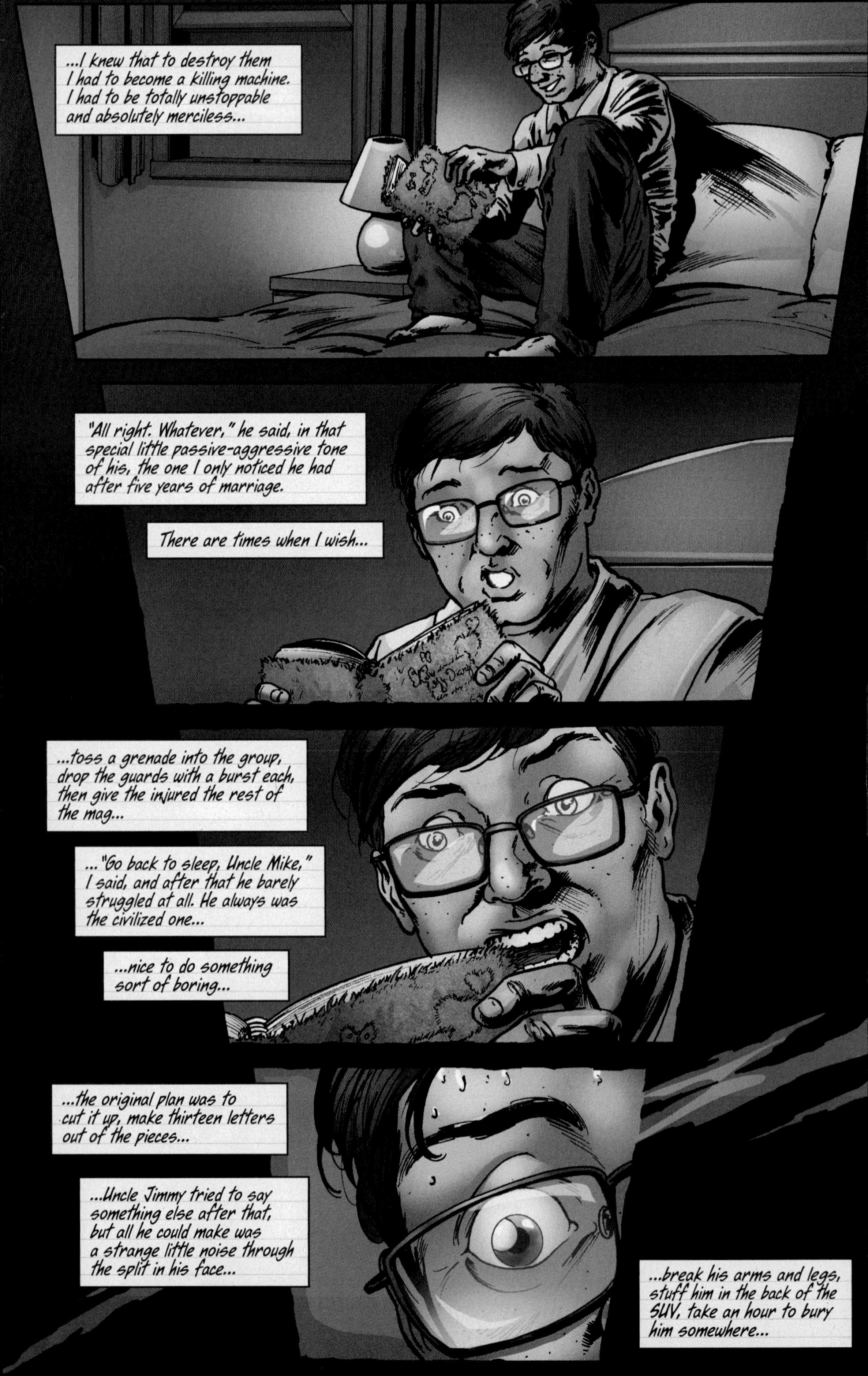
...I knew that to destroy them I had to become a killing machine. I had to be totally unstoppable and absolutely merciless...
"All right. Whatever," he said, in that special little passive-aggressive tone of his, the one I only noticed he had after five years of marriage.
There are times when I wish...
...toss a grenade into the group, drop the guards with a burst each, then give the injured the rest of the mag...
..."Go back to sleep, Uncle Mike," I said, and after that he barely struggled at all. He always was the civilized one...
...nice to do something sort of boring...
...the original plan was to cut it up, make thirteen letters out of the pieces...
...Uncle Jimmy tried to say something else after that, but all he could make was a strange little noise through the split in his face...
...break his arms and legs, stuff him in the back of the SUV, take an hour to bury him somewhere...

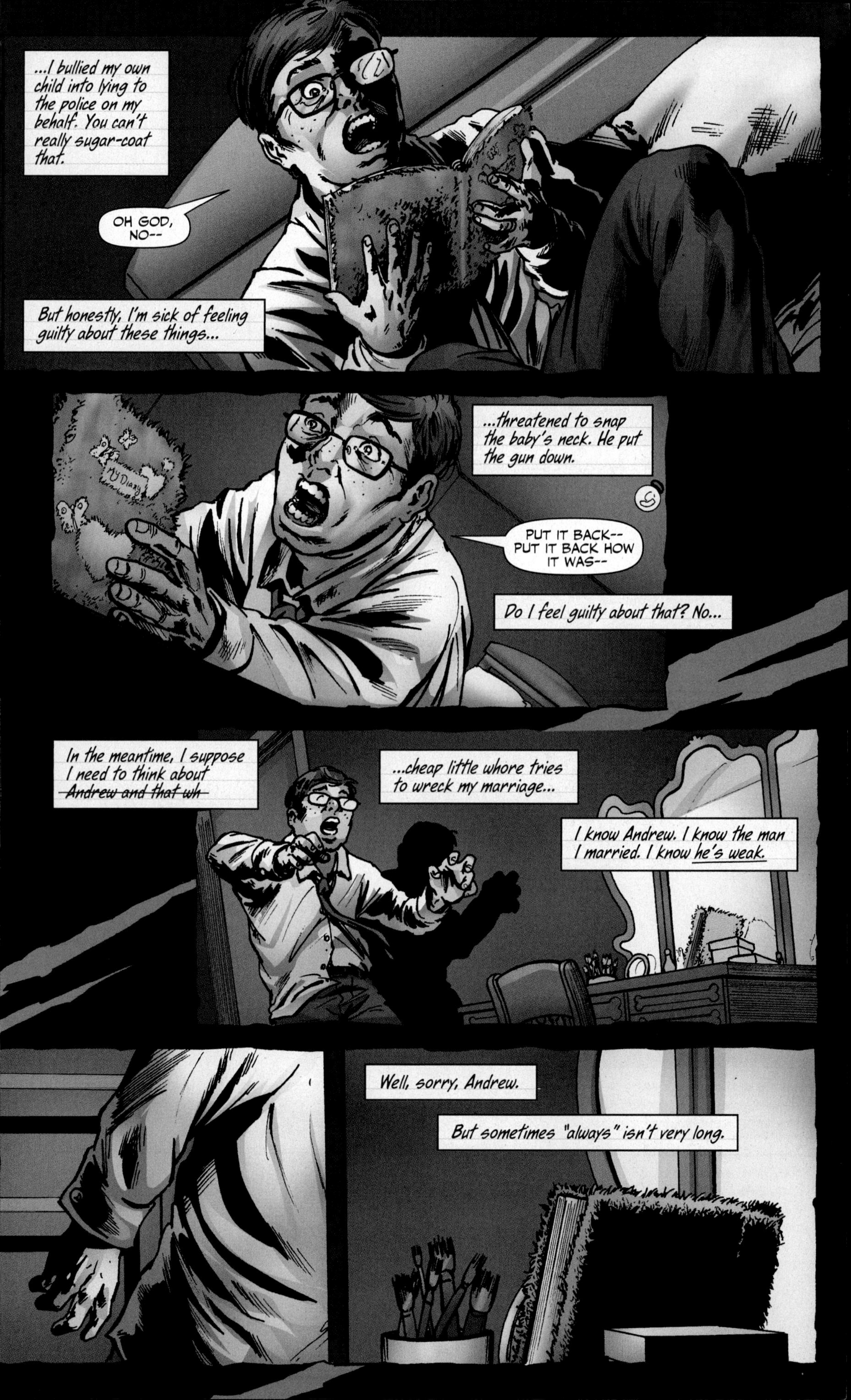
...I bullied my own child into lying to the police on my behalf. You can't really sugar-coat that.
OH GOD, NO--
But honestly, I'm sick of feeling guilty about these things...
My Diary
...threatened to snap the baby's neck. He put the gun down.
PUT IT BACK-- PUT IT BACK HOW IT WAS--
Do I feel guilty about that? No...
In the meantime, I suppose I need to think about ~~Andrew and that wh~~
...cheap little whore tries to wreck my marriage...
I know Andrew. I know the man I married. I know he's weak.
Well, sorry, Andrew.
But sometimes "always" isn't very long.

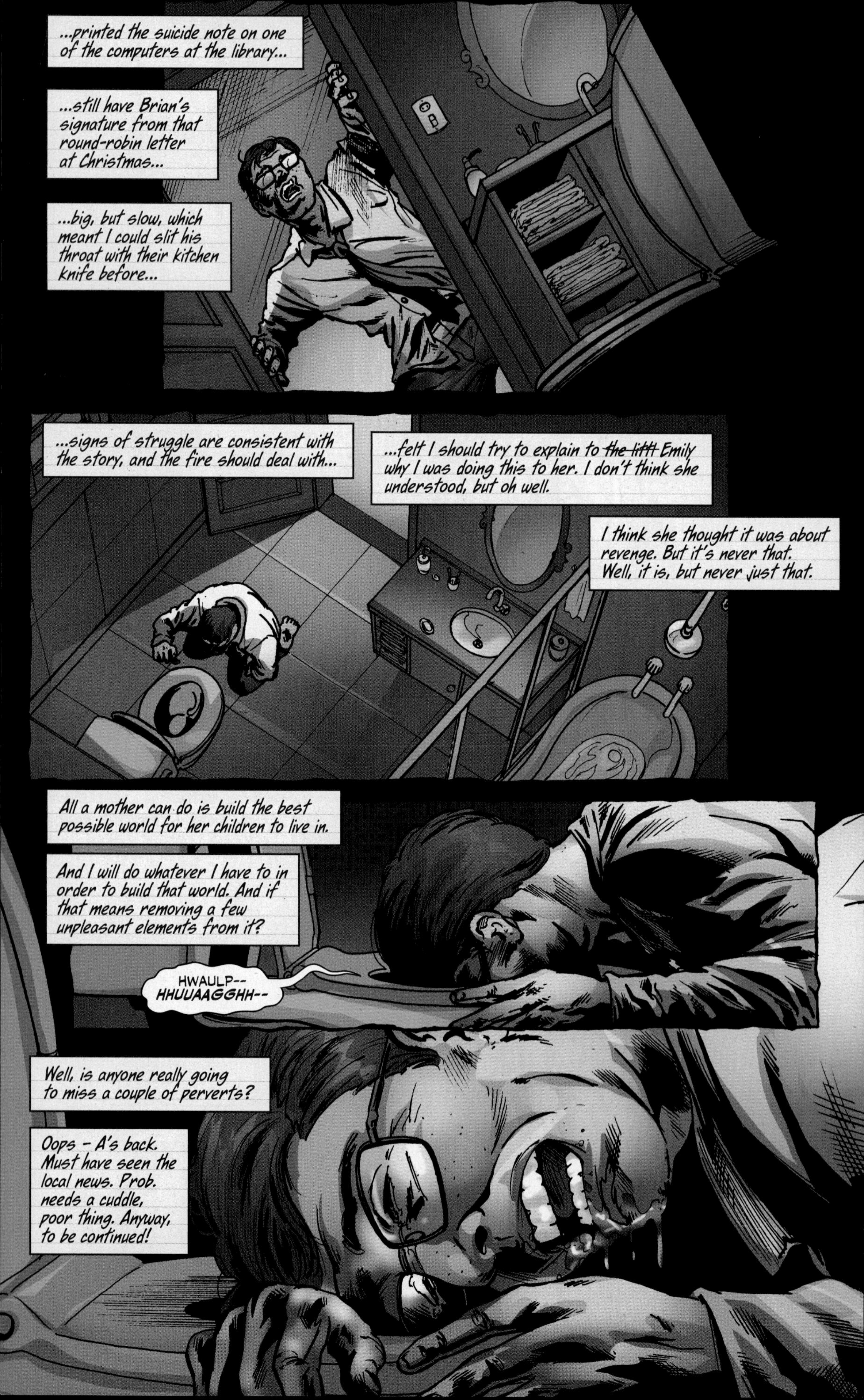
...printed the suicide note on one of the computers at the library...
...still have Brian's signature from that round-robin letter at Christmas...
...big, but slow, which meant I could slit his throat with their kitchen knife before...
...signs of struggle are consistent with the story, and the fire should deal with...
...felt I should try to explain to ~~the litt~~ Emily why I was doing this to her. I don't think she understood, but oh well.
I think she thought it was about revenge. But it's never that. Well, it is, but never just that.
All a mother can do is build the best possible world for her children to live in.
And I will do whatever I have to in order to build that world. And if that means removing a few unpleasant elements from it?
HWAULP-- HHUUAAGGHH--
Well, is anyone really going to miss a couple of perverts?
Oops - A's back. Must have seen the local news. Prob. needs a cuddle, poor thing. Anyway, to be continued!

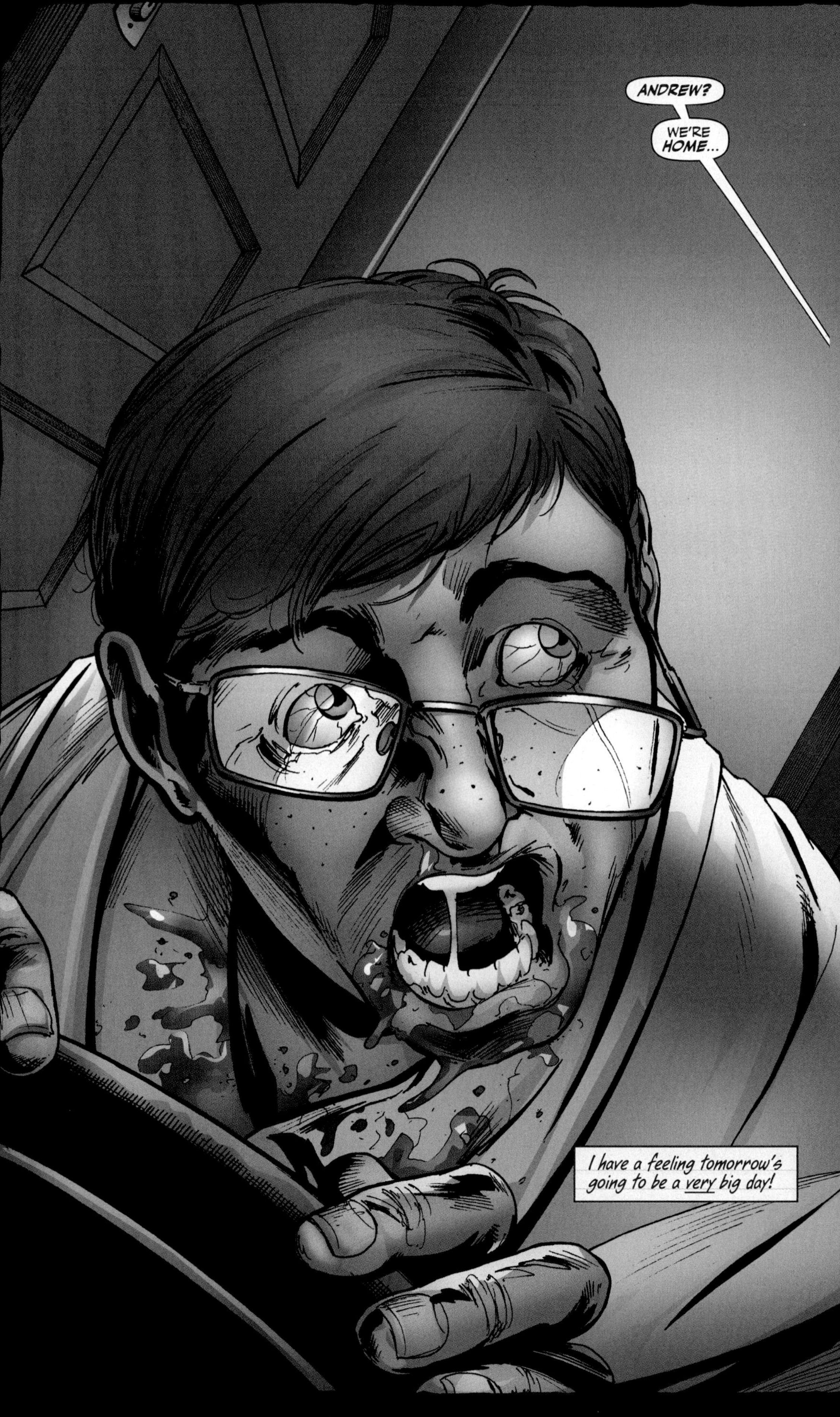
ANDREW?
WE'RE HOME...
I have a feeling tomorrow's going to be a very big day!

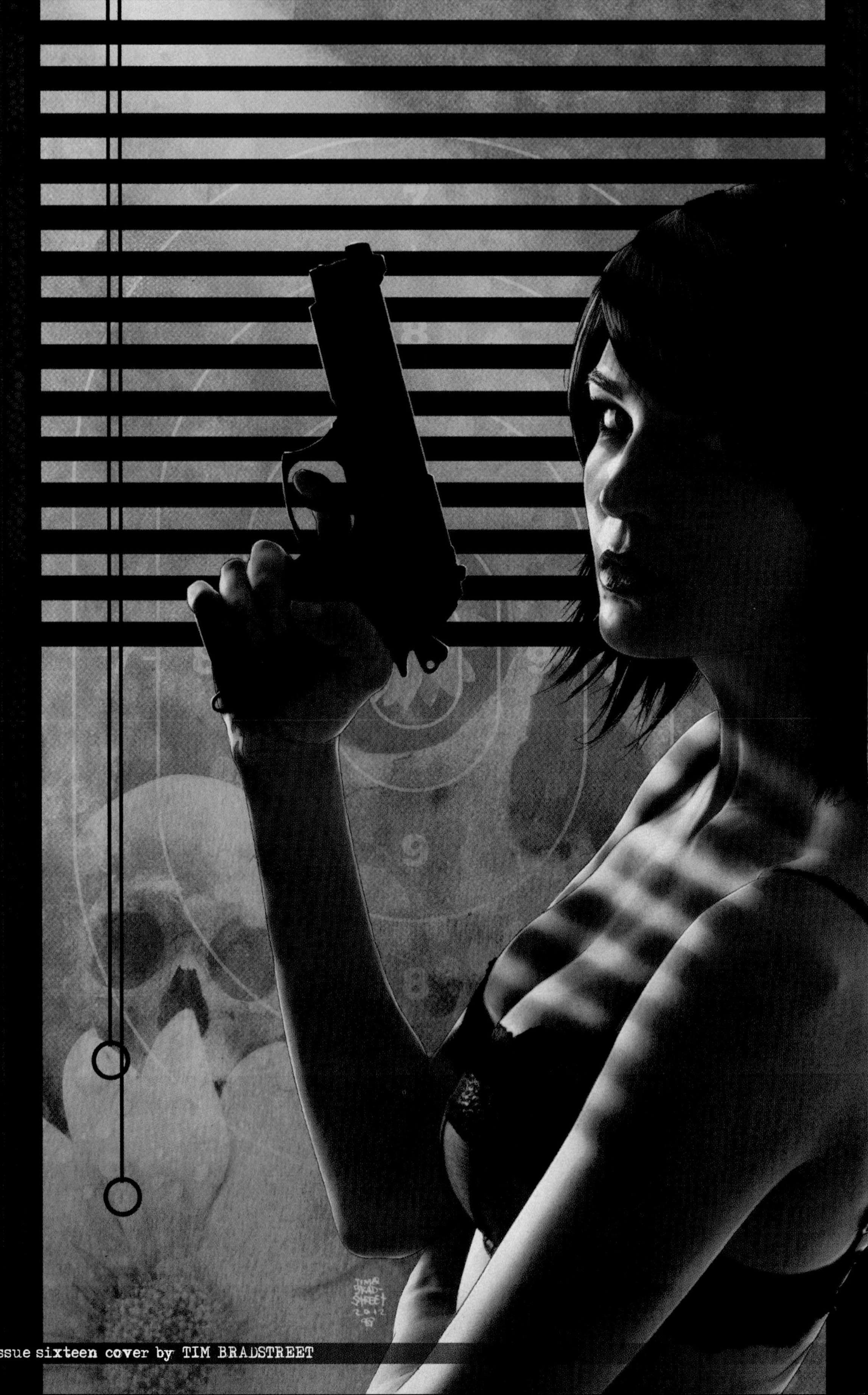
TIM BRAD-STREET 2012

issue sixteen cover by TIM BRADSTREET

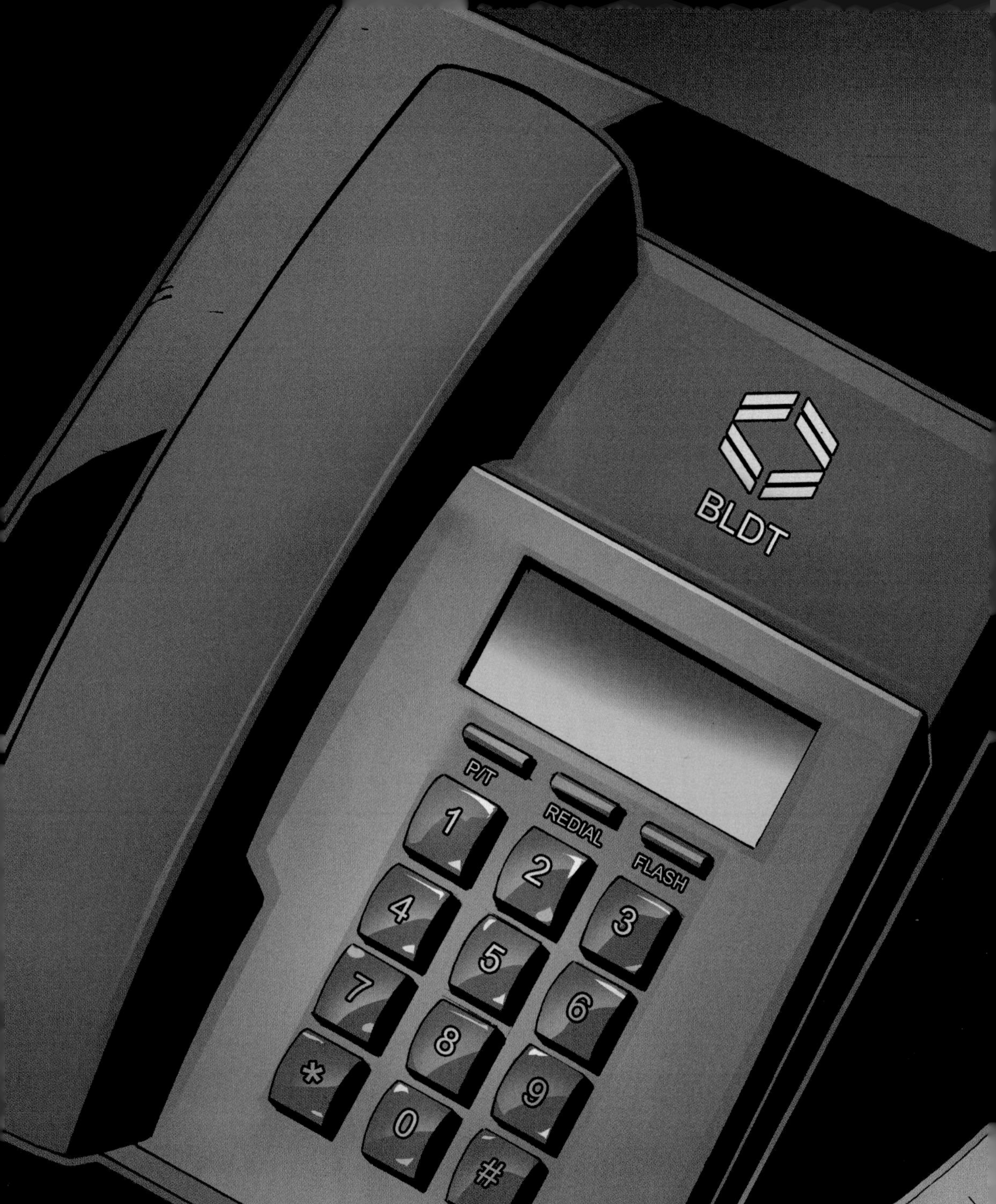
BLDT
P/T
REDIAL
FLASH

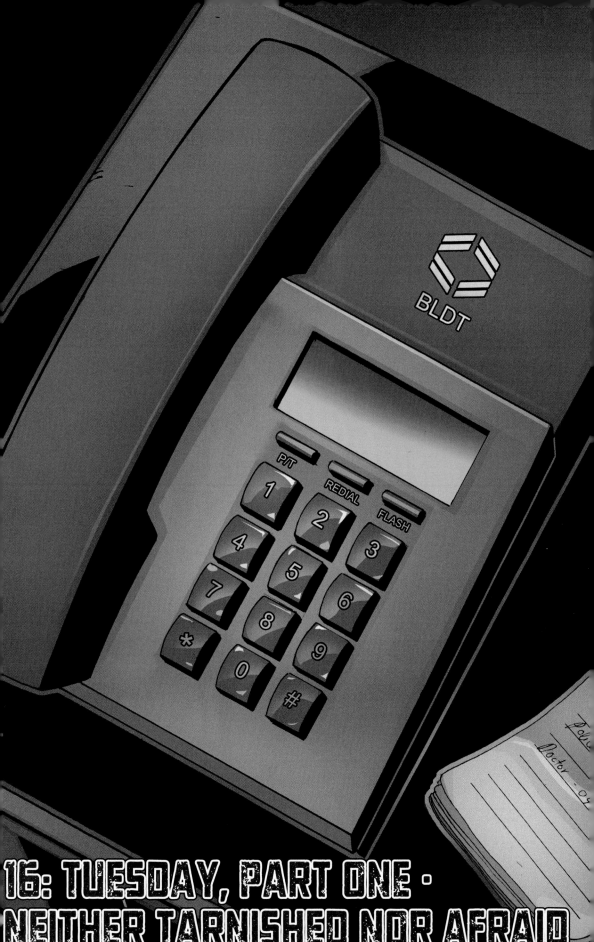

16: TUESDAY, PART ONE - NEITHER TARNISHED NOR AFRAID

CALL THE POLICE.

CALL THE *POLICE,* ANDY.

COME ON. YOU CAN DO IT.

JUST PICK UP THE--

ANDREW?

I'M *BACK!*

I PICKED UP SOME *GROCERIES* ON THE WAY HOME. FEELING BETTER?

I--I--

YOU HAVEN'T THROWN UP *AGAIN,* HAVE YOU?

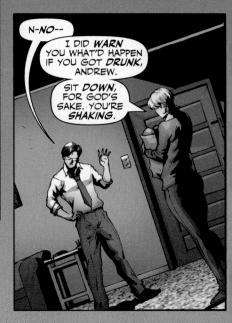

N-*NO*--

I DID *WARN* YOU WHAT'D HAPPEN IF YOU GOT *DRUNK,* ANDREW.

SIT *DOWN,* FOR GOD'S SAKE. YOU'RE *SHAKING.*

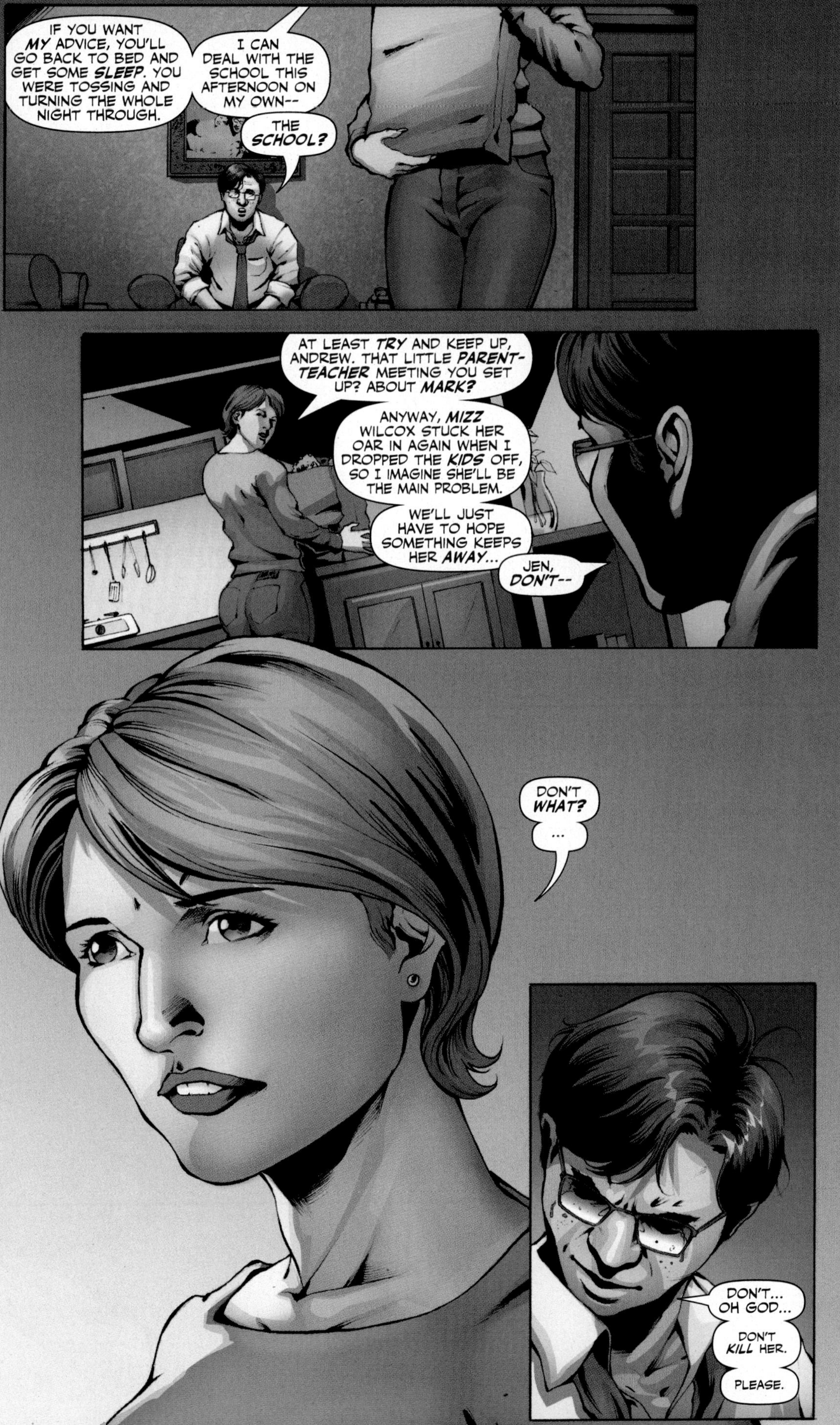
IF YOU WANT MY ADVICE, YOU'LL GO BACK TO BED AND GET SOME SLEEP. YOU WERE TOSSING AND TURNING THE WHOLE NIGHT THROUGH.
I CAN DEAL WITH THE SCHOOL THIS AFTERNOON ON MY OWN--
THE SCHOOL?
AT LEAST TRY AND KEEP UP, ANDREW. THAT LITTLE PARENT-TEACHER MEETING YOU SET UP? ABOUT MARK?
ANYWAY, MIZZ WILCOX STUCK HER OAR IN AGAIN WHEN I DROPPED THE KIDS OFF, SO I IMAGINE SHE'LL BE THE MAIN PROBLEM.
WE'LL JUST HAVE TO HOPE SOMETHING KEEPS HER AWAY...
JEN, DON'T--
DON'T WHAT?
...
DON'T... OH GOD...
DON'T KILL HER.
PLEASE.

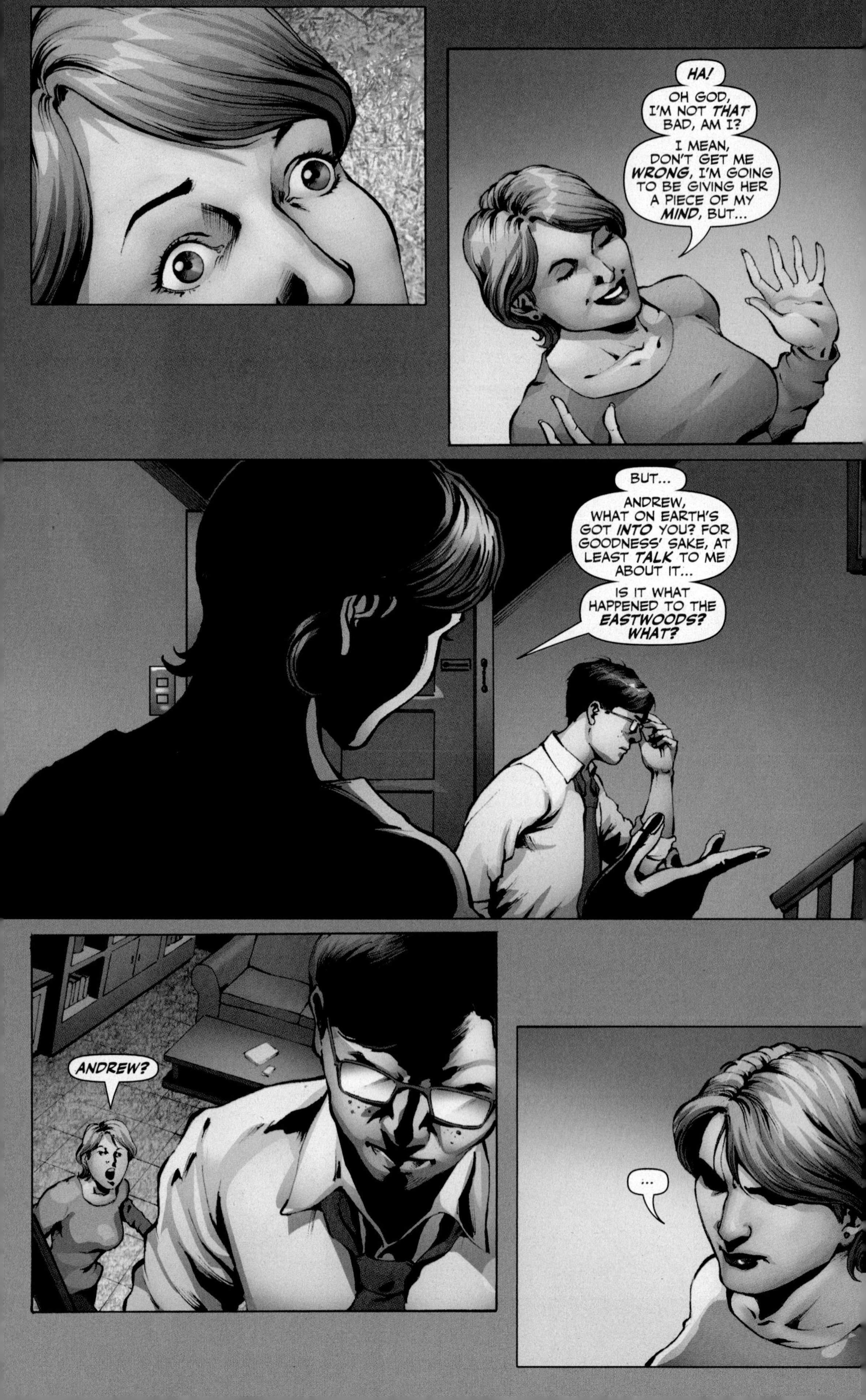
HA!
OH GOD, I'M NOT THAT BAD, AM I?
I MEAN, DON'T GET ME WRONG, I'M GOING TO BE GIVING HER A PIECE OF MY MIND, BUT...
BUT...
ANDREW, WHAT ON EARTH'S GOT INTO YOU? FOR GOODNESS' SAKE, AT LEAST TALK TO ME ABOUT IT...
IS IT WHAT HAPPENED TO THE EASTWOODS? WHAT?
ANDREW?
...

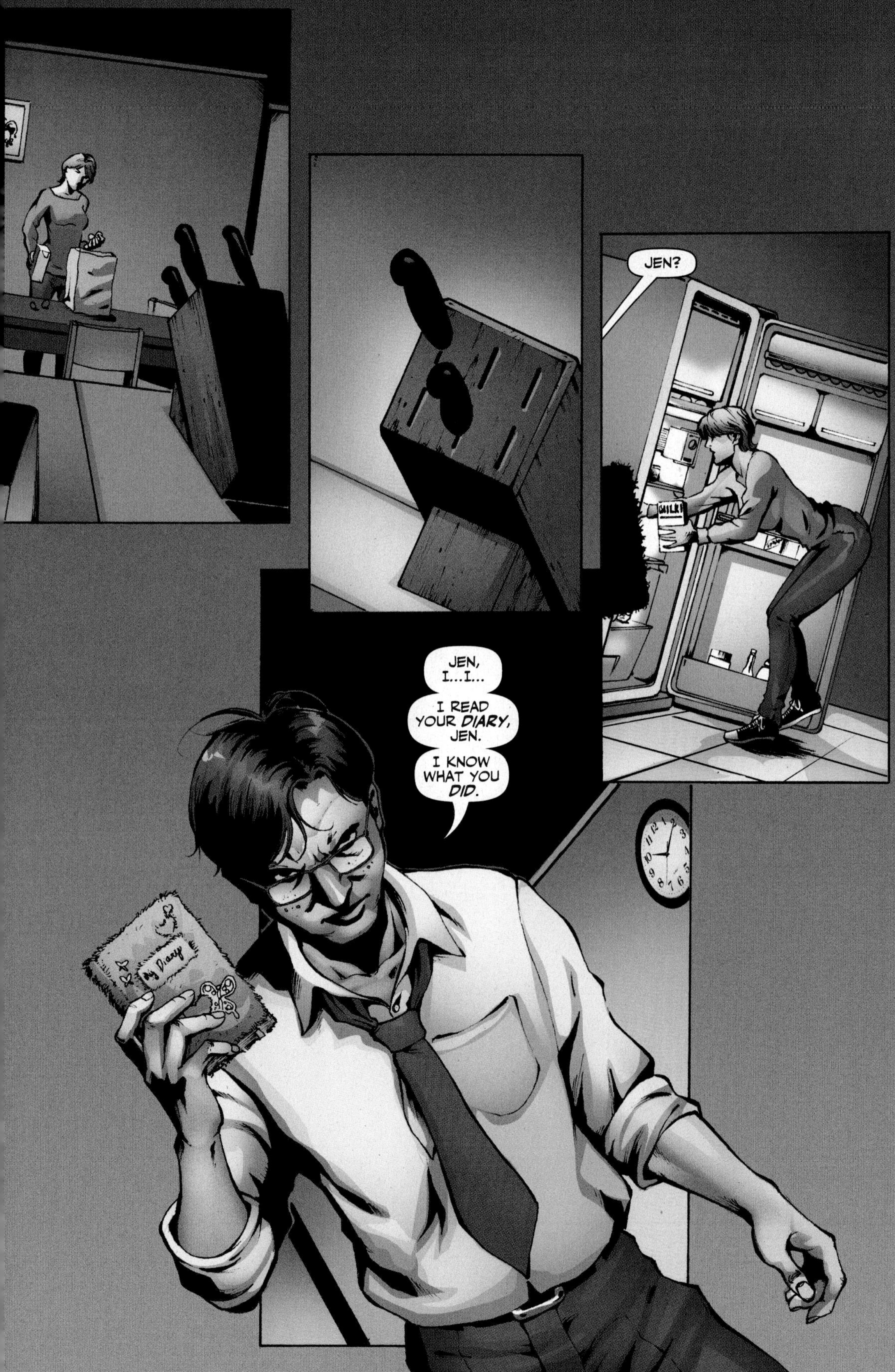
JEN?
JEN, I...I...
I READ YOUR DIARY, JEN.
I KNOW WHAT YOU DID.
My Diary
MILK

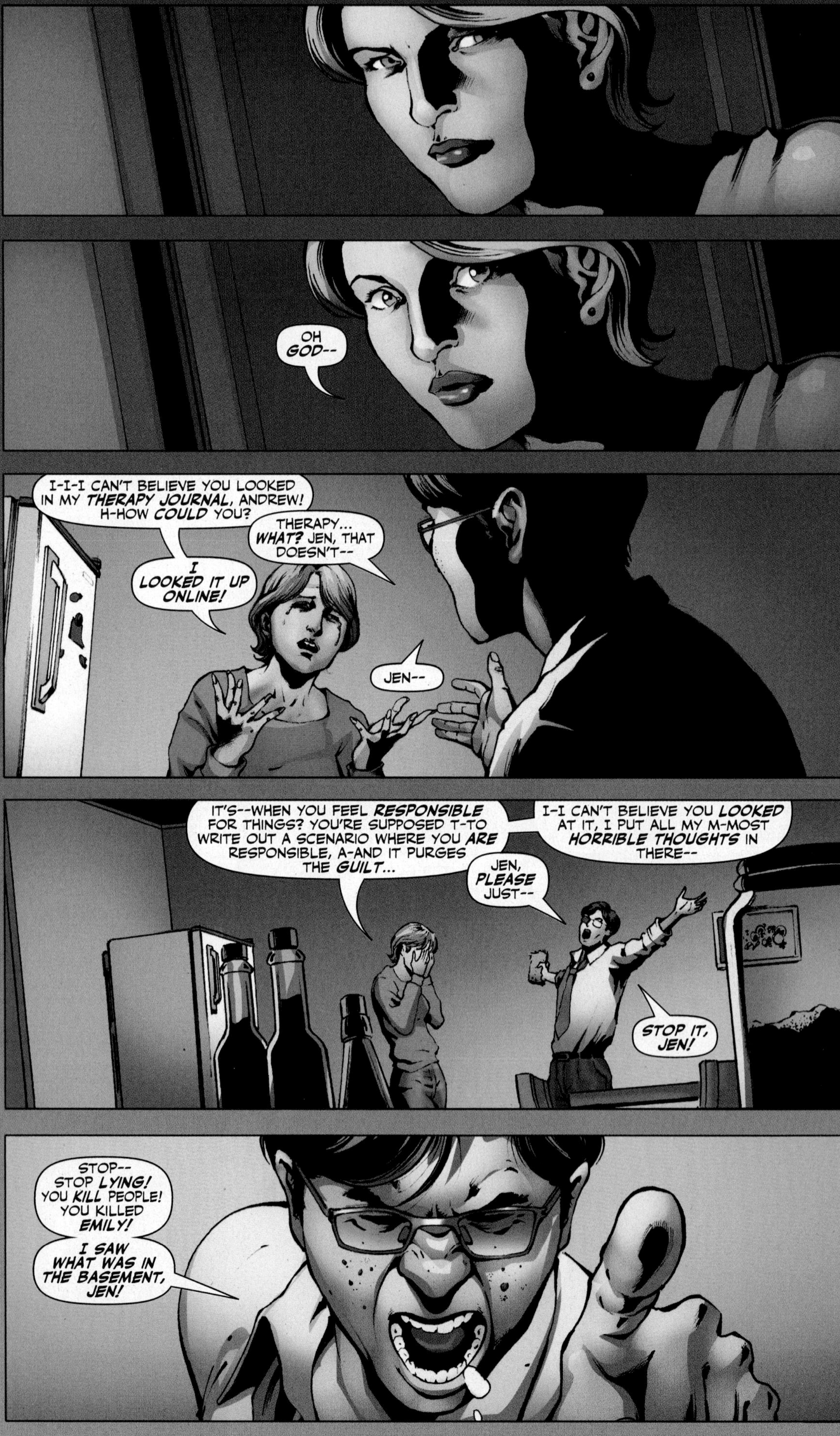
OH GOD--
I-I-I CAN'T BELIEVE YOU LOOKED IN MY THERAPY JOURNAL, ANDREW! H-HOW COULD YOU?
THERAPY... WHAT? JEN, THAT DOESN'T--
I LOOKED IT UP ONLINE!
JEN--
IT'S--WHEN YOU FEEL RESPONSIBLE FOR THINGS? YOU'RE SUPPOSED T-TO WRITE OUT A SCENARIO WHERE YOU ARE RESPONSIBLE, A-AND IT PURGES THE GUILT...
I-I CAN'T BELIEVE YOU LOOKED AT IT, I PUT ALL MY M-MOST HORRIBLE THOUGHTS IN THERE--
JEN, PLEASE JUST--
STOP IT, JEN!
STOP-- STOP LYING! YOU KILL PEOPLE! YOU KILLED EMILY!
I SAW WHAT WAS IN THE BASEMENT, JEN!

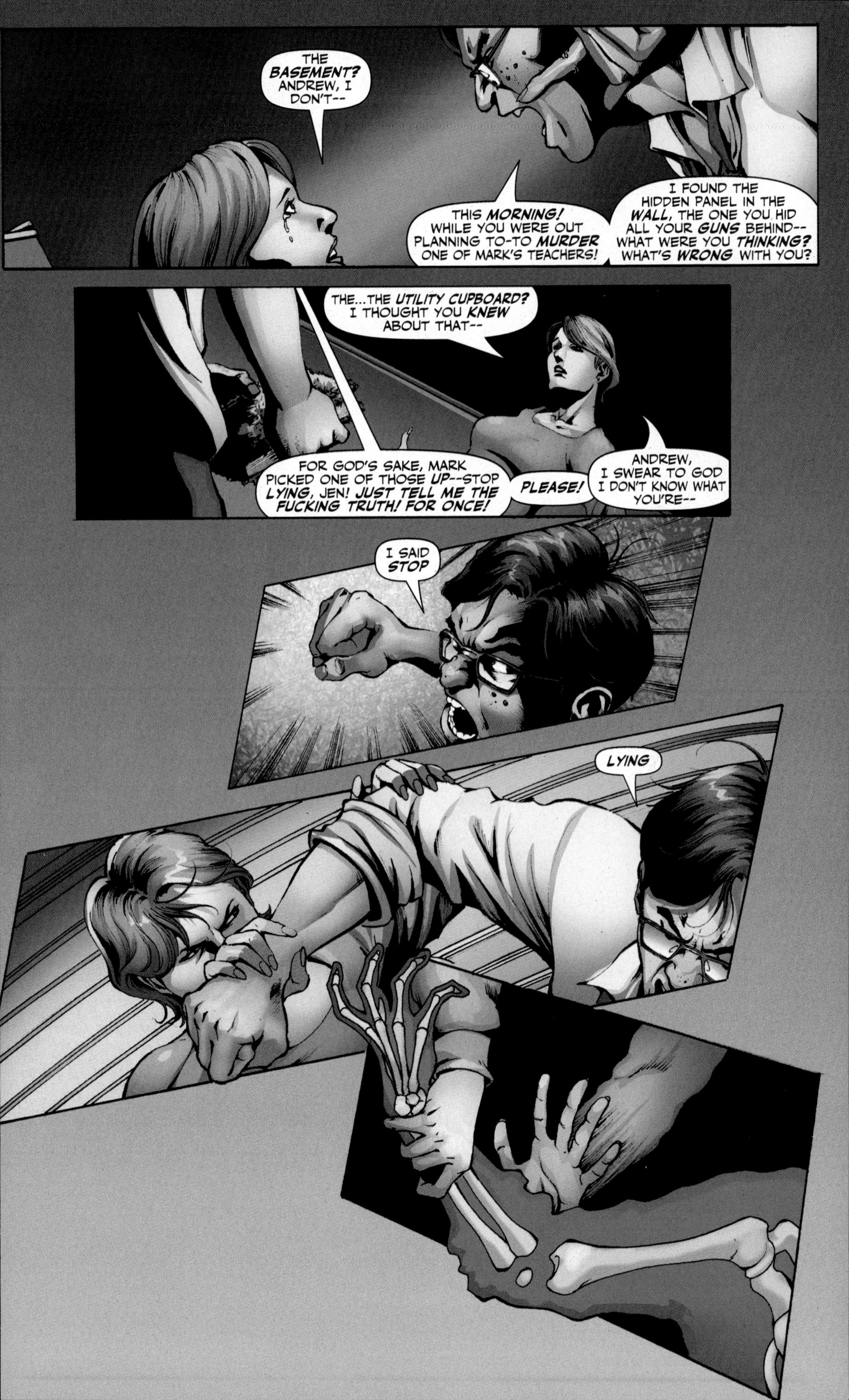
THE BASEMENT? ANDREW, I DON'T--
THIS MORNING! WHILE YOU WERE OUT PLANNING TO-TO MURDER ONE OF MARK'S TEACHERS!
I FOUND THE HIDDEN PANEL IN THE WALL, THE ONE YOU HID ALL YOUR GUNS BEHIND-- WHAT WERE YOU THINKING? WHAT'S WRONG WITH YOU?
THE...THE UTILITY CUPBOARD? I THOUGHT YOU KNEW ABOUT THAT--
FOR GOD'S SAKE, MARK PICKED ONE OF THOSE UP--STOP LYING, JEN! JUST TELL ME THE FUCKING TRUTH! FOR ONCE!
PLEASE!
ANDREW, I SWEAR TO GOD I DON'T KNOW WHAT YOU'RE--
I SAID STOP
LYING

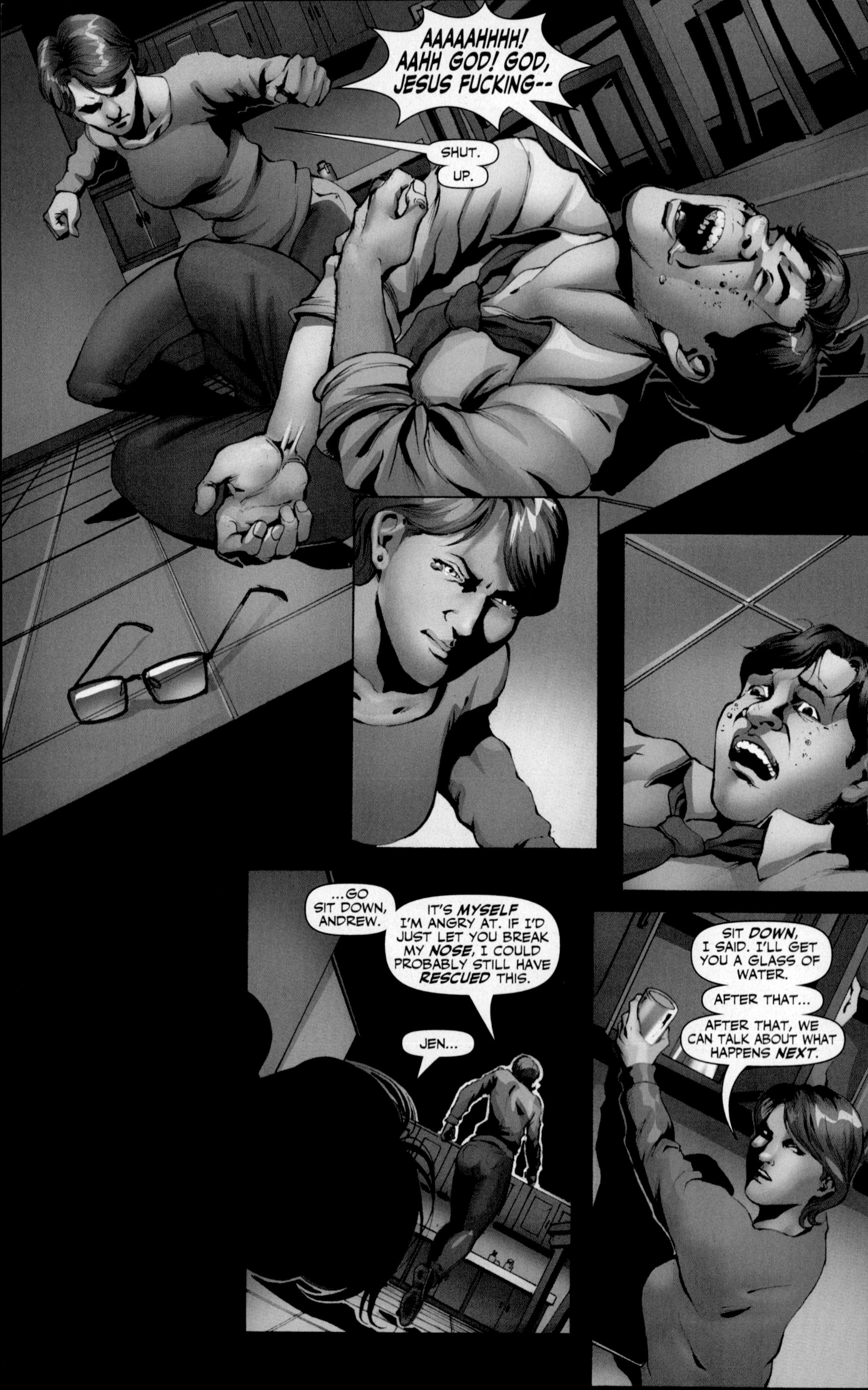
AAAAAHHHH! AAHH GOD! GOD, JESUS FUCKING--
SHUT.
UP.
...GO SIT DOWN, ANDREW.
IT'S *MYSELF* I'M ANGRY AT. IF I'D JUST LET YOU BREAK MY *NOSE*, I COULD PROBABLY STILL HAVE *RESCUED* THIS.
JEN...
SIT *DOWN*, I SAID. I'LL GET YOU A GLASS OF WATER.
AFTER THAT...
AFTER THAT, WE CAN TALK ABOUT WHAT HAPPENS *NEXT*.

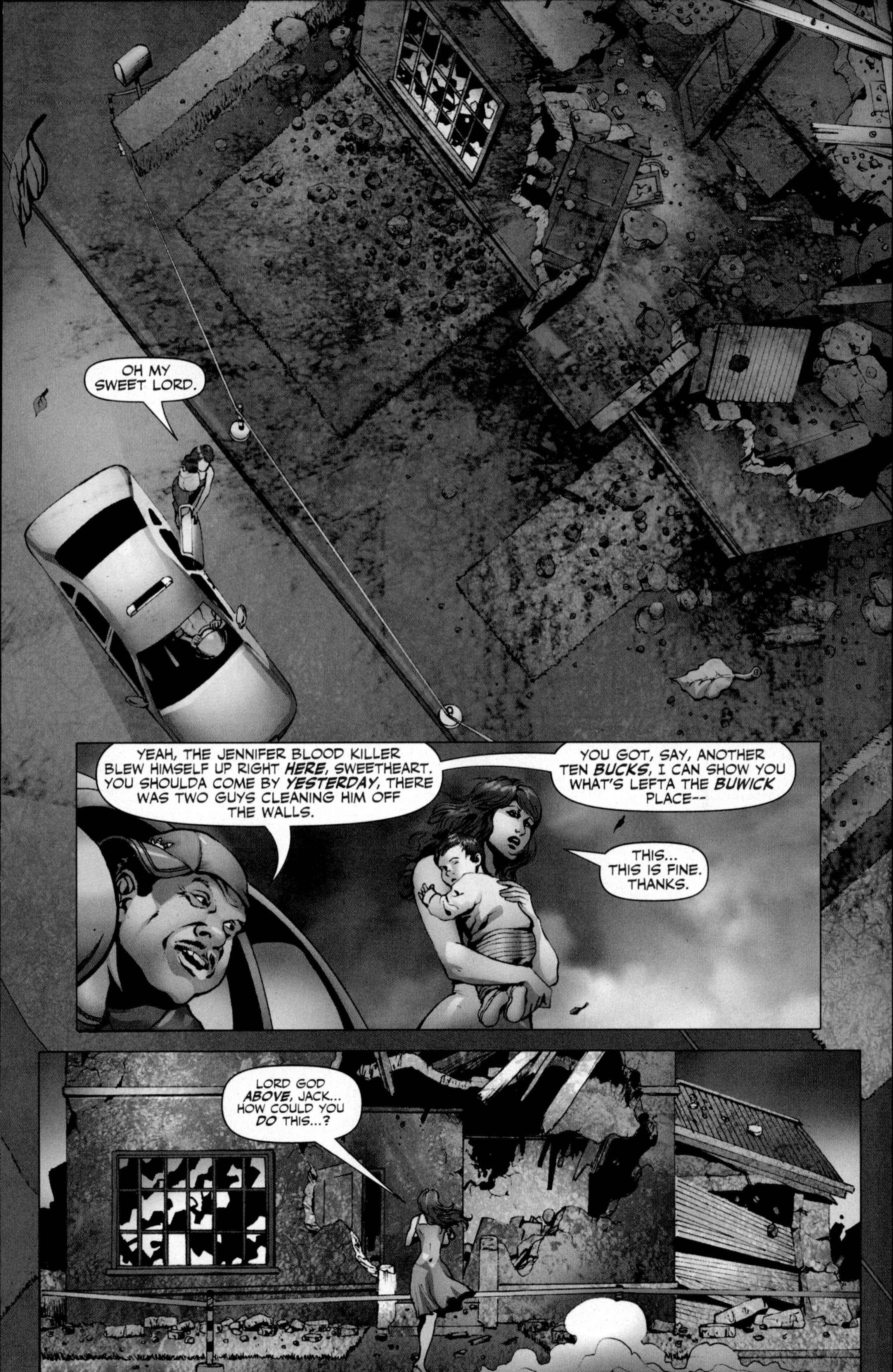
OH MY SWEET LORD.
YEAH, THE JENNIFER BLOOD KILLER BLEW HIMSELF UP RIGHT HERE, SWEETHEART. YOU SHOULDA COME BY YESTERDAY, THERE WAS TWO GUYS CLEANING HIM OFF THE WALLS.
YOU GOT, SAY, ANOTHER TEN BUCKS, I CAN SHOW YOU WHAT'S LEFTA THE BUWICK PLACE--
THIS... THIS IS FINE. THANKS.
LORD GOD ABOVE, JACK... HOW COULD YOU DO THIS...?

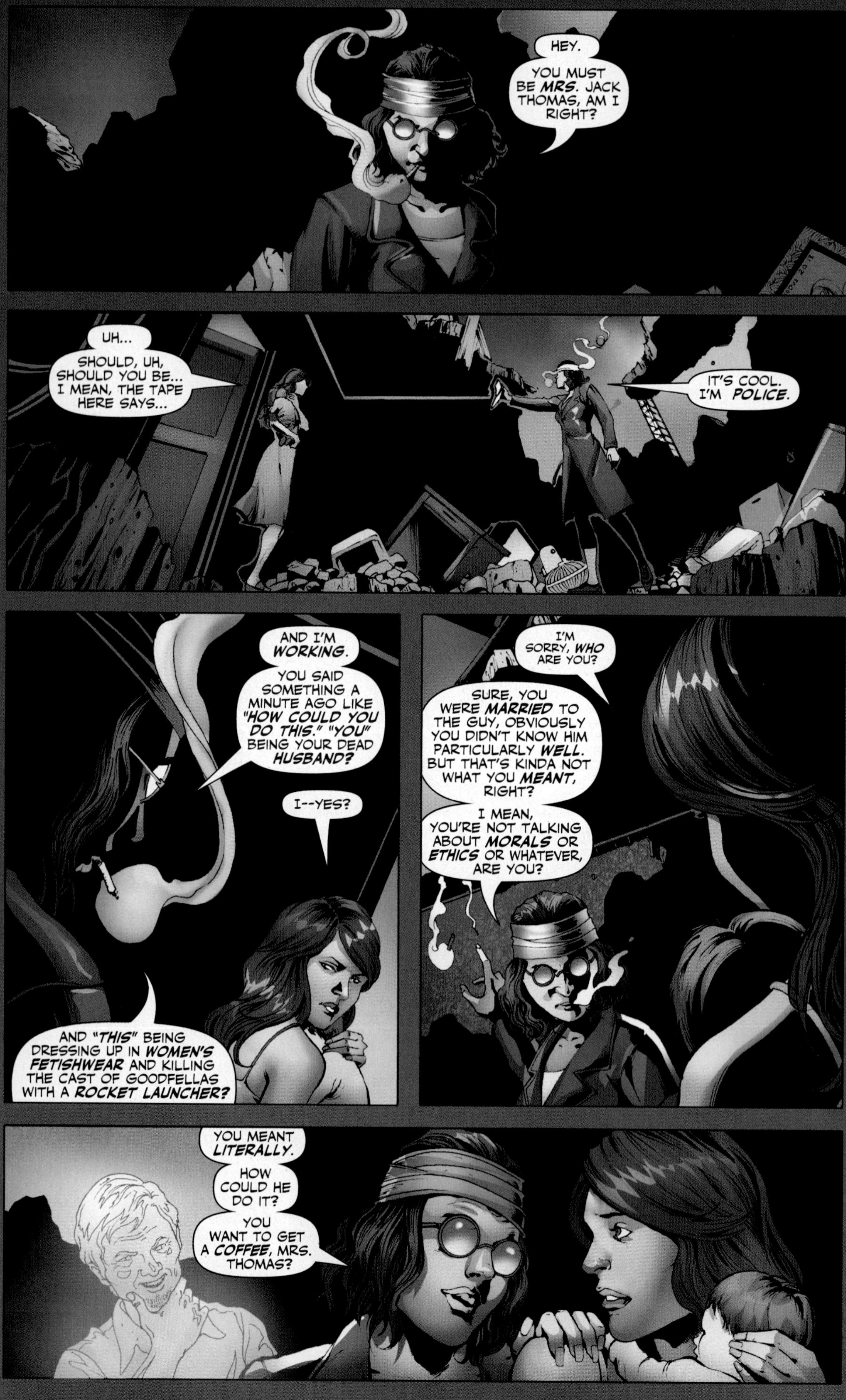

HEY.
YOU MUST BE *MRS.* JACK THOMAS, AM I RIGHT?
UH...
SHOULD, UH, SHOULD YOU BE... I MEAN, THE TAPE HERE SAYS...
IT'S COOL. I'M *POLICE*.
AND I'M *WORKING*.
YOU SAID SOMETHING A MINUTE AGO LIKE *"HOW COULD YOU DO THIS." "YOU"* BEING YOUR DEAD *HUSBAND?*
I--YES?
AND *"THIS"* BEING DRESSING UP IN *WOMEN'S FETISHWEAR* AND KILLING THE CAST OF GOODFELLAS WITH A *ROCKET LAUNCHER?*
I'M SORRY, *WHO* ARE YOU?
SURE, YOU WERE *MARRIED* TO THE GUY, OBVIOUSLY YOU DIDN'T KNOW HIM PARTICULARLY *WELL*. BUT THAT'S KINDA NOT WHAT YOU *MEANT*, RIGHT?
I MEAN, YOU'RE NOT TALKING ABOUT *MORALS* OR *ETHICS* OR WHATEVER, ARE YOU?
YOU MEANT *LITERALLY*.
HOW COULD HE DO IT?
YOU WANT TO GET A *COFFEE*, MRS. THOMAS?

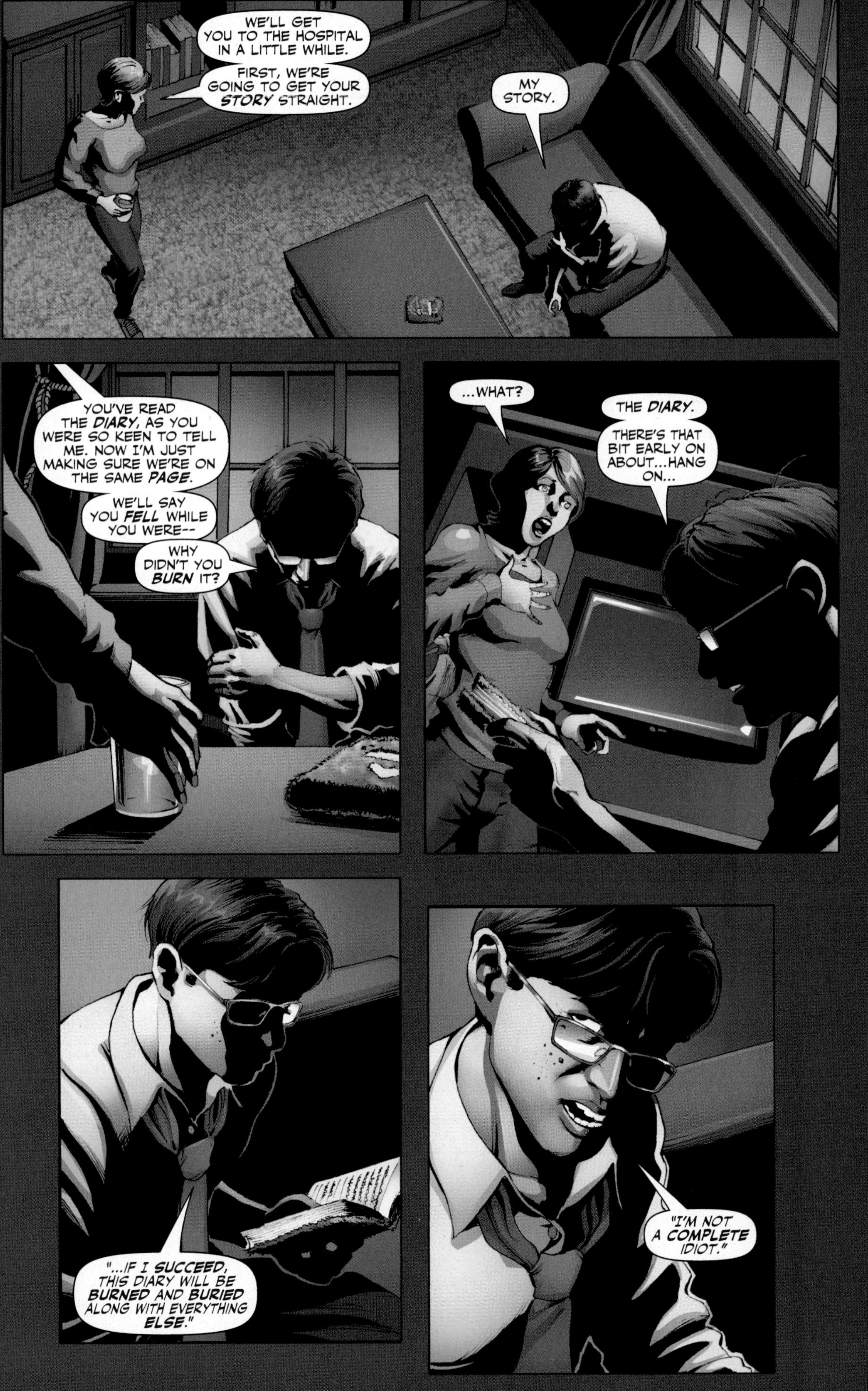
WE'LL GET YOU TO THE HOSPITAL IN A LITTLE WHILE.
FIRST, WE'RE GOING TO GET YOUR STORY STRAIGHT.
MY STORY.
YOU'VE READ THE DIARY, AS YOU WERE SO KEEN TO TELL ME. NOW I'M JUST MAKING SURE WE'RE ON THE SAME PAGE.
WE'LL SAY YOU FELL WHILE YOU WERE--
WHY DIDN'T YOU BURN IT?
...WHAT?
THE DIARY.
THERE'S THAT BIT EARLY ON ABOUT...HANG ON...
"...IF I SUCCEED, THIS DIARY WILL BE BURNED AND BURIED ALONG WITH EVERYTHING ELSE."
"I'M NOT A COMPLETE IDIOT."

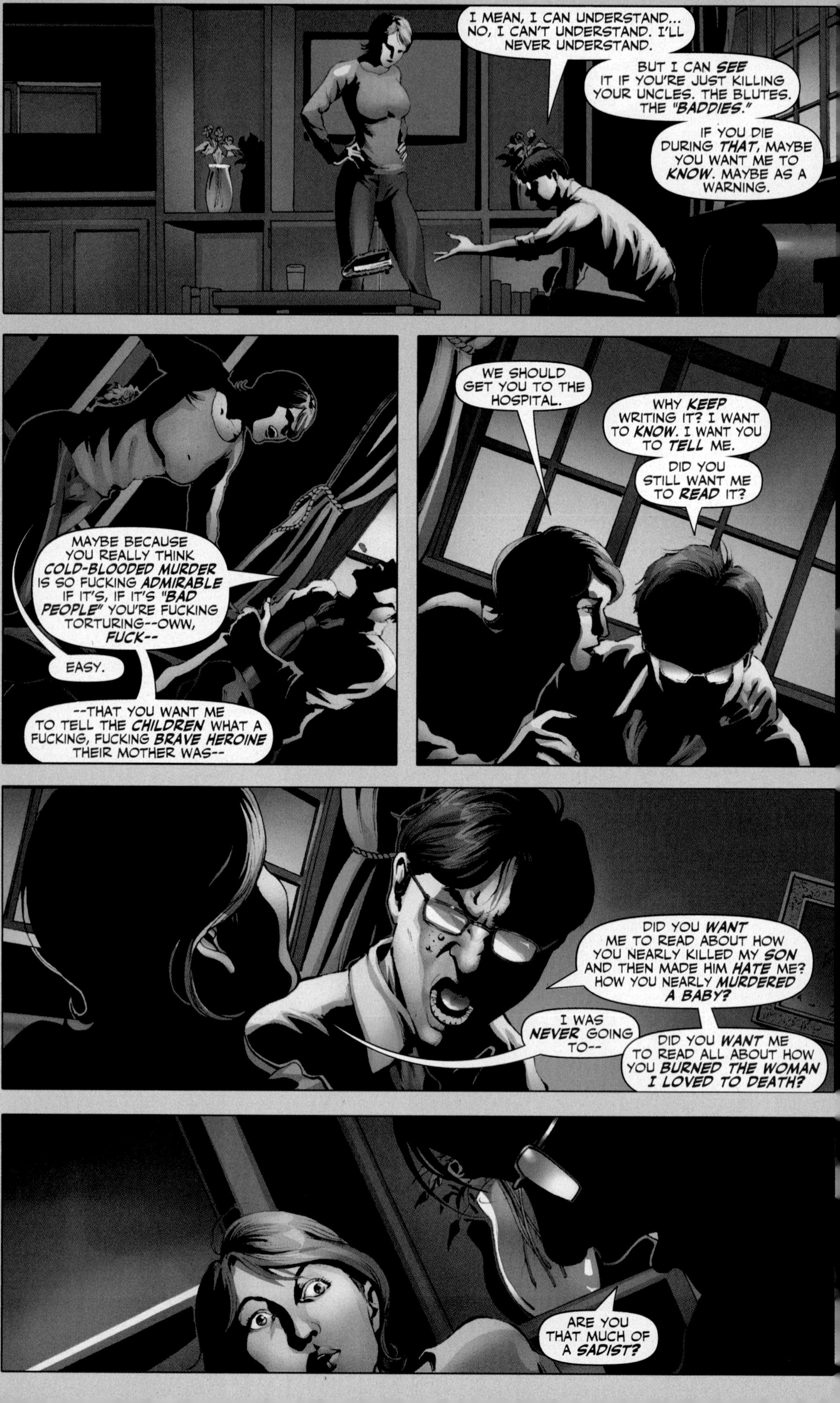
I MEAN, I CAN UNDERSTAND... NO, I CAN'T UNDERSTAND. I'LL NEVER UNDERSTAND.
BUT I CAN SEE IT IF YOU'RE JUST KILLING YOUR UNCLES. THE BLUTES. THE "BADDIES."
IF YOU DIE DURING THAT, MAYBE YOU WANT ME TO KNOW. MAYBE AS A WARNING.
MAYBE BECAUSE YOU REALLY THINK COLD-BLOODED MURDER IS SO FUCKING ADMIRABLE IF IT'S, IF IT'S "BAD PEOPLE" YOU'RE FUCKING TORTURING--OWW, FUCK--
EASY.
--THAT YOU WANT ME TO TELL THE CHILDREN WHAT A FUCKING, FUCKING BRAVE HEROINE THEIR MOTHER WAS--
WE SHOULD GET YOU TO THE HOSPITAL.
WHY KEEP WRITING IT? I WANT TO KNOW. I WANT YOU TO TELL ME.
DID YOU STILL WANT ME TO READ IT?
DID YOU WANT ME TO READ ABOUT HOW YOU NEARLY KILLED MY SON AND THEN MADE HIM HATE ME? HOW YOU NEARLY MURDERED A BABY?
I WAS NEVER GOING TO--
DID YOU WANT ME TO READ ALL ABOUT HOW YOU BURNED THE WOMAN I LOVED TO DEATH?
ARE YOU THAT MUCH OF A SADIST?

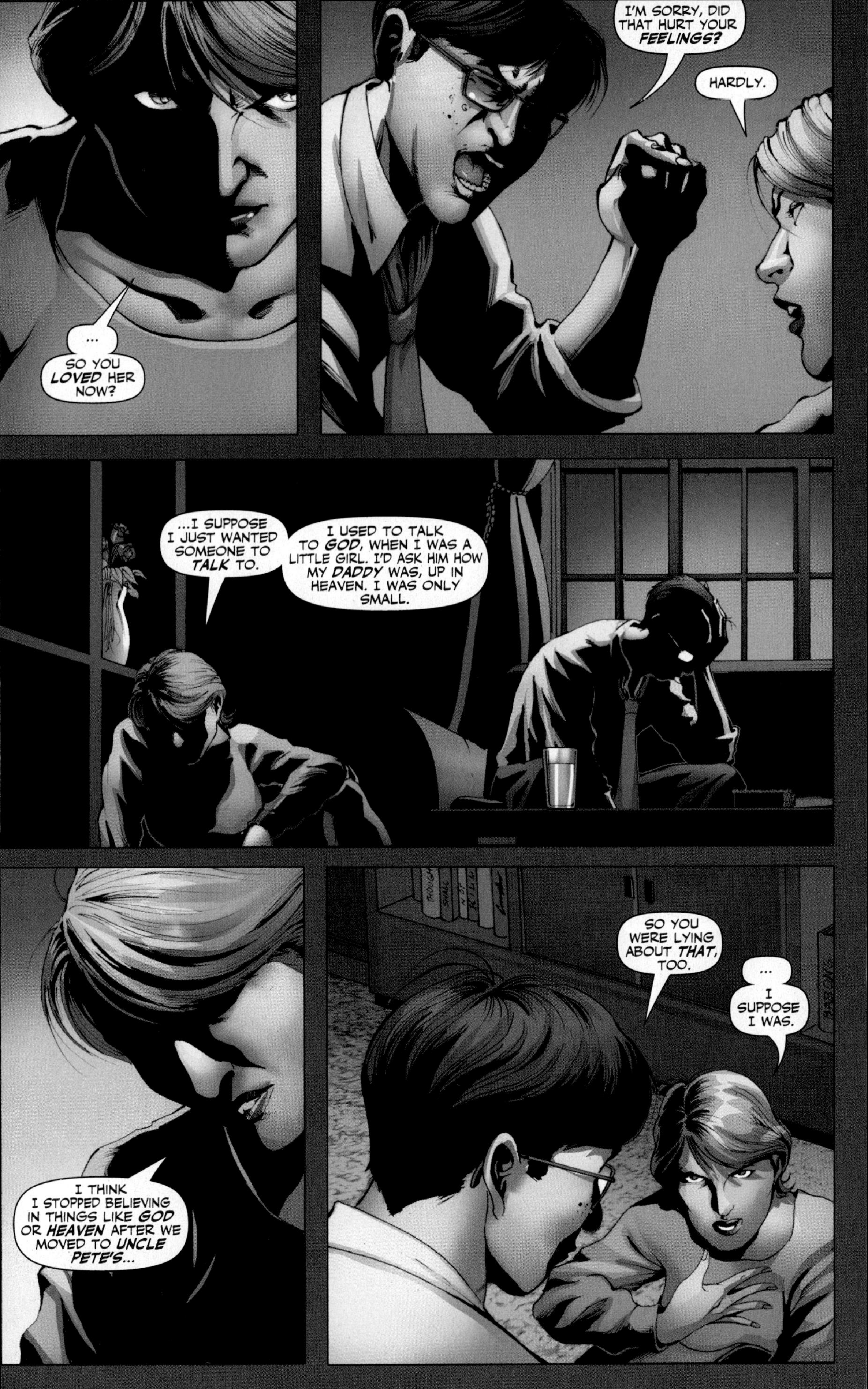
...
SO YOU LOVED HER NOW?
I'M SORRY, DID THAT HURT YOUR FEELINGS?
HARDLY.
...I SUPPOSE I JUST WANTED SOMEONE TO TALK TO.
I USED TO TALK TO GOD, WHEN I WAS A LITTLE GIRL. I'D ASK HIM HOW MY DADDY WAS, UP IN HEAVEN. I WAS ONLY SMALL.
I THINK I STOPPED BELIEVING IN THINGS LIKE GOD OR HEAVEN AFTER WE MOVED TO UNCLE PETE'S...
SO YOU WERE LYING ABOUT THAT, TOO.
...
I SUPPOSE I WAS.

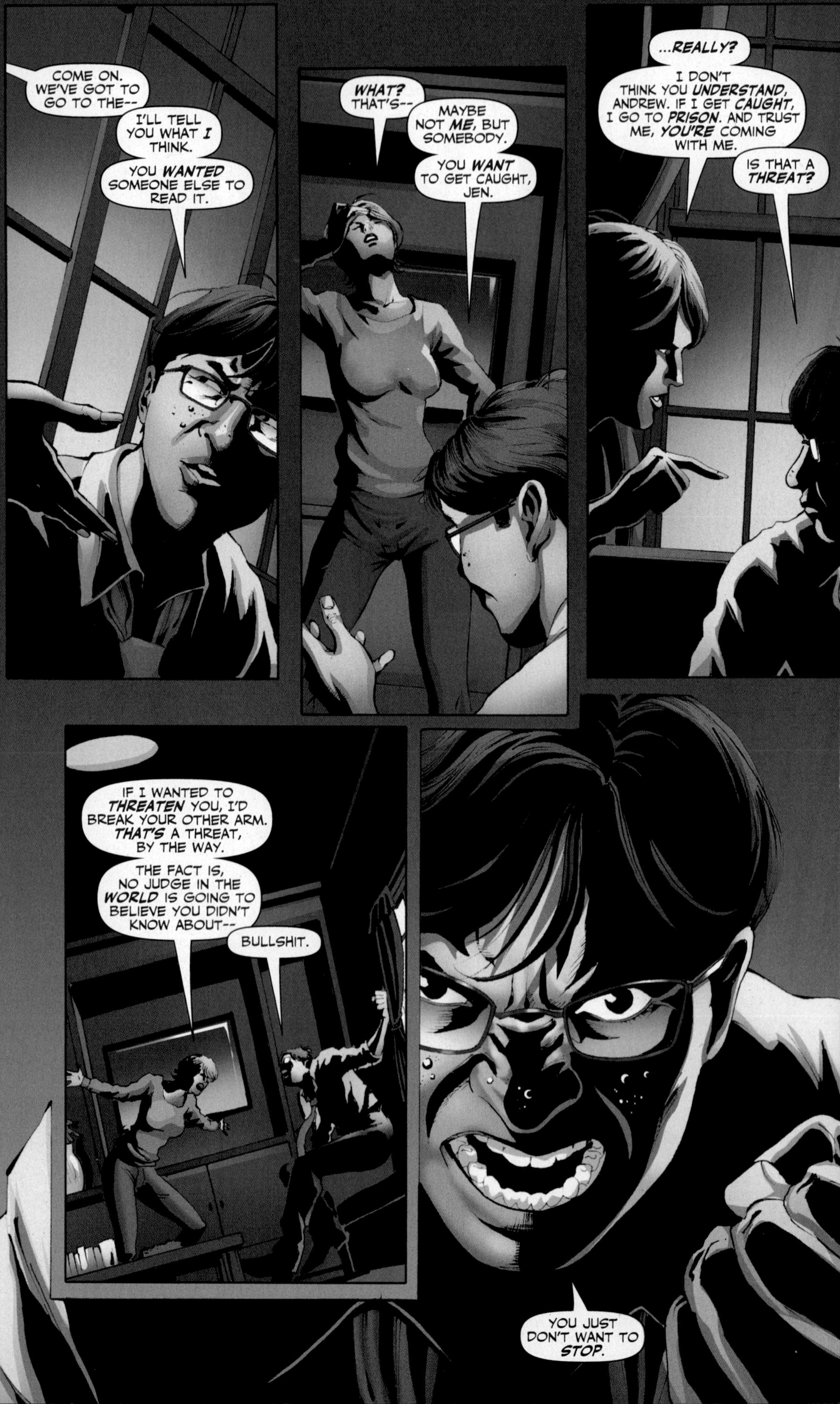
COME ON. WE'VE GOT TO GO TO THE--
I'LL TELL YOU WHAT I THINK.
YOU WANTED SOMEONE ELSE TO READ IT.
WHAT? THAT'S--
MAYBE NOT ME, BUT SOMEBODY.
YOU WANT TO GET CAUGHT, JEN.
...REALLY?
I DON'T THINK YOU UNDERSTAND, ANDREW. IF I GET CAUGHT, I GO TO PRISON. AND TRUST ME, YOU'RE COMING WITH ME.
IS THAT A THREAT?
IF I WANTED TO THREATEN YOU, I'D BREAK YOUR OTHER ARM. THAT'S A THREAT, BY THE WAY.
THE FACT IS, NO JUDGE IN THE WORLD IS GOING TO BELIEVE YOU DIDN'T KNOW ABOUT--
BULLSHIT.
YOU JUST DON'T WANT TO STOP.

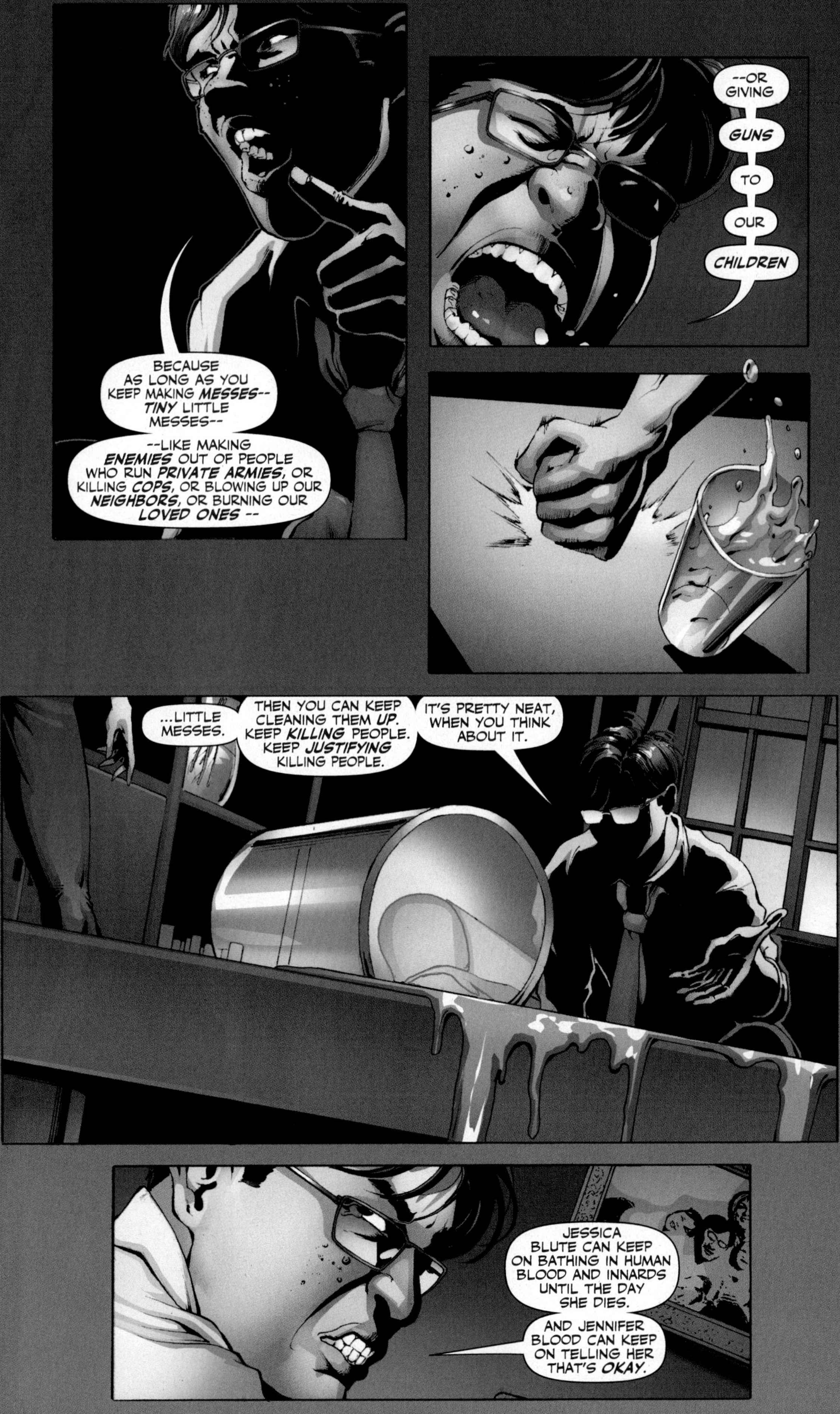
BECAUSE AS LONG AS YOU KEEP MAKING MESSES-- TINY LITTLE MESSES--
--LIKE MAKING ENEMIES OUT OF PEOPLE WHO RUN PRIVATE ARMIES, OR KILLING COPS, OR BLOWING UP OUR NEIGHBORS, OR BURNING OUR LOVED ONES --
--OR GIVING GUNS TO OUR CHILDREN
...LITTLE MESSES.
THEN YOU CAN KEEP CLEANING THEM UP. KEEP KILLING PEOPLE. KEEP JUSTIFYING KILLING PEOPLE.
IT'S PRETTY NEAT, WHEN YOU THINK ABOUT IT.
JESSICA BLUTE CAN KEEP ON BATHING IN HUMAN BLOOD AND INNARDS UNTIL THE DAY SHE DIES.
AND JENNIFER BLOOD CAN KEEP ON TELLING HER THAT'S OKAY.

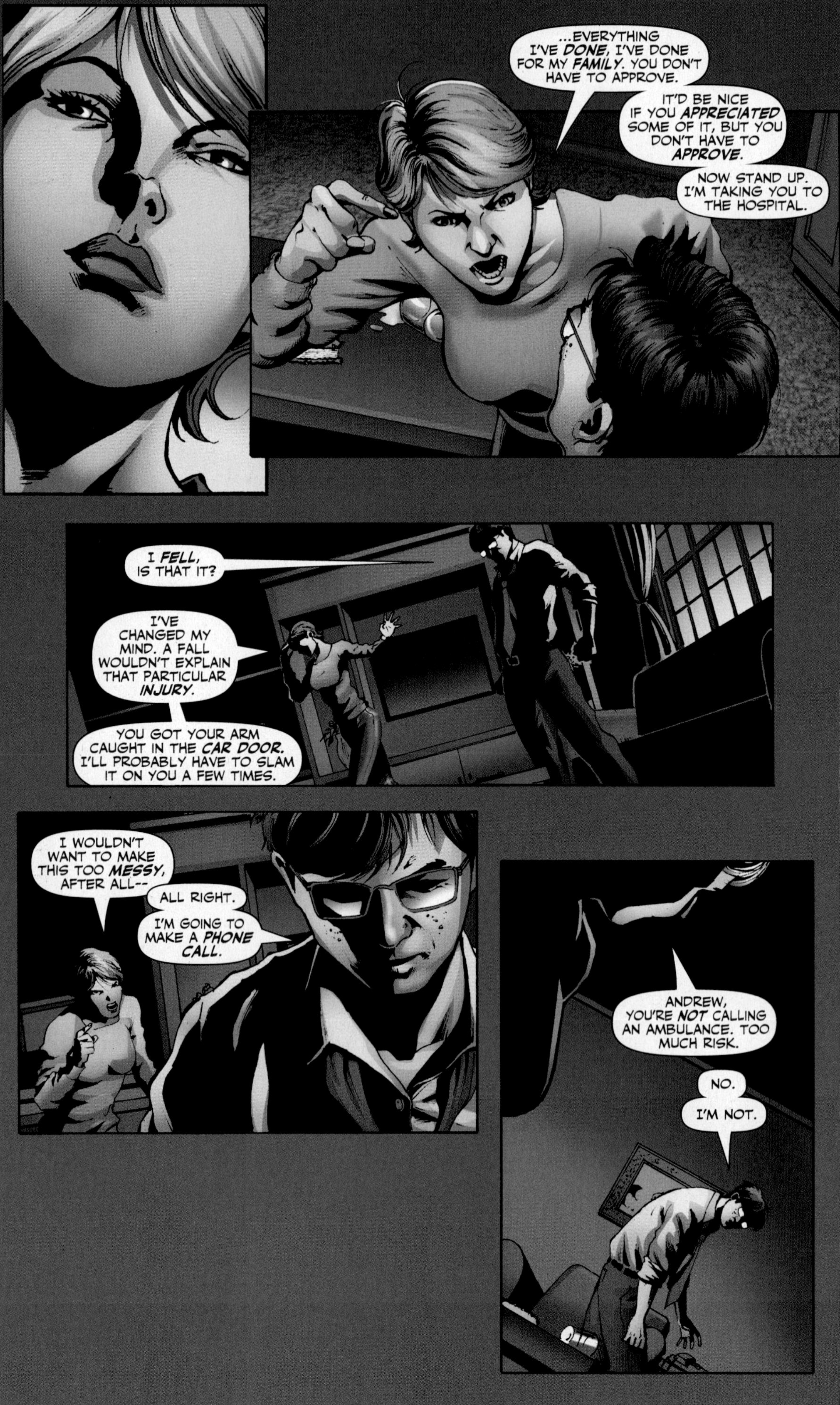
...EVERYTHING I'VE DONE, I'VE DONE FOR MY FAMILY. YOU DON'T HAVE TO APPROVE.
IT'D BE NICE IF YOU APPRECIATED SOME OF IT, BUT YOU DON'T HAVE TO APPROVE.
NOW STAND UP. I'M TAKING YOU TO THE HOSPITAL.
I FELL, IS THAT IT?
I'VE CHANGED MY MIND. A FALL WOULDN'T EXPLAIN THAT PARTICULAR INJURY.
YOU GOT YOUR ARM CAUGHT IN THE CAR DOOR. I'LL PROBABLY HAVE TO SLAM IT ON YOU A FEW TIMES.
I WOULDN'T WANT TO MAKE THIS TOO MESSY, AFTER ALL--
ALL RIGHT.
I'M GOING TO MAKE A PHONE CALL.
ANDREW, YOU'RE NOT CALLING AN AMBULANCE. TOO MUCH RISK.
NO.
I'M NOT.

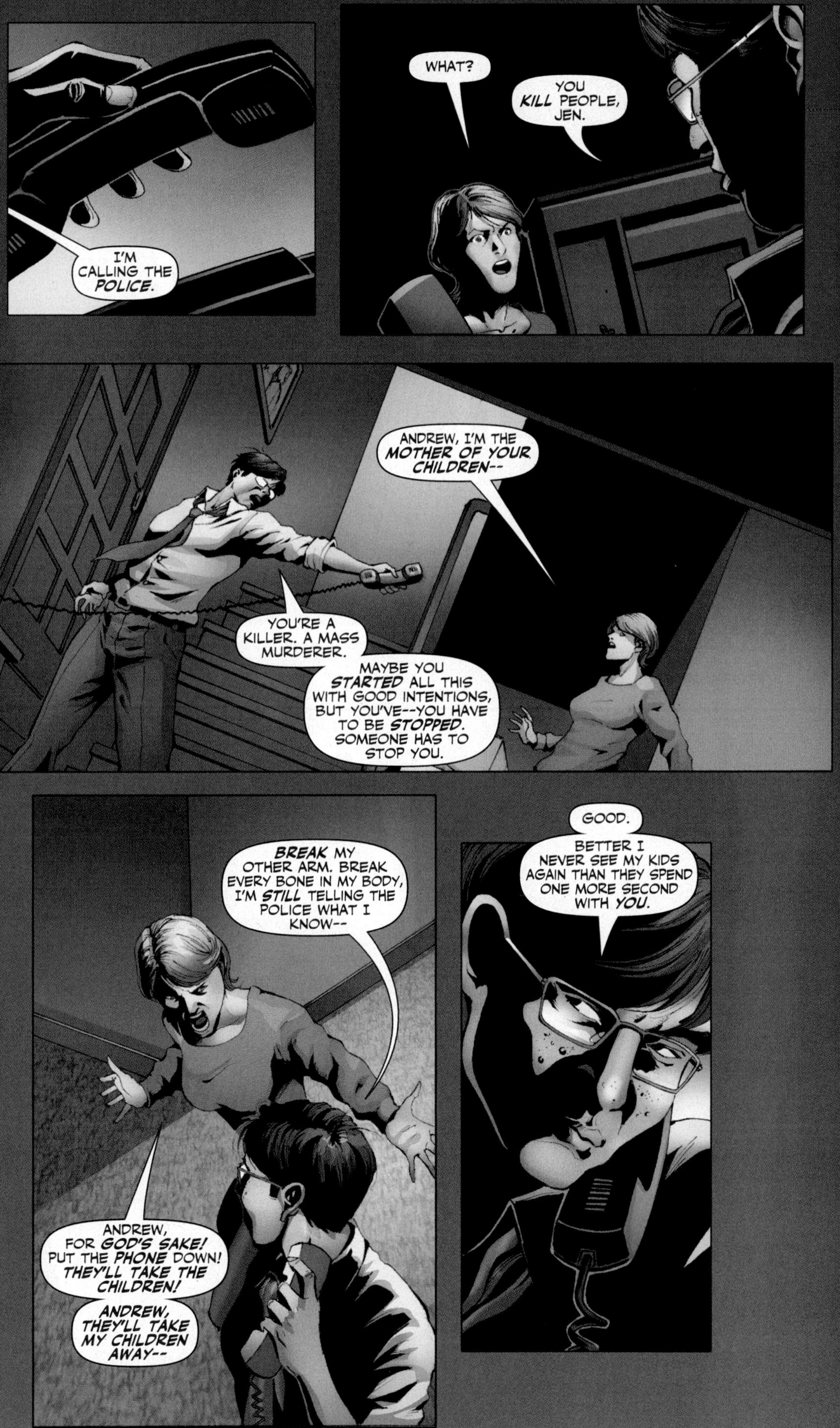
I'M CALLING THE POLICE.
WHAT?
YOU KILL PEOPLE, JEN.
ANDREW, I'M THE MOTHER OF YOUR CHILDREN--
YOU'RE A KILLER. A MASS MURDERER.
MAYBE YOU STARTED ALL THIS WITH GOOD INTENTIONS, BUT YOU'VE--YOU HAVE TO BE STOPPED. SOMEONE HAS TO STOP YOU.
BREAK MY OTHER ARM. BREAK EVERY BONE IN MY BODY, I'M STILL TELLING THE POLICE WHAT I KNOW--
ANDREW, FOR GOD'S SAKE! PUT THE PHONE DOWN! THEY'LL TAKE THE CHILDREN!
ANDREW, THEY'LL TAKE MY CHILDREN AWAY--
GOOD.
BETTER I NEVER SEE MY KIDS AGAIN THAN THEY SPEND ONE MORE SECOND WITH YOU.

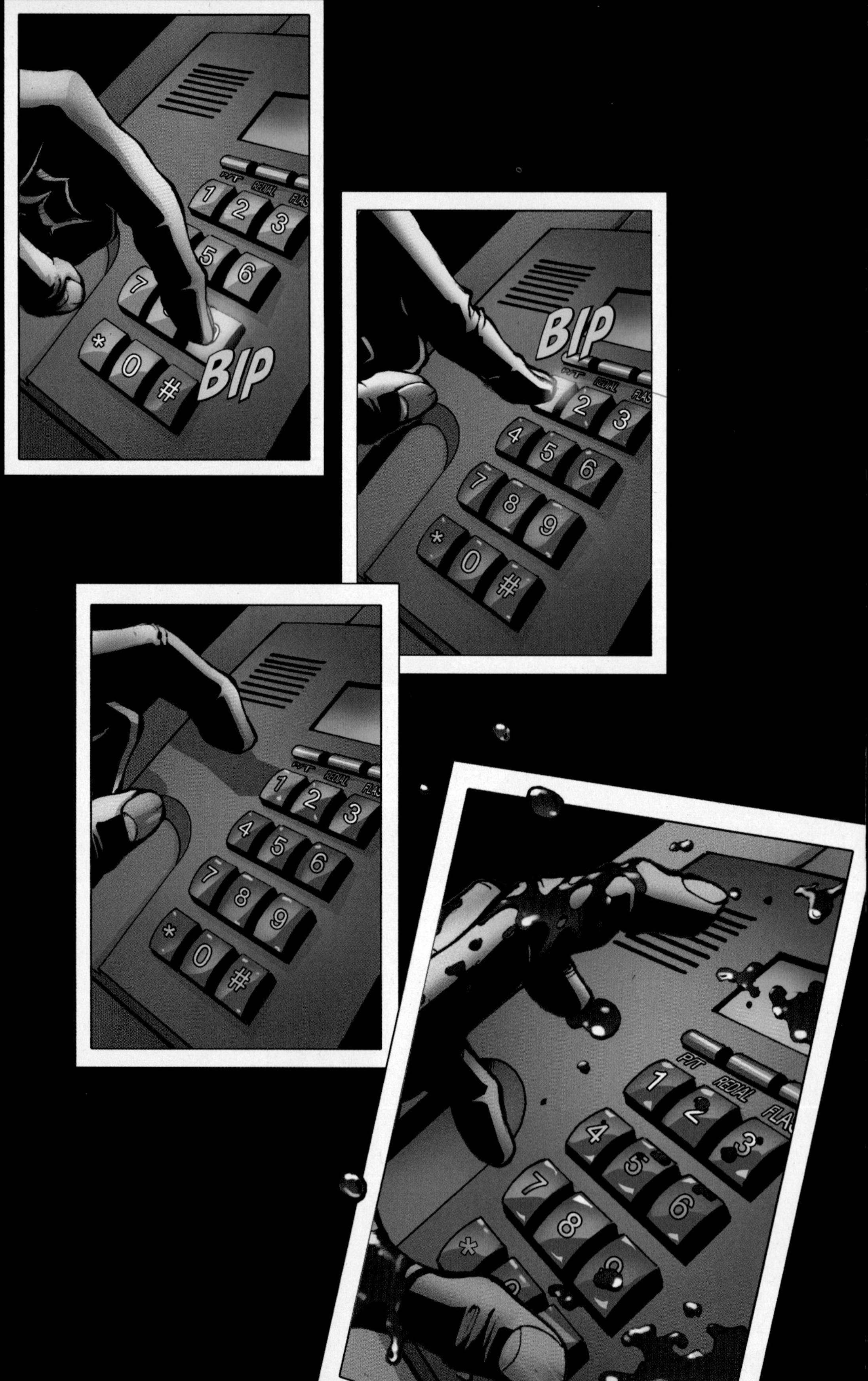
BIP
BIP

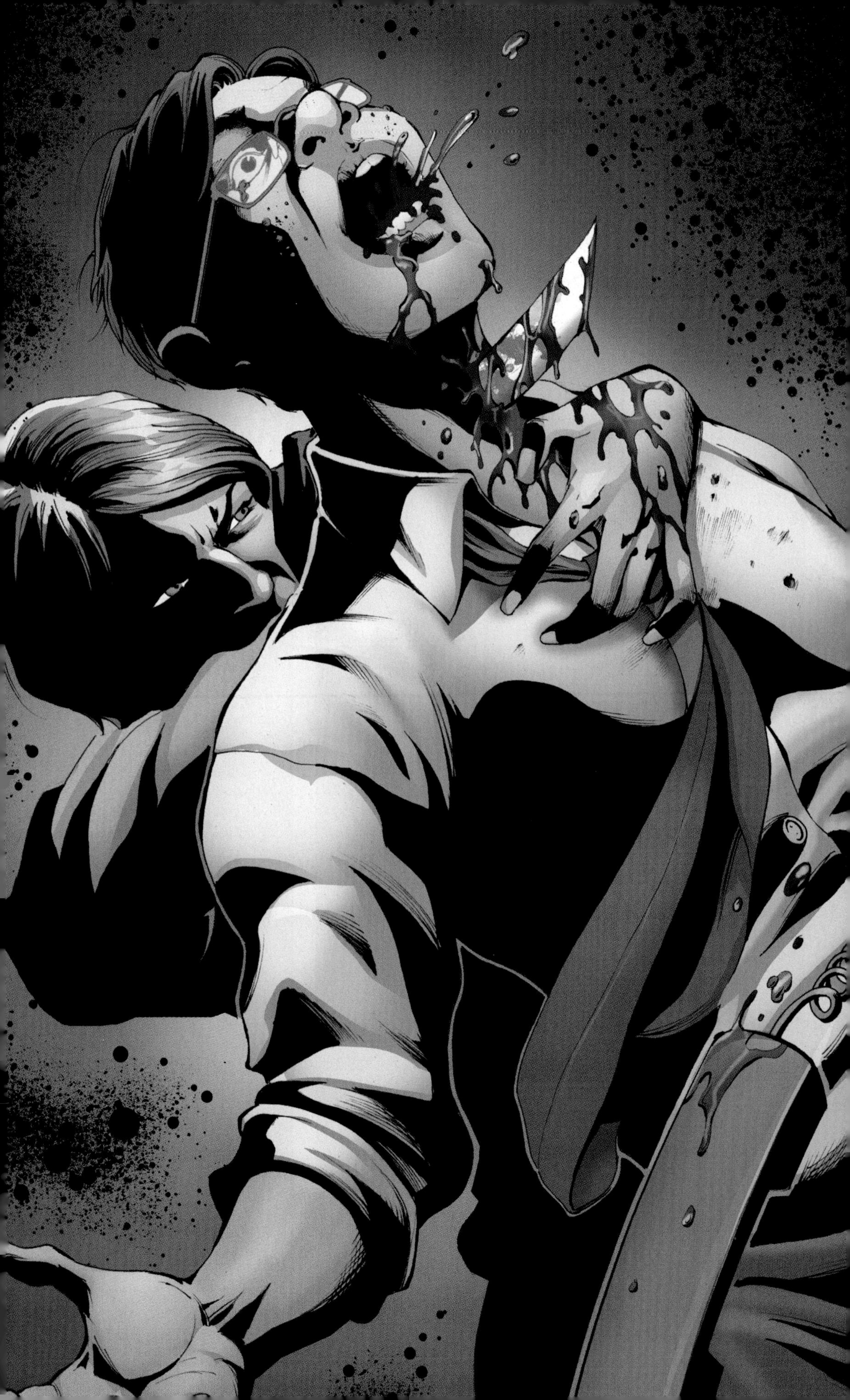

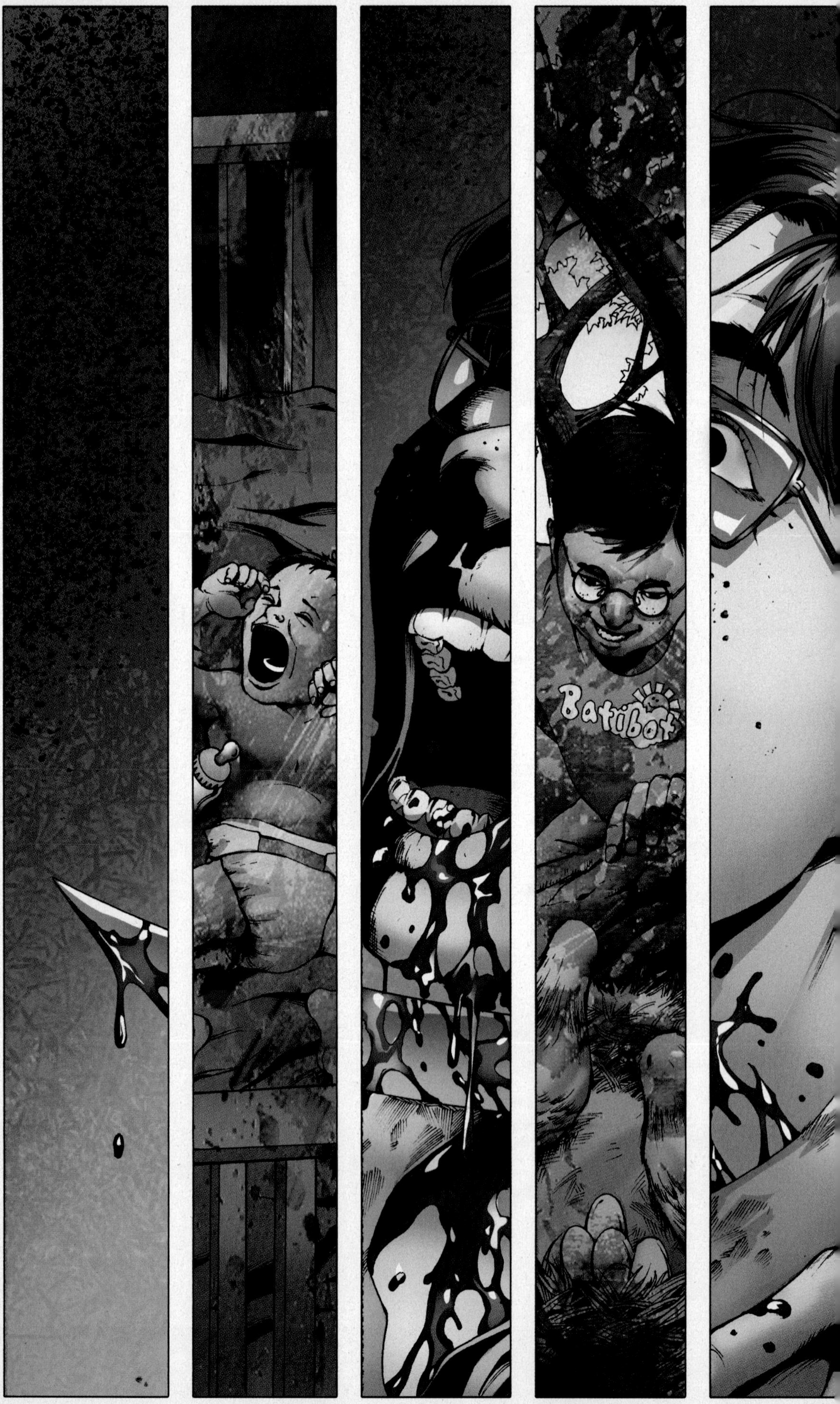
Batibot

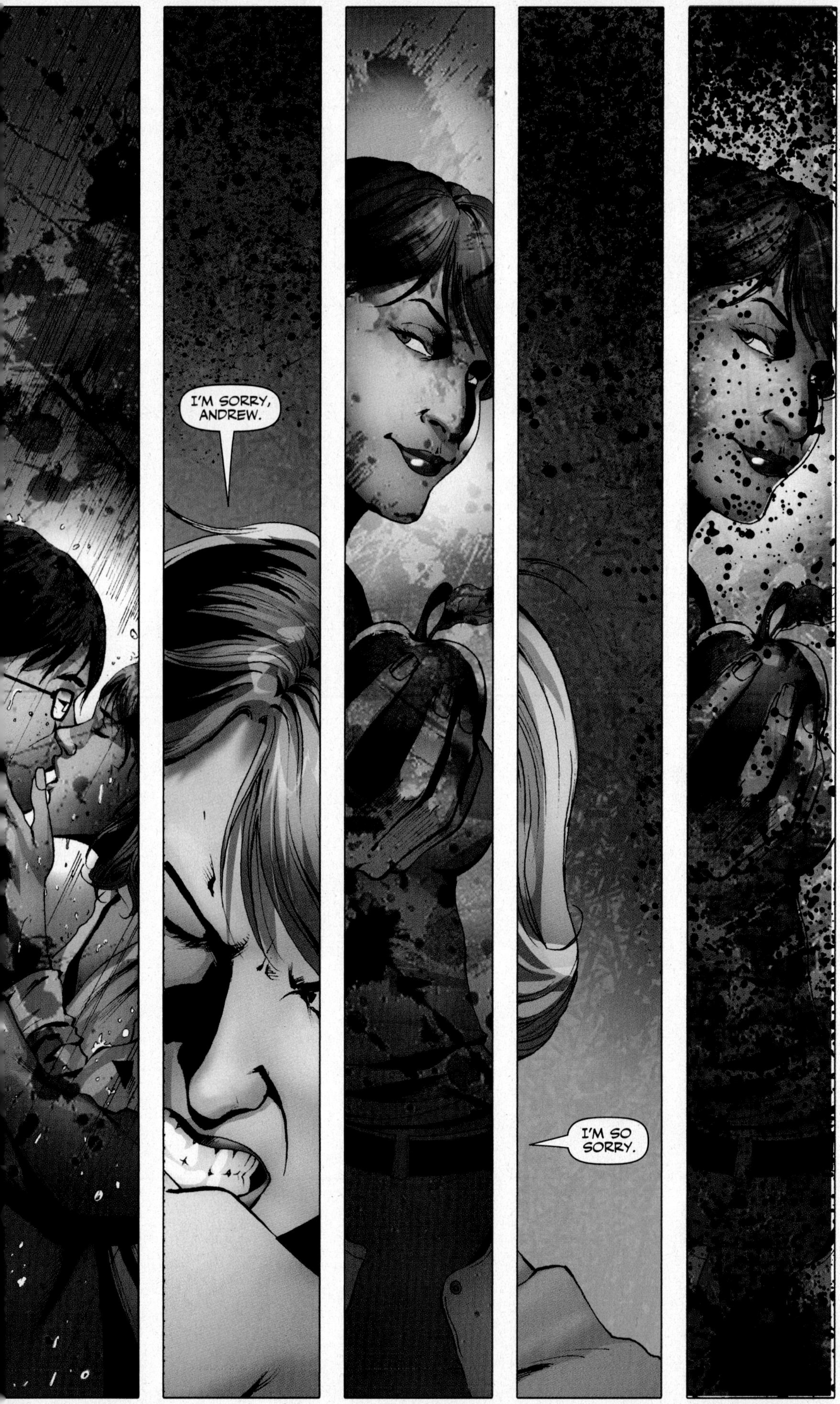
I'M SORRY, ANDREW.
I'M SO SORRY.

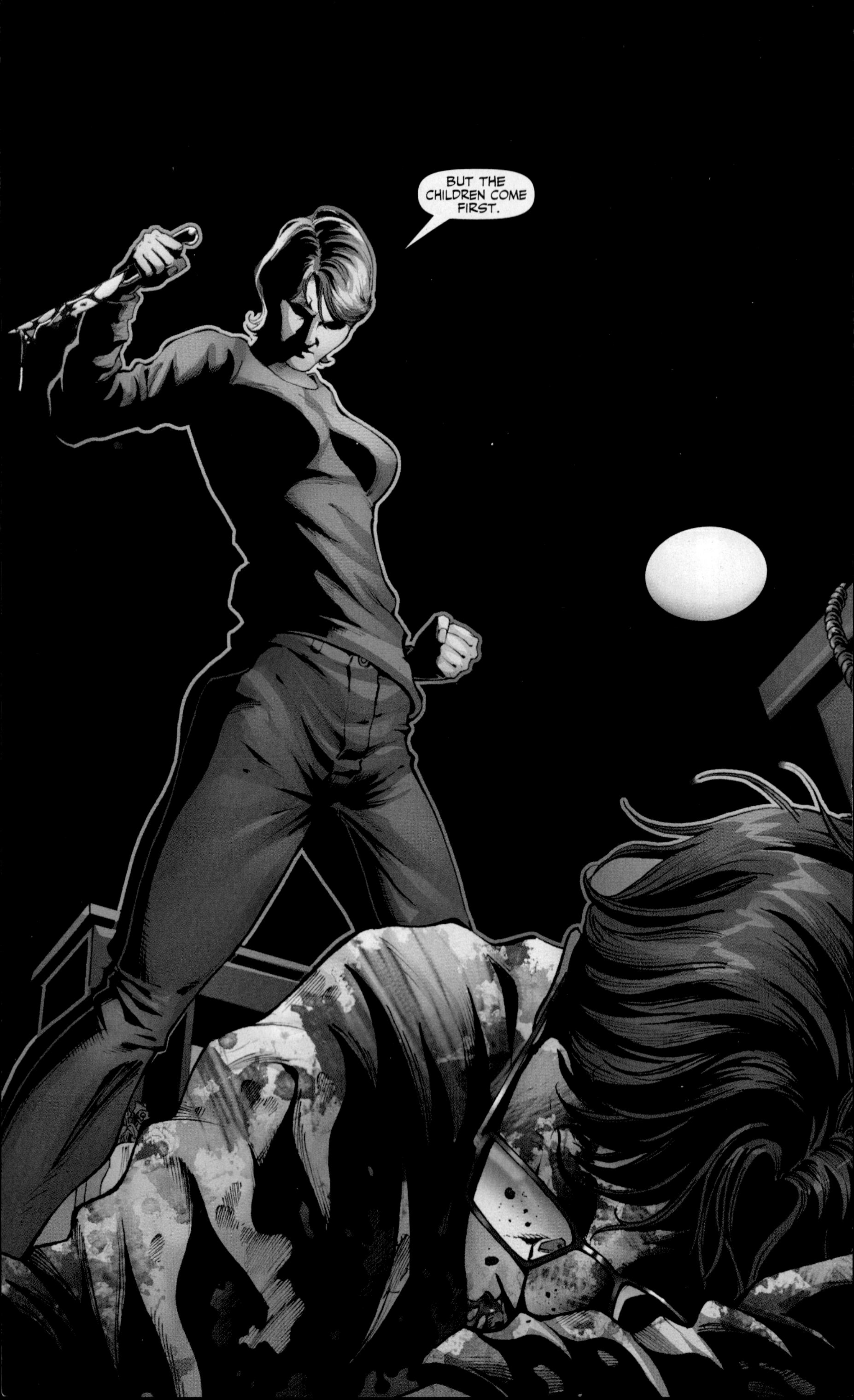
BUT THE CHILDREN COME FIRST.

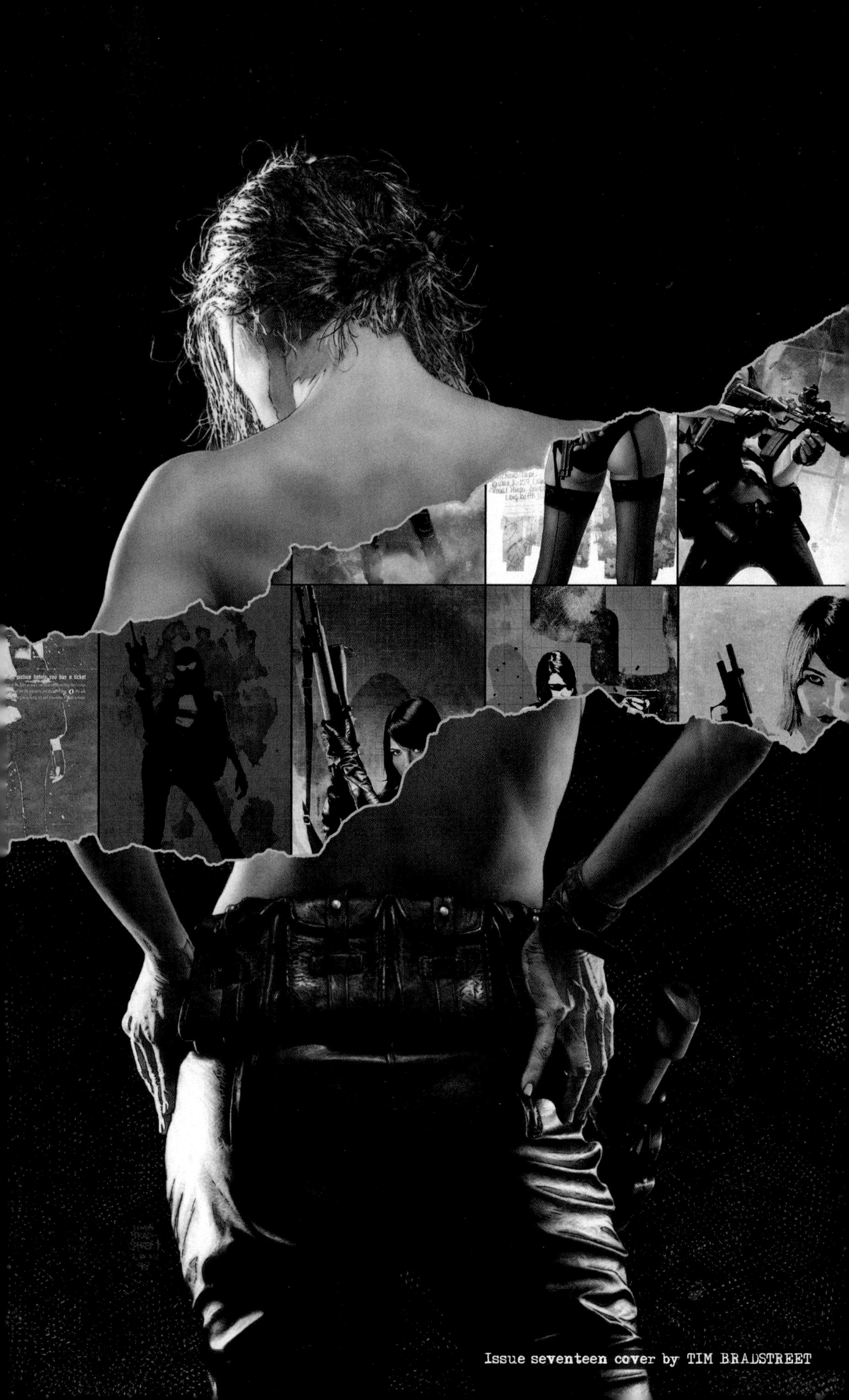

Issue seventeen cover by TIM BRADSTREET

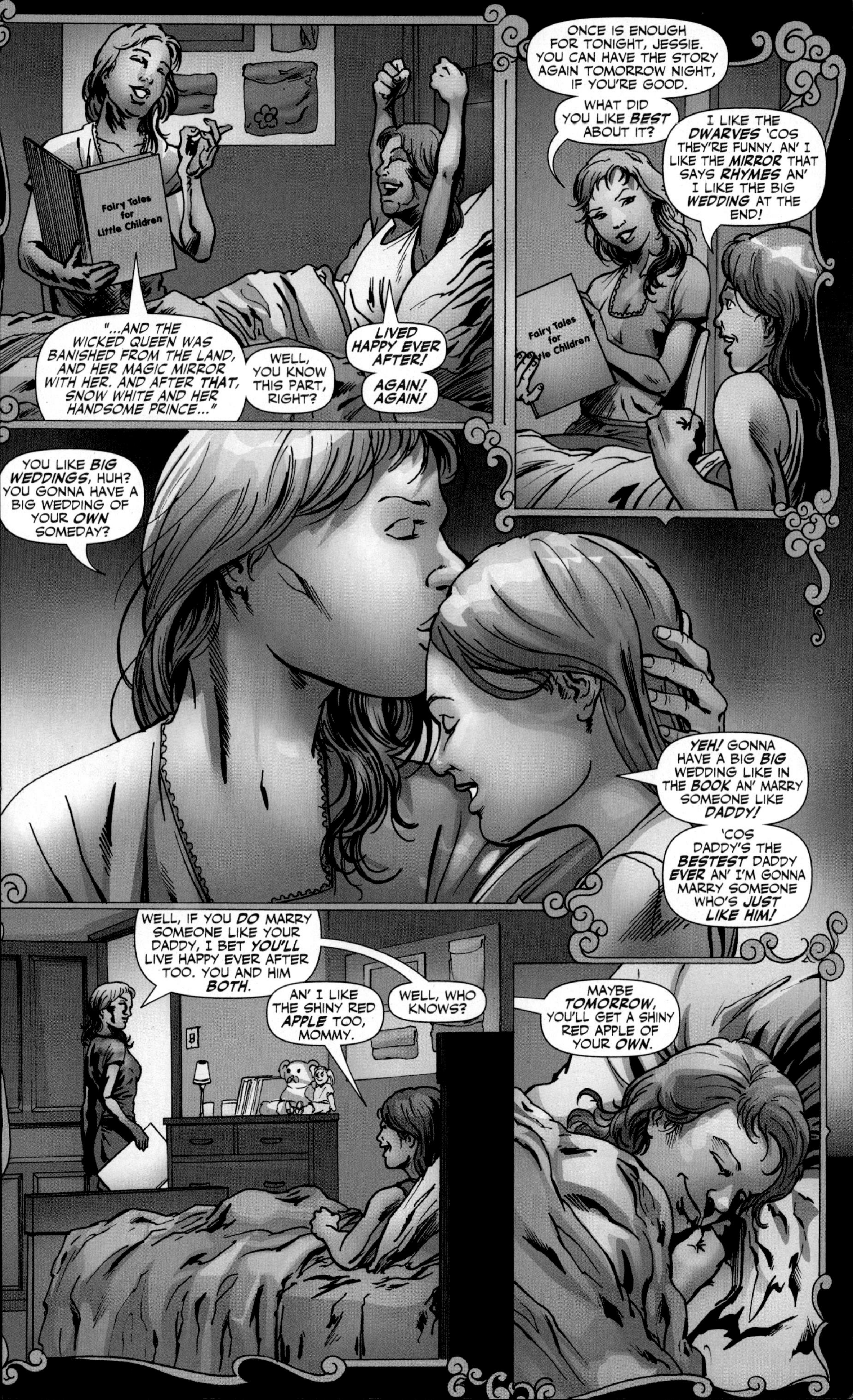

"...AND THE WICKED QUEEN WAS BANISHED FROM THE LAND, AND HER MAGIC MIRROR WITH HER. AND AFTER THAT, SNOW WHITE AND HER HANDSOME PRINCE..."
Fairy Tales for Little Children
WELL, YOU KNOW THIS PART, RIGHT?
LIVED HAPPY EVER AFTER!
AGAIN! AGAIN!
ONCE IS ENOUGH FOR TONIGHT, JESSIE. YOU CAN HAVE THE STORY AGAIN TOMORROW NIGHT, IF YOU'RE GOOD.
WHAT DID YOU LIKE BEST ABOUT IT?
I LIKE THE DWARVES 'COS THEY'RE FUNNY. AN' I LIKE THE MIRROR THAT SAYS RHYMES AN' I LIKE THE BIG WEDDING AT THE END!
YOU LIKE BIG WEDDINGS, HUH? YOU GONNA HAVE A BIG WEDDING OF YOUR OWN SOMEDAY?
YEH! GONNA HAVE A BIG BIG WEDDING LIKE IN THE BOOK AN' MARRY SOMEONE LIKE DADDY!
'COS DADDY'S THE BESTEST DADDY EVER AN' I'M GONNA MARRY SOMEONE WHO'S JUST LIKE HIM!
WELL, IF YOU DO MARRY SOMEONE LIKE YOUR DADDY, I BET YOU'LL LIVE HAPPY EVER AFTER TOO. YOU AND HIM BOTH.
WELL, WHO KNOWS?
AN' I LIKE THE SHINY RED APPLE TOO, MOMMY.
MAYBE TOMORROW, YOU'LL GET A SHINY RED APPLE OF YOUR OWN.

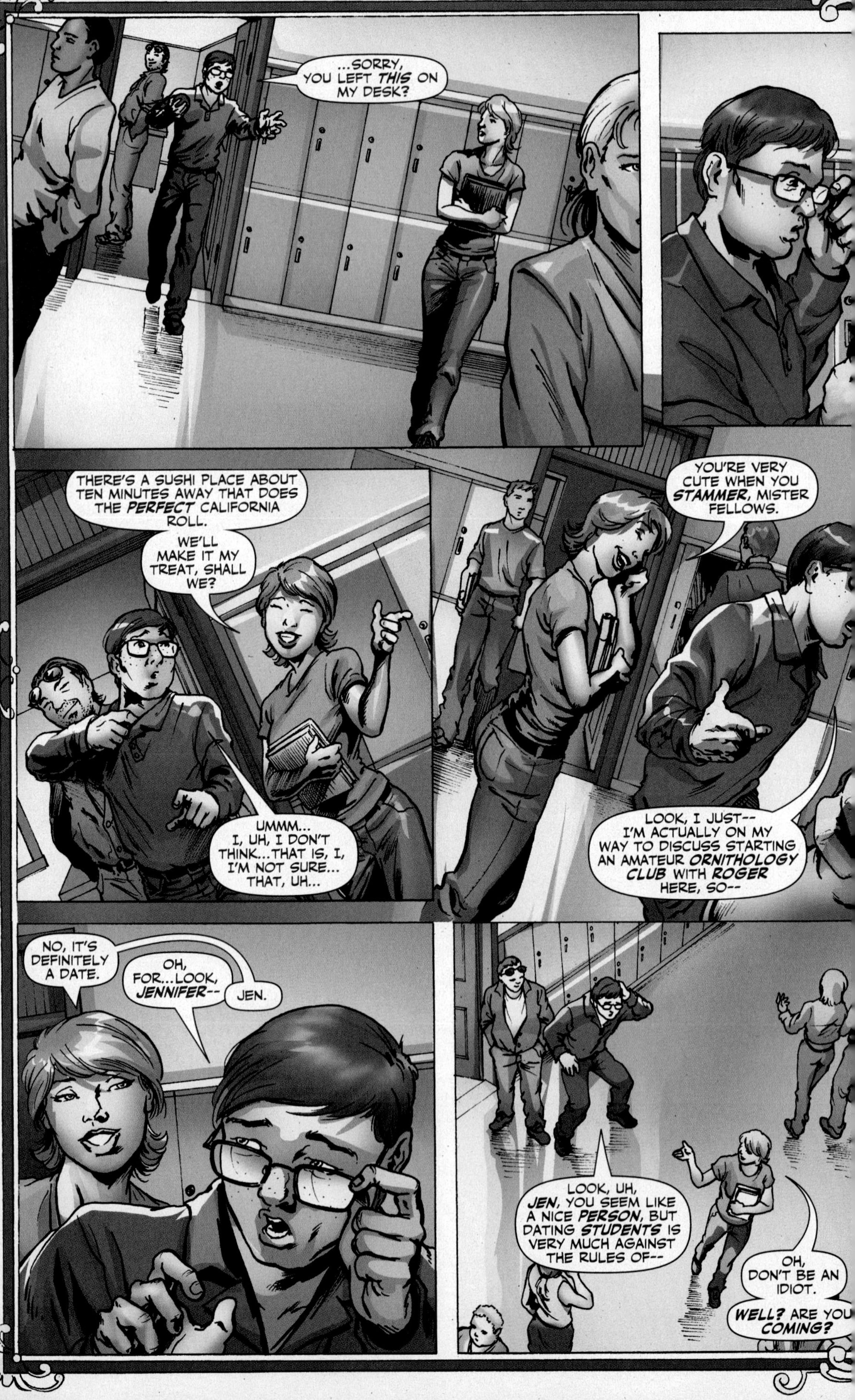
...SORRY, YOU LEFT THIS ON MY DESK?
THERE'S A SUSHI PLACE ABOUT TEN MINUTES AWAY THAT DOES THE PERFECT CALIFORNIA ROLL.
WE'LL MAKE IT MY TREAT, SHALL WE?
UMMM... I, UH, I DON'T THINK...THAT IS, I, I'M NOT SURE... THAT, UH...
YOU'RE VERY CUTE WHEN YOU STAMMER, MISTER FELLOWS.
LOOK, I JUST-- I'M ACTUALLY ON MY WAY TO DISCUSS STARTING AN AMATEUR ORNITHOLOGY CLUB WITH ROGER HERE, SO--
NO, IT'S DEFINITELY A DATE.
OH, FOR...LOOK, JENNIFER--
JEN.
LOOK, UH, JEN, YOU SEEM LIKE A NICE PERSON, BUT DATING STUDENTS IS VERY MUCH AGAINST THE RULES OF--
OH, DON'T BE AN IDIOT.
WELL? ARE YOU COMING?

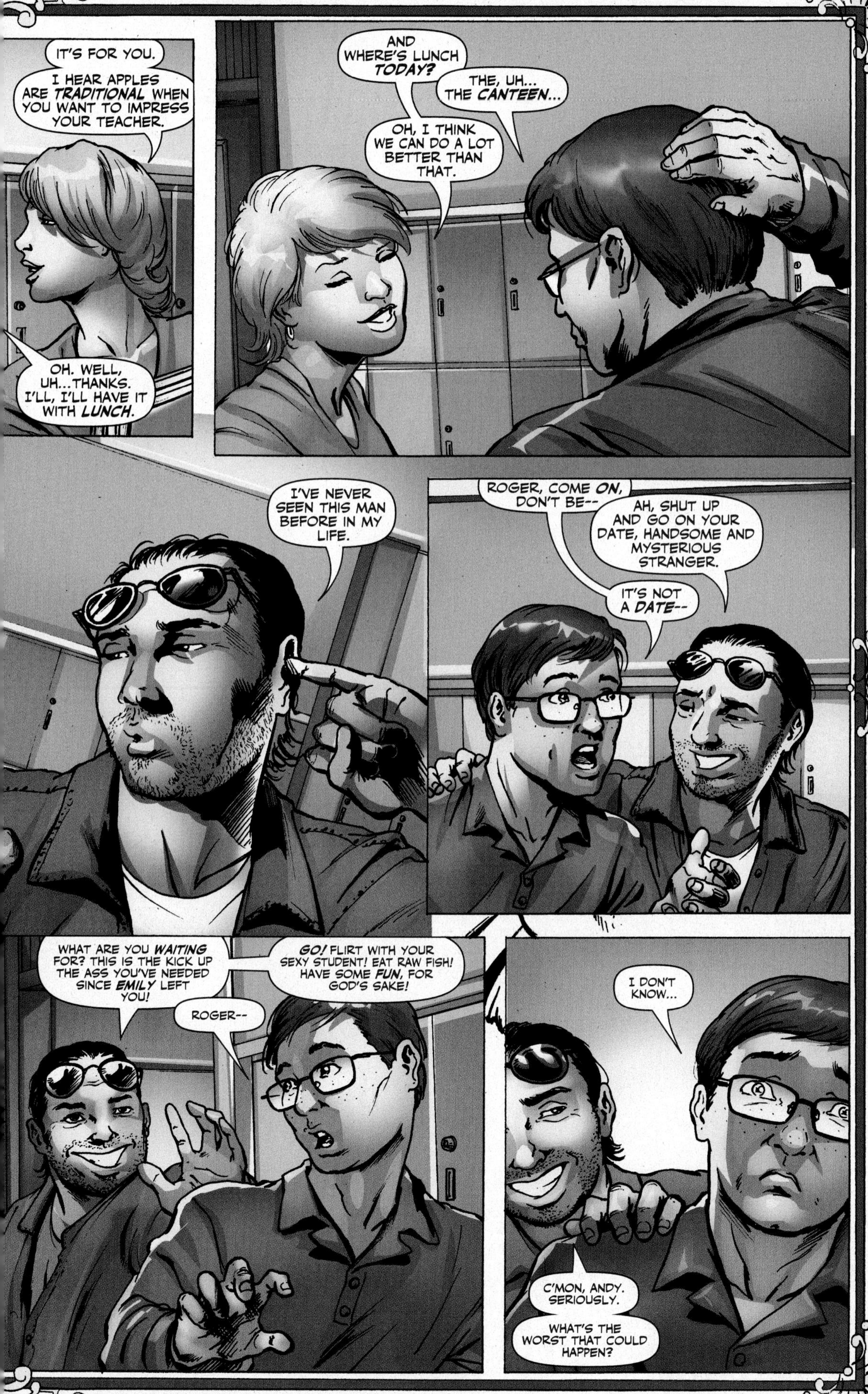
IT'S FOR YOU.
I HEAR APPLES ARE TRADITIONAL WHEN YOU WANT TO IMPRESS YOUR TEACHER.
OH. WELL, UH...THANKS. I'LL, I'LL HAVE IT WITH LUNCH.
AND WHERE'S LUNCH TODAY?
THE, UH... THE CANTEEN...
OH, I THINK WE CAN DO A LOT BETTER THAN THAT.
I'VE NEVER SEEN THIS MAN BEFORE IN MY LIFE.
ROGER, COME ON, DON'T BE--
AH, SHUT UP AND GO ON YOUR DATE, HANDSOME AND MYSTERIOUS STRANGER.
IT'S NOT A DATE--
WHAT ARE YOU WAITING FOR? THIS IS THE KICK UP THE ASS YOU'VE NEEDED SINCE EMILY LEFT YOU!
ROGER--
GO! FLIRT WITH YOUR SEXY STUDENT! EAT RAW FISH! HAVE SOME FUN, FOR GOD'S SAKE!
I DON'T KNOW...
C'MON, ANDY. SERIOUSLY.
WHAT'S THE WORST THAT COULD HAPPEN?

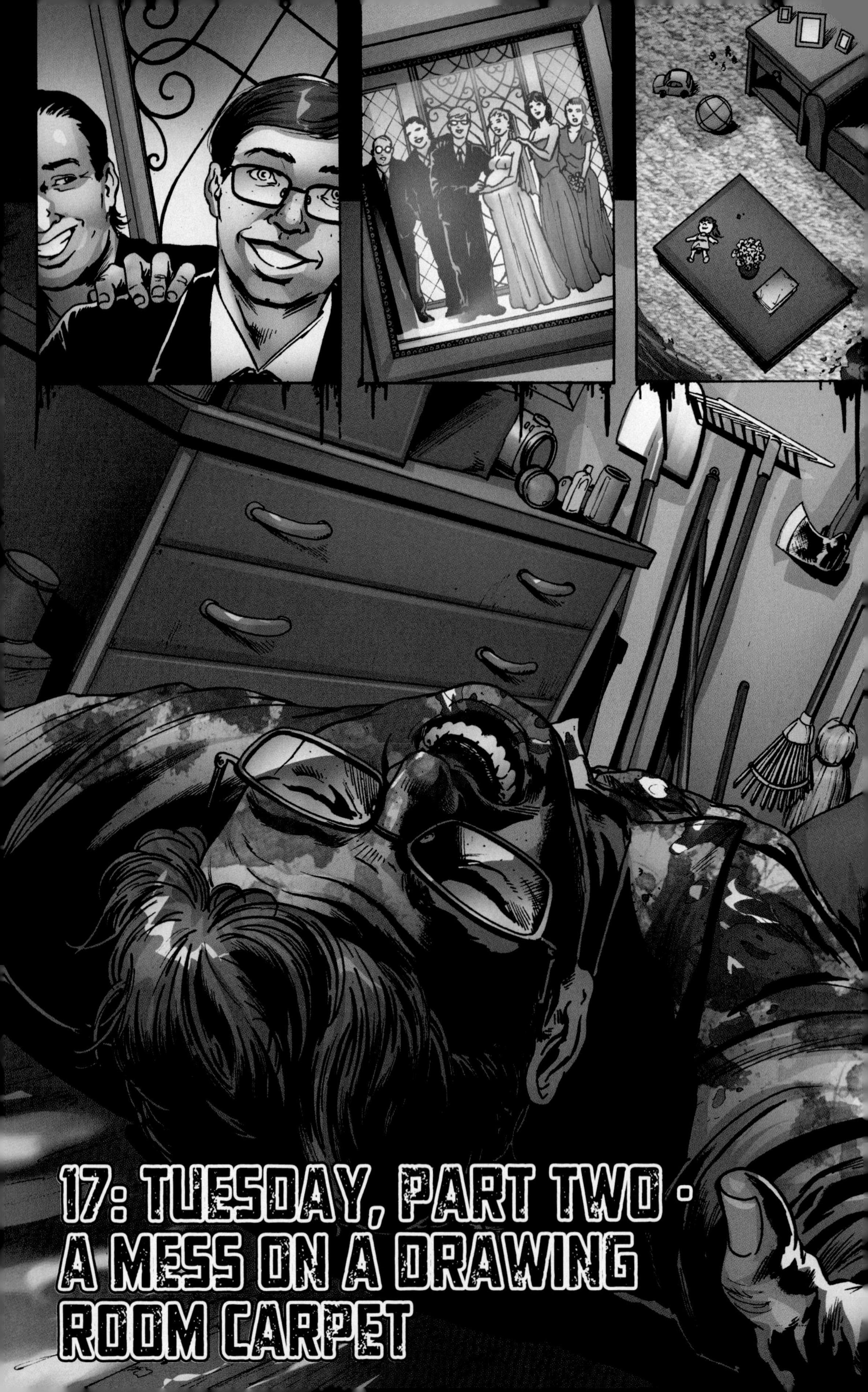
17: TUESDAY, PART TWO -
A MESS ON A DRAWING
ROOM CARPET

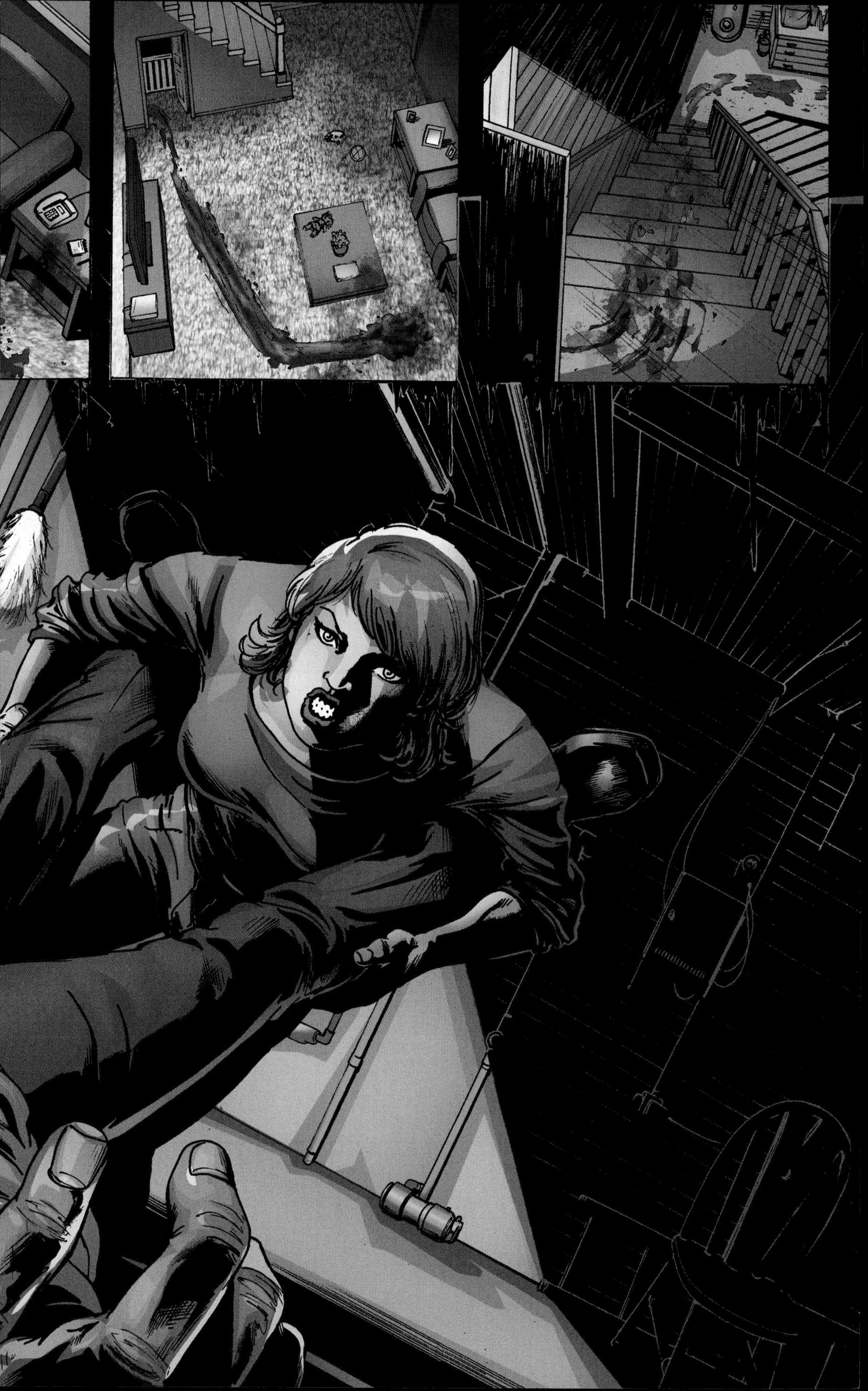

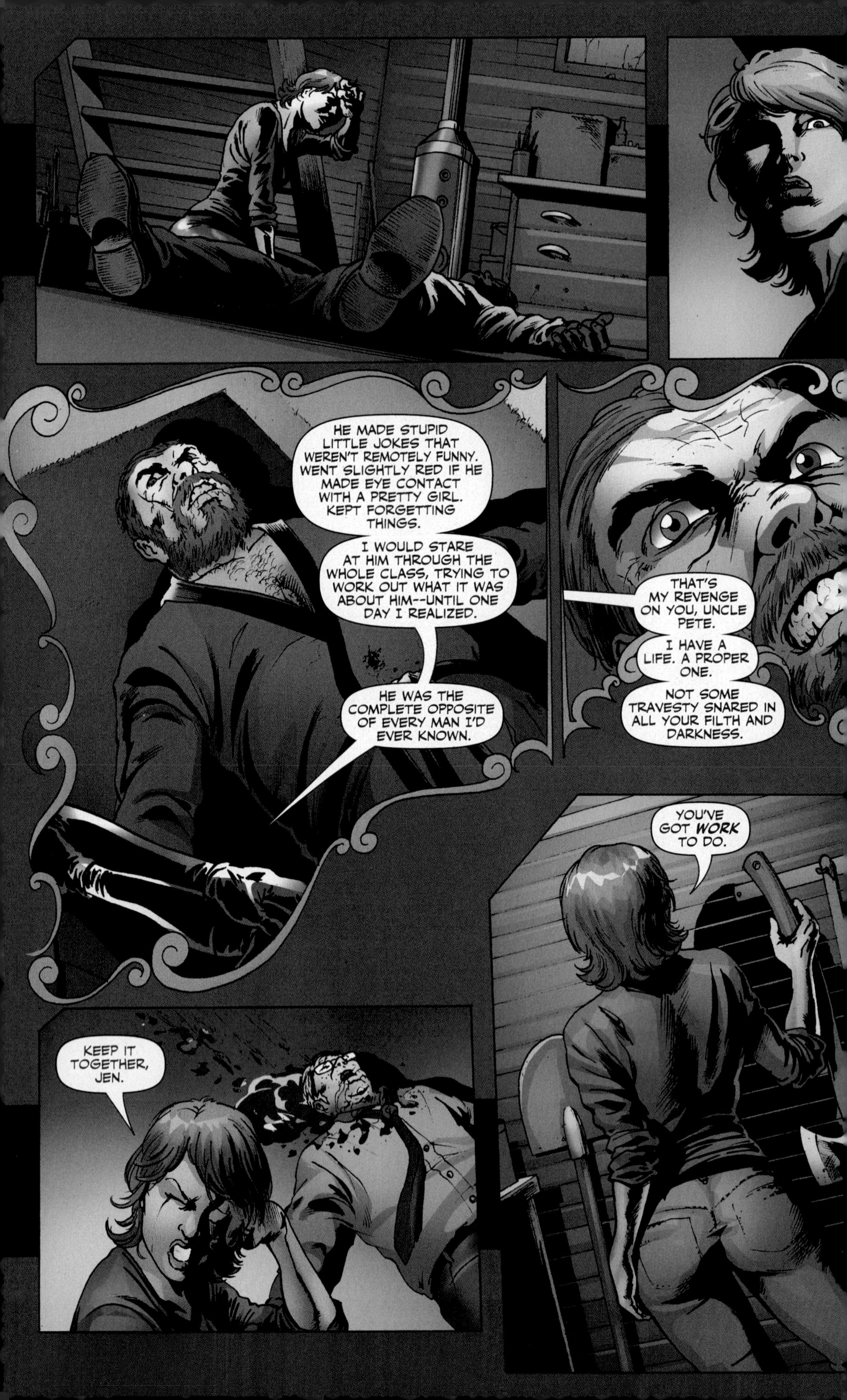
HE MADE STUPID LITTLE JOKES THAT WEREN'T REMOTELY FUNNY. WENT SLIGHTLY RED IF HE MADE EYE CONTACT WITH A PRETTY GIRL. KEPT FORGETTING THINGS.
I WOULD STARE AT HIM THROUGH THE WHOLE CLASS, TRYING TO WORK OUT WHAT IT WAS ABOUT HIM--UNTIL ONE DAY I REALIZED.
HE WAS THE COMPLETE OPPOSITE OF EVERY MAN I'D EVER KNOWN.
THAT'S MY REVENGE ON YOU, UNCLE PETE.
I HAVE A LIFE. A PROPER ONE.
NOT SOME TRAVESTY SNARED IN ALL YOUR FILTH AND DARKNESS.
KEEP IT TOGETHER, JEN.
YOU'VE GOT **WORK** TO DO.

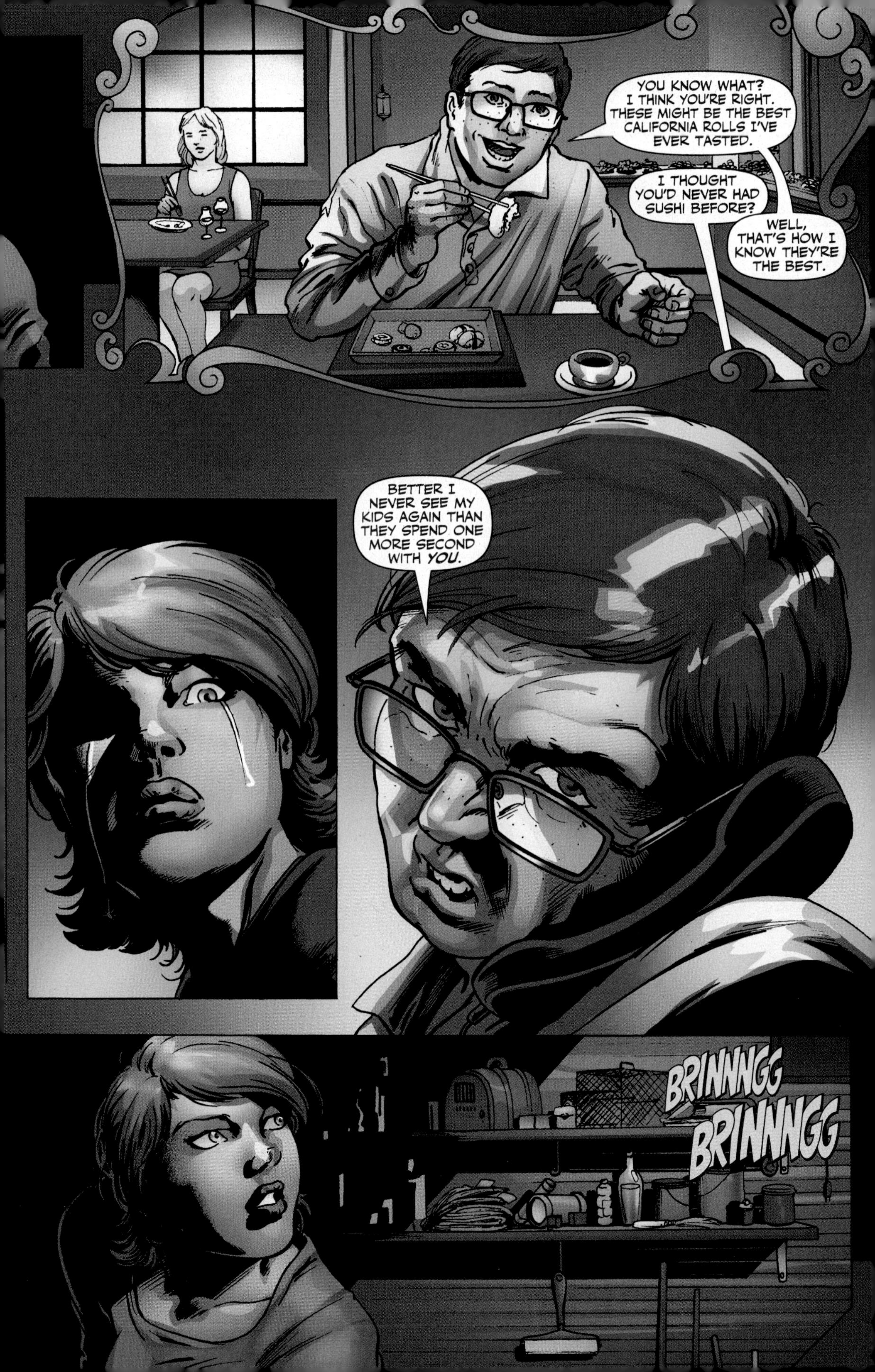
YOU KNOW WHAT? I THINK YOU'RE RIGHT. THESE MIGHT BE THE BEST CALIFORNIA ROLLS I'VE EVER TASTED.
I THOUGHT YOU'D NEVER HAD SUSHI BEFORE?
WELL, THAT'S HOW I KNOW THEY'RE THE BEST.
BETTER I NEVER SEE MY KIDS AGAIN THAN THEY SPEND ONE MORE SECOND WITH *YOU*.
BRINNNGG
BRINNNGG

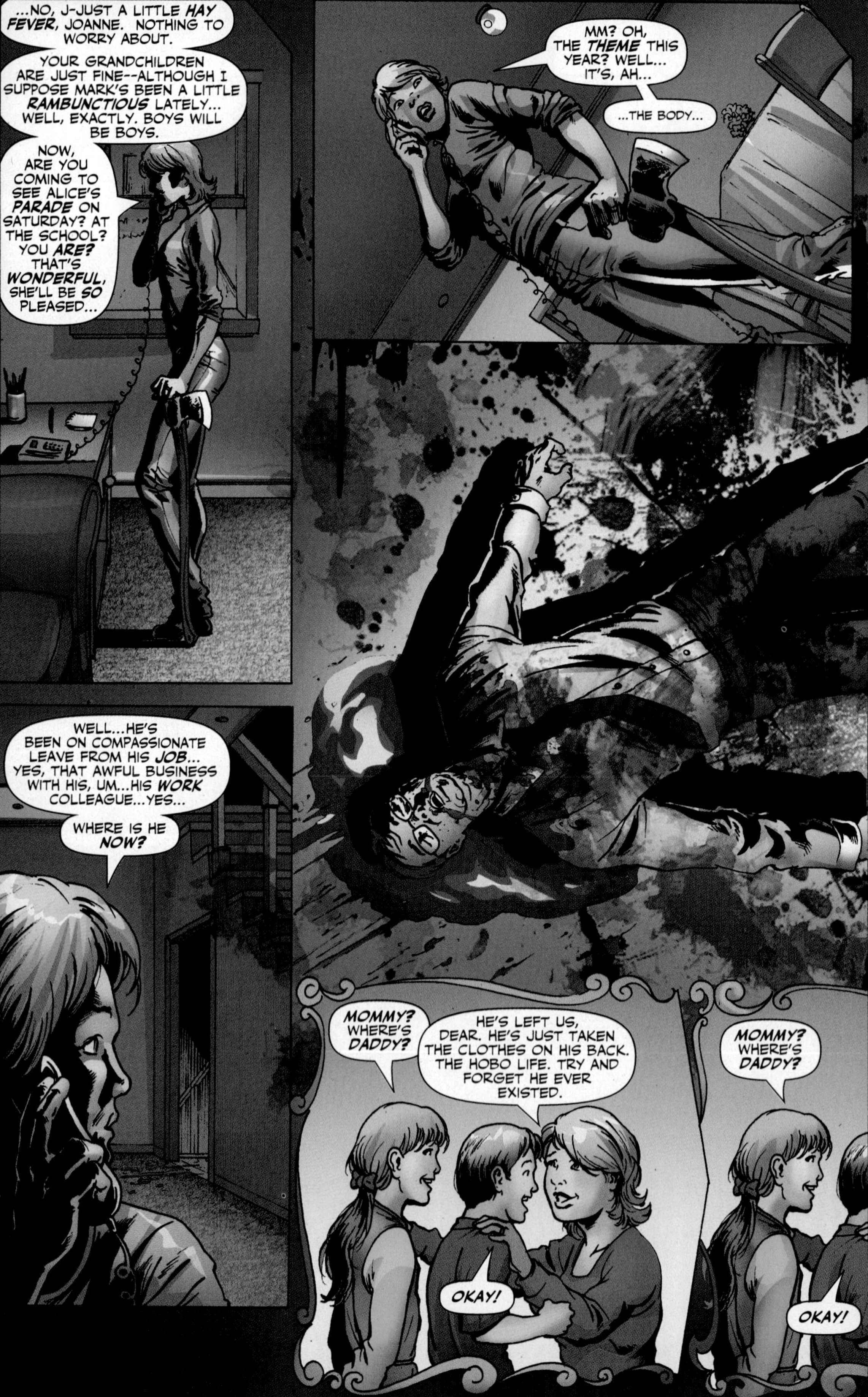

...NO, J-JUST A LITTLE HAY FEVER, JOANNE. NOTHING TO WORRY ABOUT.
YOUR GRANDCHILDREN ARE JUST FINE--ALTHOUGH I SUPPOSE MARK'S BEEN A LITTLE RAMBUNCTIOUS LATELY... WELL, EXACTLY. BOYS WILL BE BOYS.
NOW, ARE YOU COMING TO SEE ALICE'S PARADE ON SATURDAY? AT THE SCHOOL? YOU ARE? THAT'S WONDERFUL, SHE'LL BE SO PLEASED...
MM? OH, THE THEME THIS YEAR? WELL... IT'S, AH...
...THE BODY...
WELL...HE'S BEEN ON COMPASSIONATE LEAVE FROM HIS JOB... YES, THAT AWFUL BUSINESS WITH HIS, UM...HIS WORK COLLEAGUE...YES...
WHERE IS HE NOW?
MOMMY? WHERE'S DADDY?
HE'S LEFT US, DEAR. HE'S JUST TAKEN THE CLOTHES ON HIS BACK. THE HOBO LIFE. TRY AND FORGET HE EVER EXISTED.
OKAY!
MOMMY? WHERE'S DADDY?
OKAY!

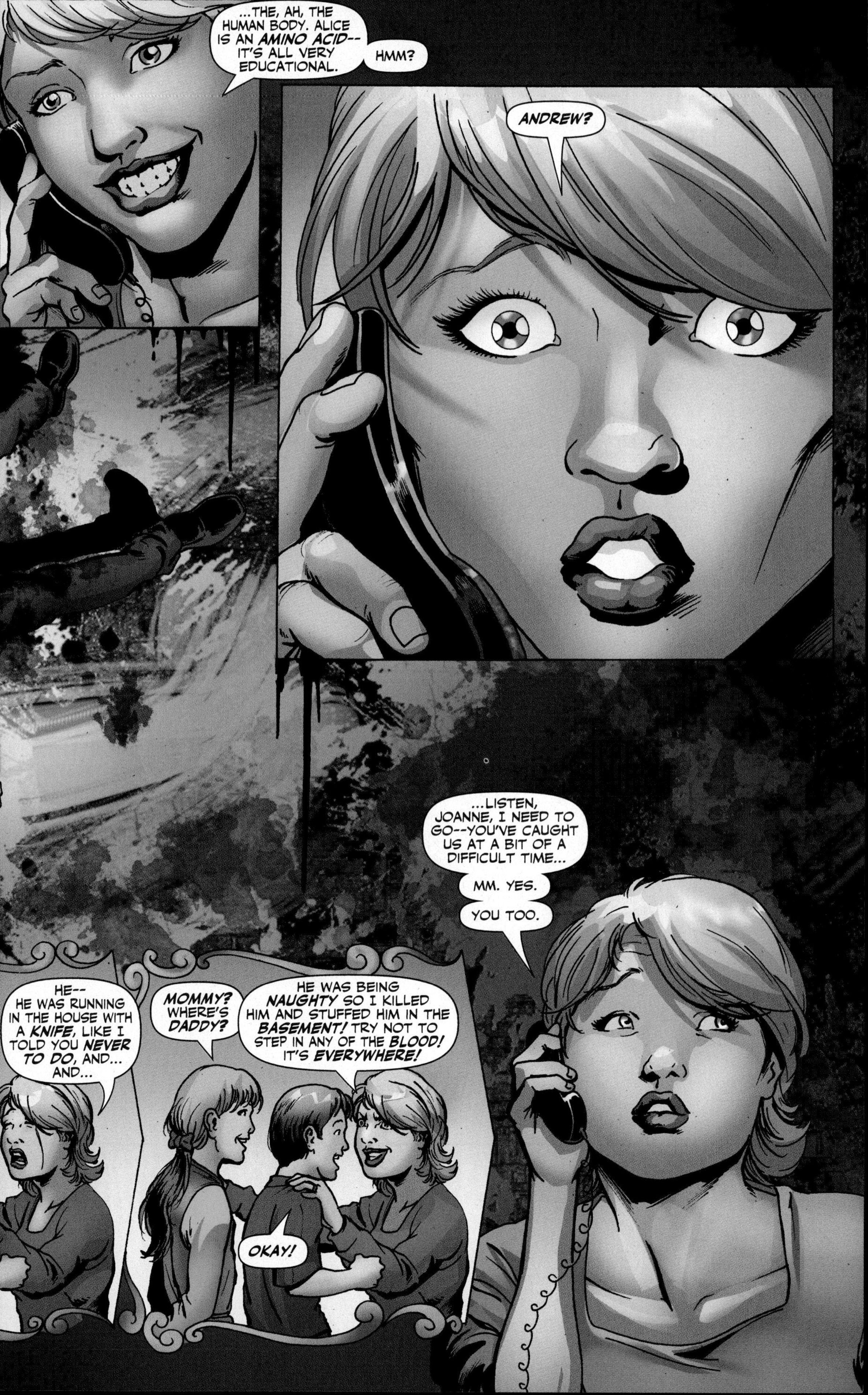
...THE, AH, THE HUMAN BODY. ALICE IS AN AMINO ACID-- IT'S ALL VERY EDUCATIONAL.
HMM?
ANDREW?
...LISTEN, JOANNE, I NEED TO GO--YOU'VE CAUGHT US AT A BIT OF A DIFFICULT TIME...
MM. YES.
YOU TOO.
HE-- HE WAS RUNNING IN THE HOUSE WITH A KNIFE, LIKE I TOLD YOU NEVER TO DO, AND... AND...
MOMMY? WHERE'S DADDY?
HE WAS BEING NAUGHTY SO I KILLED HIM AND STUFFED HIM IN THE BASEMENT! TRY NOT TO STEP IN ANY OF THE BLOOD! IT'S EVERYWHERE!
OKAY!

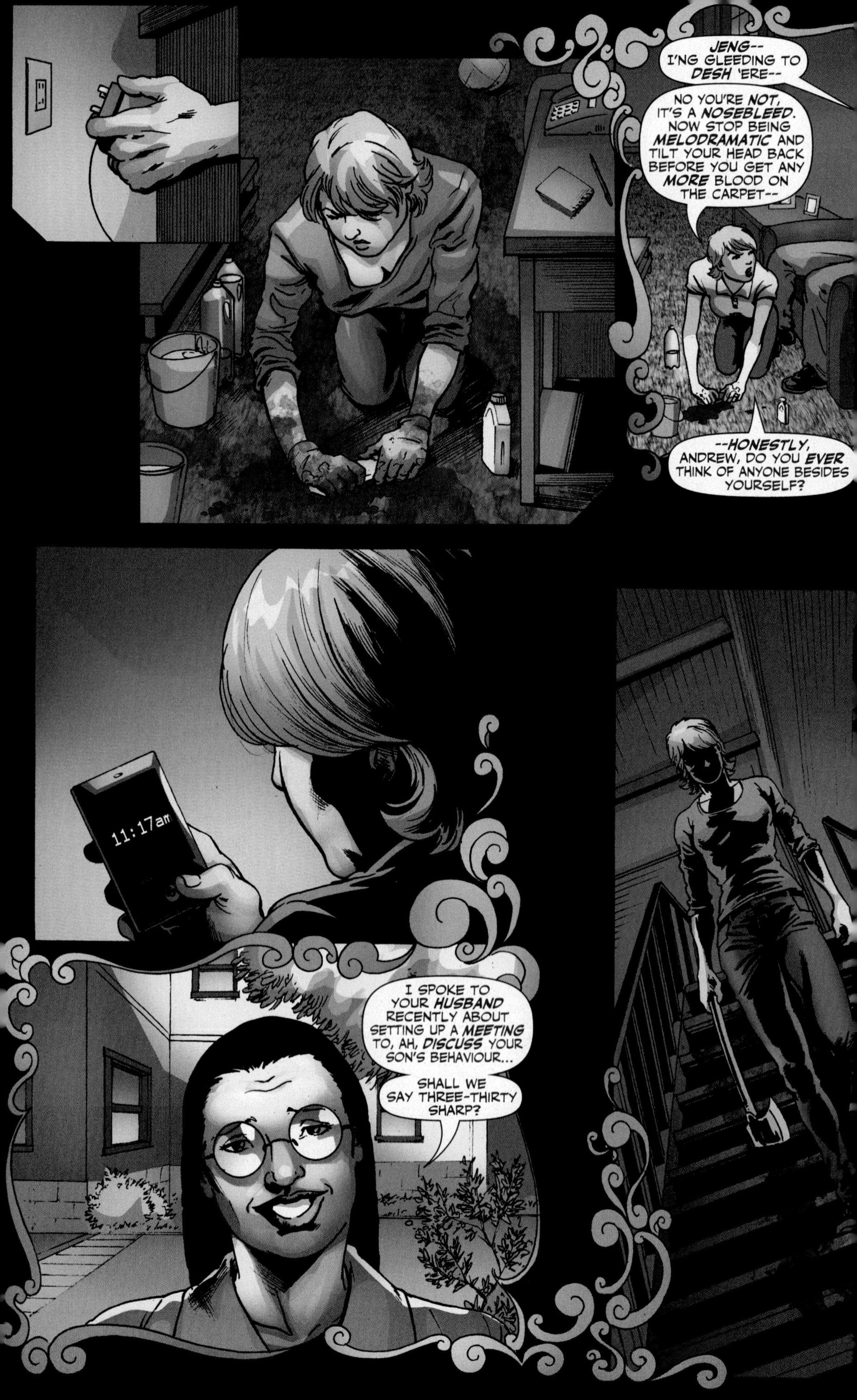
JENG-- I'NG GLEEDING TO DESH 'ERE--
NO YOU'RE NOT, IT'S A NOSEBLEED. NOW STOP BEING MELODRAMATIC AND TILT YOUR HEAD BACK BEFORE YOU GET ANY MORE BLOOD ON THE CARPET--
--HONESTLY, ANDREW, DO YOU EVER THINK OF ANYONE BESIDES YOURSELF?
11:17am
I SPOKE TO YOUR HUSBAND RECENTLY ABOUT SETTING UP A MEETING TO, AH, DISCUSS YOUR SON'S BEHAVIOUR...
SHALL WE SAY THREE-THIRTY SHARP?

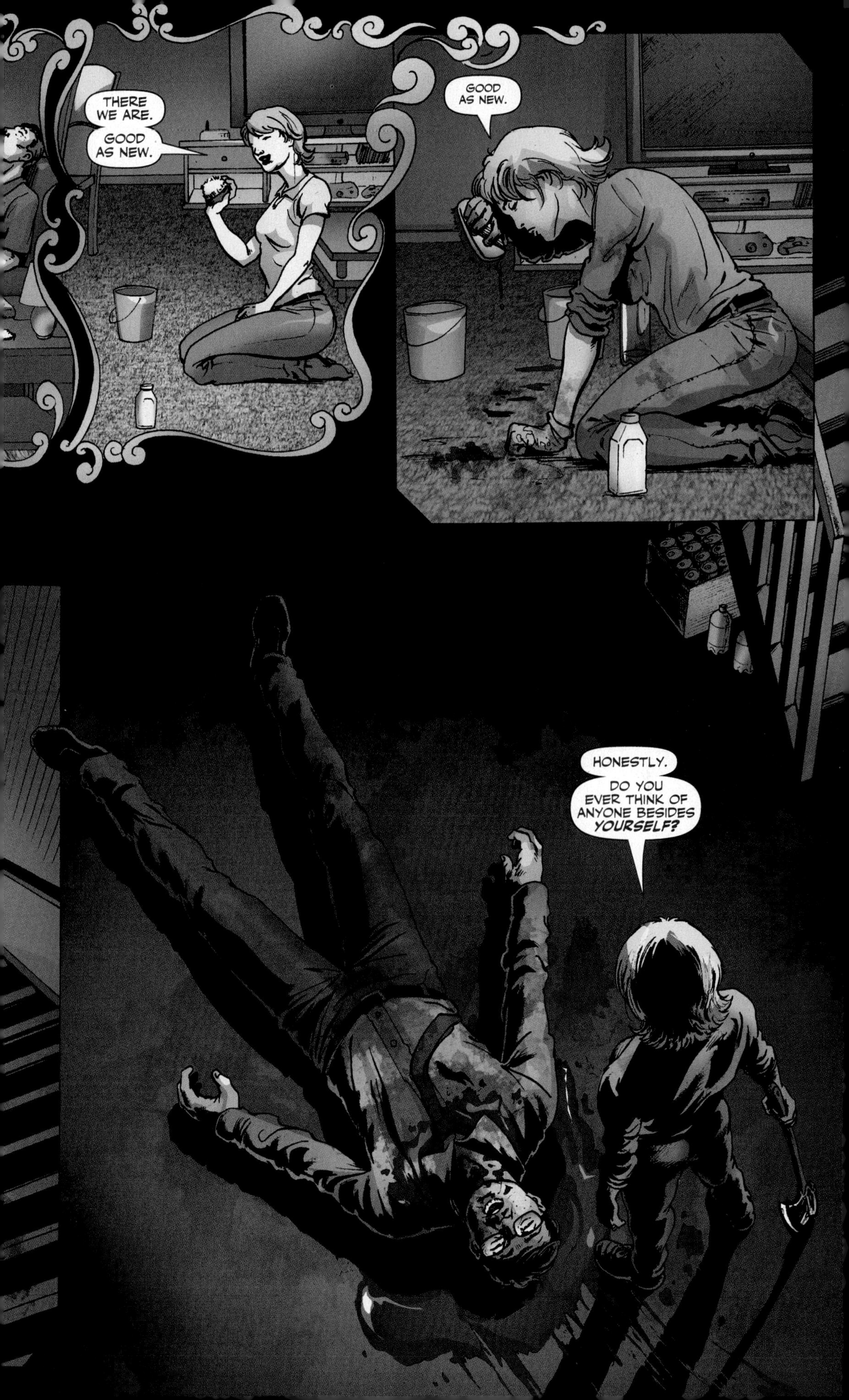
THERE WE ARE.
GOOD AS NEW.
GOOD AS NEW.
HONESTLY.
DO YOU EVER THINK OF ANYONE BESIDES *YOURSELF?*

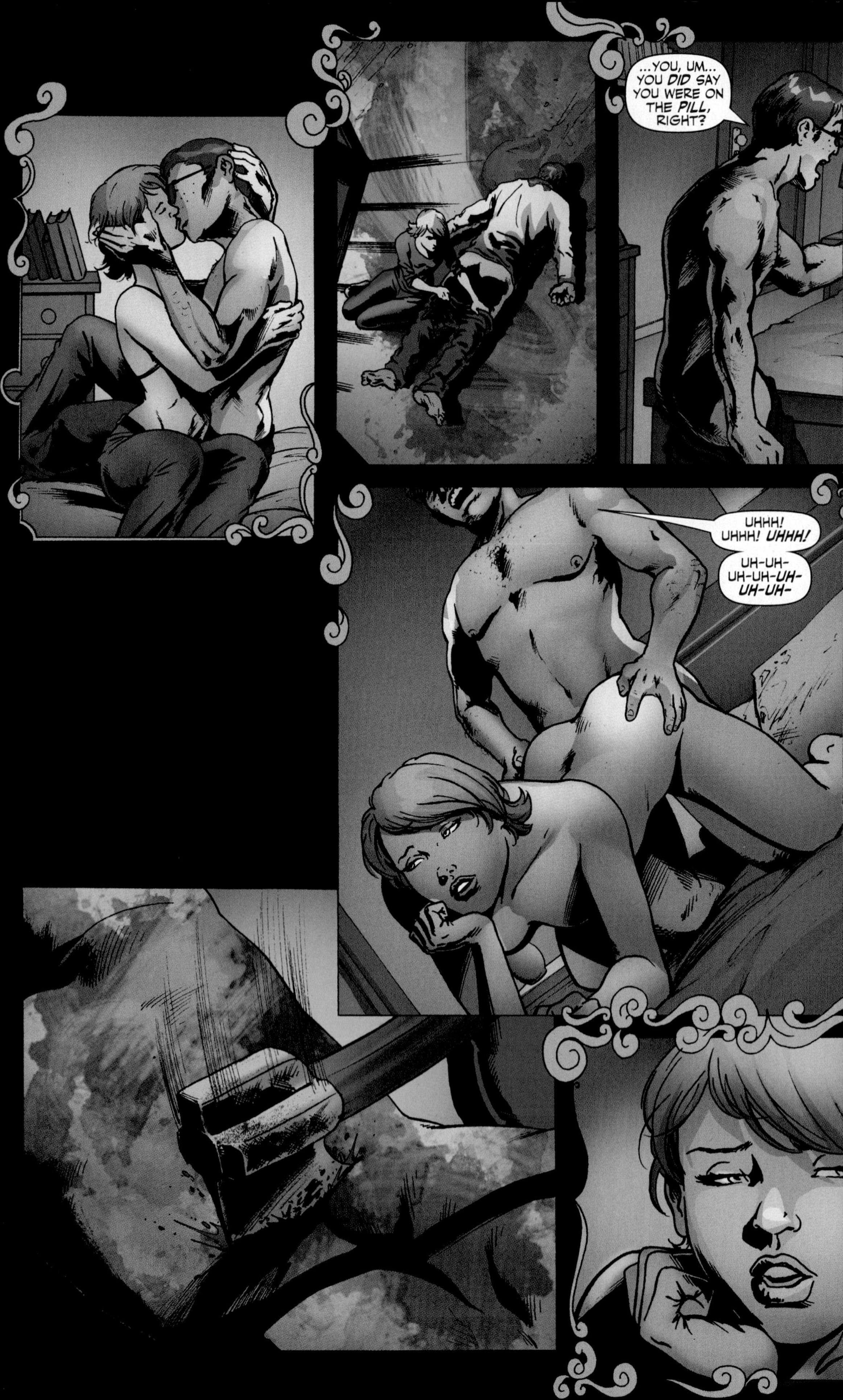

...YOU, UM... YOU DID SAY YOU WERE ON THE PILL, RIGHT?
UHHH! UHHH! UHHH!
UH-UH- UH-UH-UH- UH-UH-

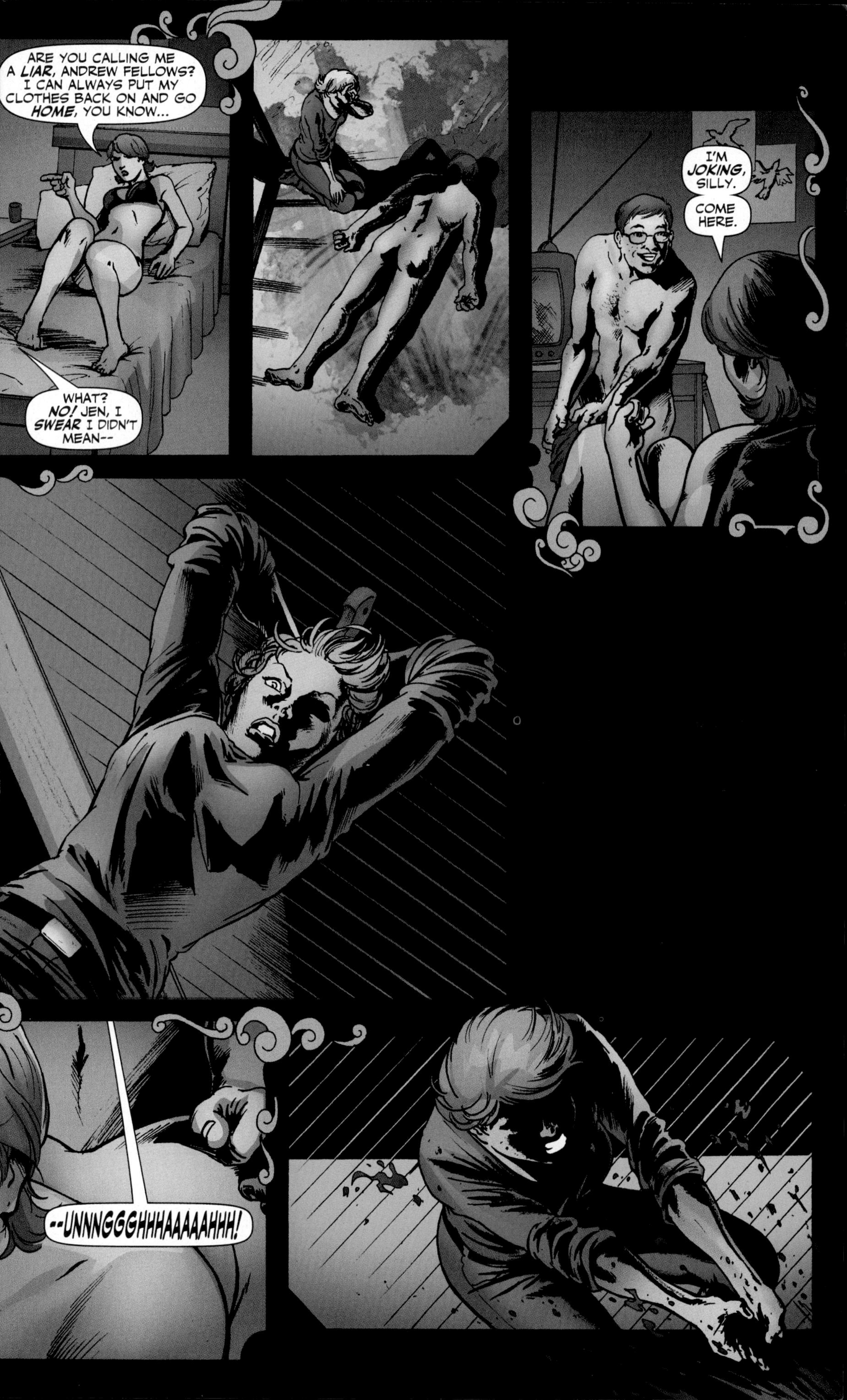
ARE YOU CALLING ME A LIAR, ANDREW FELLOWS? I CAN ALWAYS PUT MY CLOTHES BACK ON AND GO HOME, YOU KNOW...
WHAT? NO! JEN, I SWEAR I DIDN'T MEAN--
I'M JOKING, SILLY.
COME HERE.
--UNNNGGGHHHAAAAAHHH!

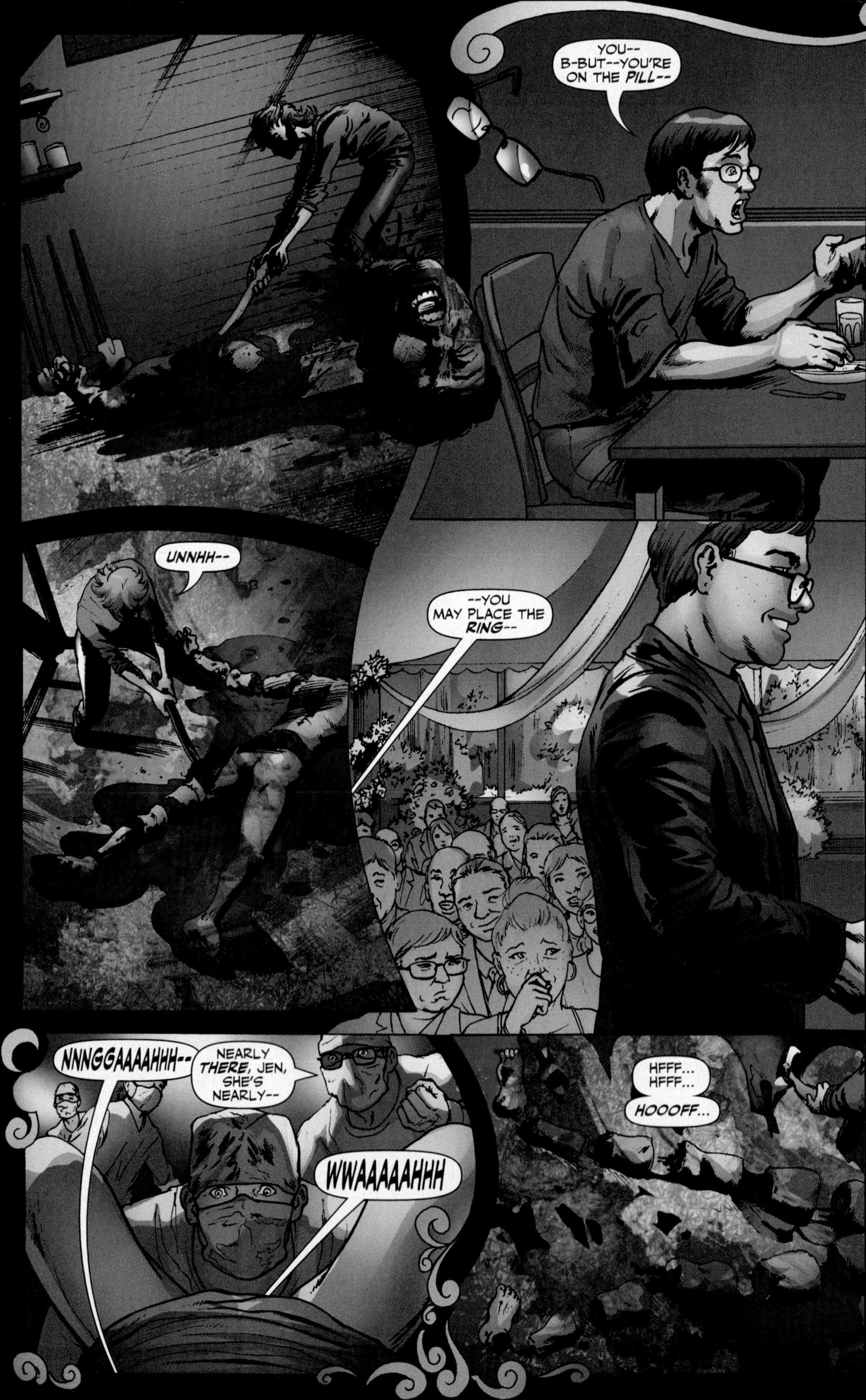
YOU--
B-BUT--YOU'RE ON THE PILL--
UNNHH--
--YOU MAY PLACE THE RING--
NNNGGAAAAHHH--
NEARLY THERE, JEN, SHE'S NEARLY--
WWAAAAAAHHH
HFFF... HFFF... HOOOFF...

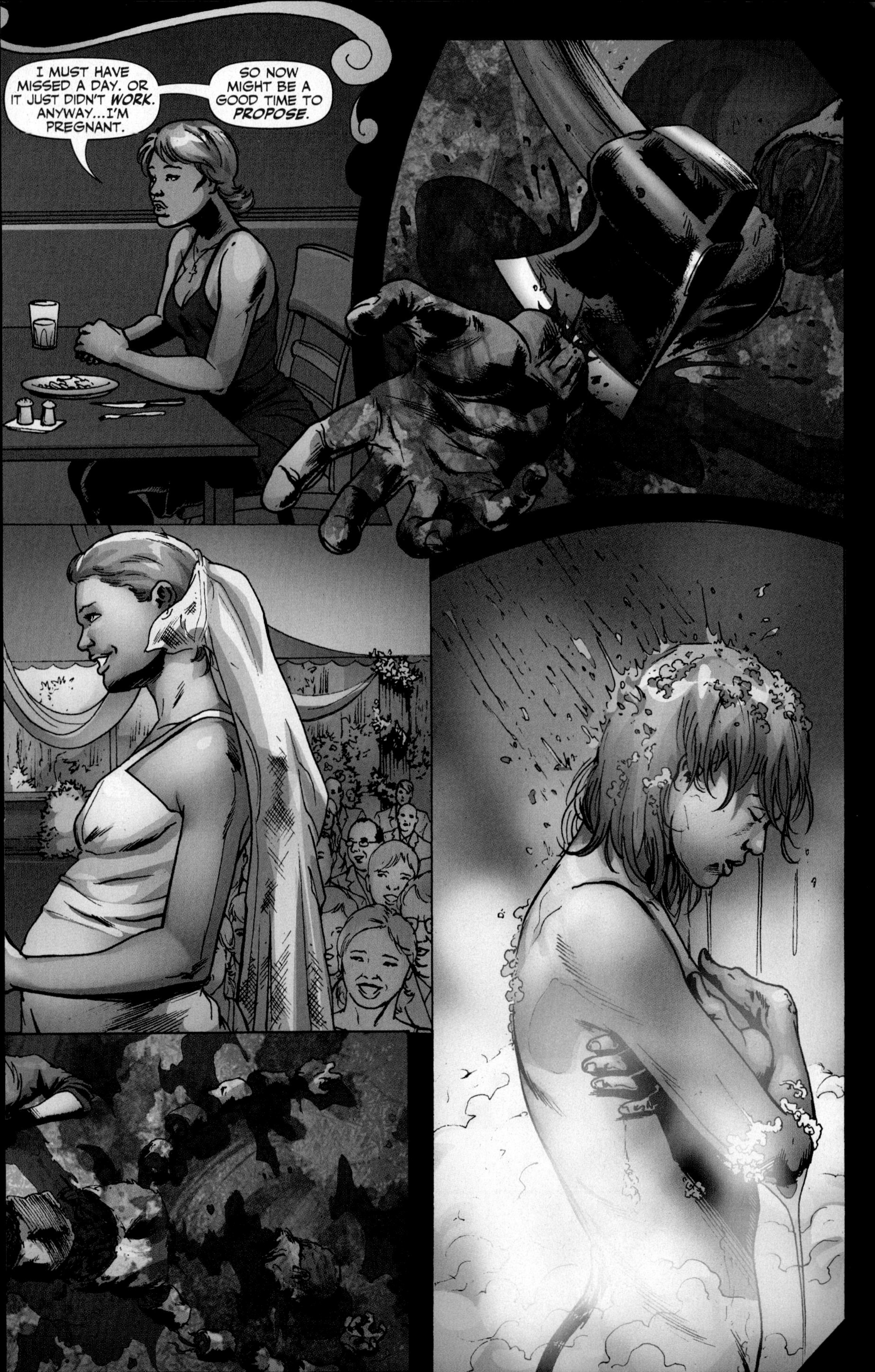

I MUST HAVE MISSED A DAY. OR IT JUST DIDN'T *WORK*. ANYWAY...I'M PREGNANT.
SO NOW MIGHT BE A GOOD TIME TO *PROPOSE*.

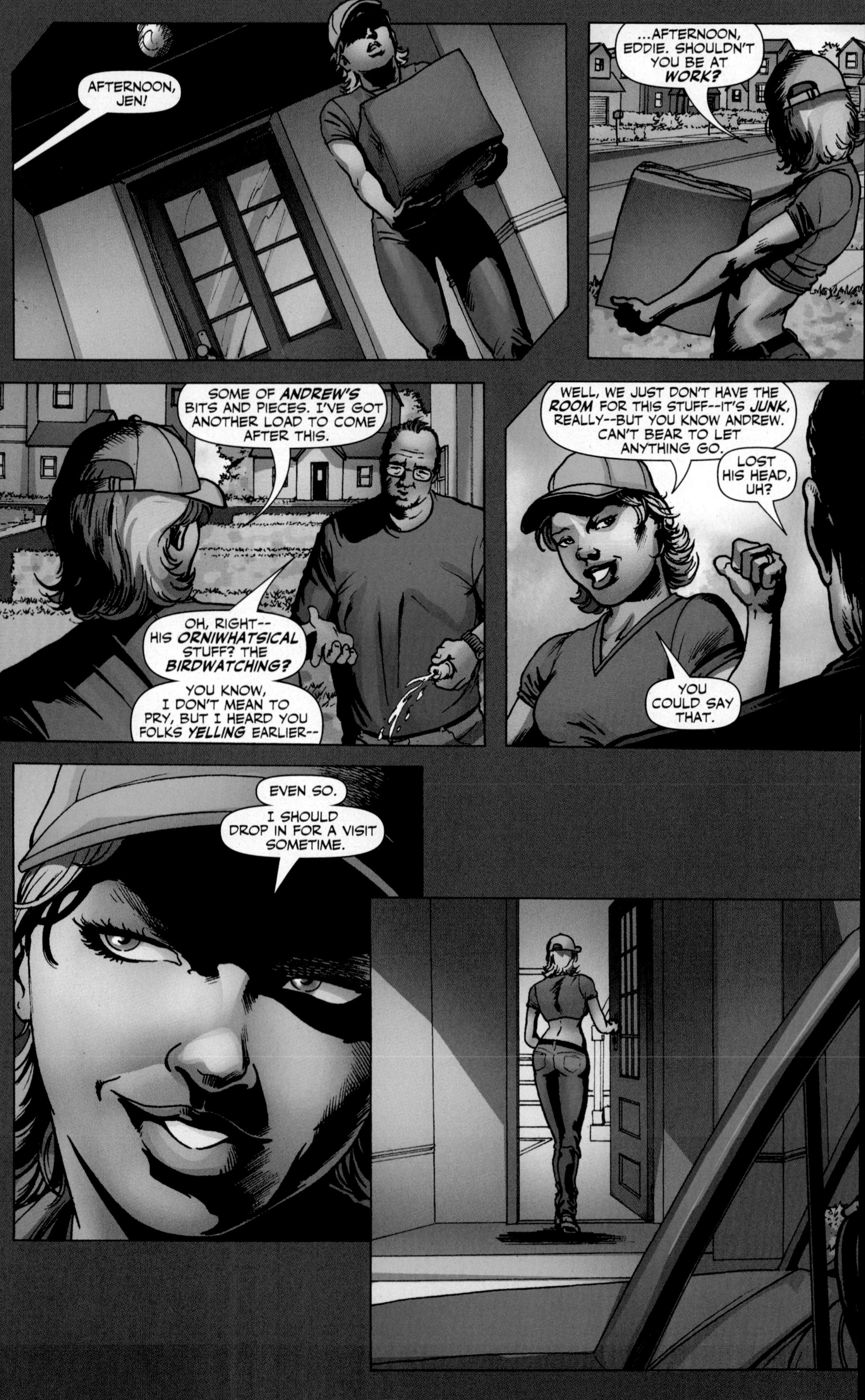
AFTERNOON, JEN!
...AFTERNOON, EDDIE. SHOULDN'T YOU BE AT WORK?
SOME OF ANDREW'S BITS AND PIECES. I'VE GOT ANOTHER LOAD TO COME AFTER THIS.
OH, RIGHT-- HIS ORNIWHATSICAL STUFF? THE BIRDWATCHING?
YOU KNOW, I DON'T MEAN TO PRY, BUT I HEARD YOU FOLKS YELLING EARLIER--
WELL, WE JUST DON'T HAVE THE ROOM FOR THIS STUFF--IT'S JUNK, REALLY--BUT YOU KNOW ANDREW. CAN'T BEAR TO LET ANYTHING GO.
LOST HIS HEAD, UH?
YOU COULD SAY THAT.
EVEN SO.
I SHOULD DROP IN FOR A VISIT SOMETIME.

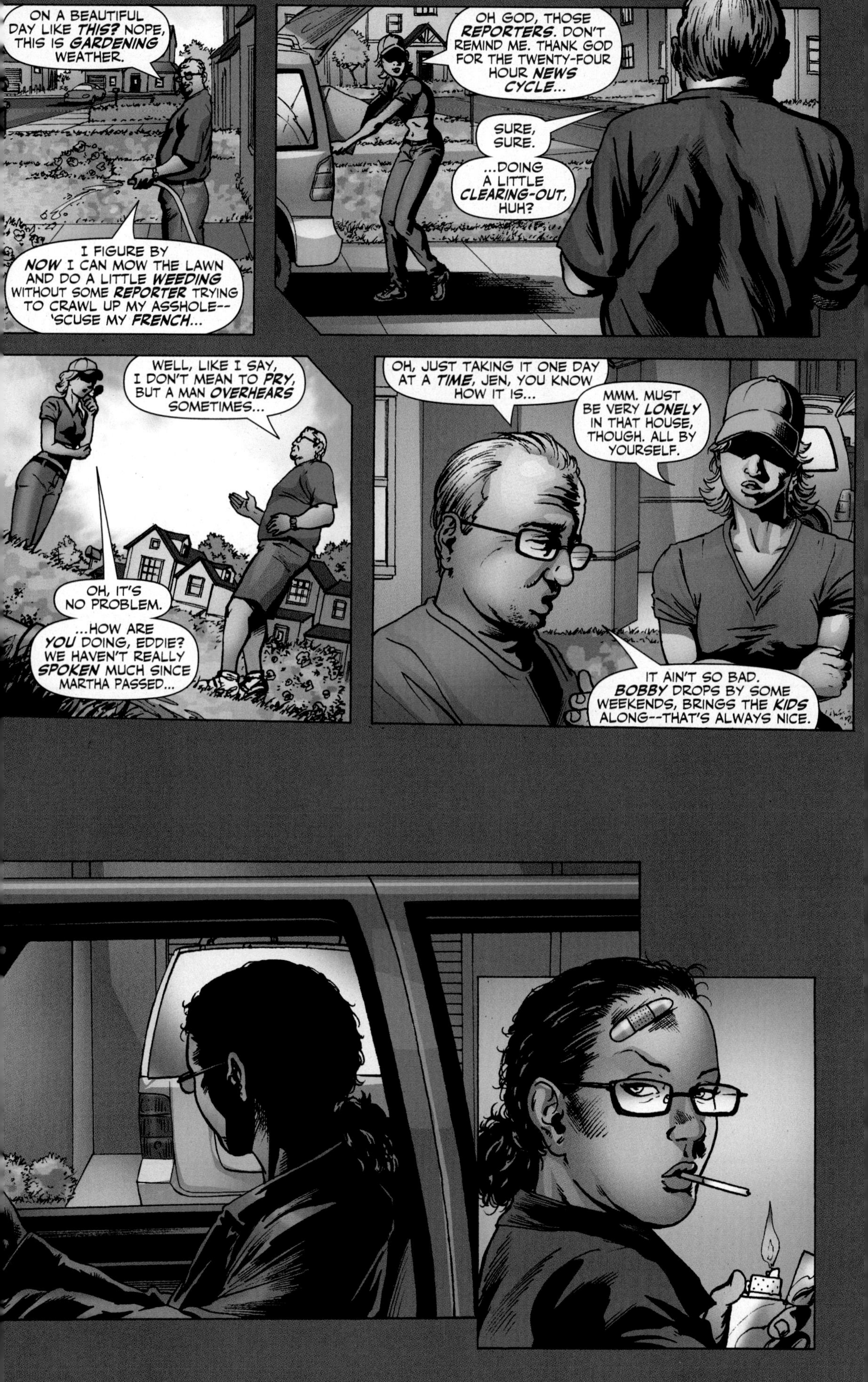

ON A BEAUTIFUL DAY LIKE THIS? NOPE, THIS IS GARDENING WEATHER.
I FIGURE BY NOW I CAN MOW THE LAWN AND DO A LITTLE WEEDING WITHOUT SOME REPORTER TRYING TO CRAWL UP MY ASSHOLE-- 'SCUSE MY FRENCH...
OH GOD, THOSE REPORTERS. DON'T REMIND ME. THANK GOD FOR THE TWENTY-FOUR HOUR NEWS CYCLE...
SURE, SURE.
...DOING A LITTLE CLEARING-OUT, HUH?
WELL, LIKE I SAY, I DON'T MEAN TO PRY, BUT A MAN OVERHEARS SOMETIMES...
OH, IT'S NO PROBLEM.
...HOW ARE YOU DOING, EDDIE? WE HAVEN'T REALLY SPOKEN MUCH SINCE MARTHA PASSED...
OH, JUST TAKING IT ONE DAY AT A TIME, JEN, YOU KNOW HOW IT IS...
MMM. MUST BE VERY LONELY IN THAT HOUSE, THOUGH. ALL BY YOURSELF.
IT AIN'T SO BAD. BOBBY DROPS BY SOME WEEKENDS, BRINGS THE KIDS ALONG--THAT'S ALWAYS NICE.

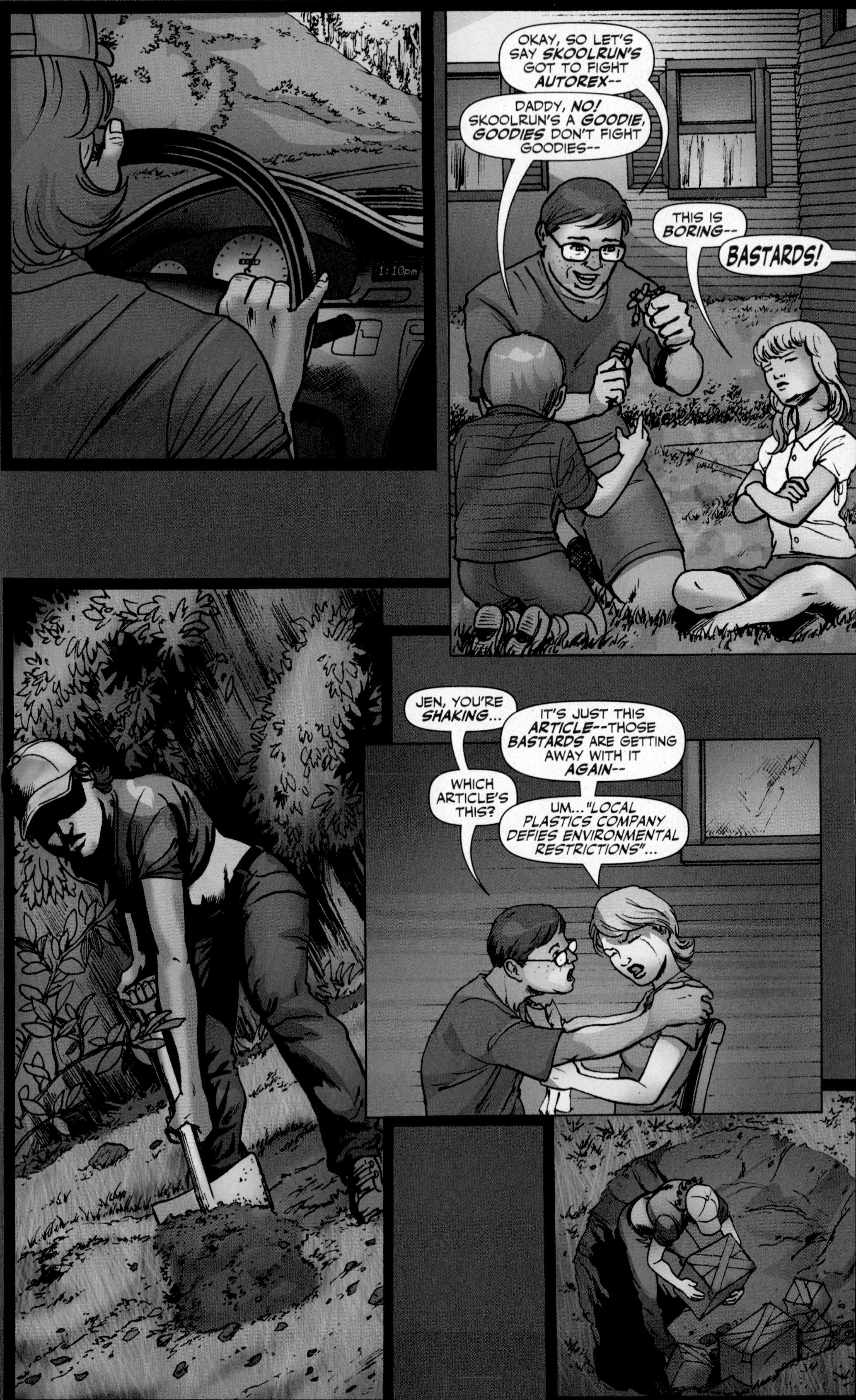
1:10pm
OKAY, SO LET'S SAY SKOOLRUN'S GOT TO FIGHT AUTOREX--
DADDY, NO! SKOOLRUN'S A GOODIE, GOODIES DON'T FIGHT GOODIES--
THIS IS BORING--
BASTARDS!
JEN, YOU'RE SHAKING...
IT'S JUST THIS ARTICLE--THOSE BASTARDS ARE GETTING AWAY WITH IT AGAIN--
WHICH ARTICLE'S THIS?
UM..."LOCAL PLASTICS COMPANY DEFIES ENVIRONMENTAL RESTRICTIONS"...

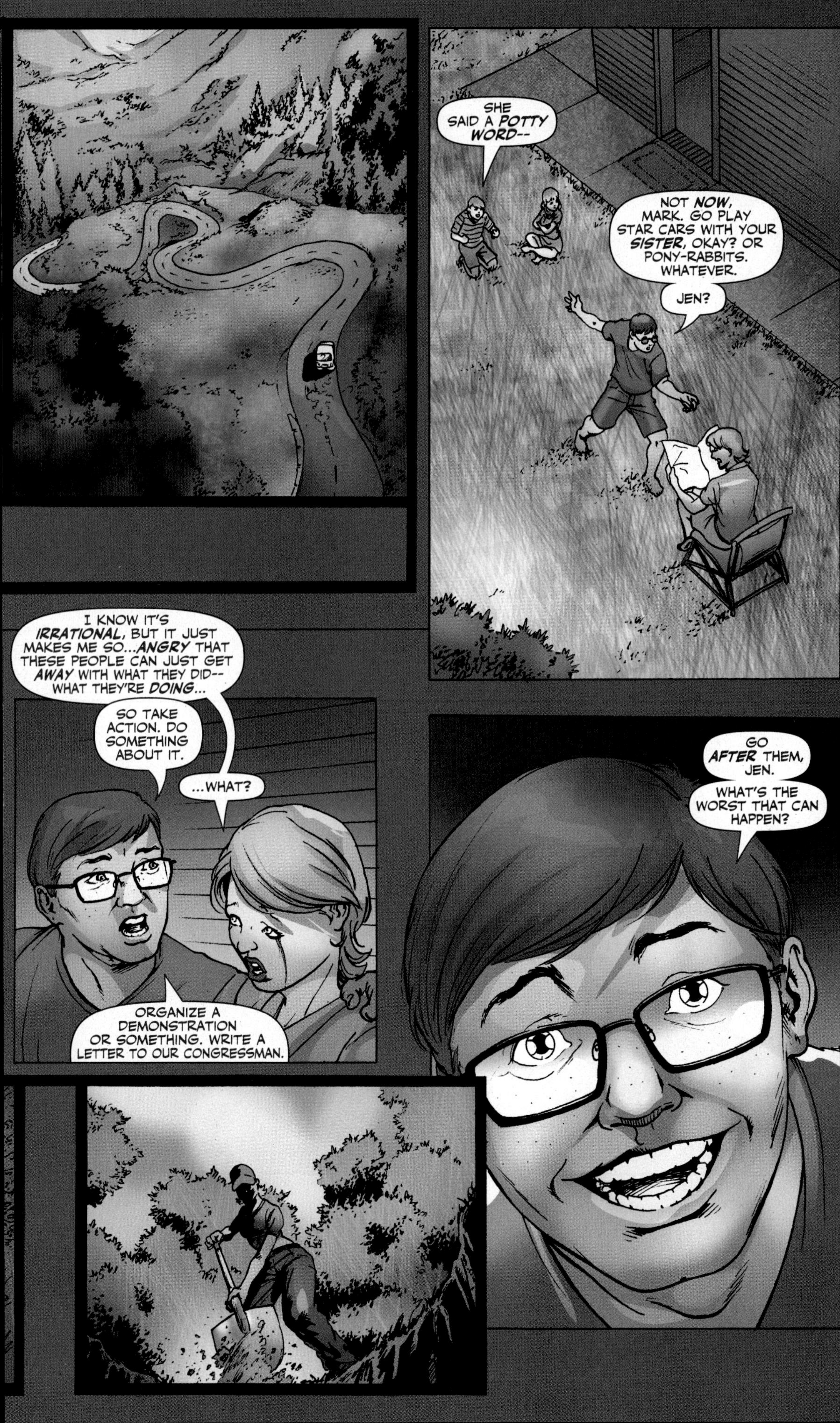
SHE SAID A POTTY WORD--
NOT NOW, MARK. GO PLAY STAR CARS WITH YOUR SISTER, OKAY? OR PONY-RABBITS. WHATEVER.
JEN?
I KNOW IT'S IRRATIONAL, BUT IT JUST MAKES ME SO...ANGRY THAT THESE PEOPLE CAN JUST GET AWAY WITH WHAT THEY DID-- WHAT THEY'RE DOING...
SO TAKE ACTION. DO SOMETHING ABOUT IT.
...WHAT?
ORGANIZE A DEMONSTRATION OR SOMETHING. WRITE A LETTER TO OUR CONGRESSMAN.
GO AFTER THEM, JEN.
WHAT'S THE WORST THAT CAN HAPPEN?

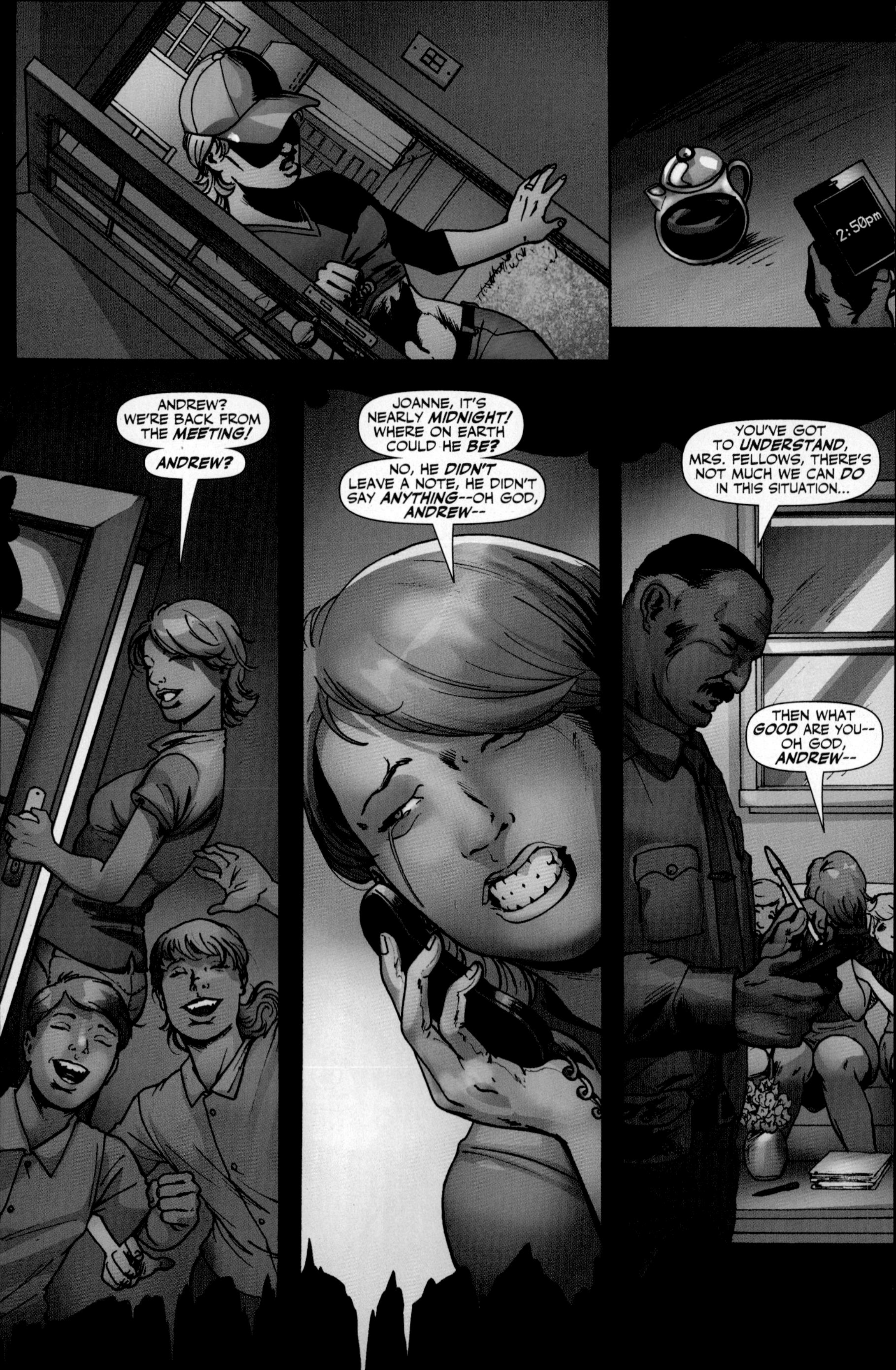
2:50pm
ANDREW? WE'RE BACK FROM THE *MEETING!*
ANDREW?
JOANNE, IT'S NEARLY *MIDNIGHT!* WHERE ON EARTH COULD HE *BE?*
NO, HE *DIDN'T* LEAVE A NOTE, HE DIDN'T SAY *ANYTHING*--OH GOD, *ANDREW*--
YOU'VE GOT TO *UNDERSTAND*, MRS. FELLOWS, THERE'S NOT MUCH WE CAN *DO* IN THIS SITUATION...
THEN WHAT *GOOD* ARE YOU--OH GOD, *ANDREW*--

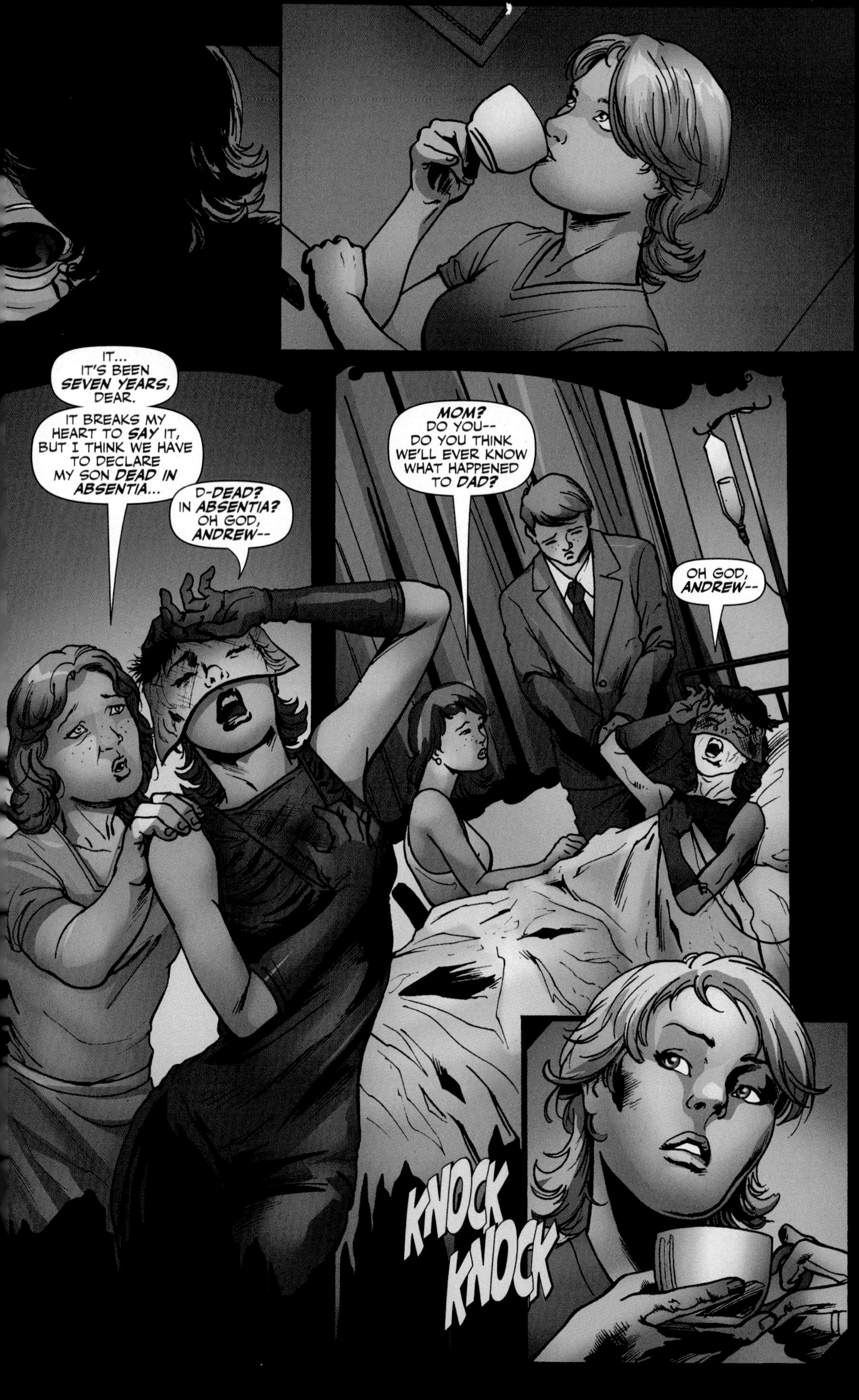

IT... IT'S BEEN SEVEN YEARS, DEAR.
IT BREAKS MY HEART TO SAY IT, BUT I THINK WE HAVE TO DECLARE MY SON DEAD IN ABSENTIA...
D-DEAD? IN ABSENTIA? OH GOD, ANDREW--
MOM? DO YOU-- DO YOU THINK WE'LL EVER KNOW WHAT HAPPENED TO DAD?
OH GOD, ANDREW--
KNOCK KNOCK

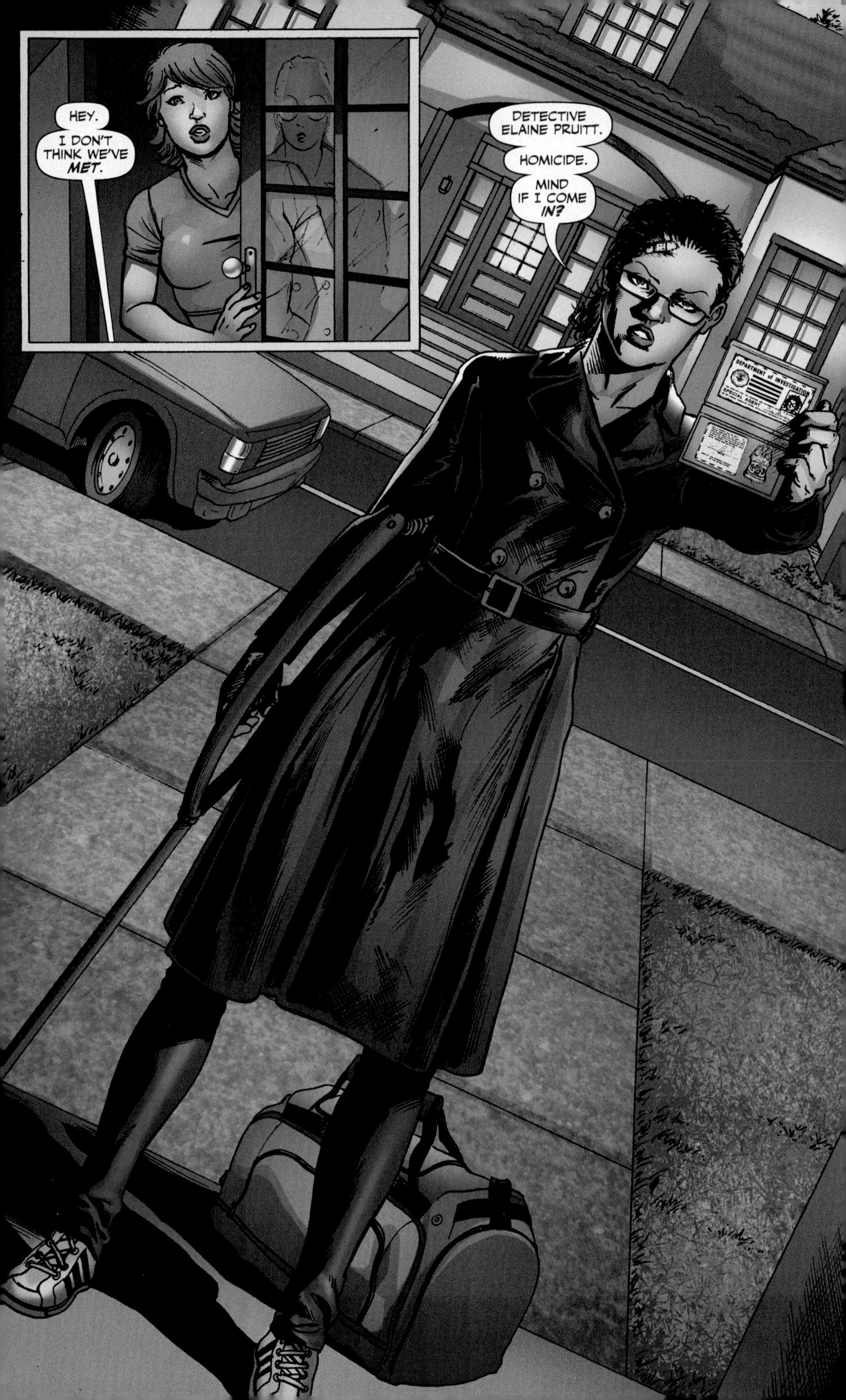
HEY.
I DON'T THINK WE'VE MET.
DETECTIVE ELAINE PRUITT.
HOMICIDE.
MIND IF I COME IN?
DEPARTMENT of INVESTIGATION
SPECIAL AGENT

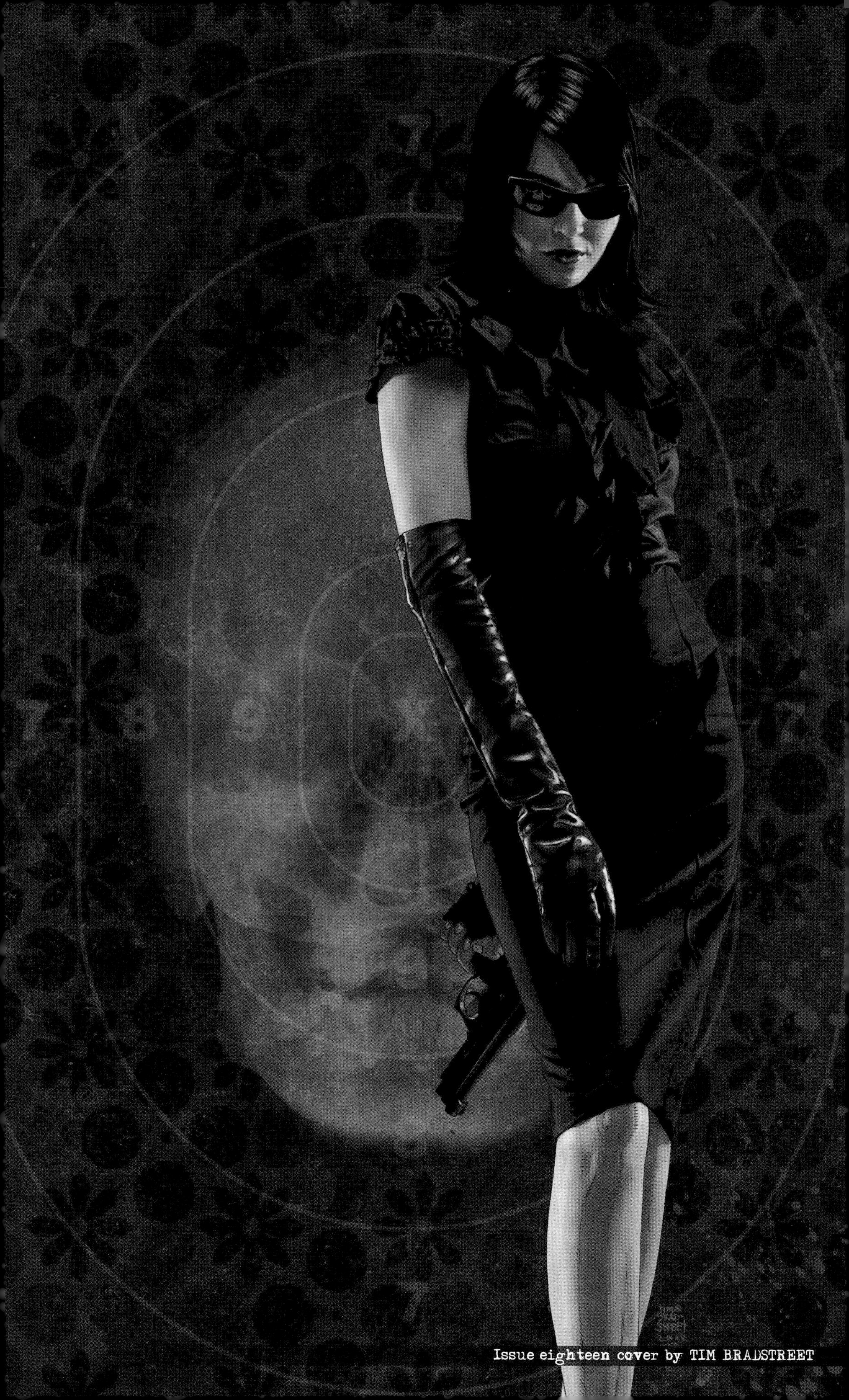

Issue eighteen cover by TIM BRADSTREET

18: TUESDAY, PART THREE - THE KNIVES AND FISTS OF A THIEVES' KITCHEN

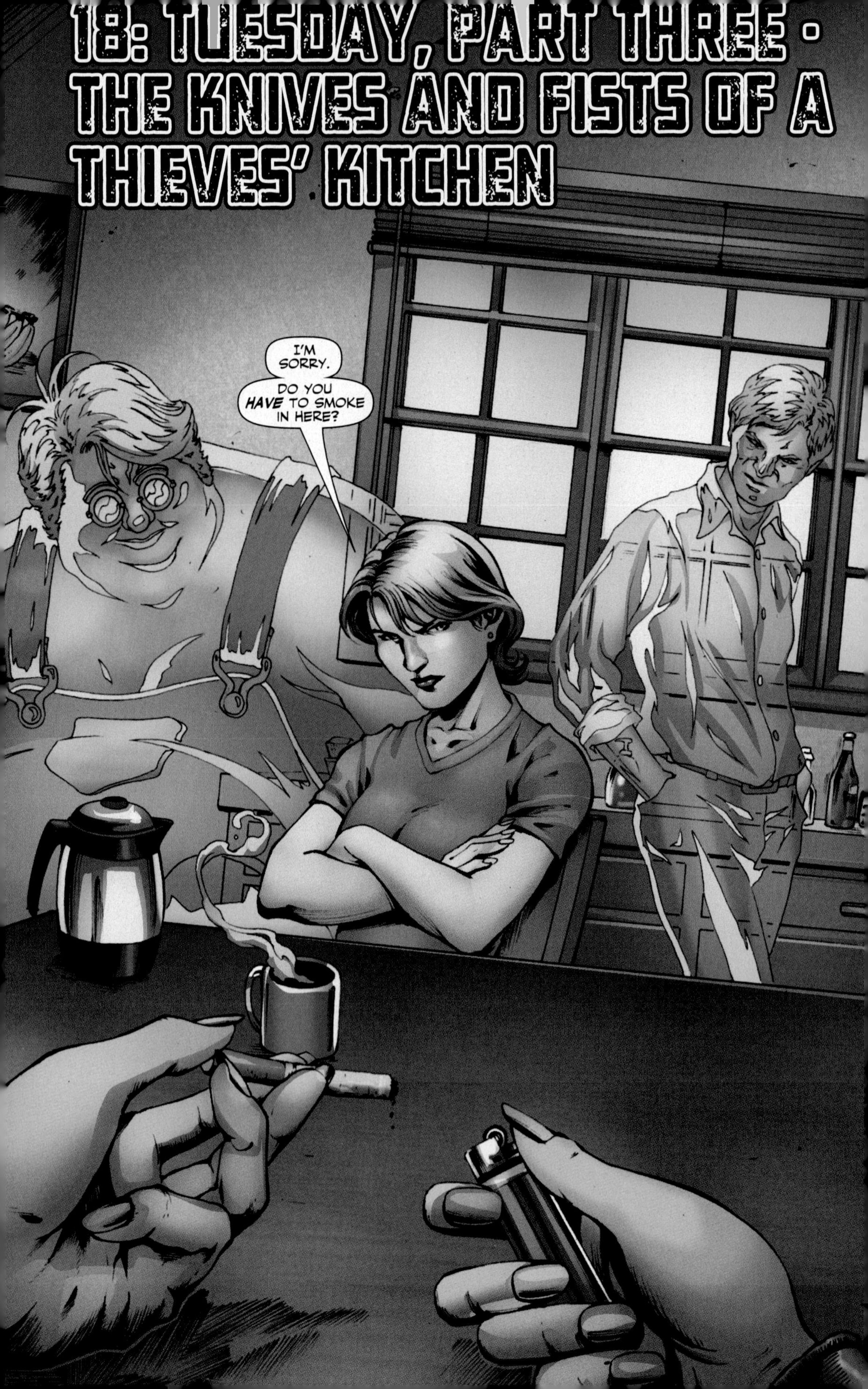
I'M SORRY.
DO YOU *HAVE* TO SMOKE IN HERE?

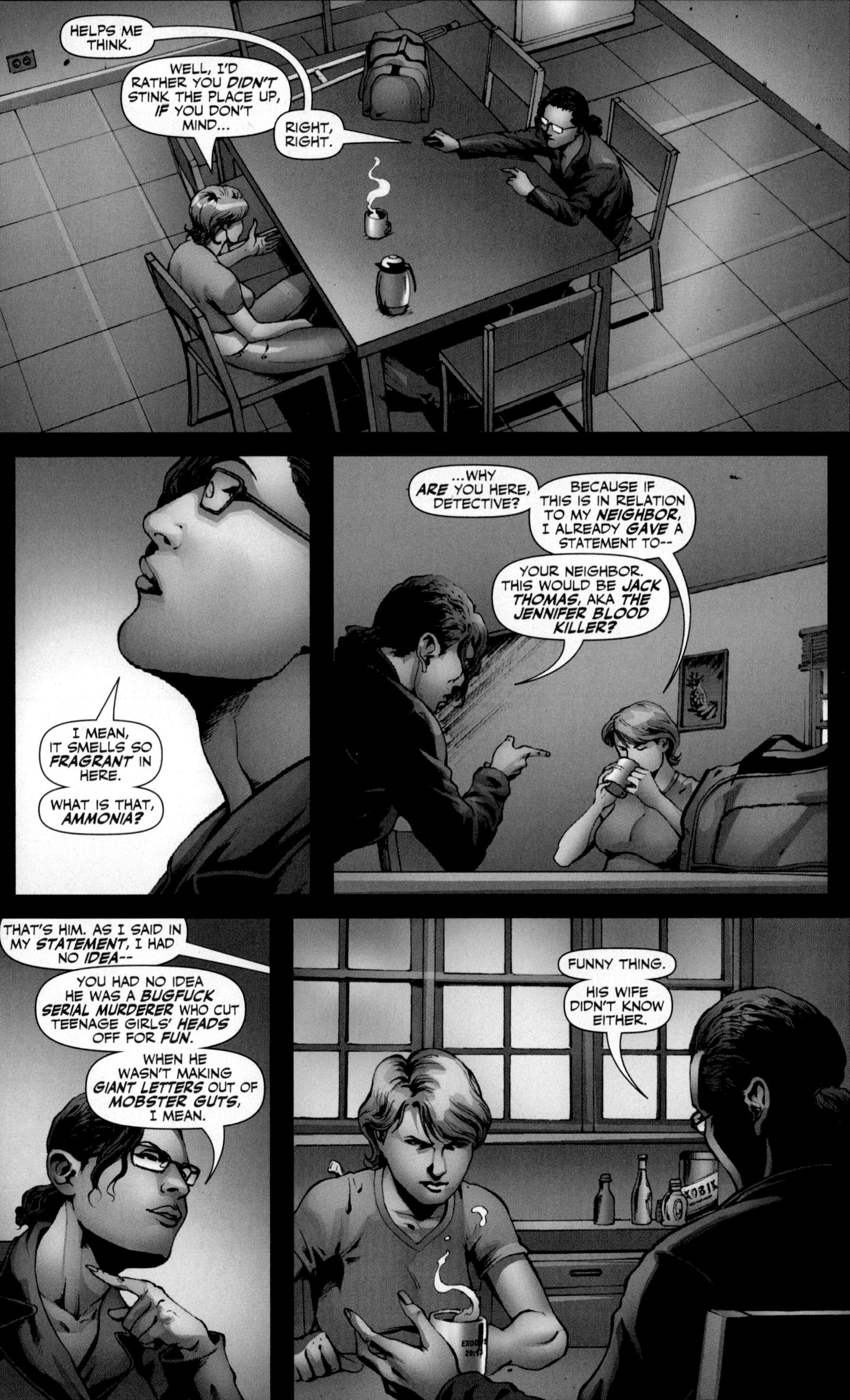
HELPS ME THINK.
WELL, I'D RATHER YOU DIDN'T STINK THE PLACE UP, IF YOU DON'T MIND...
RIGHT, RIGHT.
I MEAN, IT SMELLS SO FRAGRANT IN HERE.
WHAT IS THAT, AMMONIA?
...WHY ARE YOU HERE, DETECTIVE?
BECAUSE IF THIS IS IN RELATION TO MY NEIGHBOR, I ALREADY GAVE A STATEMENT TO--
YOUR NEIGHBOR. THIS WOULD BE JACK THOMAS, AKA THE JENNIFER BLOOD KILLER?
THAT'S HIM. AS I SAID IN MY STATEMENT, I HAD NO IDEA--
YOU HAD NO IDEA HE WAS A BUGFUCK SERIAL MURDERER WHO CUT TEENAGE GIRLS' HEADS OFF FOR FUN.
WHEN HE WASN'T MAKING GIANT LETTERS OUT OF MOBSTER GUTS, I MEAN.
FUNNY THING.
HIS WIFE DIDN'T KNOW EITHER.

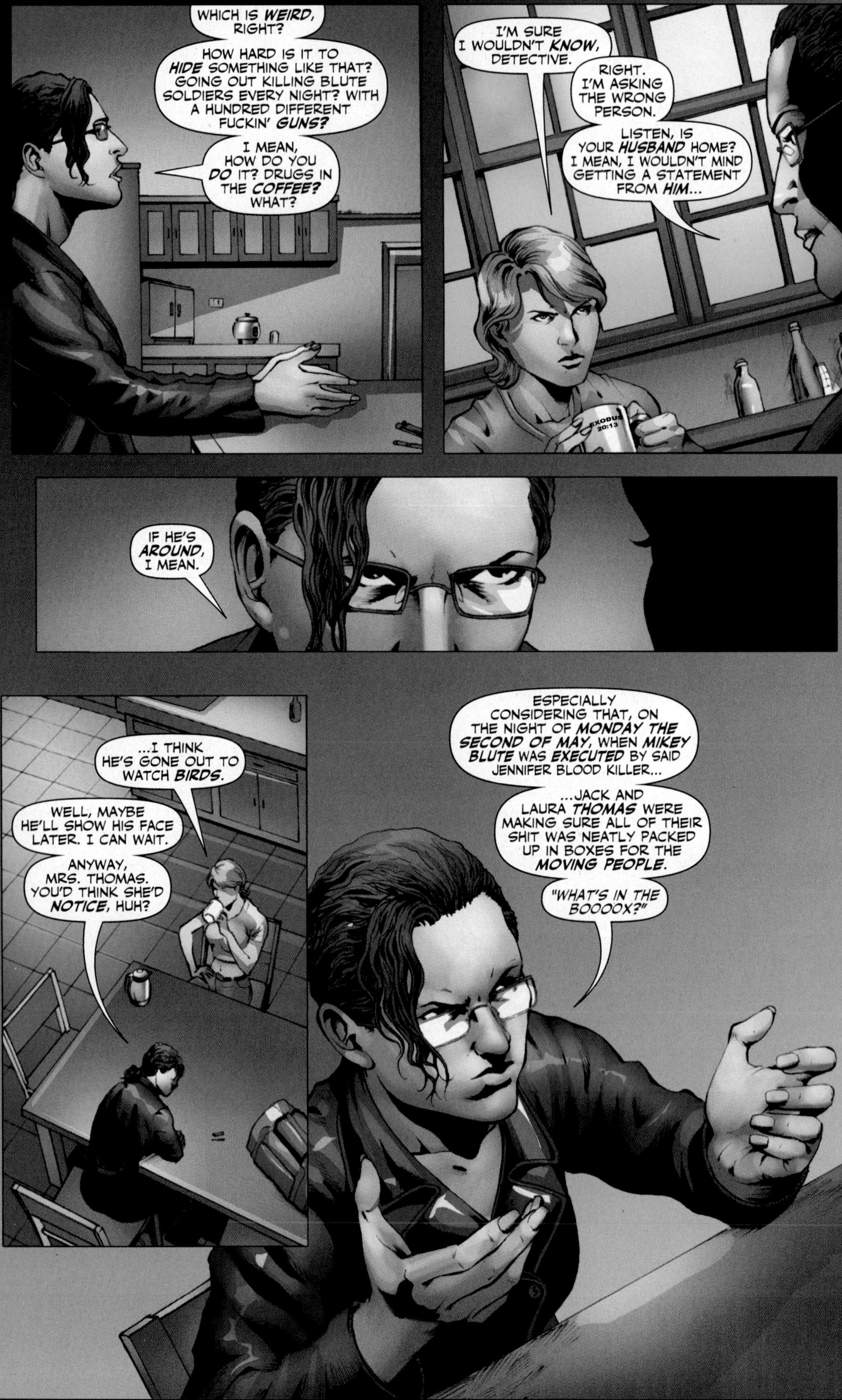
WHICH IS WEIRD, RIGHT?
HOW HARD IS IT TO HIDE SOMETHING LIKE THAT? GOING OUT KILLING BLUTE SOLDIERS EVERY NIGHT? WITH A HUNDRED DIFFERENT FUCKIN' GUNS?
I MEAN, HOW DO YOU DO IT? DRUGS IN THE COFFEE? WHAT?
I'M SURE I WOULDN'T KNOW, DETECTIVE.
RIGHT. I'M ASKING THE WRONG PERSON.
LISTEN, IS YOUR HUSBAND HOME? I MEAN, I WOULDN'T MIND GETTING A STATEMENT FROM HIM...
EXODUS 20:13
IF HE'S AROUND, I MEAN.
...I THINK HE'S GONE OUT TO WATCH BIRDS.
WELL, MAYBE HE'LL SHOW HIS FACE LATER. I CAN WAIT.
ANYWAY, MRS. THOMAS. YOU'D THINK SHE'D NOTICE, HUH?
ESPECIALLY CONSIDERING THAT, ON THE NIGHT OF MONDAY THE SECOND OF MAY, WHEN MIKEY BLUTE WAS EXECUTED BY SAID JENNIFER BLOOD KILLER...
...JACK AND LAURA THOMAS WERE MAKING SURE ALL OF THEIR SHIT WAS NEATLY PACKED UP IN BOXES FOR THE MOVING PEOPLE.
"WHAT'S IN THE BOOOOX?"

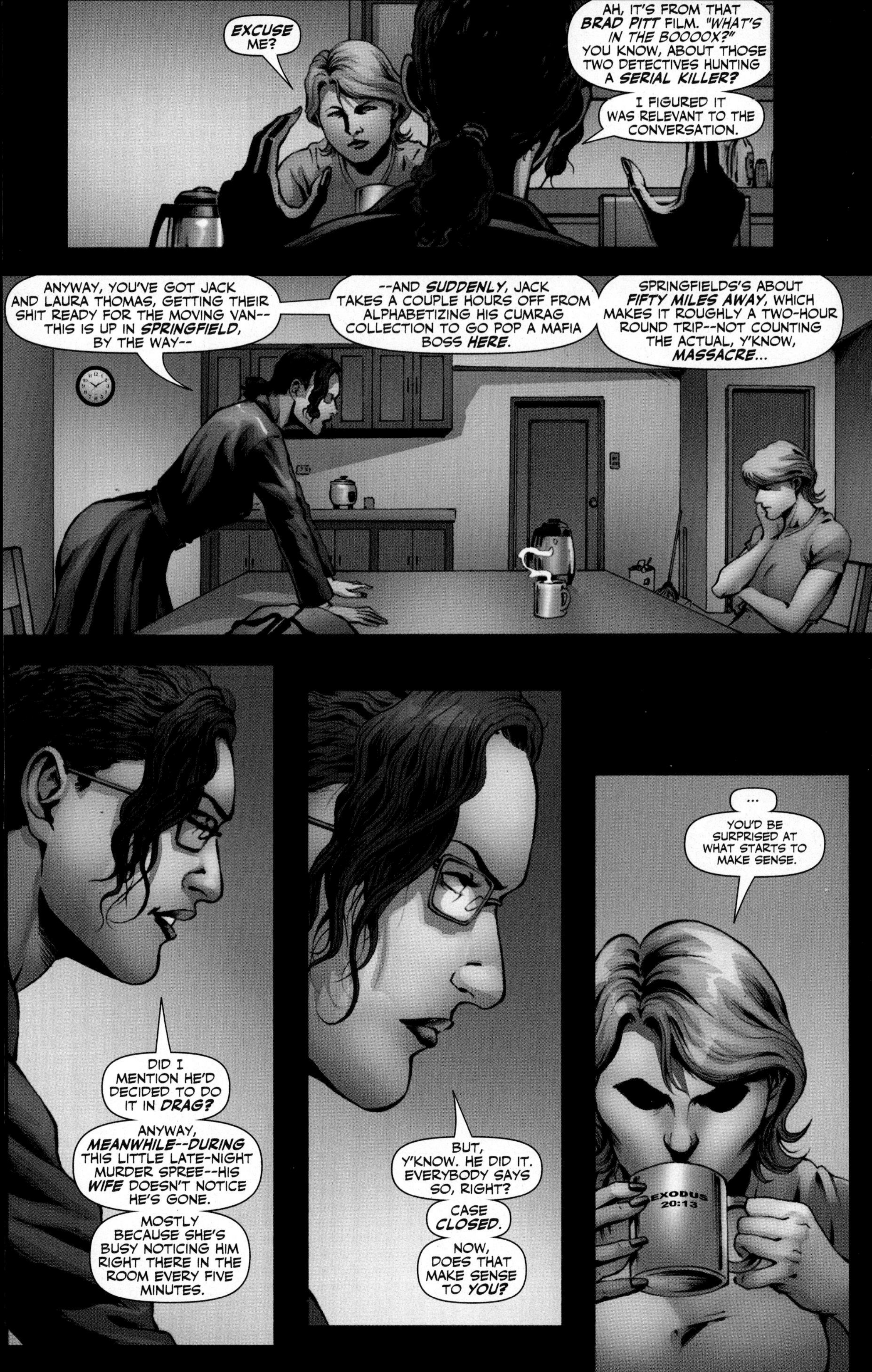
EXCUSE ME?
AH, IT'S FROM THAT BRAD PITT FILM. "WHAT'S IN THE BOOOOX?" YOU KNOW, ABOUT THOSE TWO DETECTIVES HUNTING A SERIAL KILLER?
I FIGURED IT WAS RELEVANT TO THE CONVERSATION.
ANYWAY, YOU'VE GOT JACK AND LAURA THOMAS, GETTING THEIR SHIT READY FOR THE MOVING VAN-- THIS IS UP IN SPRINGFIELD, BY THE WAY--
--AND SUDDENLY, JACK TAKES A COUPLE HOURS OFF FROM ALPHABETIZING HIS CUMRAG COLLECTION TO GO POP A MAFIA BOSS HERE.
SPRINGFIELDS'S ABOUT FIFTY MILES AWAY, WHICH MAKES IT ROUGHLY A TWO-HOUR ROUND TRIP--NOT COUNTING THE ACTUAL, Y'KNOW, MASSACRE...
DID I MENTION HE'D DECIDED TO DO IT IN DRAG?
ANYWAY, MEANWHILE--DURING THIS LITTLE LATE-NIGHT MURDER SPREE--HIS WIFE DOESN'T NOTICE HE'S GONE.
MOSTLY BECAUSE SHE'S BUSY NOTICING HIM RIGHT THERE IN THE ROOM EVERY FIVE MINUTES.
BUT, Y'KNOW. HE DID IT. EVERYBODY SAYS SO, RIGHT?
CASE CLOSED.
NOW, DOES THAT MAKE SENSE TO YOU?
...
YOU'D BE SURPRISED AT WHAT STARTS TO MAKE SENSE.
EXODUS 20:13

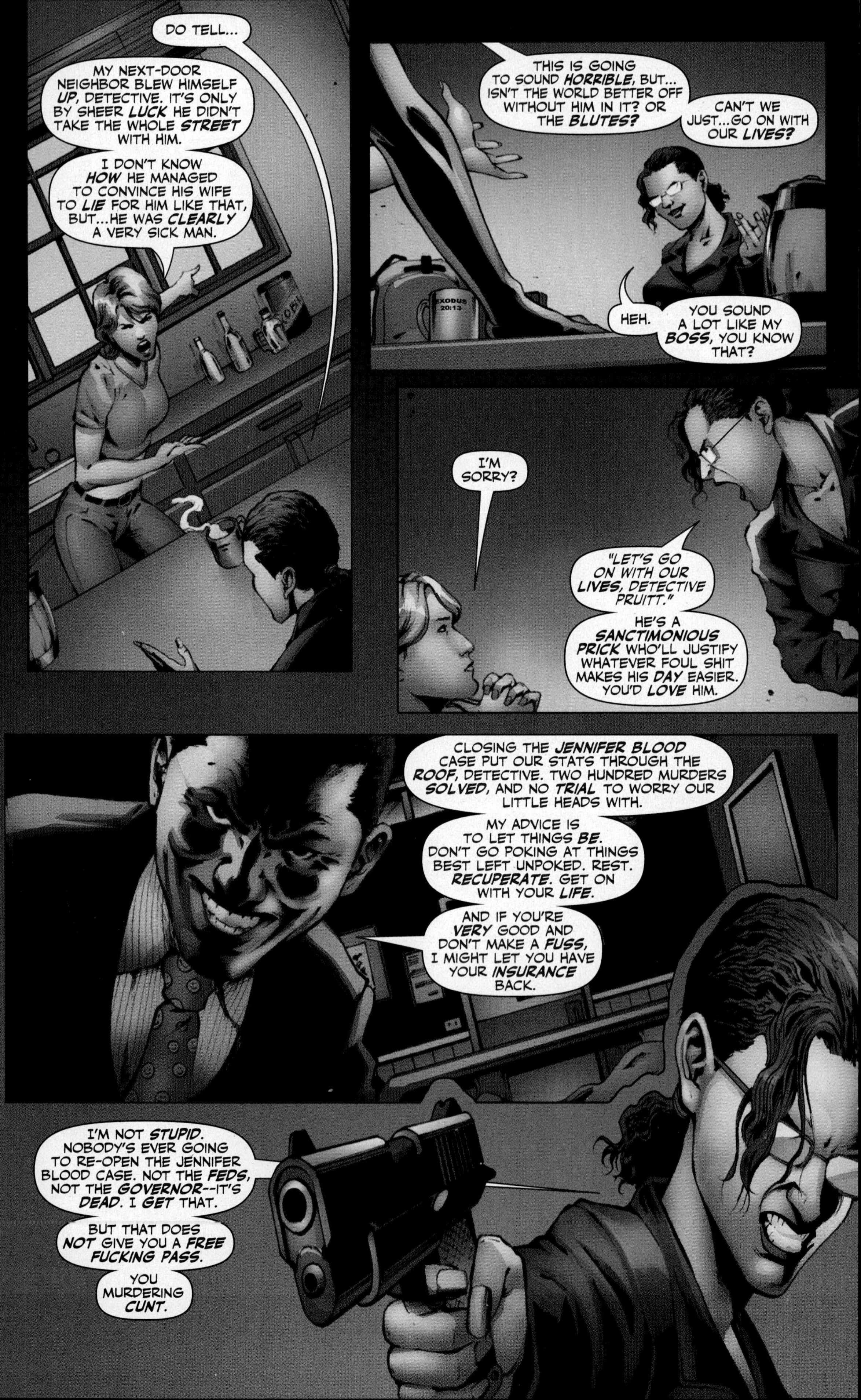
DO TELL...
MY NEXT-DOOR NEIGHBOR BLEW HIMSELF UP, DETECTIVE. IT'S ONLY BY SHEER LUCK HE DIDN'T TAKE THE WHOLE STREET WITH HIM.
I DON'T KNOW HOW HE MANAGED TO CONVINCE HIS WIFE TO LIE FOR HIM LIKE THAT, BUT...HE WAS CLEARLY A VERY SICK MAN.
THIS IS GOING TO SOUND HORRIBLE, BUT... ISN'T THE WORLD BETTER OFF WITHOUT HIM IN IT? OR THE BLUTES?
CAN'T WE JUST...GO ON WITH OUR LIVES?
EXODUS 20:13
HEH.
YOU SOUND A LOT LIKE MY BOSS, YOU KNOW THAT?
I'M SORRY?
"LET'S GO ON WITH OUR LIVES, DETECTIVE PRUITT."
HE'S A SANCTIMONIOUS PRICK WHO'LL JUSTIFY WHATEVER FOUL SHIT MAKES HIS DAY EASIER. YOU'D LOVE HIM.
CLOSING THE JENNIFER BLOOD CASE PUT OUR STATS THROUGH THE ROOF, DETECTIVE. TWO HUNDRED MURDERS SOLVED, AND NO TRIAL TO WORRY OUR LITTLE HEADS WITH.
MY ADVICE IS TO LET THINGS BE. DON'T GO POKING AT THINGS BEST LEFT UNPOKED. REST. RECUPERATE. GET ON WITH YOUR LIFE.
AND IF YOU'RE VERY GOOD AND DON'T MAKE A FUSS, I MIGHT LET YOU HAVE YOUR INSURANCE BACK.
I'M NOT STUPID. NOBODY'S EVER GOING TO RE-OPEN THE JENNIFER BLOOD CASE. NOT THE FEDS, NOT THE GOVERNOR--IT'S DEAD. I GET THAT.
BUT THAT DOES NOT GIVE YOU A FREE FUCKING PASS.
YOU MURDERING CUNT.

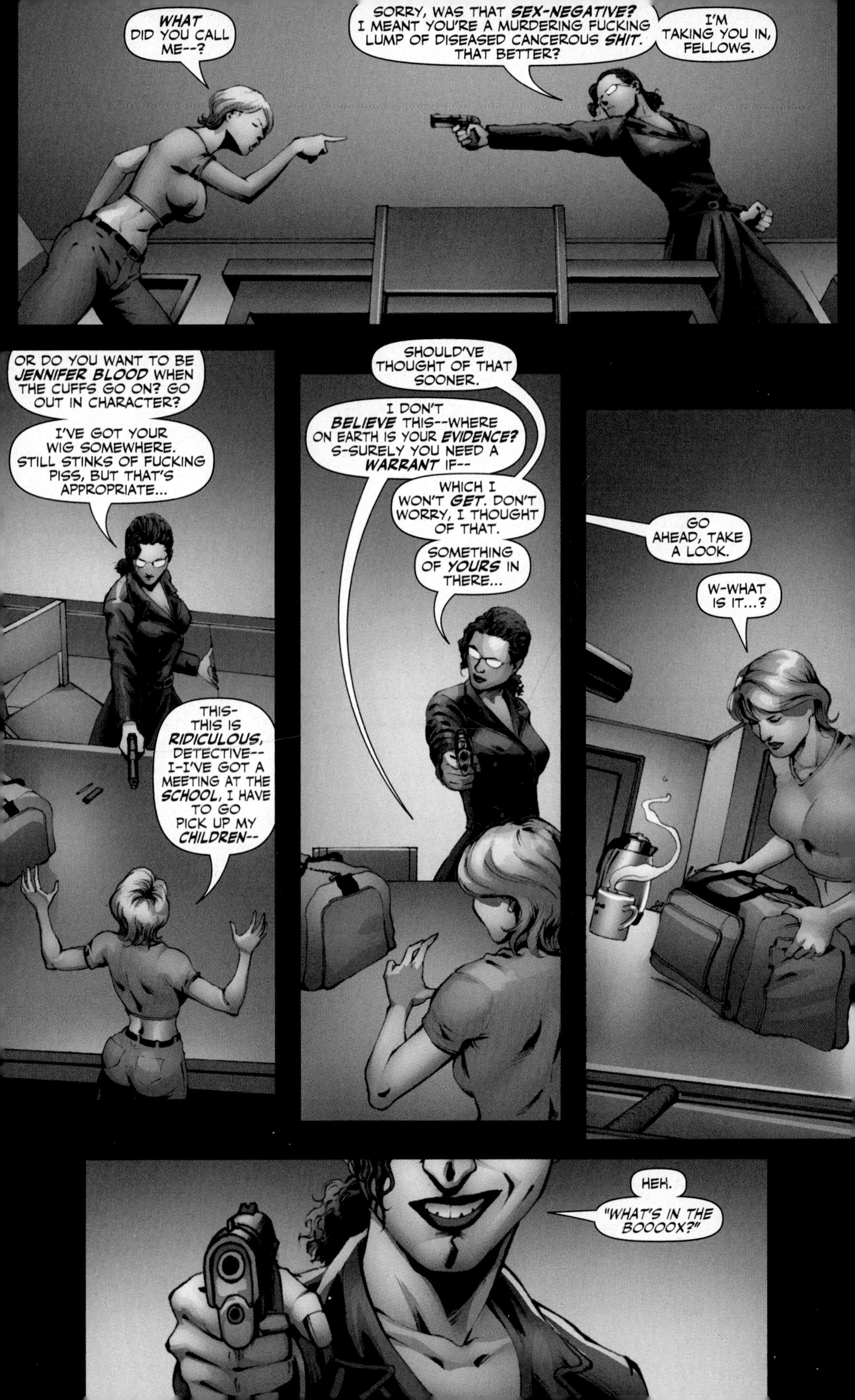
WHAT DID YOU CALL ME--?
SORRY, WAS THAT SEX-NEGATIVE? I MEANT YOU'RE A MURDERING FUCKING LUMP OF DISEASED CANCEROUS SHIT. THAT BETTER?
I'M TAKING YOU IN, FELLOWS.
OR DO YOU WANT TO BE JENNIFER BLOOD WHEN THE CUFFS GO ON? GO OUT IN CHARACTER?
I'VE GOT YOUR WIG SOMEWHERE. STILL STINKS OF FUCKING PISS, BUT THAT'S APPROPRIATE...
THIS- THIS IS RIDICULOUS, DETECTIVE-- I-I'VE GOT A MEETING AT THE SCHOOL, I HAVE TO GO PICK UP MY CHILDREN--
SHOULD'VE THOUGHT OF THAT SOONER.
I DON'T BELIEVE THIS--WHERE ON EARTH IS YOUR EVIDENCE? S-SURELY YOU NEED A WARRANT IF--
WHICH I WON'T GET. DON'T WORRY, I THOUGHT OF THAT.
SOMETHING OF YOURS IN THERE...
GO AHEAD, TAKE A LOOK.
W-WHAT IS IT...?
HEH.
"WHAT'S IN THE BOOOOX?"

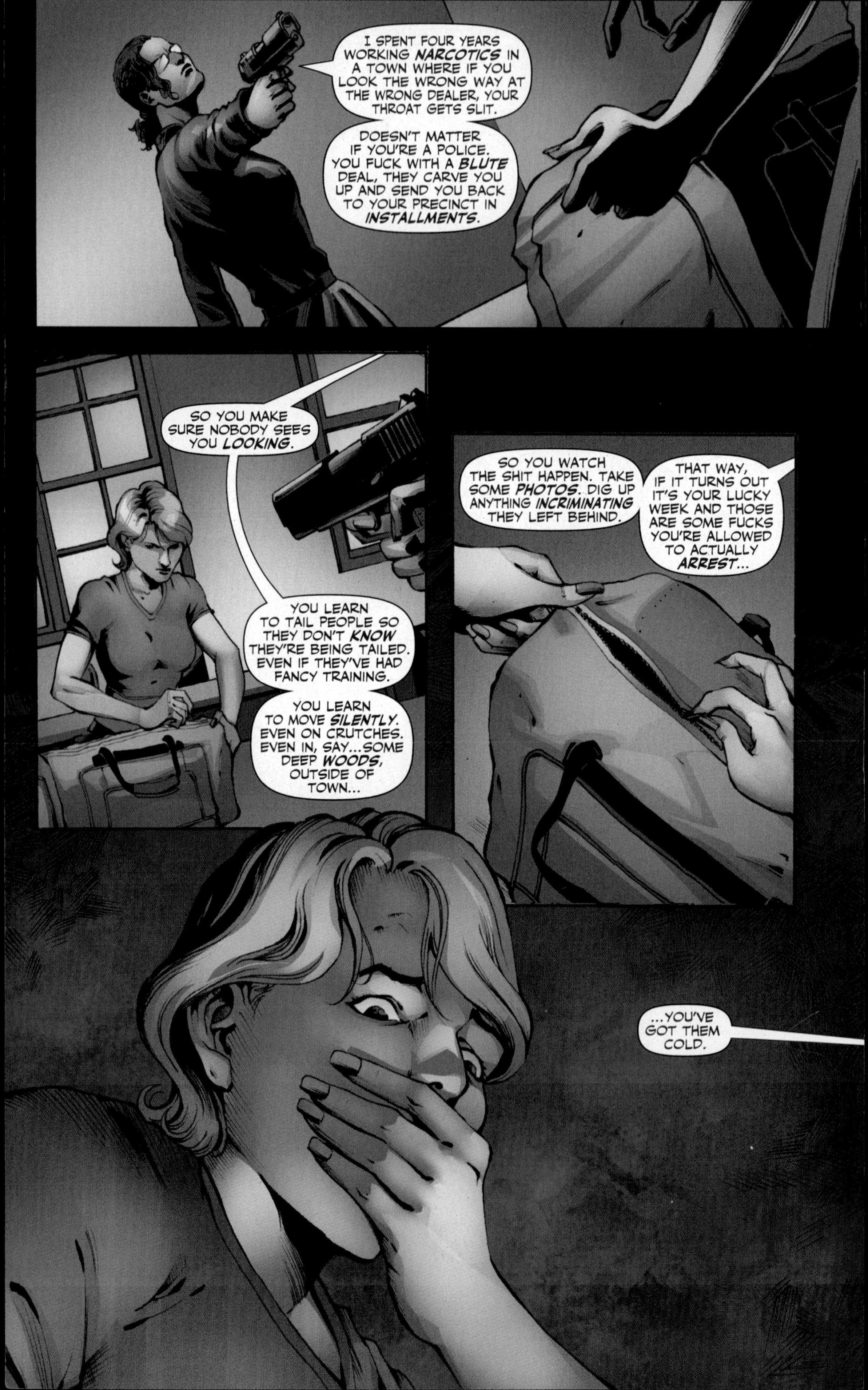
I SPENT FOUR YEARS WORKING NARCOTICS IN A TOWN WHERE IF YOU LOOK THE WRONG WAY AT THE WRONG DEALER, YOUR THROAT GETS SLIT.
DOESN'T MATTER IF YOU'RE A POLICE. YOU FUCK WITH A BLUTE DEAL, THEY CARVE YOU UP AND SEND YOU BACK TO YOUR PRECINCT IN INSTALLMENTS.
SO YOU MAKE SURE NOBODY SEES YOU LOOKING.
YOU LEARN TO TAIL PEOPLE SO THEY DON'T KNOW THEY'RE BEING TAILED. EVEN IF THEY'VE HAD FANCY TRAINING.
YOU LEARN TO MOVE SILENTLY. EVEN ON CRUTCHES. EVEN IN, SAY...SOME DEEP WOODS, OUTSIDE OF TOWN...
SO YOU WATCH THE SHIT HAPPEN. TAKE SOME PHOTOS. DIG UP ANYTHING INCRIMINATING THEY LEFT BEHIND.
THAT WAY, IF IT TURNS OUT IT'S YOUR LUCKY WEEK AND THOSE ARE SOME FUCKS YOU'RE ALLOWED TO ACTUALLY ARREST...
...YOU'VE GOT THEM COLD.

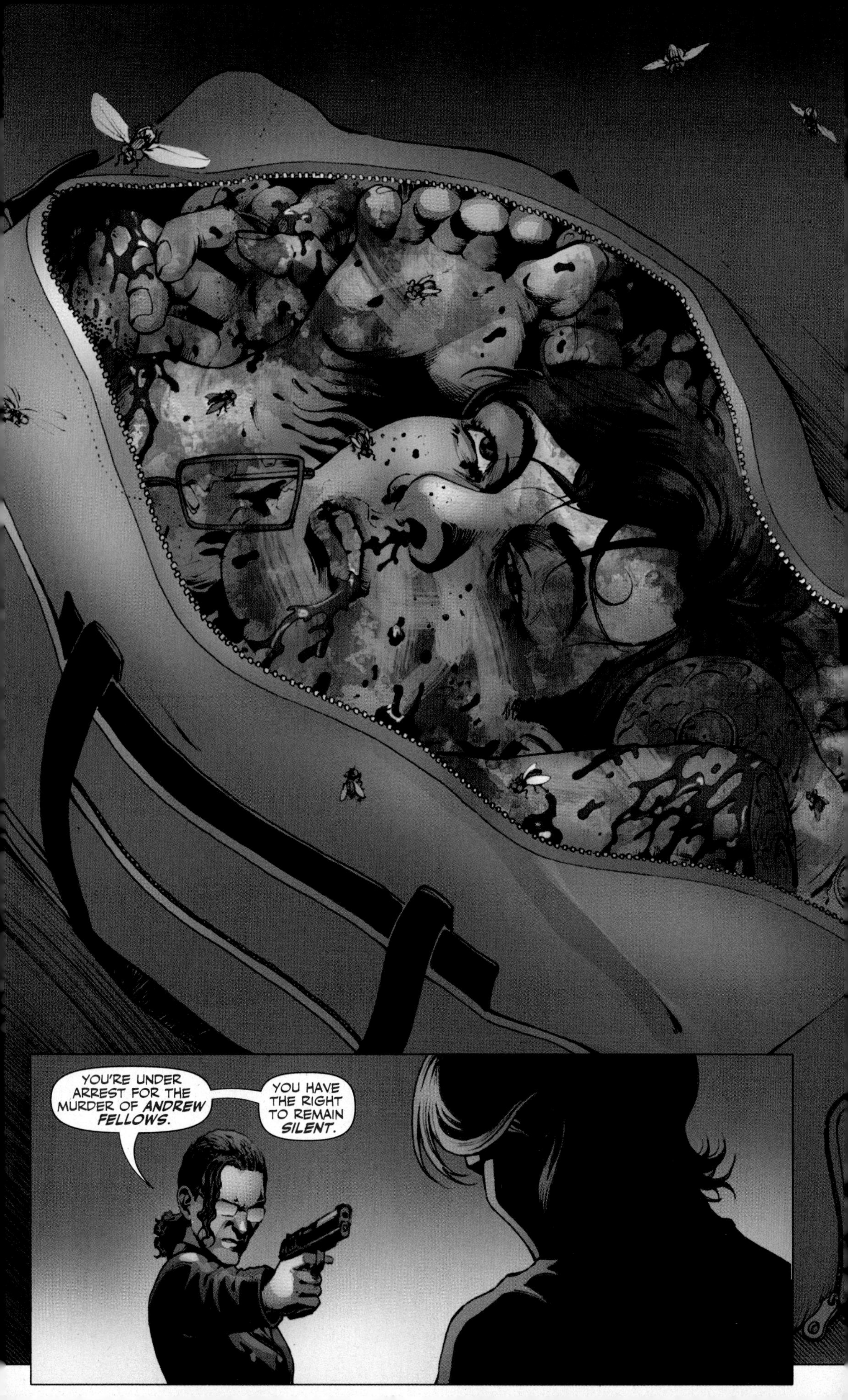
YOU'RE UNDER ARREST FOR THE MURDER OF ANDREW FELLOWS.
YOU HAVE THE RIGHT TO REMAIN SILENT.

...YOU'RE *SICK*.

I'M SICK.

HANDS ON THE TABLE. WHERE I CAN SEE THEM.

DOESN'T SOUND LIKE YOUR *SUPERIORS* WOULD APPROVE OF THIS, EITHER. YOU MADE IT SOUND LIKE YOU'RE OUT IN THE *COLD*...

DO YOU *HAVE* BACKUP, DETECTIVE? OR IS IT JUST YOU?

OH, IT'S ALWAYS JUST ME.

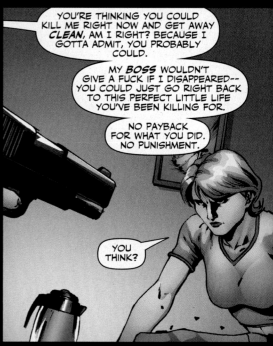

YOU'RE THINKING YOU COULD KILL ME RIGHT NOW AND GET AWAY *CLEAN*, AM I RIGHT? BECAUSE I GOTTA ADMIT, YOU PROBABLY COULD.

MY *BOSS* WOULDN'T GIVE A FUCK IF I DISAPPEARED-- YOU COULD JUST GO RIGHT BACK TO THIS PERFECT LITTLE LIFE YOU'VE BEEN KILLING FOR.

NO PAYBACK FOR WHAT YOU DID. NO PUNISHMENT.

YOU THINK?

I *KNOW*. THAT'S WHY I WAITED UNTIL YOU GOT HOME TO DO THIS.

IT GAVE ME ENOUGH TIME TO EMAIL THOSE PHOTOS I TOOK TO THE *MEDIA*. ALONG WITH YOUR NAME AND ADDRESS.

NO MORE HOUSEWIFE ACT, "MRS. *FELLOWS*." YOU DON'T EVER GET TO HIDE WHAT YOU ARE AGAIN.

JENNIFER BLOOD JUST WENT *PUBLIC*.

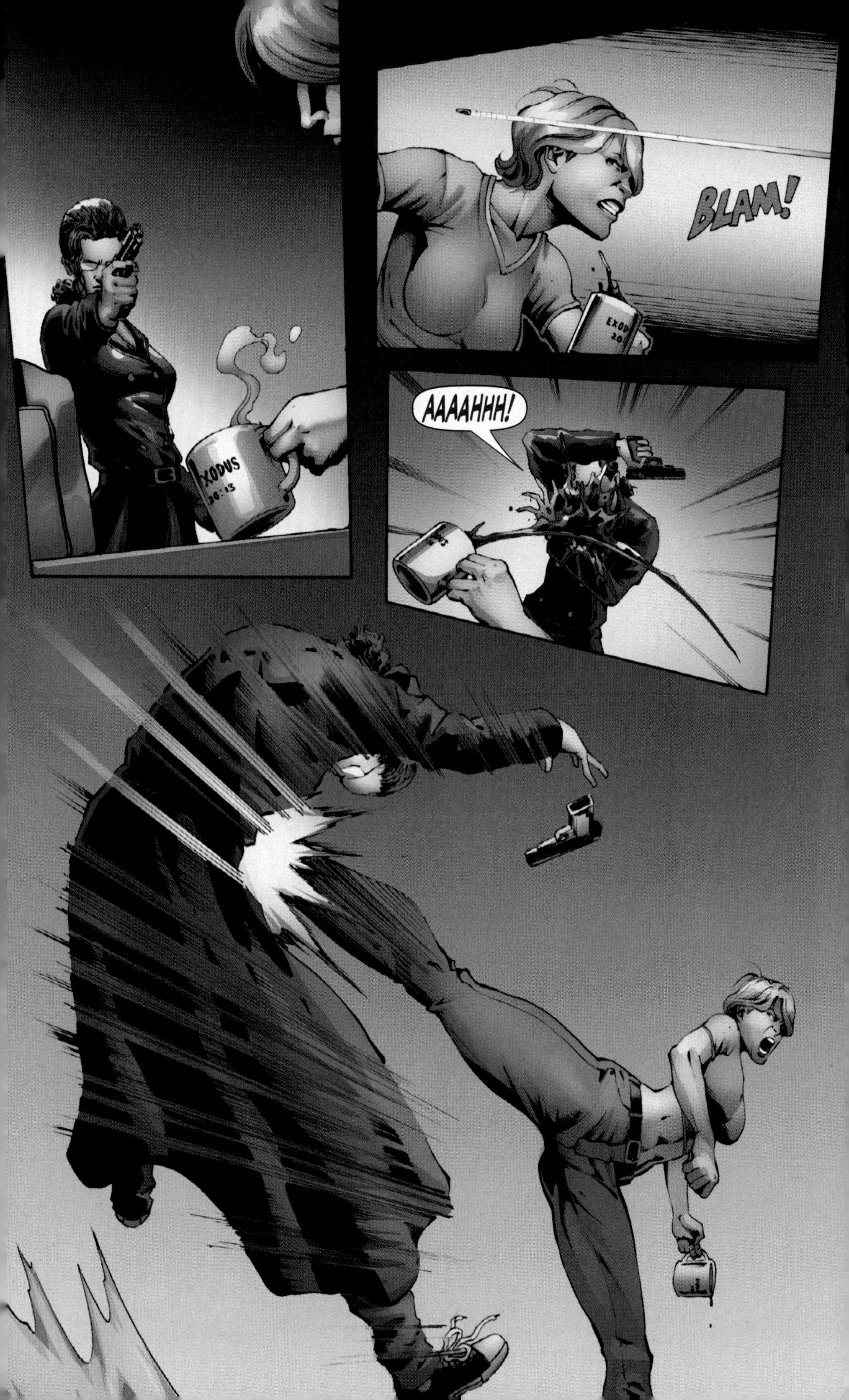

EXODUS 20:13
BLAM!
AAAAHHH!

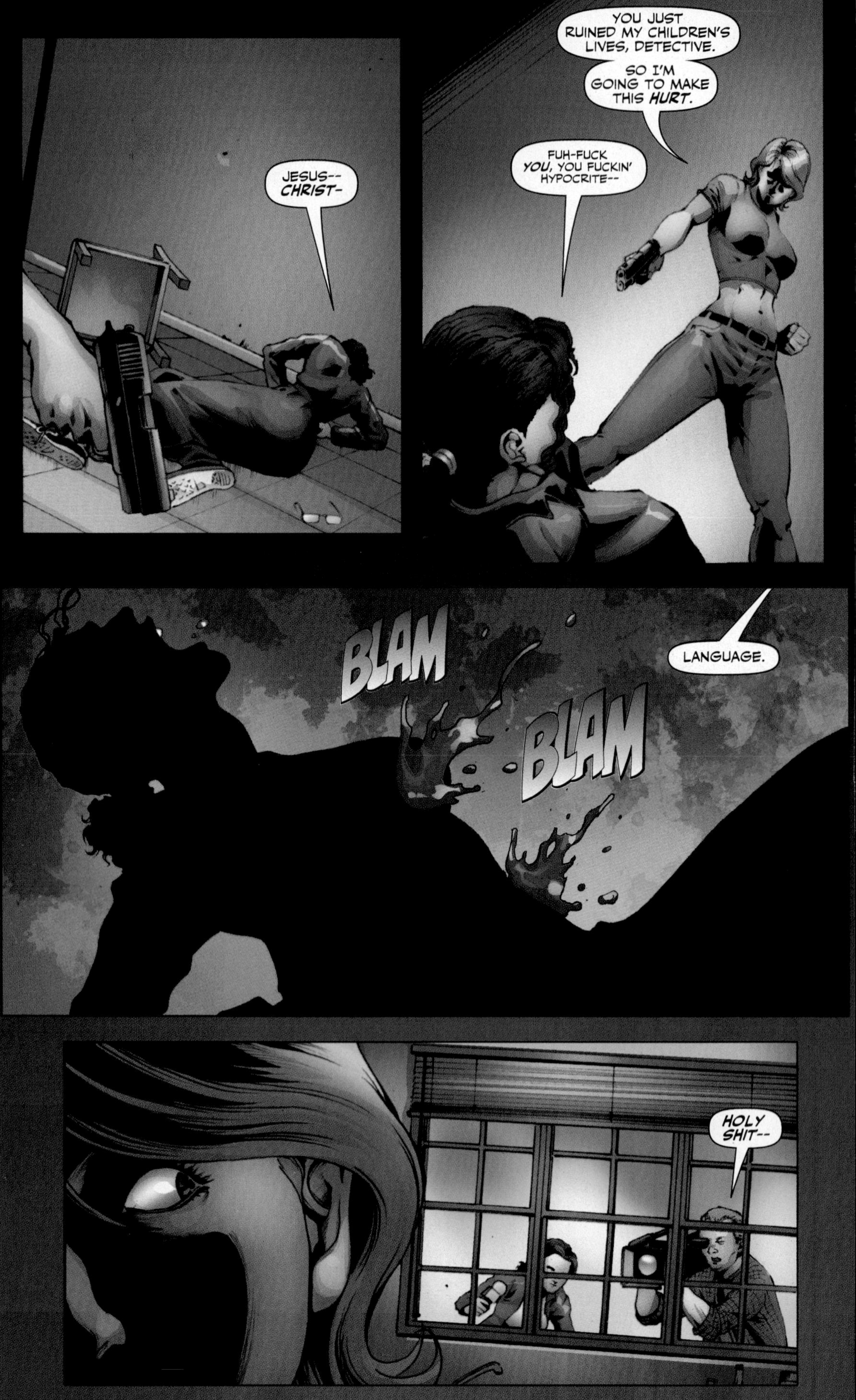
JESUS--
CHRIST-
YOU JUST RUINED MY CHILDREN'S LIVES, DETECTIVE.
SO I'M GOING TO MAKE THIS HURT.
FUH-FUCK YOU, YOU FUCKIN' HYPOCRITE--
LANGUAGE.
BLAM
BLAM
HOLY SHIT--

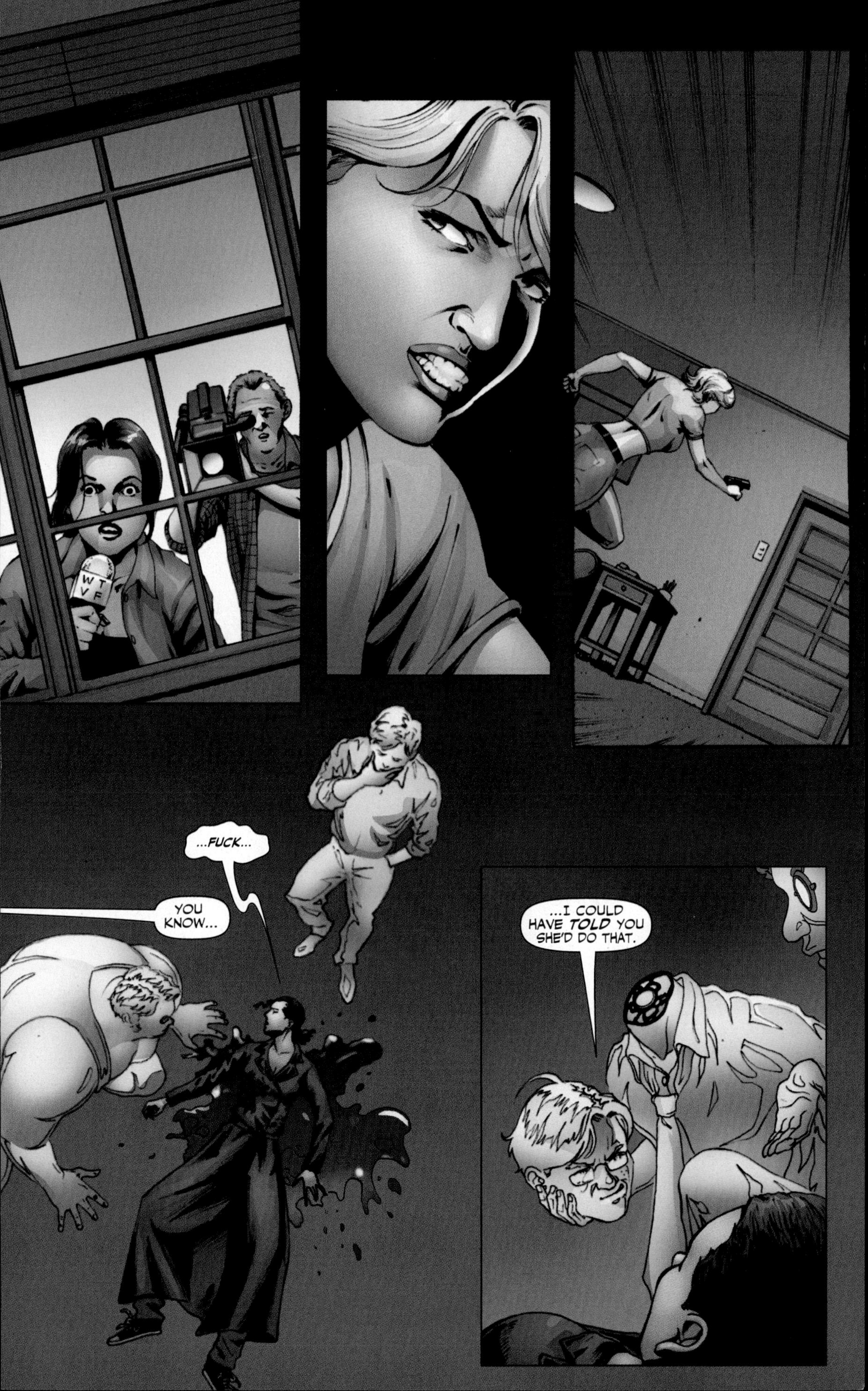
WTVF
...FUCK...
YOU KNOW...
...I COULD HAVE TOLD YOU SHE'D DO THAT.

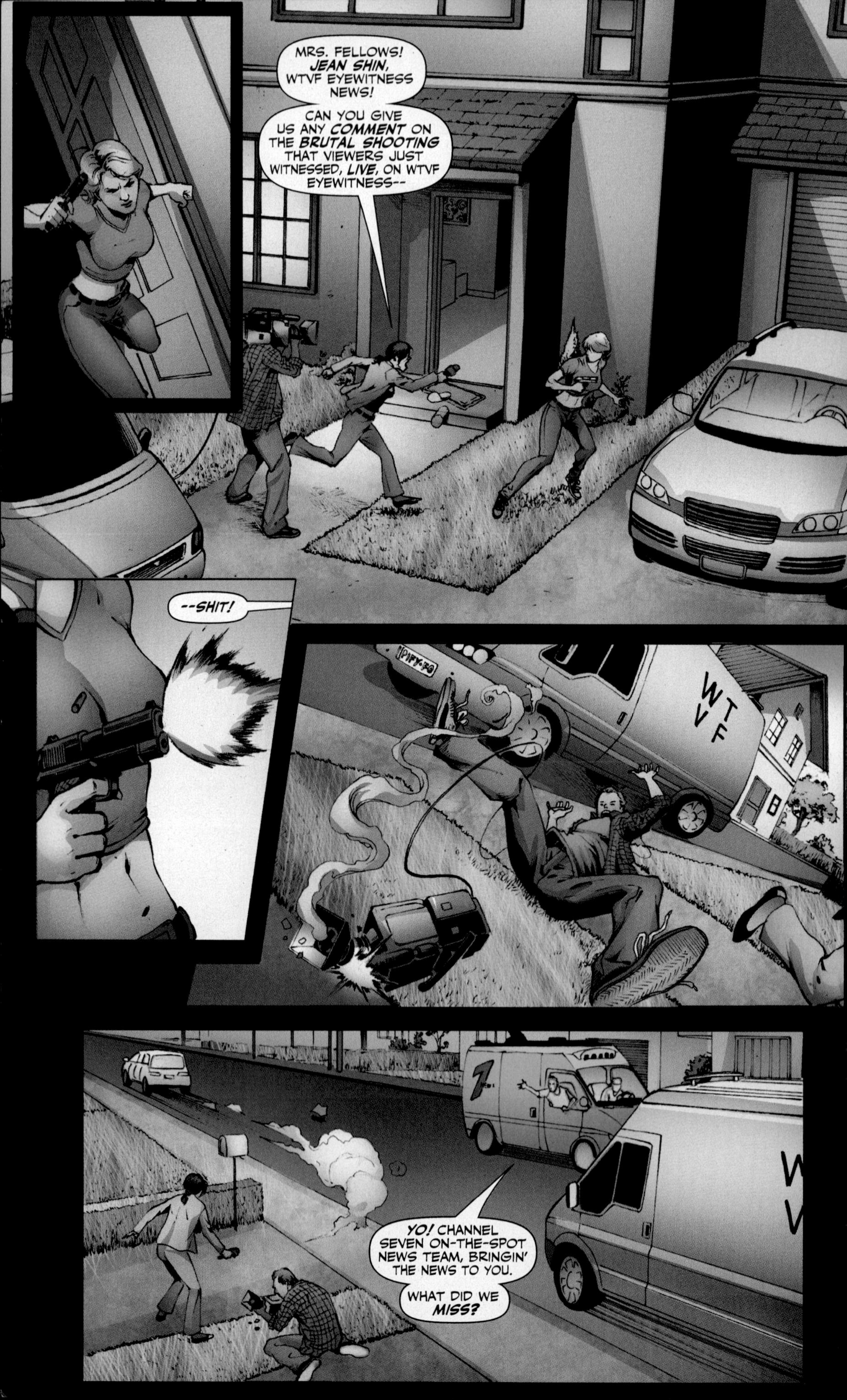
MRS. FELLOWS! JEAN SHIN, WTVF EYEWITNESS NEWS!
CAN YOU GIVE US ANY COMMENT ON THE BRUTAL SHOOTING THAT VIEWERS JUST WITNESSED, LIVE, ON WTVF EYEWITNESS--
--SHIT!
WTVF
YO! CHANNEL SEVEN ON-THE-SPOT NEWS TEAM, BRINGIN' THE NEWS TO YOU.
WHAT DID WE MISS?

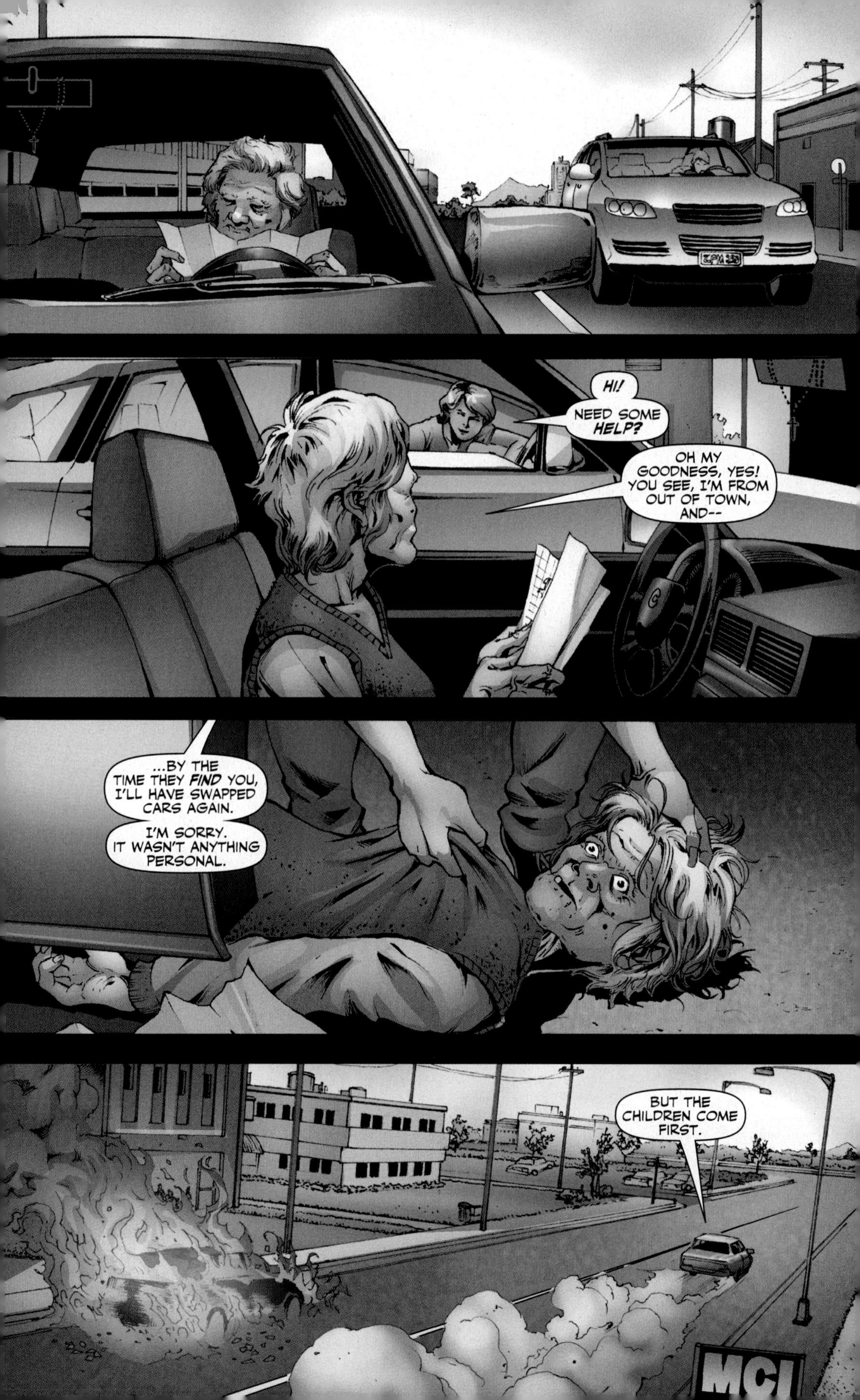
HI!
NEED SOME HELP?
OH MY GOODNESS, YES! YOU SEE, I'M FROM OUT OF TOWN, AND--
...BY THE TIME THEY FIND YOU, I'LL HAVE SWAPPED CARS AGAIN.
I'M SORRY. IT WASN'T ANYTHING PERSONAL.
BUT THE CHILDREN COME FIRST.
MCI

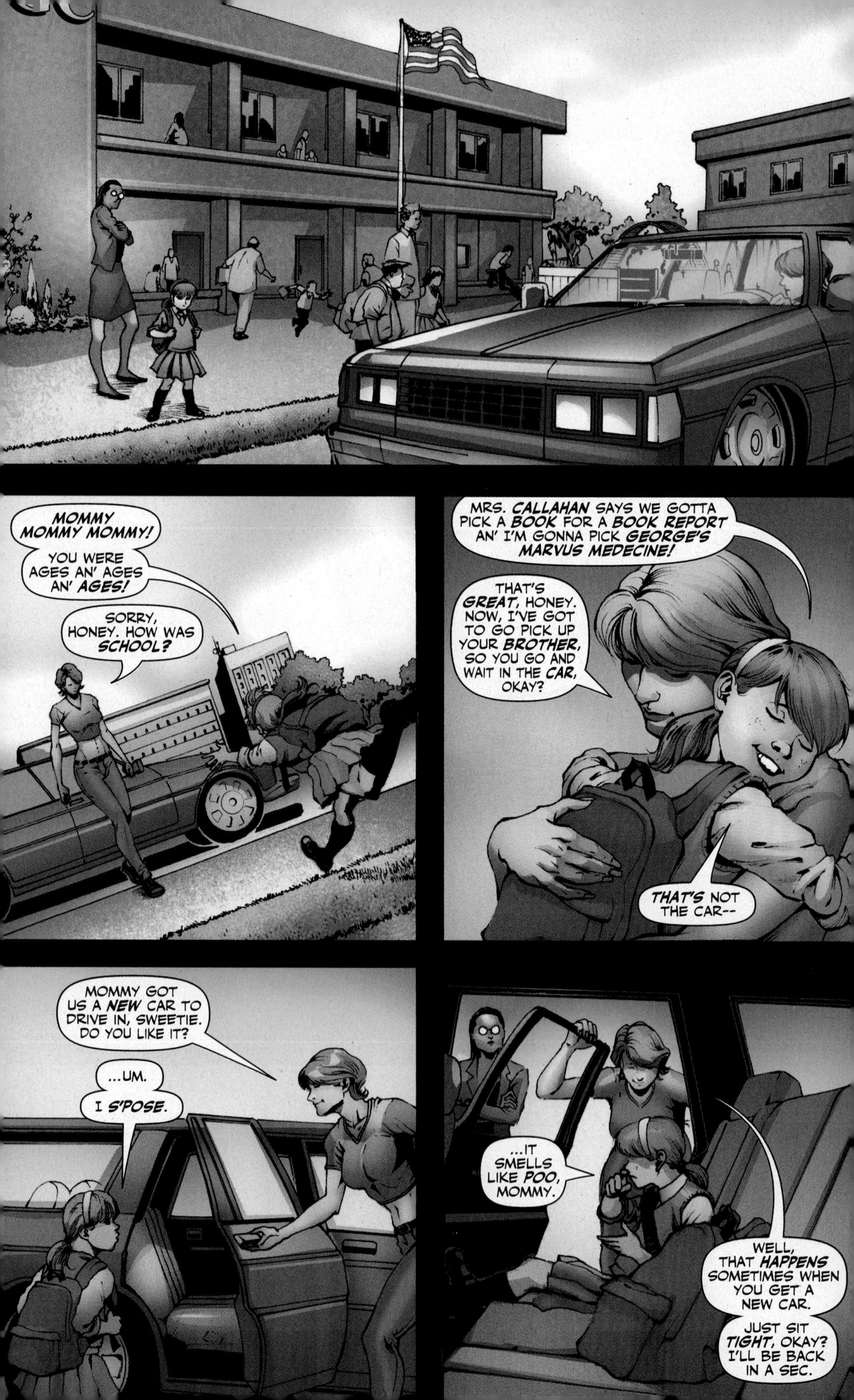
MOMMY MOMMY MOMMY!
YOU WERE AGES AN' AGES AN' AGES!
SORRY, HONEY. HOW WAS SCHOOL?
MRS. CALLAHAN SAYS WE GOTTA PICK A BOOK FOR A BOOK REPORT AN' I'M GONNA PICK GEORGE'S MARVUS MEDECINE!
THAT'S GREAT, HONEY. NOW, I'VE GOT TO GO PICK UP YOUR BROTHER, SO YOU GO AND WAIT IN THE CAR, OKAY?
THAT'S NOT THE CAR--
MOMMY GOT US A NEW CAR TO DRIVE IN, SWEETIE. DO YOU LIKE IT?
...UM.
I S'POSE.
...IT SMELLS LIKE POO, MOMMY.
WELL, THAT HAPPENS SOMETIMES WHEN YOU GET A NEW CAR.
JUST SIT TIGHT, OKAY? I'LL BE BACK IN A SEC.

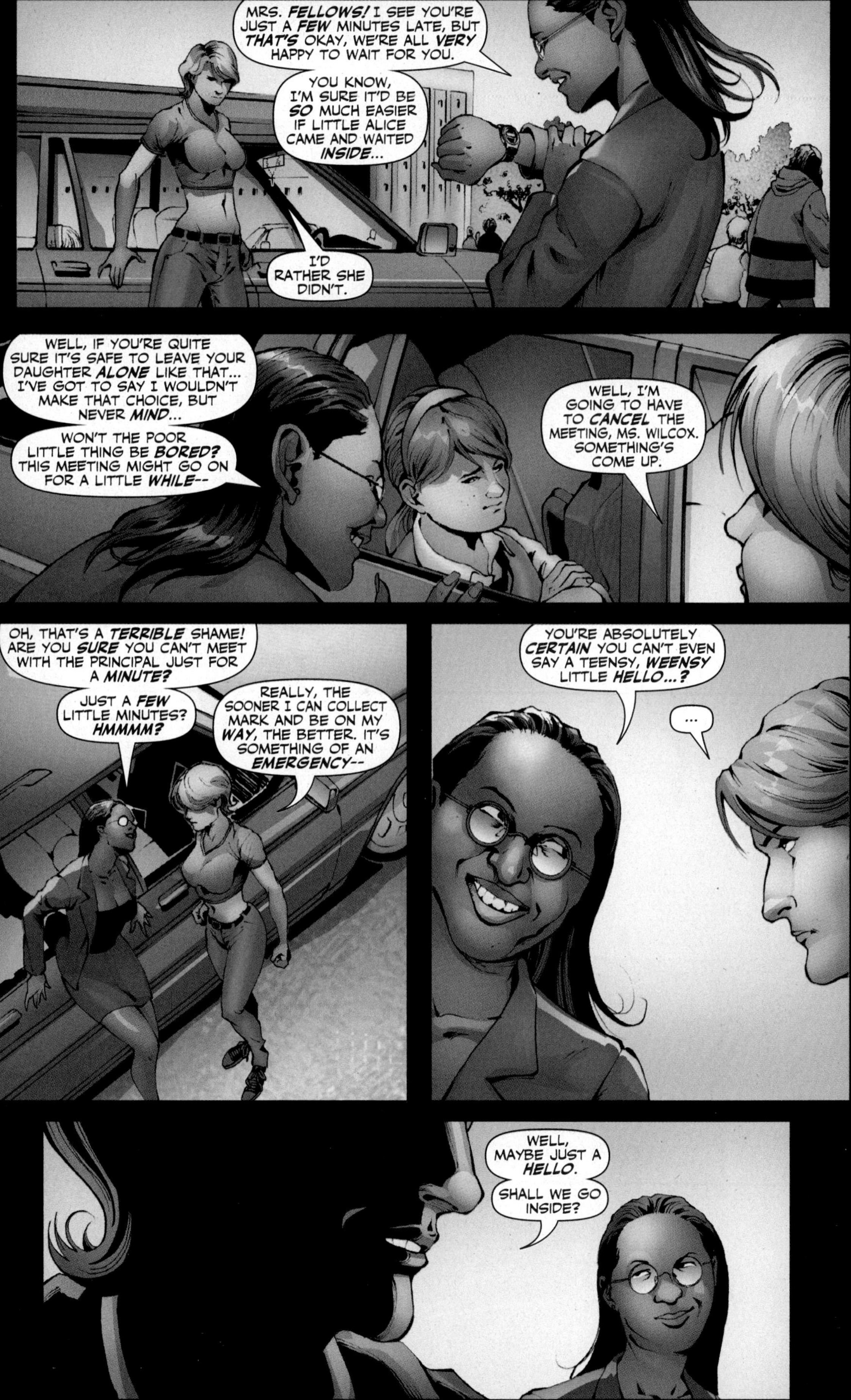
MRS. FELLOWS! I SEE YOU'RE JUST A FEW MINUTES LATE, BUT THAT'S OKAY, WE'RE ALL VERY HAPPY TO WAIT FOR YOU.
YOU KNOW, I'M SURE IT'D BE SO MUCH EASIER IF LITTLE ALICE CAME AND WAITED INSIDE...
I'D RATHER SHE DIDN'T.
WELL, IF YOU'RE QUITE SURE IT'S SAFE TO LEAVE YOUR DAUGHTER ALONE LIKE THAT... I'VE GOT TO SAY I WOULDN'T MAKE THAT CHOICE, BUT NEVER MIND...
WON'T THE POOR LITTLE THING BE BORED? THIS MEETING MIGHT GO ON FOR A LITTLE WHILE--
WELL, I'M GOING TO HAVE TO CANCEL THE MEETING, MS. WILCOX. SOMETHING'S COME UP.
OH, THAT'S A TERRIBLE SHAME! ARE YOU SURE YOU CAN'T MEET WITH THE PRINCIPAL JUST FOR A MINUTE?
JUST A FEW LITTLE MINUTES? HMMMM?
REALLY, THE SOONER I CAN COLLECT MARK AND BE ON MY WAY, THE BETTER. IT'S SOMETHING OF AN EMERGENCY--
YOU'RE ABSOLUTELY CERTAIN YOU CAN'T EVEN SAY A TEENSY, WEENSY LITTLE HELLO...?
...
WELL, MAYBE JUST A HELLO.
SHALL WE GO INSIDE?

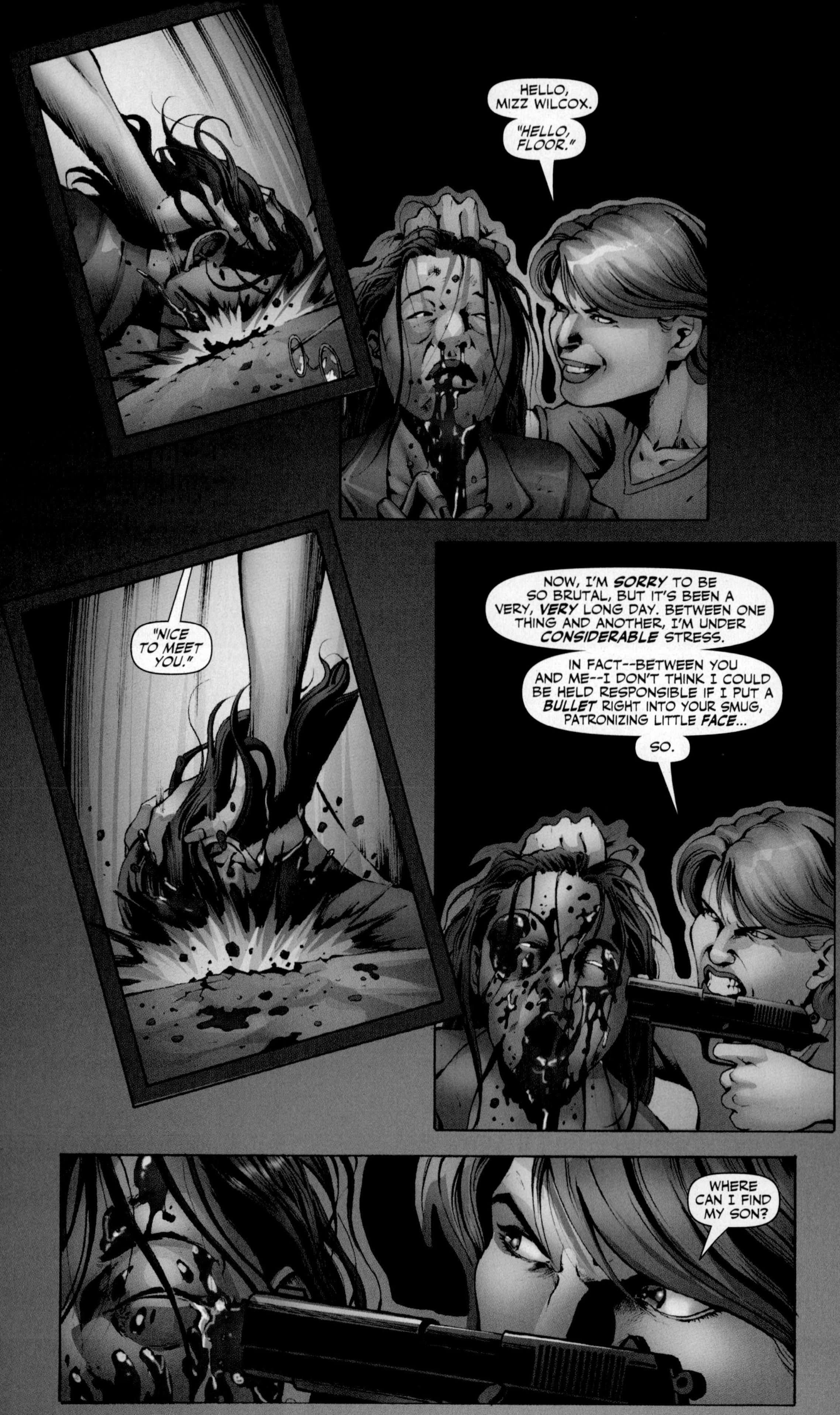
HELLO, MIZZ WILCOX.
"HELLO, FLOOR."
"NICE TO MEET YOU."
NOW, I'M SORRY TO BE SO BRUTAL, BUT IT'S BEEN A VERY, VERY LONG DAY. BETWEEN ONE THING AND ANOTHER, I'M UNDER CONSIDERABLE STRESS.
IN FACT--BETWEEN YOU AND ME--I DON'T THINK I COULD BE HELD RESPONSIBLE IF I PUT A BULLET RIGHT INTO YOUR SMUG, PATRONIZING LITTLE FACE...
SO.
WHERE CAN I FIND MY SON?

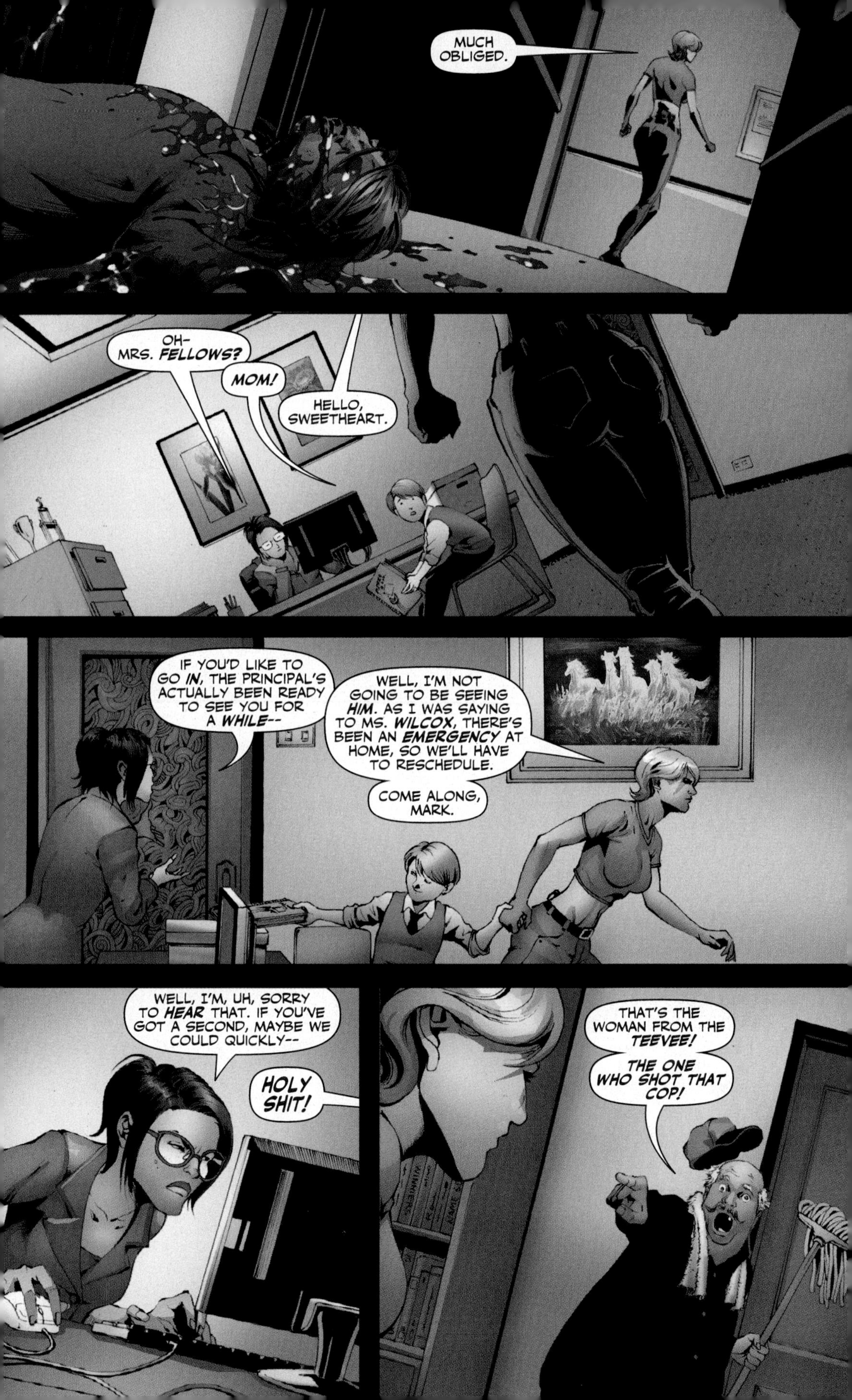
MUCH OBLIGED.
OH- MRS. FELLOWS?
MOM!
HELLO, SWEETHEART.
IF YOU'D LIKE TO GO IN, THE PRINCIPAL'S ACTUALLY BEEN READY TO SEE YOU FOR A WHILE--
WELL, I'M NOT GOING TO BE SEEING HIM. AS I WAS SAYING TO MS. WILCOX, THERE'S BEEN AN EMERGENCY AT HOME, SO WE'LL HAVE TO RESCHEDULE.
COME ALONG, MARK.
WELL, I'M, UH, SORRY TO HEAR THAT. IF YOU'VE GOT A SECOND, MAYBE WE COULD QUICKLY--
HOLY SHIT!
THAT'S THE WOMAN FROM THE TEEVEE!
THE ONE WHO SHOT THAT COP!

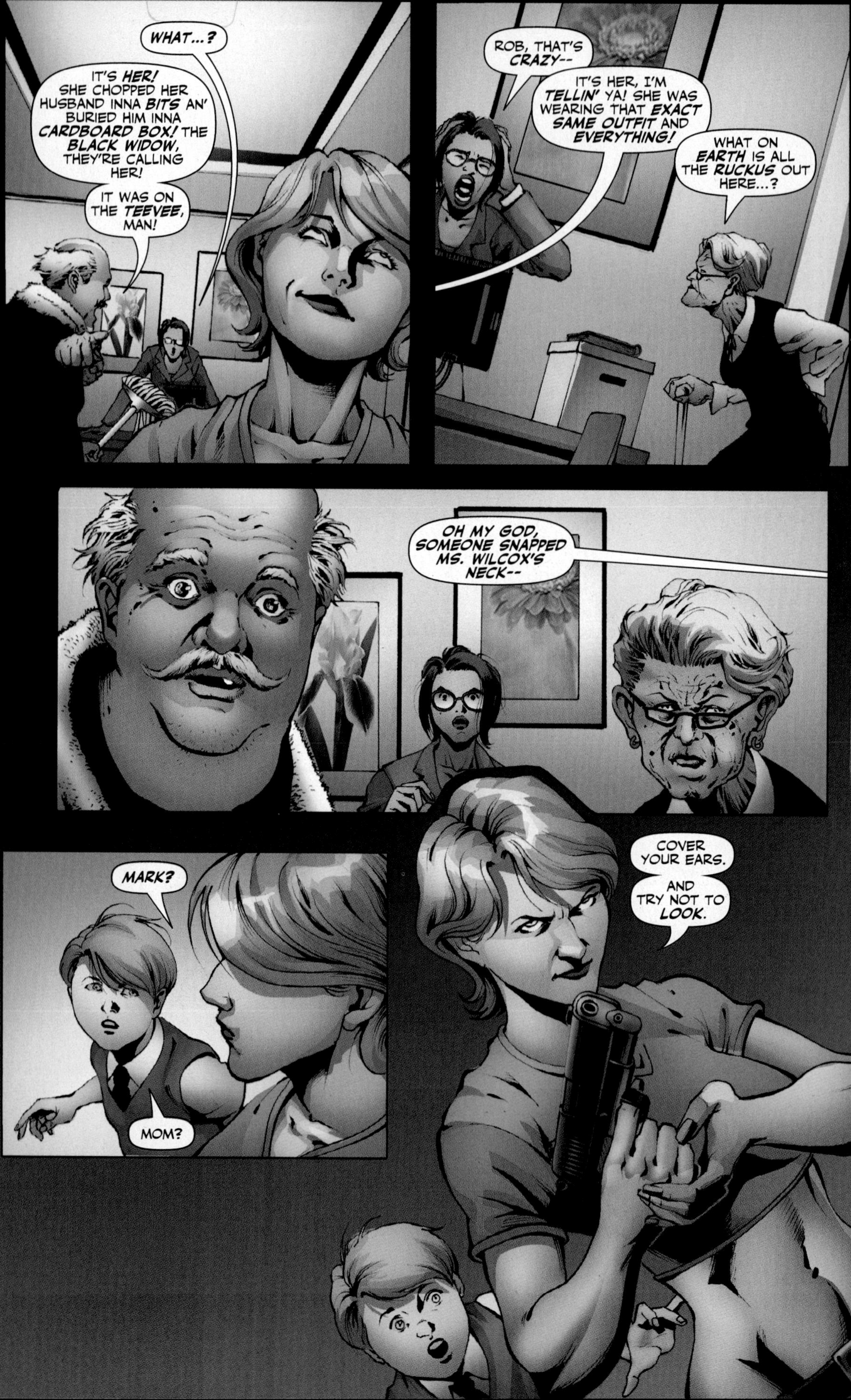
WHAT...?
IT'S HER! SHE CHOPPED HER HUSBAND INNA BITS AN' BURIED HIM INNA CARDBOARD BOX! THE BLACK WIDOW, THEY'RE CALLING HER!
IT WAS ON THE TEEVEE, MAN!
ROB, THAT'S CRAZY--
IT'S HER, I'M TELLIN' YA! SHE WAS WEARING THAT EXACT SAME OUTFIT AND EVERYTHING!
WHAT ON EARTH IS ALL THE RUCKUS OUT HERE...?
OH MY GOD, SOMEONE SNAPPED MS. WILCOX'S NECK--
MARK?
MOM?
COVER YOUR EARS.
AND TRY NOT TO LOOK.

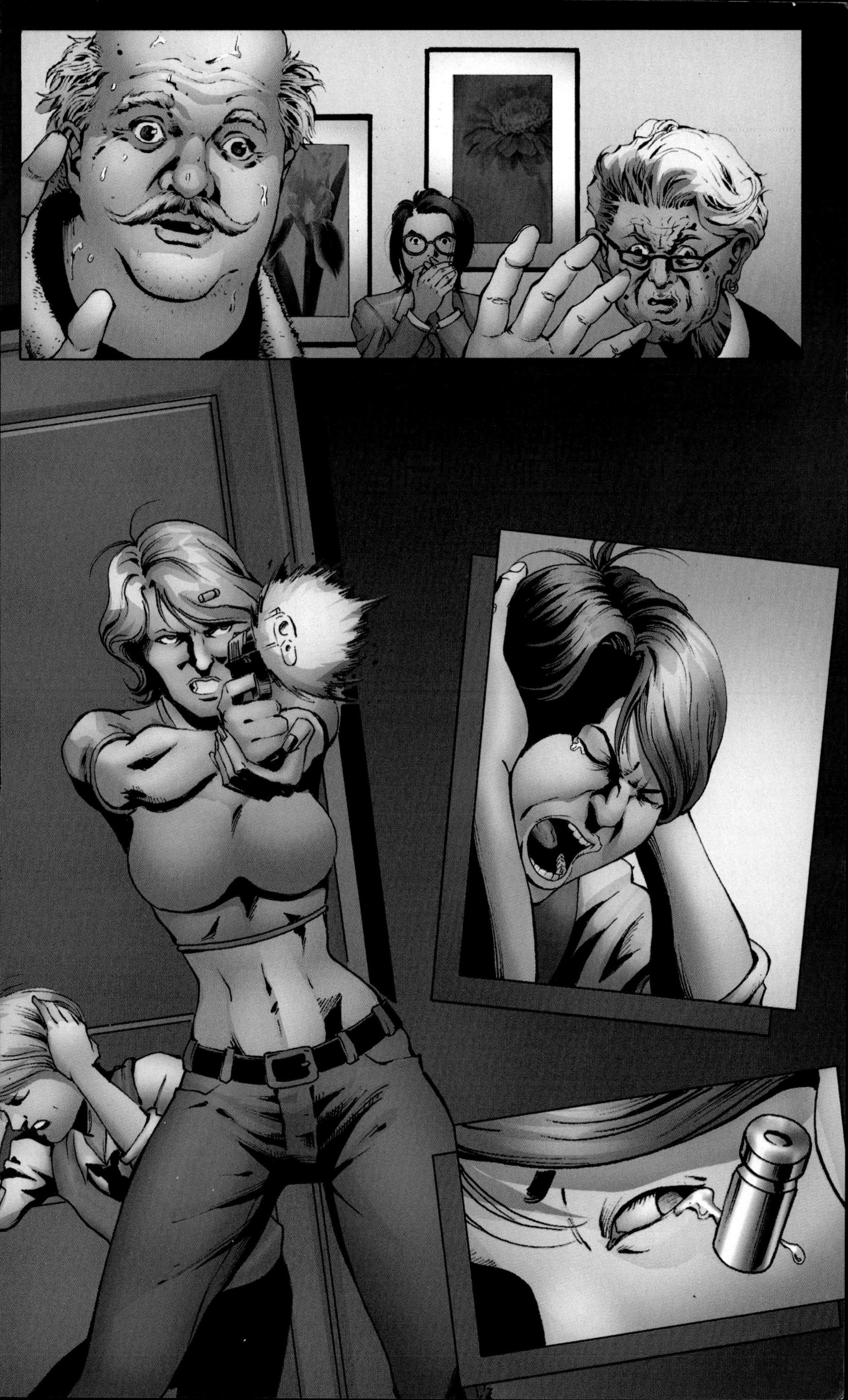

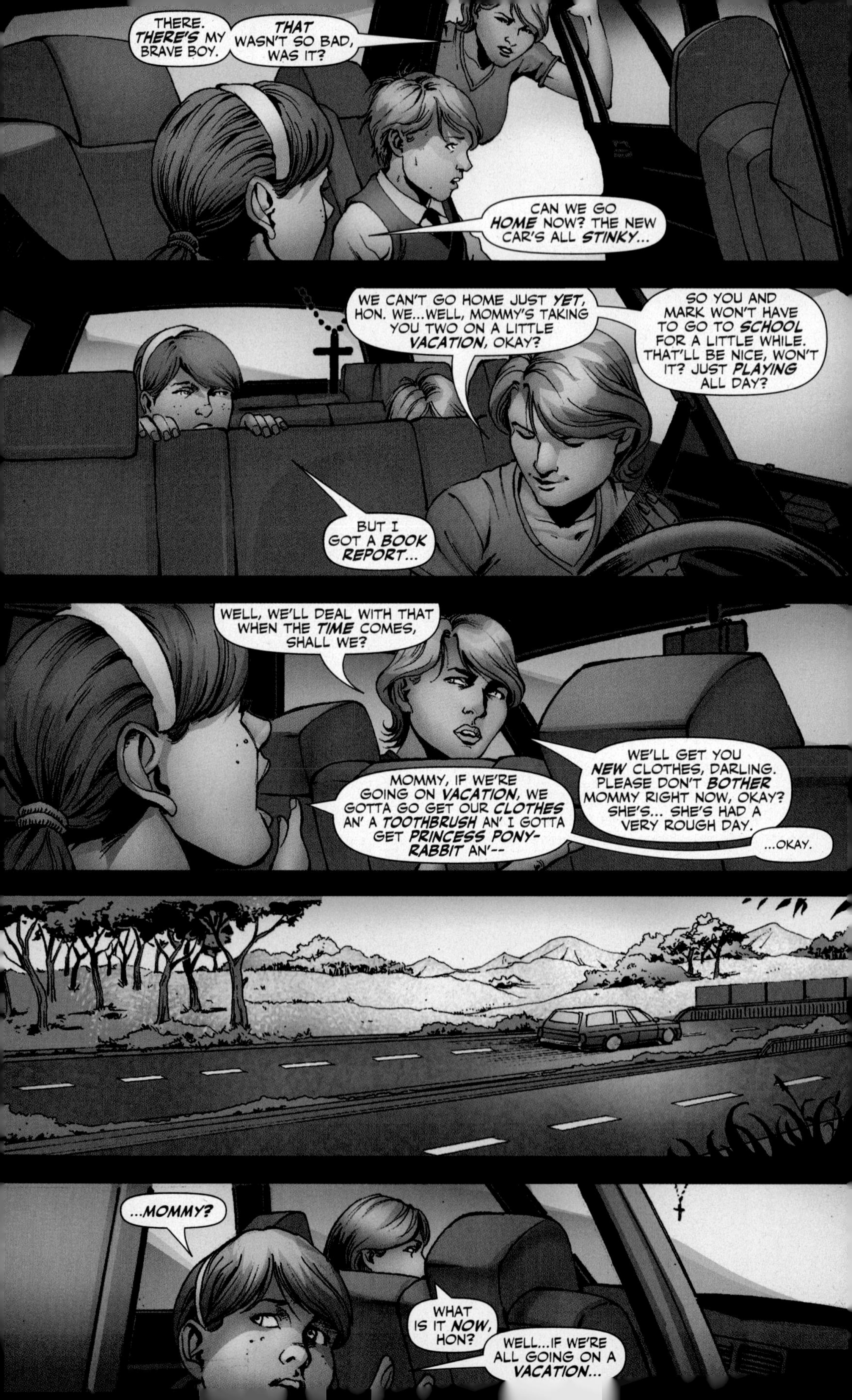
THERE. THERE'S MY BRAVE BOY.
THAT WASN'T SO BAD, WAS IT?
CAN WE GO HOME NOW? THE NEW CAR'S ALL STINKY...
WE CAN'T GO HOME JUST YET, HON. WE...WELL, MOMMY'S TAKING YOU TWO ON A LITTLE VACATION, OKAY?
SO YOU AND MARK WON'T HAVE TO GO TO SCHOOL FOR A LITTLE WHILE. THAT'LL BE NICE, WON'T IT? JUST PLAYING ALL DAY?
BUT I GOT A BOOK REPORT...
WELL, WE'LL DEAL WITH THAT WHEN THE TIME COMES, SHALL WE?
MOMMY, IF WE'RE GOING ON VACATION, WE GOTTA GO GET OUR CLOTHES AN' A TOOTHBRUSH AN' I GOTTA GET PRINCESS PONY-RABBIT AN'--
WE'LL GET YOU NEW CLOTHES, DARLING. PLEASE DON'T BOTHER MOMMY RIGHT NOW, OKAY? SHE'S... SHE'S HAD A VERY ROUGH DAY.
...OKAY.
...MOMMY?
WHAT IS IT NOW, HON?
WELL...IF WE'RE ALL GOING ON A VACATION...

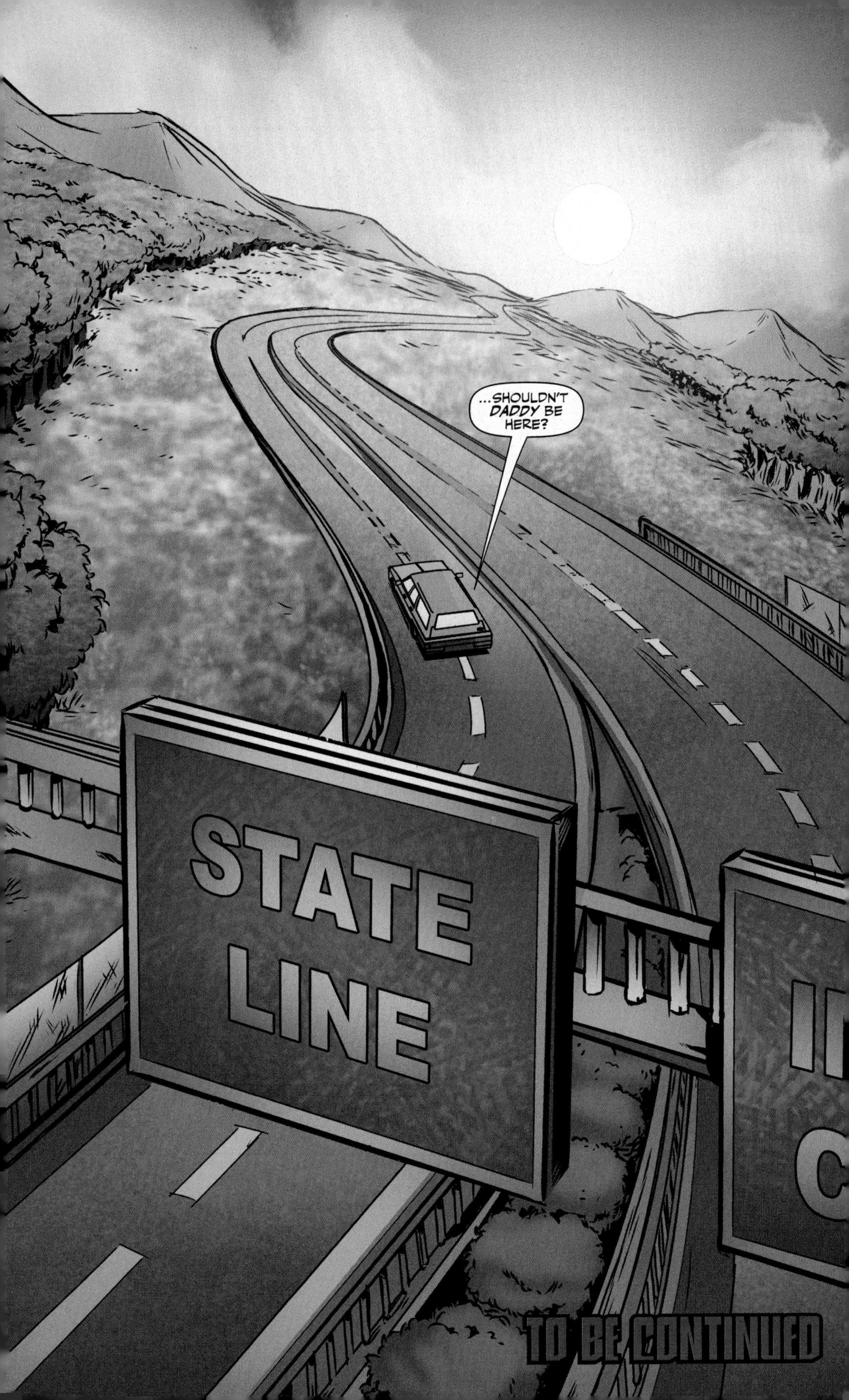
...SHOULDN'T DADDY BE HERE?
STATE LINE
TO BE CONTINUED

"risqué"
retailer incentive
covers

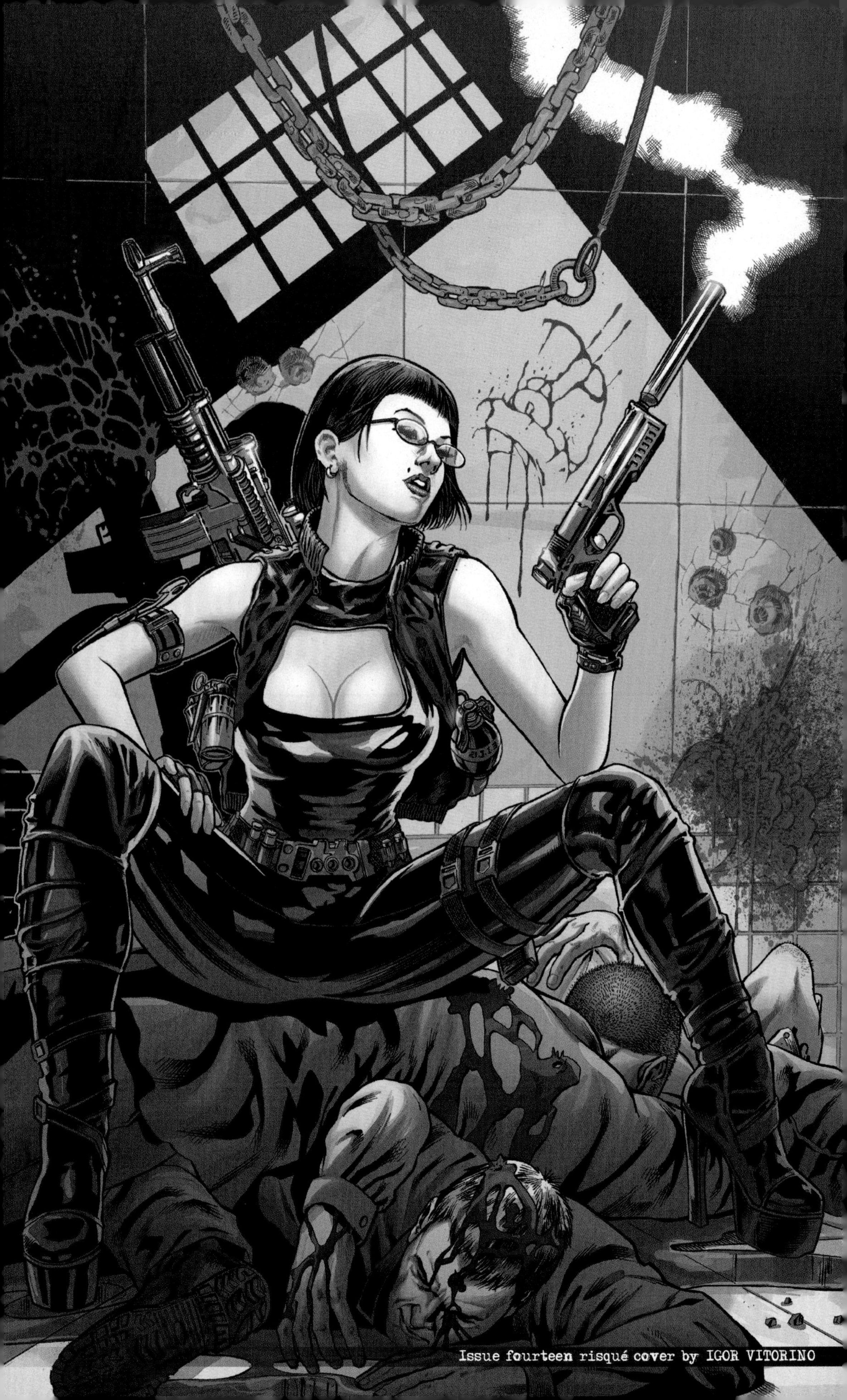

Issue fourteen risqué cover by IGOR VITORINO

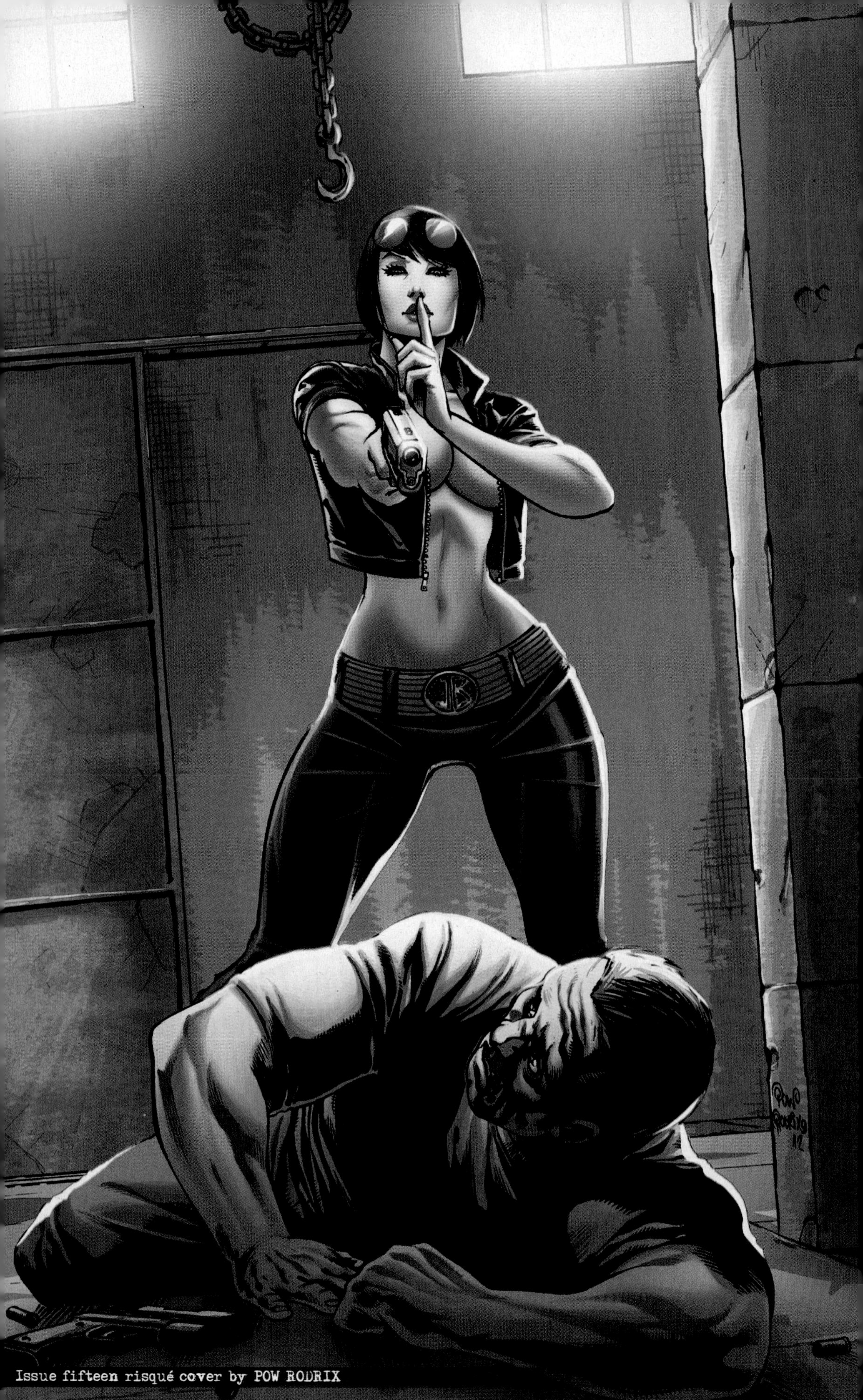
POW
RODRIX
12

Issue fifteen risqué cover by POW RODRIX

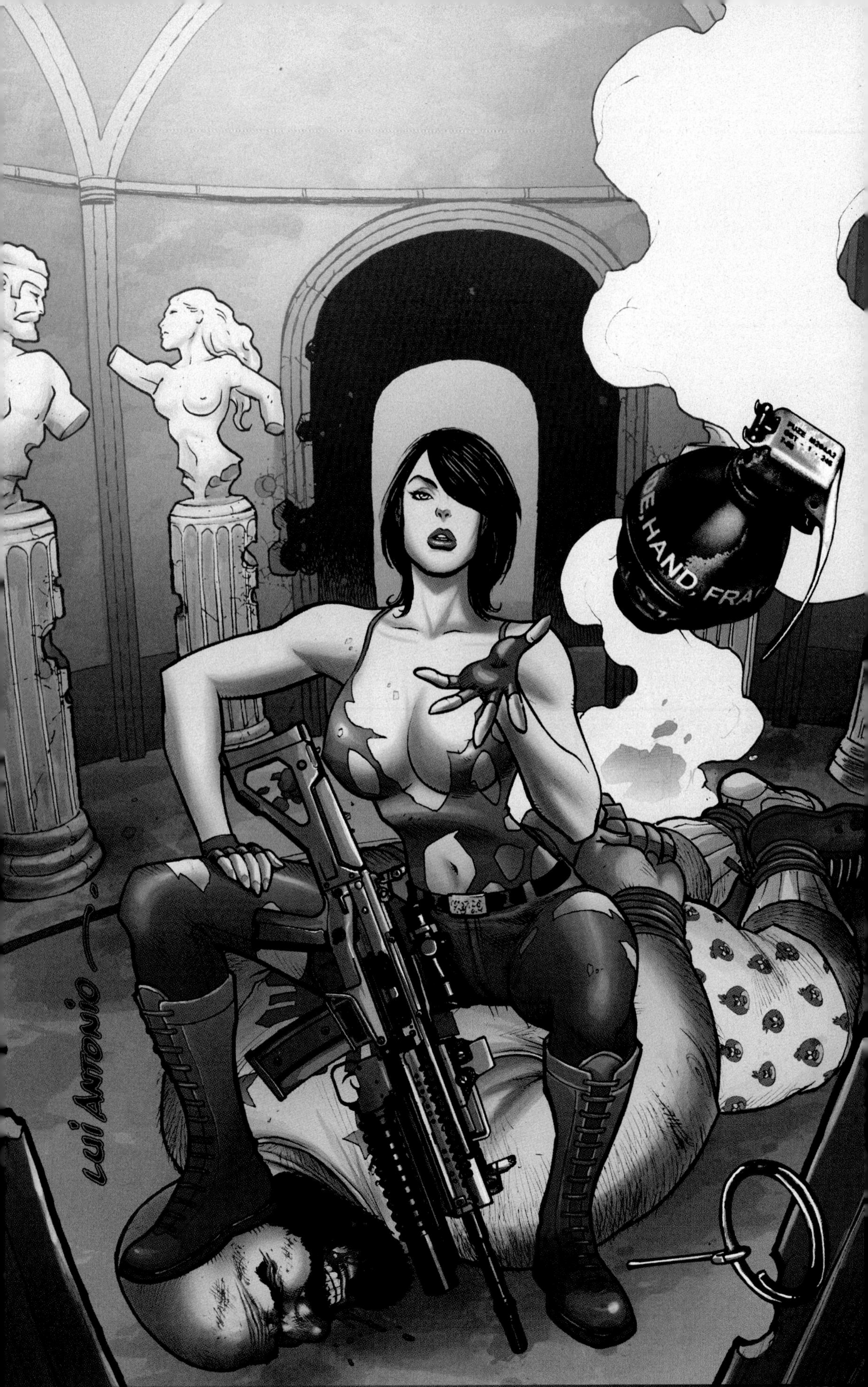
Lui Antonio

Issue sixteen risqué cover by LUI ANTONIO

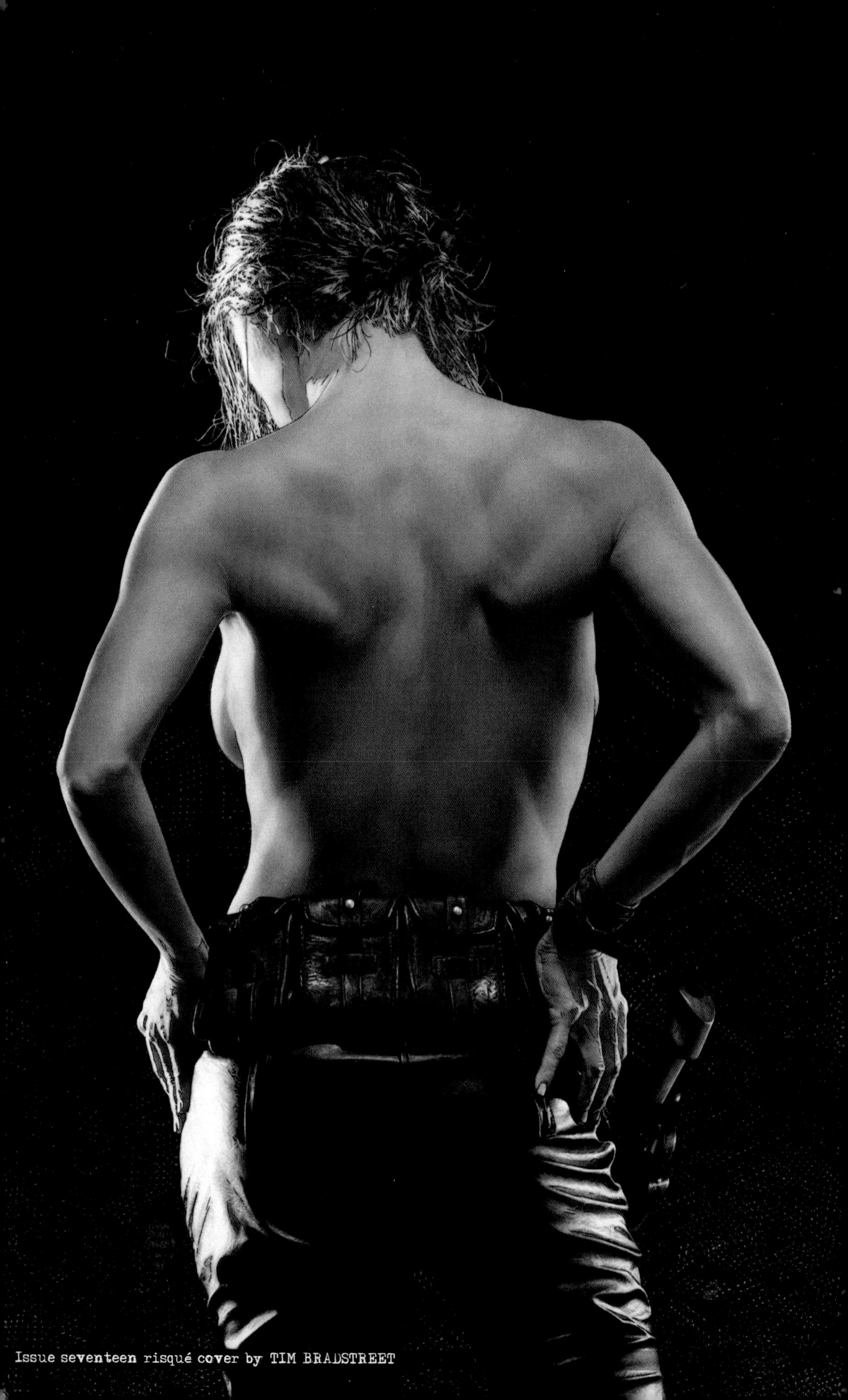

Issue seventeen risqué cover by TIM BRADSTREET

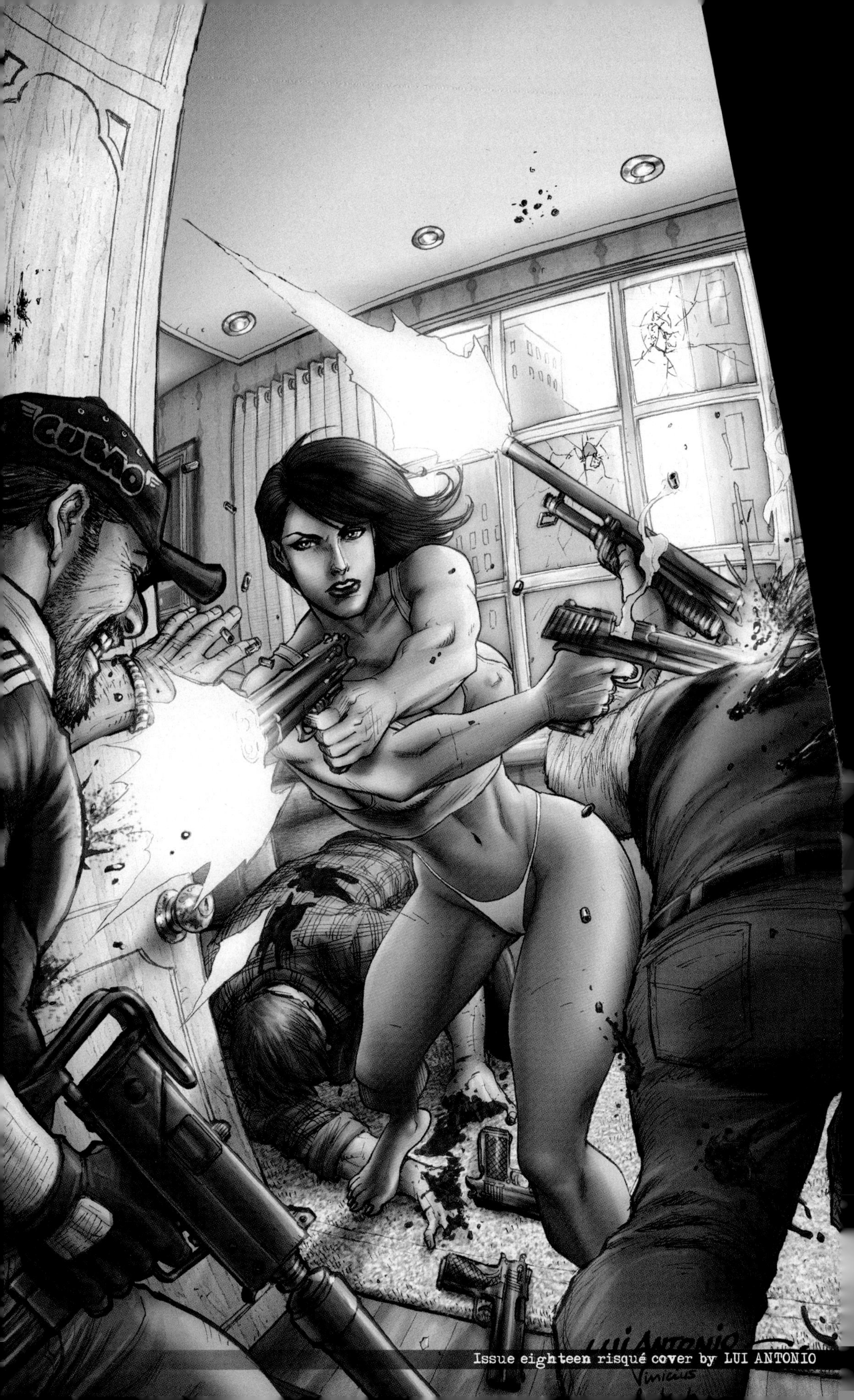
CUBAO

Issue eighteen risqué cover by LUI ANTONIO

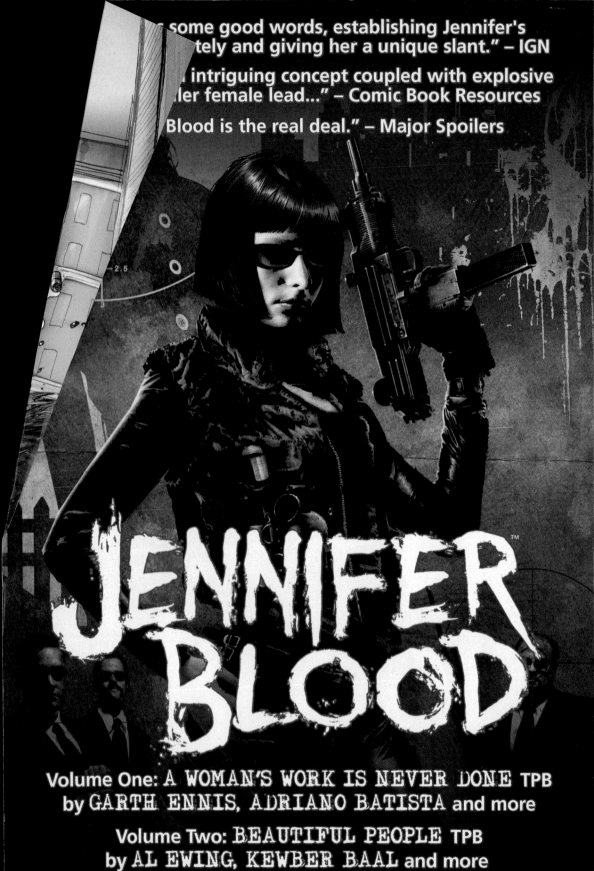

"The Ninjettes is the type of ***over-the-top, sexy, and preposterous*** *title that, when done right, works so well. Luckily for readers, Al Ewing and Eman Casallos deliver an* ***insanely fun*** *and bizarre book of even crazier characters and events.* The Ninjettes *definitely stands on its own and* ***must be read."***
– Broken Frontier

"Sometimes we need a comic of ***ultra violence*** *and* ***sexy appeal****, which* The Ninjettes *provides perfectly."* – Speak Geek To Me

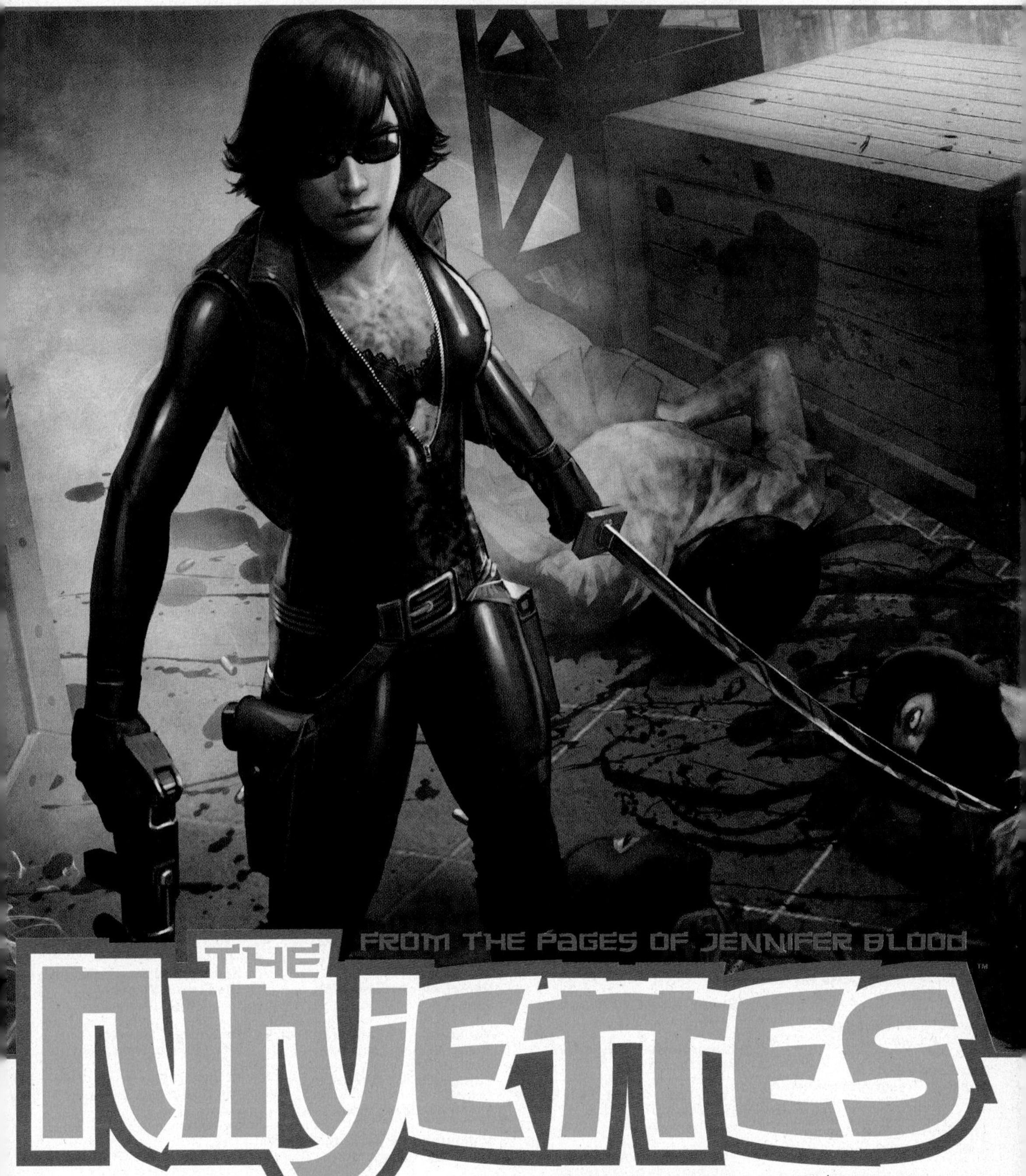

FROM THE PAGES OF JENNIFER BLOOD

THE NINJETTES™

VOLUME ONE TRADE PAPERBACK

Tearing out of the pages of **GARTH ENNIS' JENNIFER BLOOD** comes **THE NINJETTES** – a searing four-color indictment of a society that turns blushing college girls into kill-hungry ninjas!

Collecting the complete, 6-issue mini series by **AL EWING** and **EMAN CASALLOS** along with all of the covers by Admira Wijaya, Johnny Desjardins & more, a writer's commentary for issue #1 by Al Ewing and sketches and designs by Eman Casallos!

WWW.DYNAMITE.COM FOLLOW US ON TWITTER: #DYNAMITECOMICS LIKE US ON FACEBOOK: /DYNAMITECOMICS

LOOK FOR THESE DYNAMITE GREATEST HITS!

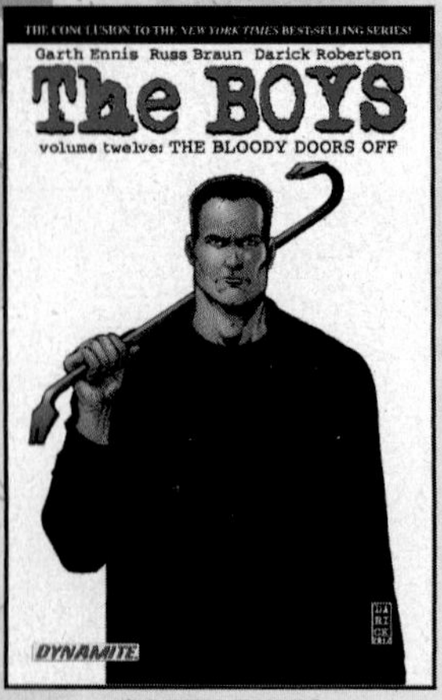
THE CONCLUSION TO THE NEW YORK TIMES BEST-SELLING SERIES!
Garth Ennis Russ Braun Darick Robertson
The BOYS
volume twelve: THE BLOODY DOORS OFF
DYNAMITE

GARTH ENNIS
THE BOYS & MORE!

(Garth Ennis') Battlefields V1: The Night Witches
Ennis, Braun

(Garth Ennis') Battlefields V2: Dear Billy
Ennis, Snejbjerg

(Garth Ennis') Battlefields V3: The Tankies
Ennis, Ezquerra

(Garth Ennis') The Complete Battlefields V1
Ennis, Braun, Ezquerra, more

(Garth Ennis') Battlefields V4: Happy Valley
Ennis, Holden

(Garth Ennis') Battlefields V5: The Firefly and His Majesty
Ennis, Ezquerra

(Garth Ennis') Battlefields V6: Motherland
Ennis, Braun

(Garth Ennis') The Complete Battlefields V2
Ennis, Braun, Holden, more

The Boys V1 The Name of the Game
Ennis, Robertson

The Boys V2 Get Some
Ennis, Robertson, Snejbjerg

The Boys V3 Good For The Soul
Ennis, Robertson

The Boys V4 We Gotta Go Now
Ennis, Robertson

The Boys V5 Herogasm
Ennis, McCrea

The Boys V6 The Self-Preservation Society
Ennis, Robertson, Ezquerra

The Boys V7 The Innocents
Ennis, Robertson, Braun

The Boys V8 Highland Laddie
Ennis, McCrea

The Boys V9 The Big Ride
Ennis, Braun

The Boys V10: Butcher, Baker, Candlestickmaker
Ennis, Robertson

The Boys V11 Over the Hill With the Swords of a Thousand Men
Ennis, Braun

The Boys Definitive Edition V1
Ennis, Robertson

The Boys Definitive Edition V2
Ennis, Robertson

The Boys Definitive Edition V3
Ennis, Robertson, more

The Boys Definitive Edition V4
Ennis, Robertson, more

Dan Dare Omnibus
Ennis, Erskine

Jennifer Blood V1 A Woman's Work Is Never Done
Ennis, Batista, Baal, more

Jennifer Blood V2 Beautiful People
Ewing, Baal, more

Just A Pilgrim
Ennis, Ezquerra

The Ninjettes
Ewing, Casallos

Seven Brothers Omnibus
Ennis, Diggle, Kang, more

The Shadow V1 The Fire of Creation
Ennis, Campbell

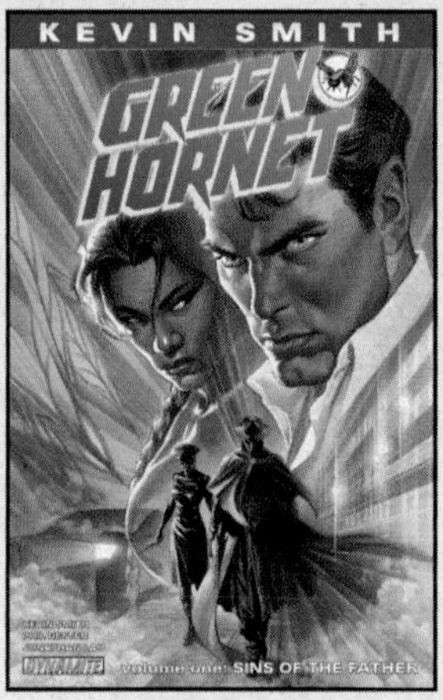
KEVIN SMITH
GREEN HORNET
volume one: SINS OF THE FATHER
DYNAMITE

GREEN HORNET
KEVIN SMITH & MORE!

(Kevin Smith's) Green Hornet V1 Sins of the Father
Smith, Hester, Lau

(Kevin Smith's) Green Hornet V2 Wearing 'o the Green
Smith, Hester, Lau

Green Hornet V3 Idols
Hester, Lau

Green Hornet V4 Red Hand
Hester, Smith, Vitorino, more

Green Hornet: Blood Ties
Parks, Desjardins

The Green Hornet: Year One V1 The Sting of Justice
Wagner, Campbell

The Green Hornet: Year One V2 The Biggest of All Game
Wagner, Campbell

The Green Hornet Parallel Lives
Nitz, Raynor

The Green Hornet Golden Age Re-Mastered
Various

Kato V1 Not My Father's Daughter
Parks, Garza, Bernard

Kato V2 Living in America
Parks, Bernard

Kato Origins V1 Way of the Ninja
Nitz, Worley

Kato Origins V2 The Hellfire Club
Nitz, Worley

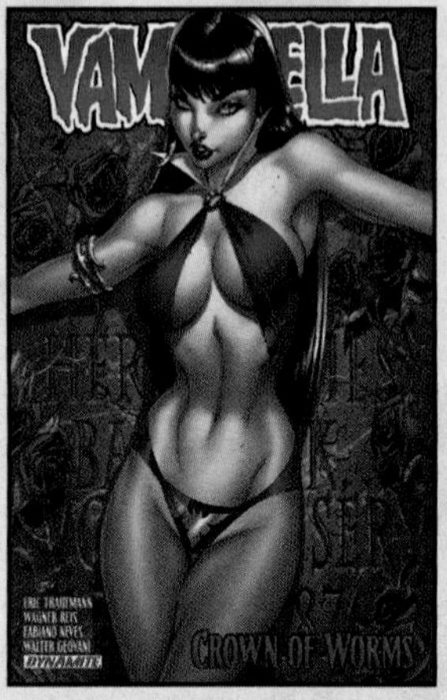
CROWN OF WORMS
DYNAMITE

VAMPIRELLA!

Vampirella Masters Series V1 Grant Morrison & Mark Millar
Morrison, Millar, more

Vampirella Masters Series V2 Warren Ellis
Ellis, Conner Palmiotti, more

Vampi Omnibus V1
Conway, Lau

Vampirella Masters Series V3 Mark Millar
Millar, Mayhew

Vampirella Masters Series V4 Visionaries
Moore, Busiek, Loeb, more

Vampirella Masters Series V5 Kurt Busiek
Busiek, Sniegoski, more

Vampirella Masters Series V6 James Robinson
Robinson, Jusko, more

Vampirella Archives V1
Various

Vampirella Archives V2
Various

Vampirella Archives V3
Various

Vampirella Archives V4
Various

Vampirella Archives V5
Various

Vampirella V1 Crown of Worms
Trautman, Reis, Geovani

Vampirella V2 A Murder of Crows
Trautman, Neves, more

Vampirella V3 Throne of Skulls
Trautman, Malaga, more

Vampirella And The Scarlet Legion
Harris, Malaga

Vampirella vs. Dracula
Harris, Rodriguez

RED SONJA!

Adventures of Red Sonja V1
Thomas, Thorne, More

Adventures of Red Sonja V2
Thomas, Thorne, More

Adventures of Red Sonja V3
Thomas, Thorne, More

Queen Sonja V1
Ortega, Rubi

Queen Sonja V2 The Red Queen
Nelson, Herbert

Queen Sonja V3 Coming of Age
Lieberman, Rubi

Queen Sonja V4 Son of Set
Nelson, Salazar

Red Sonja She-Devil With a Sword V1
Oeming, Carey, Rubi

Red Sonja She-Devil With a Sword V2: Arrowsmiths
Oeming, Rubi, more

Red Sonja She-Devil With a Sword V3: The Rise of Kulan Gath
Oeming, Rubi, more

Red Sonja She-Devil With a Sword V4: Animals & More
Oeming, Homs, more

Red Sonja She-Devil With a Sword V5: World On Fire
Oeming, Reed, Homs

Red Sonja She-Devil With a Sword V6: Death
Marz, Ortega, Reed, more

Red Sonja She-Devil With a Sword V7: Born Again
Reed, Geovani

Red Sonja She-Devil With a Sword V8: Blood Dynasty
Reed, Geovani

Red Sonja She-Devil With a Sword V9: War Season
Trautmann, Geovani, more

Red Sonja She-Devil With a Sword V10: Machines of Empire
Trautmann, Geovani, more

Red Sonja She-Devil With a Sword Omnibus V1
Oeming, Carey, Rubi, more

Red Sonja She-Devil With a Sword Omnibus V2
Oeming, Reed, Homs, more

Red Sonja She-Devil With a Sword Omnibus V3
Reed, Geovani

Red Sonja vs. Thulsa Doom V1
David, Lieberman, Conrad

Savage Red Sonja: Queen of the Frozen Wastes
Cho, Murray, Homs

Red Sonja: Travels
Marz, Ortega, Thomas, more

Sword of Red Sonja: Doom of the Gods (Red Sonja vs. Thulsa Doom 2)
Lieberman, Antonio

Red Sonja: Wrath of the Gods
Lieberman, Geovani

Red Sonja: Revenge of the Gods
Lieberman, Sampere

Savage Tales of Red Sonja
Marz, Gage, Ortega, more

ART BOOKS!

The Art of Howard Chaykin
The Art of Painted Comics
The Art of Ramona Fradon
The Art of Red Sonja
The Art of Vampirella
The Dynamite Art of Alex Ross
George Pérez: Storyteller
The Romita Legacy